REASON OF STATE, PROPAGANDA, AND THE THIRTY YEARS' WAR

Acclaimed writer and historian Noel Malcolm presents his sensational discovery of a new work by Thomas Hobbes (1588–1679): a propaganda pamphlet on behalf of the Habsburg side in the Thirty Years' War, translated by Hobbes from a Latin original. Malcolm's book explores a fascinating episode in seventeenth-century history, illuminating both the practice of early modern propaganda and the theory of 'reason of state'.

Noel Malcolm is Senior Research Fellow at All Souls College, Oxford.

D1553894

Reason of State, Propaganda, and the Thirty Years' War

An Unknown Translation by Thomas Hobbes

NOEL MALCOLM

CLARENDON PRESS · OXFORD

OXFORD

UNIVERSITY PRESS

Great Clarendon Street, Oxford OX2 6DP

Oxford University Press is a department of the University of Oxford.
It furthers the University's objective of excellence in research, scholarship,
and education by publishing worldwide in

Oxford New York

Auckland Cape Town Dar es Salaam Hong Kong Karachi
Kuala Lumpur Madrid Melbourne Mexico City Nairobi
New Delhi Shanghai Taipei Toronto

With offices in

Argentina Austria Brazil Chile Czech Republic France Greece
Guatemala Hungary Italy Japan Poland Portugal Singapore
South Korea Switzerland Thailand Turkey Ukraine Vietnam

Oxford is a registered trade mark of Oxford University Press
in the UK and in certain other countries

Published in the United States
by Oxford University Press Inc., New York

© Noel Malcolm 2007

British Library Cataloguing in Publication Data

Data available

Library of Congress Cataloging in Publication Data

Data available

Typeset by Laserwords Private Limited, Chennai, India
Printed in Great Britain
on acid-free paper by the
MPG Books Group, Bodmin and King's Lynn

ISBN 978–0–19–921593–5 (hbk)
978–0–19–957571–8 (pbk)

1 3 5 7 9 10 8 6 4 2

Contents

Preface

THIS book presents a hitherto unnoticed manuscript translation, by Thomas Hobbes, of a Latin propaganda pamphlet produced by the Habsburg side during the Thirty Years' War. The text of the translation is reproduced, with explanatory notes; the text of the original Latin is also given, to enable readers to make a closer study of Hobbes's practice as a translator; and in six introductory chapters I set out not only my reasons for identifying this anonymous manuscript as a translation by Hobbes, but also my thoughts on the background to the translation, the nature of the text itself, and the possible significance of this discovery for the study of Hobbes. On this last point I have tried not to over-state my case. The original pamphlet was not written by Hobbes, and it is very likely that the task of translating it was simply imposed on him by one or other of his patrons. Nevertheless, the fact that Hobbes must have attended very closely to this particular text is of some real interest where his intellectual biography is concerned—especially since the translation took place in the early part of his career, for which very little biographical evidence is available. That this pamphlet was regarded as worthy of such attention by one of his patrons also tells us something about the political interests of the circles in which Hobbes moved; that topic too is explored in one of the introductory chapters here. And the text itself is an unusually fascinating specimen of early seventeenth-century propaganda literature—a cynical, ingenious, and extremely well-informed piece of writing which should be of interest to historians of the Thirty Years' War, and of the polemical practices of the period, even without its Hobbesian connections. Hobbes's translation is therefore quite heavily annotated here, since the notes are intended to satisfy a number of different requirements: in addition to recording errors and omissions in the translation, they not only identify persons, places, and events, but also indicate (where possible) the degree to which the pamphlet's claims were based on accurate information, or were distorted for propagandistic purposes. Finally, since the last few pages of Hobbes's translation are missing, I have supplied my own translation of that part of the text, so that readers may consider—as Hobbes himself must have done—the claims and arguments of the entire work.

It is of course possible that a complete manuscript copy of Hobbes's translation may eventually come to light. If it does so before the relevant volume of the Clarendon Edition of the works of Hobbes is (also eventually) published, then Hobbes's wording of the final part will be included in that edition. Clarifications of points which I have not been able to explicate in the text (and, perhaps, corrections to explanations which I have put forward) may also be included there. But on the other hand, the Clarendon Edition will not contain the original Latin; the annotations may be more summary there; and the introductory materials in that edition will necessarily be much briefer than the six chapters presented here.

During the preparation of this book I have accumulated many debts of gratitude. For help and advice on specific points I am very grateful to Jim Adams, Peter Beal, Thomas Cogswell, Bob Evans, Alastair Hamilton, Kinch Hoekstra, Tim Raylor, Paul Seaward, Kevin Sharpe, Hotso Spanninga, and Marta Vaculínová. I am especially grateful to Patrick Finglass, who scrutinized my translation of the final pages of the text and made some very helpful corrections and suggestions. My thanks go also to Andrew Peppitt, for his help during my visit to Chatsworth, and to the staffs of the Bodleian Library and the British Library, where much of the research for this book was carried out. I record with gratitude the permission of the Trustees of the Chatsworth Settlement and the Trustees of the British Library to reproduce photographs of manuscripts in their collections. I am very grateful to Peter Momtchiloff, of the Oxford University Press, for taking such an interest in this book, and seeing it through the press. Most of all, I wish to thank the Warden and Fellows of All Souls College for giving me the freedom to engage in intensive research, and for providing the congenial conditions in which this book was written.

A Note on Dates and Transcriptions

In the 1620s most of continental Europe used the Gregorian calendar (New Style), which was ten days ahead of the Julian calendar (Old Style) used in England. In this book, where events in England and material from English sources are concerned, both dates are given (with the New Style date added in square brackets if it has been inferred); otherwise, where events on the Continent are concerned, only the New Style date is used.

The transcription of all manuscript material here aims to reproduce as accurately as possible the original text, altering or omitting only those kinds of detail that are of no importance to the study of its meaning. The original spelling is preserved, but long 's' and the ligatures 'æ' and 'œ' are normalized, and the double hyphen '=' is presented as a single hyphen. Superscripts are preserved, but other sorts of contraction are expanded—silently if they are simple and unambiguous, but otherwise with the expansion placed within square brackets. The original punctuation is normally adhered to; only in very rare cases is punctuation emended, with the emendation presented in square brackets. The main form of emphasis used in the Hobbes manuscript consists of writing in larger script; this is rendered here as italics, and the occasional use of underlining is presented as underlining. (In quotations from other manuscripts elsewhere in this book, underlining is rendered as italics.)

Editorial interventions, and the recording of information about the text in the text itself, are presented in square brackets. The most important of these are as follows. Where a deletion is legible, it is presented thus:

> I have [sent *deleted*] delivered your letters

Where the deletion is not legible, an attempt is made to indicate its extent. Thus:

> I have [*word deleted*] your letters

Or:

> I have [*2 letters deleted*] your letters

Interlinear material is presented thus, using a sign reminiscent of a caret mark:

> I have [>not yet] delivered your letters

Such material is placed where the original caret mark stands (if present) or should stand; but the original caret mark itself is not reproduced. Where an interlineation replaces material originally written on the line and then deleted, the deletion is presented first, and the two sets of square brackets are fused into one. Thus:

> I have [already *deleted* >not yet] delivered your letters

If there is a deletion and an interlineation, with the interlineation itself also deleted, this is presented as follows:

> I have [already *deleted* >not yet *deleted*] delivered your letters

In general, such combinations will be self-explanatory. Equally self-explanatory are italicized statements about the text such as '[*page torn*]'. This information may be combined with a conjectural restitution of the text, in the form:

> I have [*page torn* deli]vered your letters

Also self-explanatory is material presented as follows:

> I have [delivered *altered to* destroyed] your letters

Uncertain readings are placed in square brackets, with an italicized question-mark:

> I have [never?] delivered your letters

These editorial elements, normally italicized, are non-italicized if the text itself is in italics at that point.

1

Hobbes's Early Career

IN a volume of the papers of William Cavendish, first Earl of Newcastle, there is a text in English entitled 'A second most secret instruction Gallo-britanno-batauian, giuen to Fredericke the V. Translated out of Low Dutch into Latine, and diuulged for the most publique good'.[1] This is a translation of a political pamphlet, *Altera secretissima instructio Gallo-Britanno-Batava Friderico V data, ex belgica in latinam linguam versa, et optimo publico evulgata*, an analysis of the geopolitical position and interests of the Elector Palatine (the German Protestant prince and son-in-law of James I, whose acceptance of the crown of Bohemia from the anti-Habsburg rebels there had plunged Central Europe into war), which was published somewhere on the continent of Europe in 1626.[2] This manuscript translation was not printed, nor could its publication have been contemplated at the time, given that the *Altera secretissima instructio* was a work of ingenious and virulent pro-Habsburg propaganda calling for, among other things, the overthrow of Charles I. Neither does there appear to be any surviving reference to this translation by any of the people who were involved in its commissioning, production, or circulation—if it was circulated at all. The name of the translator is not stated in the manuscript; there are, nevertheless, reasons (which will be presented below) for thinking that this English translation was made by Thomas Hobbes.

That Hobbes should have been engaged in such a task in the latter part of the 1620s is in keeping with many of the key aspects of his personal biography up to that time: his skill as a Latinist; his experience as a translator; his role as 'secretary' in a noble household; and his personal acquaintance with the future Earl of Newcastle. In order to sketch the background to his translation of this Latin text,

---

[1] British Library [hereafter: BL], MS Add. 70499, fos. 73–83.
[2] The place of publication is given as The Hague ('Hagae Comitis'), but this can be presumed to have been a fiction. See below, Ch. 3, at n. 46.

it may be useful to supply a few details about these aspects of his early life.

Hobbes's schooling had been at the hands of an Oxford graduate, Robert Latimer, whom a later pupil, John Aubrey, would describe as 'a good Graecian'.[3] Under him, Hobbes would have received the sort of education in the humanities that had become standard in the grammar schools of late Tudor England. The bedrock of this was a mastery of Latin; indeed, by this time, fluency in Latin was regarded more or less as an entrance requirement for university.[4] Such mastery was acquired not only by linguistic study, but also by the study of classical rhetoric (above all, Cicero and Quintilian), and by immersion in the major works of Latin poetry, history, and moral philosophy.[5] In the final years of school education, it was normal (at least, at a good school) for some knowledge of Greek to be acquired too. With Latimer's encouragement, Hobbes seems to have attained an unusually high level of proficiency here; before he left the school, he translated the whole of Euripides' *Medea* into Latin verse.[6]

Little is known about Hobbes's studies at Magdalen Hall, Oxford (1603–8), and the few details that have come down to us, in Hobbes's autobiographical writings and John Aubrey's notes, are heavily skewed by the polemical concerns of Hobbes's later years. The picture Hobbes then presented was of a university curriculum filled with barbarous scholastic logic and antiquated Aristotelian metaphysics and physics—from which he turned in disgust, preferring to spend his time in bookshops gazing at maps that presented the latest discoveries in geography and astronomy.[7] In fact, the Oxford curriculum at this time was 'quintessentially humanistic in nature'; much of Hobbes's time would have been spent in broadening and deepening his knowledge of classical texts in the fields of rhetoric, poetry, history, and moral philosophy.[8] When William Trumbull's son went up to Magdalen College, Oxford, in 1622, Trumbull advised him: 'Converse wth the

---

[3] J. Aubrey, *'Brief Lives', chiefly of Contemporaries*, ed. A. Clark, 2 vols. (Oxford, 1898), i, pp. 328–9.

[4] M. Feingold, 'The Humanities', in N. Tyacke, ed., *The History of the University of Oxford*, iv: *Seventeenth-Century Oxford* (Oxford, 1997), pp. 211–357, here p. 243.

[5] For an authoritative account see Q. Skinner, *Reason and Rhetoric in the Philosophy of Hobbes* (Cambridge, 1997), pp. 19–40.

[6] Aubrey, *'Brief Lives'*, i, pp. 328–9; T. Hobbes, *Opera philosophica quae latine scripsit omnia*, ed. W. Molesworth, 5 vols. (London, 1839–45), i, p. xxiii.

[7] Aubrey, *'Brief Lives'*, i, pp. 329–30; Hobbes, *Opera philosophica*, i, pp. lxxxvi–lxxxvii.

[8] Feingold, 'The Humanities', p. 213.

Poets, for a yeare, therein I would haue yo^u well versed. Read Tully, and Livy with dilligence for yor Lattin; Plinyes, and Manutius his Epistles: and augment your Greek . . . Learne to make a verse, a theame, & an oration.'[9] The account-book of two Oxford undergraduates in the early seventeenth century shows that they bought, for their studies, texts by Horace, Juvenal, Persius, Martial, Lucan, Ovid, Plautus, Seneca, Petronius, Theophrastus, Aulus Gellius, Tacitus, Florus, Livy, Sallust, and Suetonius.[10] Hobbes's finances might not have allowed so many purchases; but his reading would have followed a similar course.

Soon after his graduation in 1608, Hobbes was employed by William Cavendish, Baron Cavendish of Hardwick, as a tutor to his elder son, who was Hobbes's junior by only two years. That he was personally recommended for this post by the Principal of Magdalen Hall suggests that he was thought to have been an outstanding student. The son, also called William Cavendish (he became Sir William in 1609, and Lord Cavendish on his father's elevation to the earldom of Devonshire in 1618), had already been through the hands of several tutors and had acquired some proficiency in Latin.[11] That he had serious intellectual interests would soon become plain, but it was also obvious that he was a headstrong character, a philanderer (in his teenage years, at least), and a spendthrift on a massive scale.[12] Hobbes had both the pleasure of going 'a hunting and hawking with him', and the indignity of begging for loans on his behalf.[13] Nevertheless, some tuition does seem to have taken place. Baron Cavendish's account-book lists various book-purchases that look as if they may have been made for this purpose: Ammianus Marcellinus (in 1609), Keckermann's *Systema physica* and *Politica*, and Plutarch's *Lives* (1611), another volume of Plutarch, Ramus's *Grammar*, and the *Elegantiae Ciceronis* (1613).[14] The same source provides evidence of

9 BL, MS Add. 72441, fo. 4r (24 August [/3 September] 1622).

10 Feingold, 'The Humanities', p. 250.

11 Chatsworth, MS Hardwick 143/12 is a document drawn up on 16 [/26] November 1602, in which it is agreed that 'if M^r. William doe speake lattin till lent assizes next' to various members of the Cavendish household, 'Then my m[aste]^r: will geve m^r: William a rapyer and dagger, an imbrodered girdle & hanger and a payre of spurres'; it is signed by Baron Cavendish and his son.

12 Details of his early education, philandering, and debts are given in the History of Parliament Trust's unpublished article on him for the 1602–29 section (by V. C. D. Moseley); I am very grateful to the History of Parliament Trust for allowing me to see this article in draft.

13 Aubrey, *'Brief Lives'*, i, pp. 331, 347.

14 Chatsworth, MS Hardwick 29, pp. 143, 219b, 263b, 355. Possibly Hobbes was also giving some tuition to the two younger sons.

studies in Italian and French, with the purchase of Botero's *Primavera* and *Detti e fatti memorabili*, several instalments of the *Tesoro politico*, a 'french dictionary', and an 'Italian dictionary' (1611), 'Corderius in Latin and frenche' (a bilingual version of the popular book of pedagogical dialogues by Mathurin Cordier) and 'examen des esprits' (a French translation of Huarte's *Examen de los ingenios*) (1612), and 'french and latine dictionary', 'new testament in french', 'psalmes in french', and 'Monntains essaies' (1613).[15] It may have been during this period of preparatory study of Italian that Hobbes's pupil translated the first book of Castiglione's *Libro del cortegiano* into Latin.[16] Language-learning was evidently taken seriously in this household; the accounts record the services of 'Lewis the frenchman', presumably a language-teacher, who was paid off in May 1614.[17]

Soon thereafter, Hobbes and his pupil embarked on their Grand Tour, which lasted from June 1614 to October 1615.[18] Their main destination was Venice; from there they made an expedition to Rome in October 1614, returning to stay in Venice until the summer of 1615. Cavendish worked hard on his Italian, and, as an exercise, made an Italian translation of Bacon's *Essayes* (which was later printed, though without direct attribution to Cavendish, in London in 1618).[19] He also met Venice's leading intellectual, Paolo Sarpi, and became well acquainted with Sarpi's confidant Fulgenzio Micanzio. Soon after the departure of Cavendish (and Hobbes) from Venice, Micanzio began writing a series of lengthy newsletters to him, which would continue until Cavendish's death. Those letters survive in English translations made by Hobbes. Since Cavendish was perfectly capable of reading

15 Chatsworth, MS Hardwick 29, pp. 219b, 263b, 303, 316, 355.

16 Chatsworth, MS Hardwick 64: the initials 'W. C.' are stamped in gold on the front cover of the manuscript's binding, and the text is in a calligraphic hand very similar to that used in the signature by the future second Earl in MS Hardwick 143/12 (see above, n. 11). There are occasional corrections to the Latin, some of which may possibly be in a neat version of Hobbes's hand. The Hardwick library catalogue (MS Hobbes E.1.A.) includes an entry for 'yᵉ Courtier, by Castilio[ne]. in Ital. french. & Eng. 4°' — a reference to the London, 1588 edition, which printed in parallel columns the Italian text and the translations by Gabriel Chappuys and Sir Thomas Hoby. Translating from this edition into Latin would thus have been a useful pedagogical exercise, involving the study of both Italian and French. The same catalogue does also include an entry for Bartholomew Clerke's Latin version, *De curiali sive aulico libri quatuor* (London, 1571 and subsequent editions); but perhaps this was a later acquisition.

17 Chatsworth, MS Hardwick 29, p. 370.

18 Ibid., pp. 371, 453.

19 See N. Malcolm, *De Dominis (1560–1624): Venetian, Anglican, Ecumenist and Relapsed Heretic* (London, 1984), pp. 47–54.

the originals in Italian, it is clear that the translations were made for circulation to others; and there is evidence that they underwent a twofold circulation, first as individual letters and later in copies of the complete series.[20] The originals of the letters are not extant; nevertheless, the impression given by Hobbes's translations is that he must have attained a very good command of the Italian language. His own statement, in his prose autobiography, that during their stay in France and Italy he had acquired enough knowledge of French and Italian 'to be able to understand them moderately well' seems unduly modest.[21]

To Hobbes himself, however, it seems that his knowledge of these modern languages was of much less importance than his mastery of Latin and Greek, which he took great trouble to maintain. In his prose autobiography he says that he began to worry about forgetting those languages within the first year of his employment; Aubrey would later recount that, to remedy this, he 'bought him bookes of an Amsterdam print that he might carry in his pocket (particularly Caesar's Commentaryes) which he did read in the lobbey, or ante-chamber, whilst his lord was making his visits'.[22] On his return from the Grand Tour Hobbes embarked on a major programme of reading the works of ancient poets and historians (and commentators on them), 'in order to be able to write, not in a flowery way, but in proper Latin'; the texts he studied included Horace, Vergil, and Plautus, as well as a number of Greek writers, including Homer, Euripides, Sophocles, Aristophanes, and 'many historians', among whom 'I liked Thucydides best of all'.[23] With his pupil aged 25 on their return to England,

---

[20] Two complete scribal copies survive: Chatsworth, Hobbes MSS, unnumbered, 'Translations of Italian Letters', and BL, MS Add. 11309. The former bears some annotations in Hobbes's hand. An edition (based on the BL MS) is given in F. Micanzio, *Lettere a William Cavendish*, ed. R. Ferrini and E. De Mas (Rome, 1987): for evidence of piecemeal circulation see pp. 13, 115. See also V. Gabrieli, 'Bacone, la riforma e Roma nella versione Hobbesiana d'un carteggio di Fulgenzio Micanzio', *The English Miscellany*, 8 (1957), pp. 195–250. Filippo de Vivo has argued that Micanzio's letters were written by both Micanzio and Sarpi, on the grounds that some of the same material appears in Sarpi's own letters ('Paolo Sarpi and the Uses of Information in Seventeenth-Century Venice', in J. Raymond, ed., *News Networks in Seventeenth-Century Britain and Europe* (London, 2006), pp. 35–49, here p. 37). This argument might cut both ways: the correspondence of Sarpi, a very busy man, may have been partly managed by Micanzio. But, given the closeness between the two men, some cooperation may reasonably be assumed in this case.

[21] Hobbes, *Opera philosophica*, i, p. xiii: 'ut intelligere eas mediocriter potuerit'.

[22] Ibid., p. xiii; Aubrey, *'Brief Lives'*, i, p. 331.

[23] Hobbes, *Opera philosophica*, i, pp. xiv ('non ut floride, sed ut Latine posset scribere'), lxxxviii ('multi Scriptores Historiarum'; 'prae reliquis Thucydides placuit').

Hobbes's role had ceased to be even vestigially that of a tutor; he was now officially to be described as Cavendish's 'secretary'.[24] Only fragmentary evidence survives of what those secretarial duties involved. In addition to translating the Micanzio letters, Hobbes may also have helped to prepare the final version of Cavendish's translation of Bacon's *Essayes* in 1617–18; this might have brought him into contact with Bacon himself, who had been personally acquainted with Cavendish since 1616 (at the latest) and is known to have corrected one of the early copies of the translation.[25] Admiration for Bacon's work was also signalled by a set of ten 'Essayes' written by Cavendish himself; a fair-copy manuscript of them was written out by Hobbes, and was probably presented to Cavendish's father, the Earl of Devonshire, on New Year's day 1619.[26] In his dedicatory epistle to that work, Cavendish defended his decision to write his essays in English rather than Latin, commenting that 'For any man to entitle himselfe to Learninge and not understand Latin, is some presumption, but to understand it well, though not speake it, is to have it as farre as is usefull.'[27] That Cavendish himself did 'understand it well' was made clear in the following year, when his ten essays were printed together with four longer 'discourses' (one of which had already been published—anonymously but with

---

[24] See Skinner, *Reason and Rhetoric*, p. 222.

[25] Micanzio, *Lettere*, pp. 54–5 (31 March 1616: 'I am exceedingly bound to you for relating to Sr Francis Bacon how much I esteeme his judgement and learning'; 'the favour of calling me to a commerce of letters with him I . . . accompt it a great happinesse & a great debt of mine to you'); Malcolm, *De Dominis*, pp. 50–2. Bacon's friendship with Cavendish is attested to in both versions (1621 and 1625) of Bacon's will (F. Bacon, *The Works*, ed. J. Spedding, R. L. Ellis, and D. D. Heath, 14 vols. (London, 1857–74), xiv, pp. 228, 542; cf. also G. C. Robertson, *Hobbes* (Edinburgh, 1886), p. 19 (n.)). The fact that Bacon's chaplain and amanuensis printed an extract from one of Micanzio's letters to Cavendish (W. Rawley, 'The Life of the Honourable Author', in F. Bacon, *Resuscitatio*, ed. W. Rawley (London, 1657), sigs. b2–c4, here sig. c3r, quoting a passage from Micanzio's letter of 6 May 1622 in Hobbes's version: Micanzio, *Lettere*, p. 167) suggests that he found the letter among Bacon's papers, which suggests in turn that Bacon was a recipient of copies of Hobbes's translations of the Micanzio letters. Also noteworthy is the presence among the Hardwick manuscripts at Chatsworth of four items containing works by Bacon (see F. Bacon, *Philosophical Studies, c.1611–c.1619*, The Oxford Francis Bacon, vi, ed. G. Rees (Oxford, 1996), pp. cvi–cx).

[26] Chatsworth, MS Hardwick 29, p. 575, entry for 1 [/11] January 1619: 'To Mr Hobs bringing a booke from his Lord: £1 2s'. The fair-copy MS, which bears a dedicatory epistle to the Earl, is Chatsworth, MS Hobbes D 3; the text is printed in F. O. Wolf, *Die neue Wissenschaft des Thomas Hobbes: zu den Grundlagen der politischen Philosophie der Neuzeit* (Stuttgart, 1969), pp. 135–67. The dedicatory epistle refers to the work as 'this dayes present' (p. 136).

[27] Wolf, *Die neue Wissenschaft*, pp. 135–6.

clear indications of Cavendish's authorship—nine years before). Of the three new discourses, one gave an account of Cavendish's visit to Rome in 1614, one was 'Of Lawes' (with occasional quotations from Livy, Cicero, and the *Digest*), and one, entitled 'A Discourse vpon the Beginning of Tacitus', was a commentary on the first four chapters of Book 1 of the *Annals*, with parts of the original text presented in Latin and translation.[28] A recent study using 'wordprint' analysis has claimed that these three discourses were composed by Hobbes, not Cavendish; but this claim has not won general acceptance among Hobbes scholars, and there is more than one reason for doubting it.[29] More recently, an investigation of the discourse 'Of Lawes' has shown that it adapted material from an unpublished work by Bacon, the 'Aphorismi de jure gentium maiore sive de fontibus justiciae et juris'; this is of interest not only for the evidence it supplies of intellectual closeness to Bacon, but also because the occasional errors in the discourse's translations of passages from Bacon's Latin are of a kind that Hobbes is unlikely to have committed.[30] Nevertheless, even if Hobbes was not the author of these discourses, he was probably involved to some extent in their creation—as sounding-board for the arguments they contained, and as a copyist of the final text.

Hobbes's other secretarial duties would have included buying books and organizing the library; he eventually drew up a complete catalogue of

[28] [W. Cavendish,] *Horae subsecivae: Observations and Discourses* (London, 1620). On the previously published *A Discourse against Flatterie* (London, 1611), see Skinner, *Reason and Rhetoric*, pp. 236–7. The entry for *Horae subsecivae* in the Register of the Stationers' Company referred to 'A booke Called *A Discourse against flattery*, and *Of Rome*, with *Essaies*' (E. Arber, ed., *A Transcript of the Registers of the Company of Stationers of London, 1554–1640 AD*, 5 vols. (London, 1875–94), iii, p. 311: 29 March [/8 April] 1620). This might suggest that the other two discourses were given to the publisher later; but other explanations are also possible.

[29] T. Hobbes (attrib.), *Three Discourses*, ed. N. B. Reynolds and A. W. Saxonhouse (Chicago, 1995), esp. pp. 3–19. The 'wordprint' technique used here was developed by A. Q. Morton; for an authoritative survey of the objections which have been made to Morton's method (concluding that it is 'fundamentally unreliable') see B. Vickers, *Shakespeare, Co-Author: A Historical Study of Five Collaborative Plays* (Oxford, 2002), pp. 101–11. It should also be noted that the description of Rome was the sort of exercise normally performed on an educational Grand Tour by the pupil, not the tutor, and that the opinions expressed in the 'Discourse of Lawes' differ significantly from Hobbes's later views. Only in the discourse on Tacitus does one find, here and there, some touches of Hobbesian phrasing.

[30] A. Huxley, 'The *Aphorismi* and *A Discourse of Laws*: Bacon, Cavendish, and Hobbes, 1615–1620', *Historical Journal*, 47 (2004), pp. 399–412; the errors include taking 'invalescere' to mean 'to grow weaker' instead of 'to grow stronger'. The work by Bacon survives in a manuscript copy at Chatsworth, MS Hardwick 51 (item 11).

the books at Hardwick Hall (an impressive collection, numbering more than 1,400 items).[31] He presumably assisted his master in his financial and legal affairs, and gave similar assistance in his parliamentary business (Cavendish sat in the House of Commons in every parliament from 1610 to 1626, when he was elevated to the Lords on his father's death).[32] Cavendish also performed some functions at Court—notably the introduction of several foreign ambassadors there in 1622, which may testify to his linguistic prowess as well as his special interest in European affairs.[33] And some of Cavendish's time during this period was also taken up with commercial ventures, notably in the Virginia Company and its sister organization (for the Bermudas), the Somers Islands Company. Hobbes was granted a share in the former by Cavendish in June 1622; he also became (at an unknown date) a shareholder in the latter. Between 1622 and 1624 Hobbes attended no fewer than thirty-seven meetings of the Virginia Company in London; he did some secretarial work for the Company too, helping to draw up a response to a petition of grievances by the colonists in Virginia.[34]

It was probably during that period that Hobbes also performed some secretarial services, including translation, for Bacon. Our knowledge of this episode in Hobbes's life comes primarily from his friend John Aubrey, who wrote in his description of the gardens of Bacon's house near St Albans:

Here his lordship much meditated, his servant Mr. Bushell attending him with his pen and inke horne to sett downe his present notions.—Mr. Thomas Hobbes told me, that his lordship would employ him often in this service whilest he was there, and was better pleased with his *minutes*, or notes sett

---

[31] See below, Ch. 2 n. 2. Many of these books may have been bought for Hobbes's benefit: in his verse autobiography he recalled that Cavendish 'supplied books of all kinds for my studies' (Hobbes, *Opera philosophica omnia*, i, p. lxxxviii: 'libros | Omnimodos studiis praebuit ille meis'). But Cavendish clearly also had intellectual interests of his own.

[32] An example of Hobbes's involvement in Cavendish's financial affairs is supplied by a legal document of 4 [/14] March 1618, in which Cavendish arranged that his cousin (the future Earl of Newcastle) would stand surety for a debt owed by him to 'one Edmond Story of London'; Hobbes added his signature (the first dated example of it) as a witness (Staffordshire Record Office, Stafford, D 4038/I/33; I am grateful to Dr Peter Beal for drawing my attention to this document).

[33] See S. Lee, 'William Cavendish, second earl of Devonshire', revised by V. Stater, *Oxford Dictionary of National Biography* (www.oxforddnb.com). One of these, the new Venetian Ambassador, came with a personal recommendation from Micanzio: see Micanzio, *Lettere*, pp. 161–2, 185, 197, 235.

[34] See N. Malcolm, *Aspects of Hobbes* (Oxford, 2002), pp. 53–79, esp. pp. 54–5.

down by him, then by others who did not well understand his lordship. He told me that he was employed in translating part of the Essayes, viz. three of them, one wherof was that of the Greatness of Cities, the other two I have now forgott.[35]

Two other sources supply some confirmation of this. In late 1663, after visiting Hobbes in London, his friend Samuel Sorbière wrote: 'He is indeed a relic of Bacon, under whom he wrote in his youth. And from everything I have heard him say about him, and from what I observe in his style, I can well see that he has learned much from him.'[36] In the following summer Hobbes's French admirer François du Verdus also referred, in a letter to Hobbes, to 'something which I think I was told a long time ago, namely, that you were a secretary to this Chancellor Bacon in his studies.'[37] As we have seen, Bacon had been acquainted with Cavendish since 1616 (or earlier), and Hobbes may have had contacts with him over the Italian translation of his *Essayes*. In addition, Hobbes is known to have visited the Lord Chancellor in connection with the first Earl of Devonshire's legal business in 1619 and 1620.[38] Possibly Hobbes was 'loaned' to Bacon on various occasions over quite a long period; but the translation of the *Essayes* into Latin can be dated more specifically. In June [/July] 1623 Bacon wrote to a friend that 'It is true my labours are now most set to have those works which I had formerly published, as that of Advancement of Learning, that of Henry 7th, that of the Essays being retractate and made more perfect, well translated into Latin by the help of some good pens which forsake me not'.[39] The translation of the *Essayes*, entitled *Sermones fideles*, was not printed until 1638, but the particular essay mentioned (under a slightly mis-remembered title) by Aubrey, 'Of the Greatnesse of Kingdomes', appeared in Latin translation in 1623, when it was included in the Latin

[35] Aubrey, *'Brief Lives'*, i, p. 83; cf. a similar account in Aubrey's notes on Hobbes (i, p. 331: 'The Lord Chancellour Bacon loved to converse with him. He assisted his lordship in translating severall of his Essayes into Latin').

[36] S. Sorbière, *Relation d'un voyage en Angleterre* (Paris, 1664), p. 97: 'Il est en effet vn reste de Bacon, sous lequel il a escrit en sa ieunesse, & par tout ce que ie luy en ay ouy dire, & que ie remarque dans son stile, ie vois bien qu'il en a beaucoup retenu'. This work was completed on 12 December 1663 and printed by 16 May 1664: see sig. a4v and the 'Privilège'.

[37] T. Hobbes, *The Correspondence*, ed. N. Malcolm, 2 vols. (Oxford, 1994), ii, pp. 624, 3 August 1664 ('ce qu'il me semble qu'on m'assura des-long-tems Que vous avés esté secretaire des Etudes de ce Chancelier Bacon'), 628.

[38] Chatsworth, MS Hardwick 29, pp. 605, 633.

[39] Bacon, *Works*, xiv, p. 429.

version of the *Advancement of Learning*.[40] The other two essays have not been identified with any certainty, though one scholar has suggested, on the basis of the high quality of the translations, that they were 'Of Simulation and Dissimulation' and 'Of Innovations'.[41] But whether or not Hobbes was the best member of the team of translators, the fact that he was chosen to perform such a task for England's leading intellectual testifies to the high regard in which he was held, both as a Latinist and as a translator.

Four years later, Hobbes's skills as a Latinist were displayed in his lengthy poem in Latin hexameters, *De mirabilibus pecci*, which described a tour, made with Cavendish and some other companions, of the seven 'wonders' of the Peak District in Derbyshire.[42] A similar poem survives in English, written by the physician and poet Richard Andrews, who enjoyed the friendship and patronage of Cavendish's cousin, Viscount Mansfield. That English poem (which describes some, but not all, of the wonders) may well have been a product of the same tour—in which case it supplies not only the date of the tour, which it gives as August 1627, but also the information that Mansfield was one of the party.[43]

---

[40] See F. Bacon, *The Essayes and Councels, Civill and Morall*, ed. M. Kiernan (Oxford, 1985), pp. xc–xci; see also pp. 233–4 for evidence that the translation was made some time between the spring and autumn of 1623. The Latin translation corresponded to an enlarged and remodelled ('retractate') version of the previously published English essay; the new version was published in English for the first time in 1625, as 'Of the true Greatnesse of Kingdomes and Estates'. Richard Tuck has suggested that the Latin was written by Bacon and that Hobbes translated that new, enlarged, version of the essay back into the English version printed in 1625 ('Hobbes and Tacitus', in G. A. J. Rogers and T. Sorell, eds., *Hobbes and History* (London, 2000), pp. 99–111, here p. 108); but a comparison of the Latin and English texts does not support this. At some points the Latin supplies something logically required, but only implicit in the English phrasing; sometimes it has to make an effort to find a Latin equivalent of a term (e.g. 'Gentlemen', translated as '(quos vocamus) Generosi'); and sometimes it makes an explanatory expansion or simplification (e.g. 'But when they [*sc.* the Spartans] did spread, and their Boughs were becommen too great, for their Stem, they became a Windfall vpon the suddaine', translated as 'At postquam Limites suos caepissent proferre, et latius dominari, quam ut Stirpe Spartanorum, Turbam Exterorum, Imperio commode coercere posset, Potentia eorum corruit': here it is easy to imagine the English being translated into the Latin, but not vice versa).

[41] F. Bacon, *Essays and Colours of Good and Evil*, ed. W. Aldis Wright (London, 1875), pp. xix–xx.

[42] Hobbes, *Opera philosophica*, v, pp. 323–40; the poem has 538 lines.

[43] BL, MS Harl. 4955, fos. 164–71 (fo. 165r: 'At last to Buxtons wee are come | And welcom'd there, both all and some; | Cheifely for Viscount Mansfeilds sake | W^th whom the Towne, and Countrey take:'). On Andrews see H. Kelliher, 'Donne, Jonson, Richard Andrews and the Newcastle Manuscript', in P. Beal and J. Griffiths, eds., *English Manuscript Studies, 1100–1700*, iv (1994), pp. 134–73. An extract from this poem

By that time Cavendish was the Earl of Devonshire, having succeeded his father in March 1626. Hobbes's poem was written to be presented as a gift to him; this suggests, once again, that Cavendish himself had a more than adequate grasp of the Latin language.

Hobbes's most important intellectual enterprise during this period of his life was, however, a much more weighty task: a complete translation of Thucydides, made (unlike previous English versions) directly from the Greek. Unfortunately it is not known when exactly he worked on this translation. It was presumably complete by March 1628, when it was registered at the Stationers' Company; the printing seems to have been substantially accomplished by November of that year, and Hobbes was able to give an exemplum of the book to a friend as a New Year's gift on 1 January 1629.[44] But in his Preface Hobbes included the following, rather tantalizing, sentence: 'After I had finished it, it lay long by mee, and other reasons taking place, my desire to communicate it ceased.'[45] Whether that 'long' period was a matter of months or years is not apparent; nor is the motive for the delay at all apparent. Hobbes gave no clear idea as to what those 'other reasons' might be. The only explanation he added here was that he had doubted whether the work would satisfy a general readership, for two reasons: first, because most readers of history books preferred the excitements of military history to the demands of political analysis, and secondly, because of the proliferation of place-names in Thucydides' text, which would

is printed in B. Jonson, *Works*, ed. C. H. Herford, P. Simpson, and E. Simpson, 11 vols. (Oxford, 1925–52), xi, pp. 387–9. Another poem by Andrews from the same MS (fo. 67v), celebrating the houses of both Cavendish families, is printed in A. Fowler, *The Country House Poem: A Cabinet of Seventeenth-Century Estate Poems and Related Items* (Edinburgh, 1994), pp. 159–63. Fowler, following the editors of Jonson, gives Andrews's first name, incorrectly, as 'Francis'.

[44] For the registration (18 [/28] March 1628) see Arber, ed., *Transcript of the Registers*, iv, p. 161. In his letter to the widowed Countess of Devonshire, sent from London on 6 [/16] November, Hobbes said that the printers would 'shortly be ready' for the Epistle Dedicatory, which was printed last of all (Hobbes, *Correspondence*, i, p. 6). The title page of the book gives the date of publication as 1629; but it was common practice to put the next year's date on a book published in November or December. The exemplum in Dr Williams's Library, London, pressmark 1083.O.4, bears the inscription: 'Ex Authoris dono Januarij primo [1628 *altered to* 1629] Ex libris Samuel. Harrisonj.' This is in the hand of Samuel Harrison, an apothecary in Bishopsgate Street (where Devonshire House was located); cf. the holograph letter from Harrison to William Hale of 29 June [/9 July] 1637 in BL, MS Add. 33572, fo. 243r. On Harrison see R. S. Roberts, 'The London Apothecaries and Medical Practice in Tudor and Stuart England', London University PhD thesis (1964), pp. 311–13.

[45] Thucydides, *Eight Bookes of the Peloponnesian Warre*, tr. T. Hobbes (London, 1629), sig. A4r.

make his narrative hard to follow.[46] Hobbes therefore drew a detailed map of Greece (which was engraved and printed in his book) and added a gazetteer giving information (drawn mostly from Thucydides, Herodotus, Livy, Pausanias, and Strabo) about all the places and features marked on it.[47] This must have taken some time to compile; but the bibliographical evidence suggests that its compilation took place only after the work had been consigned to the printers, so it cannot be used to explain any 'long' delay between completing the translation and sending that translation to be printed.[48]

In the period between the registering of the translation at the Stationers' Company and the completion of its printing, a major change had taken place in Hobbes's life: his pupil-patron, the second Earl of Devonshire, died on 20 [/30] June 1628. His will, made three days before his death, was witnessed by Hobbes; in a codicil to it he urged his wife to retain all his servants in her employment.[49] But within little more than a month she had dispensed with Hobbes's services: he settled his accounts with the Cavendish family on 23 July [/2 August].[50] How he spent his time for the rest of that year is not known. He may well have spent most of it in London, attending the printers on a regular basis to inspect and correct the setting of his text.[51] The fact that his letter to the widowed Countess of Devonshire of 6 [/16] November 1628 was sent 'From yor La.^{ps} house' in London (Devonshire House, in Bishopsgate) should not be taken to imply that he was still in her service; the settling of accounts in July is evidence of a definitive parting

---

[46] Thucydides, *Eight Bookes*, sig. A4r.

[47] In this gazetteer he also refers occasionally to Ptolemy, Polybius, Athenaeus, the Scholiast on Thucydides, Pliny, the *Argonautica* (attributed to Orpheus), the *Itinerarium Antonini*, the *Tabula Peutingeriana*, and the Greek dictionary of Stephanus (Henri Étienne).

[48] Ibid., sigs. b2r–c4r. The signing here suggests that Hobbes had not yet supplied this material—or told the printers to expect it—when the printing of the text had begun earlier in 1628; the text begins on sig. B1, which shows that (following normal practice) they had allowed one gathering (sig. A) for the prefatory materials. Sig. A duly contains the Epistle Dedicatory and the Preface to the Readers.

[49] The National Archives (Public Record Office), Kew [hereafter: PRO], microfilm Prob. 11/154, fos. 38–9.

[50] Chatsworth, MS Hardwick 27 (receipts of the second Earl and his widow), receipts for the period 25 March [/4 April] to Michaelmas 1628: '23 July by m^r hobbes the^{se} p[er] end of his Acco: £23 19s 04d'. Cf. also Chatsworth, MS Hobbes D 6 ('A Narration of Proceedings'), fo. 2r: 'Thomas Hobbes who . . . was vpon ye death of his said Lord & Master discharged'.

[51] On this common practice see P. Simpson, *Proof-Reading in the Sixteenth, Seventeenth and Eighteenth Centuries* (Oxford, 1935), pp. 6–19.

of the ways, and it is therefore much more likely that Hobbes simply went to Devonshire House to write the letter in order to ensure that it would reach her, via her own servants, as speedily as possible.[52] Probably he was staying with friends, or in a London lodging-house. But one other possibility should also be considered—that he was now attached, if only informally, to his other Cavendish patron, William Cavendish, Viscount Mansfield, the future Earl of Newcastle. For Hobbes's next employment, which began some time in 1629, was as tutor and travelling companion to the son of Sir Gervase Clifton; and Sir Gervase was one of Viscount Mansfield's closest colleagues and friends.[53]

The early history of Hobbes's relations with this other William Cavendish (who, to prevent confusion, will hereafter be referred to by the title he received in 1620, 'Mansfield') is quite obscure. Possibly Hobbes had made his acquaintance during the first year of his employment under Baron Cavendish of Hardwick, when he visited Cambridge in 1608; the future Viscount Mansfield had been entered at St John's College there, as a fellow-commoner, in that year.[54] Mansfield showed no aptitude for scholarship; as his second wife would put it, 'though he was sent to the University . . . and had his Tutors to instruct him; yet they could not perswade him to read or study much, he taking

---

[52] Hobbes, *Correspondence*, i, p. 6; the letter expresses Hobbes's desire for all possible speed.

[53] One of Mansfield's first actions, on becoming Lord-Lieutenant of Nottinghamshire in July 1626, was to appoint Clifton his deputy; on this, and their friendship, see J. R. Dias, 'Politics and Administration in Nottinghamshire and Derbyshire, 1590–1640', Oxford University D.Phil. thesis (1973), pp. 314, 327. That some arrangement was made under which Hobbes would return to the service of the Countess of Devonshire after the completion of his work for Clifton is indicated by his letter to Clifton from Hardwick Hall of 2 [/12] November 1630 (Hobbes, *Correspondence*, i, p. 17: 'That I am welcome home, I must attribute to yor fauorable letter, by wch my lady vnderstandes yor good acceptance of my seruice to Mr Clifton'). But the arranger is very likely to have been Mansfield.

[54] On Mansfield's membership of St John's see L. Hulse, 'William Cavendish, first duke of Newcastle upon Tyne', *Oxford Dictionary of National Biography* (www.oxforddnb.com), and L. Worsley, 'The Architectural Patronage of William Cavendish, Duke of Newcastle, 1593–1676', University of Sussex D.Phil. thesis (2001), p. 98. Baron Cavendish's account-book includes an entry shortly after 23 November [/3 December] 1608: 'To Hobbes by my Lo: appointm^t to pay in p[ar]te for a Coach to fetch m^r Wm Cauendishe from Cambridge xxs' (Chatsworth, MS Hardwick 29, p. 38). It is conceivable that this refers to Mansfield; but 'Mr Wm Cavendish' is the form used consistently in these accounts for Hobbes's pupil, who thus seems to have spent some time at Cambridge—perhaps in the company of his cousin.

more delight in sports, then in learning'.[55] One consequence of this
was that, in later life, he was never comfortable reading Latin; in Paris
in the mid-1640s, when he commissioned a manuscript treatise on
optics from Hobbes, the work was written in English at his specific
request.[56] Nevertheless, he did develop strong intellectual interests—in
philosophy, the natural sciences, and literature—many of which he
shared with his much more studious younger brother, Sir Charles
Cavendish. The first piece of evidence that directly connects Hobbes
with this other Cavendish family consists of a letter sent in 1624 from
Hobbes's pupil, Lord Cavendish, to a clergyman, Henry Bates, who
seems to have been patronized by both him and Mansfield: referring to
the other William Cavendish (Mansfield), he added: 'Hobs shall put me
in mind to write to W^ms brother'.[57] Personal relations between the two
Williams seem to have been close at this time; in 1624 Mansfield lent his
cousin the huge sum of £4,500, to enable him to pay his most pressing
debts.[58] The evidence that Mansfield joined Devonshire, Hobbes, and
Andrews on their little tour of the Peak District in August 1627 has
already been mentioned; and in the following month Mansfield was
at Chatsworth, where he was a co-signatory to a letter (written out by
Hobbes, and signed first by Devonshire) to the Secretary of State, Sir
John Coke, about the work of a 'commission' to investigate the raising
of revenues for the Crown from the Derbyshire lead-mining industry.[59]
Three of the literary or intellectual figures who were known to Hobbes
in the late 1620s, Ben Jonson, Dr Richard Andrews, and the Rev. Henry
Bates, appear to have been patronized by both William Cavendishes;
this makes it seem likely that the two Cavendishes, especially when they
coincided in London, had a shared or overlapping social world, at least

55 M. Cavendish, *The Life of the Thrice Noble, High and Puissant Prince William
Cavendishe* (London 1667), p. 141.
56 His brother, Sir Charles Cavendish, wrote to John Pell on 1 [/11] November
1645: 'M^r: Hobbes intends to publish as soon as he can a treatise of opticks . . . It is in
english at my brothers request' (N. Malcolm and J. A. Stedall, *John Pell (1611–1685)
and his Correspondence with Sir Charles Cavendish: The Mental World of an Early Modern
Mathematician* (Oxford, 2005), p. 434). The treatise is BL, MS Harl. 3360. The
university 'entrance requirement' of fluency in Latin could of course be relaxed for
students of sufficiently high social status.
57 BL, BL Add. 70499, fo. 118r (William Cavendish to Henry Bates, June 1624).
58 Dias, 'Politics and Administration', p. 317. Cf. also the document mentioned
above (n. 32), in which the future Viscount Mansfield stood surety for a debt of £305 in
1618.
59 BL, MS Add. 64893, fos. 102–3: letter of 25 September [/5 October] about 'y^e
Lead businesse', signed by Devonshire, Mansfield, R. Harpur, and Francis Coke.

where cultural and intellectual life (though probably not, as we shall see, political life) was concerned.[60] By late 1630, when Hobbes came back from his continental tour with Sir Gervase Clifton's son, Mansfield and his brother seem to have formed the centre of gravity of Hobbes's intellectual world in England: during that winter he spent some time at Mansfield's house in Nottinghamshire, Welbeck Abbey, discussing his new philosophical theories about sense-perception with Mansfield and Sir Charles Cavendish.[61] In early 1631 (probably in February) Hobbes returned to the service of the Countess of Devonshire.[62] But, as his correspondence in the 1630s shows, it was Mansfield and his brother that were now his chief intellectual patrons; and in 1640 it would be at the request of Mansfield (now elevated to the earldom of Newcastle) that Hobbes would write the first of his great political treatises, *The Elements of Law.*

[60] Aubrey recorded that Jonson was Hobbes's 'loving and familiar friend and acquaintance', and that Hobbes asked Jonson to give his opinion of the style of his translation of Thucydides: '*Brief Lives*', i, p. 365.

[61] BL, MS Harl. 3360, fo. 3r; Hobbes, *Correspondence*, i, pp. 102–3, 108; Malcolm, *Aspects of Hobbes*, p. 116.

[62] Chatsworth, MS D 6, fo. 2r: 'About y[e] beginning of y[e] yeare 1631 It hapned that y[e] said Countesse dismissed y[e] then Tutor of y[e] Earle her sonne, & receaued into that place one Thomas Hobbes'. This text was signed (and probably composed) by Hobbes. Cf. also the indenture granting Hobbes the manor of Cleisby, dated 25 February [/7 March] 1639 (14 Charles I), which refers to 'the faithfull and good service done unto him [*sc.* the third Earl] . . . by him the said Thomas Hobbs for the space of Eight Yeares now last past' (Chatsworth, Indenture H/301/16).

2

The Translation: Authorship, Date, and Style

THERE is nothing surprising, then, about the idea that an English translation of a difficult Latin text of the late 1620s, found among Mansfield's papers, should be the work of Thomas Hobbes. The particular reasons for the attribution may now be considered. They are threefold: the handwriting, the nature of the alterations in the manuscript, and some stylistic features of the English.

The volume that contains this manuscript is not unknown to Hobbes scholars: among the other items in it relating to Mansfield are seven holograph letters sent to him by Hobbes in 1634–6.[1] But it has not been noticed that the translation of the *Altera secretissima instructio* is also in Hobbes's handwriting—an earlier form than that of the mid-1630s, with a more regular italic character, but nevertheless with some of the characteristic features of his later hand (such as the 'e' with a detached loop hovering above and beyond the main body of the letter). The closest match to the handwriting of this translation is to be found in the Hardwick library catalogue which Hobbes wrote out in 1627 or 1628: all the letter-shapes found in the translation, including some very characteristic capital letters, recur there.[2] Especially typical is a capital 'A' in which the left-hand vertical starts a long way below the line, and

---

[1] BL, MS Add. 70499, fos. 172–3, 184–5, 202–3, 210–11, 212–13, 214–15, 216–17 (printed in Hobbes, *Correspondence*, i, pp. 19–20, 28–9, 32, 33–4, 37–8, 39, 41–2). This MS volume contains not only Cavendish papers, but also some earlier items from the papers of the Vere and Holles families (which later came into the Cavendish family by marriage); the general arrangement is chronological, which means that the Vere and Holles papers come first, then 'A second most secret instruction', then Cavendish papers. Hobbes scholars may have been misled by the fact that the Historical Manuscripts Commission listed 'A second most secret instruction' as belonging to the Vere and Holles part of the volume: HMC, *Thirteenth Report*, 'MSS of his Grace the Duke of Portland', ii (London, 1893), p. 117.

[2] Chatsworth, MS Hobbes E. 1. A. This catalogue, which is arranged alphabetically, by author's name, is mostly in Hobbes's hand. In some cases, at the end of the entries for

the whole letter leans to the right; a capital 'B' in which the top of the vertical stroke starts some way above the rest of the letter; a fluid and rather slender capital 'E' of the Greek 'sigma' type; a capital 'H' in which a diagonal line passes from the bottom of the left-hand vertical to the top of the right-hand one; a capital 'K' with a thickened and lengthened downwards diagonal stroke; a capital 'P' with the vertical leaning to the right and a horizontal foot extending only on its right-hand side; a capital 'Q' with a lengthened and slightly thickened tail pointing more downwards than to the right; and a rather minimal capital 'T', resembling a capital 'J', in which the vertical is slightly curved and the horizontal stroke is lengthened but extends only on the left-hand side.

The manuscript is not dated. The text itself was of highly topical interest, so it seems reasonable to assume that the demand for a translation of it would have been strongest when the text first became available. Since the Latin text was published in the second half of 1626, and since there is some evidence (discussed below) that it was circulating as a novelty in England in the period between January and August 1627, this translation may be tentatively dated to 1627. As we have seen, Hobbes spent some time in the company of Mansfield in August and September 1627, when the latter stayed with his cousin at Chatsworth; so it is possible that the translation was made at that time.[3] The close correspondence between Hobbes's hand here and that found in the

a letter, we find one or more entries in a different hand; these are often followed by a few further entries in Hobbes's hand (a visibly later version of it). It thus appears that another person took charge of registering new acquisitions, during a period when Hobbes was absent from Hardwick. Those additions in another hand include the entry 'Thucidides Eng: Fol:', for Hobbes's translation (1629). Analysis of the publication dates of the books shows that the catalogue was substantially written by Hobbes before his departure in July 1628; some additions were made by an unknown hand during his absence (1628–31), and some further additions by him in the 1630s. The latest certainly datable item among the main entries by Hobbes is S. Gardiner, *The Devotions of the Dying Man* (London, 1627); there is also an entry for G. Hakewill, *An Apologie of the Power and Providence of God in the Government of the World*, which presumably refers to the first edition (Oxford, 1627), not the second (London, 1630). In the main body of Hobbesian entries there is one for A. Ross, *Three Decads of Divine Meditations*, a work dated '1630' in STC; but the book itself (dedicated to Lady Kinloss, either the mother or the sister-in-law of the Countess of Devonshire) is undated. (It was printed for Francis Constable; Ross's three other books printed for Constable appeared between 1617 and 1622.) The Hobbesian entry for one work which was published in 1629 or 1630, B. Soverus [Sovero, Souvey, Schouwey], *Curvi ac recti proportio* (Padua: title page '1630'; colophon '1629'), even though it precedes the entries for 'S' in the other hand, is in fact a subsequent addition by Hobbes (in his later hand), inserted at the foot of a page.

[3] See above, Ch. 1 nn. 43, 59. Cf. also the slight but possibly significant evidence that the copy from which Hobbes translated may have derived from a manuscript copy held

Hardwick library catalogue is fully consistent with such a dating. As usual, the evidence provided by watermarks in the paper does not afford much chronological precision; but it does tend to confirm what the other evidence tells us about the likely origins of this translation. The watermark in this manuscript is a flagpole with a two-tongued banner floating to the right; on the left of the pole, at its base, is a letter 'G', and on the right is a '3' (which, taken with the side of the pole that bounds it, might be read as a 'B').[4] Among Mansfield's surviving papers there are several items with similar watermarks, each with flagpole, double banner, and 'G 3'; each of these is slightly different, and none is an exact match to the watermark in this manuscript (the main difference, which they all share, being that they have a '3' clearly separated from the pole), but it seems reasonable to conclude that Mansfield was buying paper from a supplier who, in turn, was regularly supplied by the same manufacturer, and that that manufacturer made the paper on which this manuscript was written. None of these similarly watermarked items is dated, but one of them contains a selection of satirical poems (in Mansfield's hand) which belong to the final years of James I's reign.[5] Several of his other manuscripts have a watermark which follows the same design but adds a second '3' to the right of the first one: some of these items have been tentatively dated to 1634, and their watermarks resemble that in an item dated 1636 in Heawood's catalogue, so it might be thought that this was a later variant, were it not for the fact that the Hardwick library catalogue drawn up by Hobbes in 1627 or 1628 also has a version of this watermark.[6] Similar watermarks can be

by the London stationer Nathaniel Butter, which was in existence by July 1627 (below, Ch. 4 n. 34).

    [4] This watermark appears on fos. 73, 74, 80, 81, 83. The flagpole is 5.5 cm tall, and the design lies between two chain-lines that are 5.6 cm apart. No countermark is visible. The paper-size is fairly uniform: 30.0 to 30.1 cm tall, and 20.5 to 21.1 cm wide. (Because of the binding, the measurement of the widths here is not absolutely precise.)

    [5] Hallward Library, University of Nottingham, MSS Pw V 522; Pw V 872; Pw V 944; Pw2 V 213 (the satirical poems are in MS Pw V 522).

    [6] Hallward Library, University of Nottingham, MSS Pw 25/19 (fo. 19); Pw 25/44 (fo. 57); Pw 25/48 (fo. 62) [1634?]; Pw 25/49 (fo. 64) [1634?]; Pw 25/57 (fo. 78); Pw 25/139 (fo. 1); Pw 26/196 (fos. 155–9); E. Heawood, *Watermarks mainly of the 17th and 18th Centuries* (Hilversum, 1950), no. 1380. In the Nottingham MSS just listed, the mark has a countermark consisting of a stalk topped by a trefoil (in place of the flagpole and banner) with 'G' on the left at the base of the stalk, one '3' half-way up it on the right, and another '3' below and to the right of that one. In Chatsworth, MS Hobbes E.1.A (the library catalogue), the paper has been cut in such a way that only the lower part of the flagpole (with the 'G 33') is present; this paper also has a trefoil countermark.

found also in letters written by Christian Cavendish, the Countess of Devonshire (Hobbes's employer at Hardwick and Chatsworth) in the early or mid-1630s: in most cases these are the 'G 33' design, but in just one case we find the 'G 3' form (though, once again, with the '3' differing from the ones in our manuscript, insofar as it is clearly detached from the pole).[7] It would thus seem that both branches of the Cavendish family were buying paper supplies from the same source. This evidence does not help with the dating of our manuscript; even if these other items were dated and provided a precise match in the watermarks, this would prove nothing, since a household might use a single stock of paper over a long period.[8] But it does at least tend to confirm—if confirmation is needed—the manuscript's Hobbesian origins.

The character of the manuscript is that of a fair text, designed for presentation: the hand is neat, the writing takes place within margins defined by carefully ruled pencil lines, and catchwords are used at the foot of each page. (The term 'fair text', rather than 'fair copy', is used here advisedly: as the corrections, discussed below, will show, this manuscript was probably not a final copy made from a separate rough draft.) Unfortunately the translation is incomplete; only eleven folios survive, out of an original total of perhaps fourteen, and the text breaks off near the end of section 26, in a work that contained 35 sections in all. That the missing folios did originally exist and have simply gone astray is indicated by the whole character of the manuscript—and, indeed, by the fact that the last surviving page has the catchword for the start of the no longer extant twelfth folio.

That Hobbes wrote out this manuscript does not in itself prove, of course, that he made the translation himself. But he was clearly not just copying out a translation of a Latin text he had not seen. At one point in the manuscript (in section 5) he left a row of asterisks for a particularly puzzling Latin sentence, and then added the Latin words in the margin. Several of the corrections and alterations in the manuscript

---

[7] Hallward Library, University of Nottingham, MSS Pw 1 54 (G 3); Pw 1 59 (G 33); Pw 1 60 (G 33); Pw 1 61 (G 33); Pw 1 63 (G 33). These letters are all undated; internal evidence suggests that some were written in the period 1634–5. MS Pw 1 54 is a brief letter of compliments; unlike the others, it bears an address ('To the right Honourable the Countesse of Newcastle') written in Hobbes's hand.

[8] For striking evidence of this see W. Proctor Williams, 'Paper as Evidence: The Utility of the Study of Paper for Seventeenth-Century English Literary Scholarship', in S. Spector, ed., *Essays in Paper Analysis* (Washington, 1987), pp. 191–9, which notes that at Castle Ashby the same paper was used in 1644, 1666, and 1700.

suggest, indeed, that Hobbes was translating directly from the Latin as he wrote. Just before that untranslated sentence, there was another sentence, awkwardly constructed in the Latin, which seems to have caused Hobbes some difficulty: where the Latin has 'Ille ne ad nuptialia quidem sacra sororem admisit, nec aliâ conditione, quàm ad triumphale epulum', the manuscript has 'And he admitted not his sister to come so much as to his weddinge [though *deleted*>and *deleted*] wthout other condition then to be present at ye Triumphall feast.' (Altered material is placed here in square brackets, and the symbol '>' is used to indicate an interlinear addition.) Here it appears that Hobbes first wrote 'though'; at some stage (probably after writing 'wthout') he deleted it, and replaced it with 'and' as an interlineation; and at some point thereafter, as he continued to wrestle with the meaning of this sentence, he deleted the 'and' as well.

Some other examples offer clearer evidence of Hobbes translating the text as he went along. In section 5, translating the phrase 'proceres offendis, qui tibi subsidia negant, sine eorum nervo rex invalidus est', Hobbes wrote: 'you offend the nobility, who will deny to giue you subsidyes, and wthout [their *deleted*>the] strength of them ye kinge is weake'. Here it seems that he first wrote 'their strength', assuming that 'eorum' referrred to 'proceres' ('the nobility'), and then, realizing that it referred to 'subsidia' ('subsidyes'), decided that 'their strength' should be changed to 'the strength of them'. (At first sight, admittedly, 'their strength' and 'the strength of them' are entirely equivalent in meaning; but if one reads 'the strength of them' placing the emphasis on 'them', this is more likely to be taken to refer to the 'subsidyes'.) Also in section 5, where a discussion of the Duke of Buckingham contained the sentence, 'Dani Legatus sociorum mentem Britanno aperuit, Unius amore impediri pecuniam', Hobbes wrote: 'The Danish Amb.^{r} shewed vnto ye kinge of Brittany the minde of ye Confederates. That [one mans *deleted*>his] loue to one man hindred him of mony.' It thus seems that Hobbes first thought that 'Unius amore' should be translated as 'one mans loue', but then realized that the phrase referred to Charles's love for Buckingham, not vice versa, and changed the phrase which he had just written ('one mans loue') to 'his loue to one man'. A discussion of the policies of Gábor Bethlen in section 13 contained the phrase, 'aurum quaerit, post aurum auxilia venditat, non praesentat'; Hobbes's manuscript has 'He seekes for mony, wch gotten, he shewes his [ayde *deleted*] forces, but bringes them not on.' Here it seems that Hobbes's first impulse was to translate 'auxilia' in accordance with the most simple meaning of that term (helps, assistance), and that it was only a moment later that he realized that it referred here to armed forces. In a discussion of Venetian policy in section 15, where the Latin has 'Dux ipse', Hobbes wrote 'the [Generall *deleted*>Duke] himselfe': here he seems to have been misled at first, by a reference to soldiers in the previous sentence, into taking 'Dux' in its military sense, before recognizing that it referred to the Doge or 'Duke' of Venice. In section 16 the Latin describes the position of the Emperor Ferdinand as follows: 'At Caesar licet afflictus, vastas tamen habet, & fertilitate nativa dites Provincias'; Hobbes wrote 'But Caesar though he [be troubled *deleted*] receaue hurt, yet hath he large and fertile Provinces'. Here it appears that Hobbes first interpreted 'afflictus' in its psychological sense, and that it was only on considering the meaning of the rest of the sentence that he understood that it referred to material loss. In section 21, where the Latin has 'Fallere autem promptum erit, si Hispano, Caesaríve, aut Boio liberi tradantur educandi', Hobbes wrote 'It will be easie to deceaue them, if you deliuer your children [to the Spaniard *deleted*] to be brought up by yᵉ Spaniard the Empʳ or Bauiere'. Here the construction 'deliver your children to' seems to have led him naturally to the list of indirect objects, and it was only after writing down the first of these, 'the Spaniard', that he realized that a translation of 'educandi' had to be fitted in first.

Of these corrections, only the ones involving the awkwardly constructed sentence in section 5 and the reference to the Doge of Venice in section 15 (which has a simple interlineation) could have been made after the whole manuscript had been written out. In the other cases, it is necessary to assume that Hobbes had the Latin in front of him and was thinking carefully about it as he wrote the English version. Of course he could have been producing a fair copy of an earlier rough draft, trying to correct errors in it as he went along. One or two minor corrections are consistent with that scenario. For example, the fact that an 'of' needed to be changed into an 'or' in section 24 might have arisen from an initial misreading of a badly written 'or' in his draft (though, on the other hand, the presence of an uncorrected 'vngergo' instead of 'vndergo' in section 16 shows that Hobbes was quite capable of simple slips of the pen).[9] The overall nature of the manuscript, as

---

[9] One or two other corrections might suggest, on the other hand, aural rather than visual errors: a 'yoʳ' deleted and replaced by 'you are' (in section 8), and what looks like 'by' deleted and replaced by 'buy' (in section 25). But the manuscript as a whole does not look like a product of dictation. Errors of this sort can often be made by writers who

a fair text disfigured by few corrections, would also support such a hypothesis. However, if Hobbes did produce a rough draft first, one might expect him to have done all his wrestling with the meaning of the text (especially with textual problems as simple as most of the ones mentioned above) at that stage, and to have confined himself at the next stage to merely producing a fair copy of what was in the corrected draft—whereas the corrections analysed above indicate that he was not only checking carefully against the original but also doing some rather primary thinking about the meaning of the text when he produced the manuscript we have.[10] That he could have produced this fair text at the first attempt is not implausible, even though the Latin is rebarbative in places. (He did admit defeat where one sentence was concerned; but there the difficulty lay not so much in converting the Latin into English, as in seeing how the resulting English sentence could make sense with regard to the situation it purported to describe.) After all, it is not necessary to assume that Hobbes was reading the text for the first time as he translated it: he may have had plenty of time to study it in the Latin first. But he was in any case a talented classicist—someone who, within a couple of years of writing this translation, would publish the first ever English translation of Thucydides directly from the Greek.

If it is possible, nevertheless, that Hobbes was working here from an earlier rough draft, is it also possible that that draft was not by him, and that he was merely making small corrections to someone else's work? This scenario cannot be entirely excluded, but the balance of the evidence is set very firmly against it. Once again, the nature of the

are in the habit of listening to the words in their mind's ear as they write—especially if they are at the same time distracted by other tasks, as a translator thinking about his translation may well be. Another error ('youc', corrected to 'you' and followed by 'can': in section 4) seems neither aural nor particularly visual, merely indicating distraction.

[10] One other case of an interlinear correction may be noted here, which seems easily compatible with the idea that he was translating the text for the first time as he wrote this manuscript (though other explanations may also be possible). In section 2, translating 'incentor Allobrox', he wrote: the [Grison *deleted*>Sauoyard] instigatinge'. (The correction was right: the Grisons are in the south-eastern corner of present-day Switzerland, whereas the Allobroges were a tribe who lived to the south and south-west of Lake Geneva, in an area roughly corresponding to the duchy of Savoy.) A similar translation of 'Allobrox' (in section 3) as 'The Grisons' went uncorrected. Later in the text Hobbes would have encountered 'Arma Rhetica' (section 7), which he translated as 'The Grison . . . warres', 'Grisones' (section 8), translated as 'Grisons', and 'Allobrogibus' (section 9), translated as 'to . . . y^e . . . Sauoyards'. It seems that, by this stage, the context had made the distinctions between these references much clearer, enabling him to go back to section 2 and make the correction; but he apparently forgot that the term 'Allobrox' had also occurred in section 3.

heaued it on, and set it going. you know your owne and your freinds
wordes. I warned you of the vncertainty of Princes aydes. They haue
eaten vp the Palatinate. They gaue Spinola the best place of y⁰ land
to winter in. Conditioninge headlong for themselues they followed
fortune: and some of them warred for y⁰ Spaniard. Indeed all men
haue fortune in Lord⁰, and are afrayde to helpe one that is falling:
but one fallen they will neuer take vp. I affirmed that succours
from Vinice would come but leasurely. Their Amb.r a hundred times
entreated, would afford none. To giue you much he said, would be
a burthen to them, and to giue a little would do you no good, and
be no hono⁰ for their Republique. The Grisons complayned that
they were ensnared by your fraud. Of France and others they were
iealous that I told you, and are all come to passe. And this was
in y⁰ first Instruction.

4.

I haue made way for credit. now like a good Tiresias I adde
my aduise, and shew you to y⁰ selfe. I will first tell you what
you cannot do. Next what you can. Choose what you please. The
first deliberation is the more laborious, for many things you
cannot do, w⁰⁰ you thinke you can. The other will be shorter for
you cannot do much. A wise mans care is to consider first quid
ferunt humeri quid ferre recusant. Fooles by indeauoring
vayne workes, wast the strength they should employ on that w⁰⁰ might
do them good. this I would haue you to auoyd. Abstayne from
vnprofitable paynes, that you may hold out in profitable. But
lets come into y⁰ path.

5.

you cannot be restord by your Brother in law. for y⁰ owne
sake he will not. He hates you out of emulation, he hates you
out of ielousie. Neyther are the causes nor the effects of this
hatred secret. He keepes in mind the words of you and y⁰ls and
your rough letters to his Father, full of contumely towards him. y⁰ls
                                                                    Father

2

Plate 1. Hobbes, translation of *Altera secretissima instructio* (BL, MS Add. 70499, fo. 74r). Original size: 30 × 21 cm. Reproduced by permission of the Trustees of the British Library.

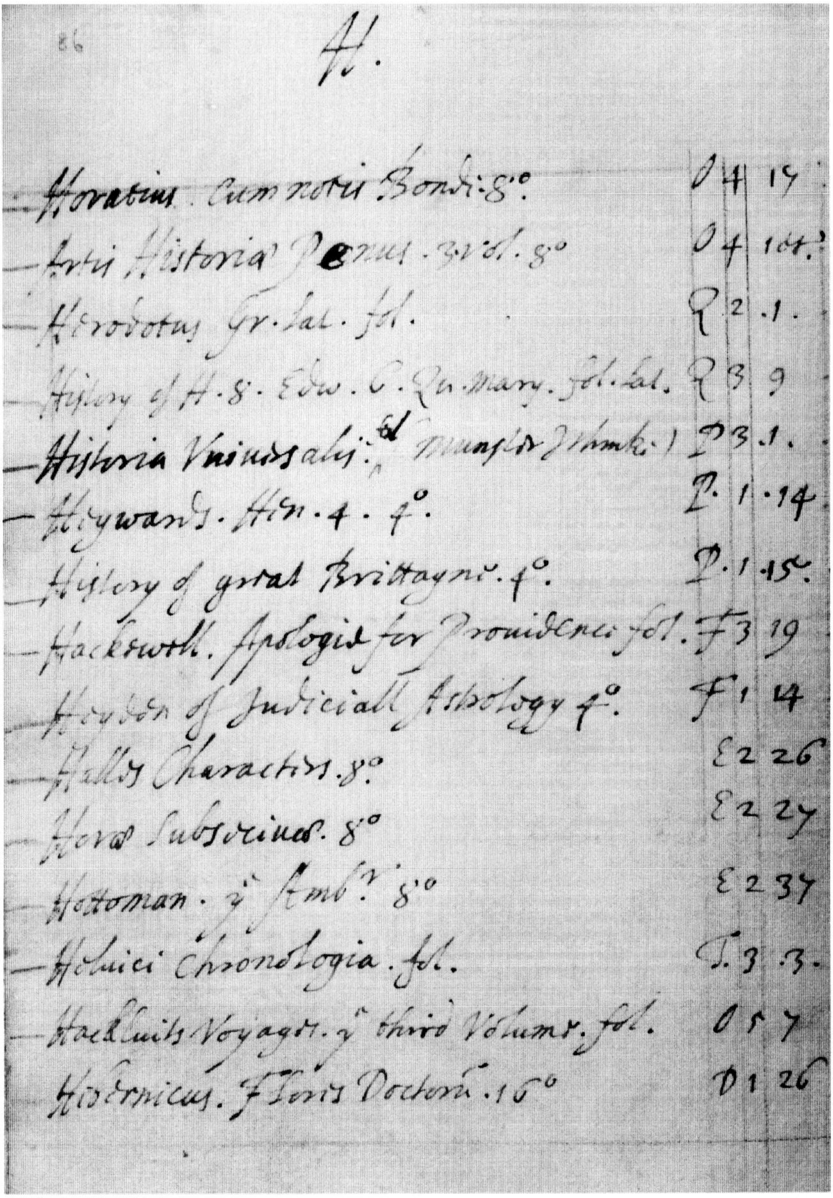
86

H.

Horatius. Cum notis Bondi. 8°.	O	4	19
Artis Historiae Penus. 3 vol. 8°	O	4	14
Herodotus Gr. lat. fol.	R	2	1
History of H. 8. Edw. 6. Qu. mary. fol. lat.	R	3	9
Historia Universalis. fol. Munster Dutch.	P	3	1
Heywards. Hen. 4. 4°.	P	1	14
History of great Brittayne. 4°.	P	1	15
Hackwell. Apologie for Providence. fol.	F	3	19
Heydon of Judiciall Astrology 4°.	F	1	14
Halls Characters. 8°.	E	2	26
Horae Subsecivae. 8°	E	2	27
Hottoman. ye Ambr. 8°	E	2	37
Helvici Chronologia. fol.	T	3	3
Hackluits Voyages. ye third Volume. fol.	O	5	7
Hibernicus. Flores Doctorum. 16°	D	1	26

Plate 2. Hobbes, Hardwick library catalogue (Chatsworth, MS Hobbes E.1.A, p. 86). Original size: 20 × 15 cm. Reproduced by permission of the Trustees of the Chatsworth Settlement.

corrections would seem hard to square with such a scenario: a translator who had got so many difficult things right would hardly have left, in his draft, the sort of simple errors that can arise only on a first glance at a phrase or sentence. Another point that counts rather strongly against this scenario is that there are many minor omissions (of words, phrases, or sentences) in the translation. As is noted below, it is conceivable that all of these were caused by omissions in the manuscript copy of the Latin from which the translation may have been made—conceivable, but not very likely. (In the three surviving manuscript copies made in England in this period, one of which may correspond quite closely to the copy used in the making of this translation, all the missing words and phrases are present.)[11] If we assume that at least some of the missing material was present in the Latin copy that was used in this case, and if we suppose that Hobbes was going through a draft translation by somebody else and comparing it carefully with the original, it must seem very strange that he neither drew attention to any of those omissions nor attempted to remedy them.

There are other reasons, too, for doubting that Hobbes would have been put to work as a mere transcriber or polisher of someone else's work. The translation was presumably commissioned by Mansfield; the most likely scenario is that he had obtained a copy of this notorious Latin pamphlet and, finding the Latin difficult, had requested a translation from some suitably skilled person in his employment or under his patronage. If that person was not Hobbes but someone else (say, a secretary or chaplain), it is hard to see why that same person should not also have written out the fair copy. Both translating and copying were secretarial tasks, and, since the latter had a slightly lower status, it is even harder to see why it should have been given to Hobbes, whose intellectual standing—at a time when he had probably started, and might already have finished, his path-breaking work on Thucydides—must have been well known to Mansfield. The corrections are few and far between; if the translator was someone other than Hobbes, that person could have been asked to produce a fair copy, which Hobbes could merely have annotated. And, in any case, if the other person had been thought to be such an inferior Latinist that his work needed to be corrected by Hobbes, it would surely have made more sense to commission the translation from Hobbes in the first place.

[11] See below, Ch. 4 n. 34.

In 1627, of course, Hobbes was the employee not of Mansfield but of his namesake and cousin (who will be referred to as 'Devonshire'—or, for the period preceding his succession to the earldom, as 'Lord Cavendish'—hereafter). So the possibility should also be considered that the manuscript was prepared at Devonshire's request—even though Devonshire was a much better Latinist than his cousin—and that it was then lent or given to Mansfield. But here too the same objection would apply: there is no reason to think that Devonshire would have had a more suitable translator to hand, or that that translator would then have been thought more unsuited than Hobbes to the task of copying out the final manuscript version. It should be recalled that, over the course of many years, Hobbes had prepared translations of the Italian letters Devonshire had received from Fulgenzio Micanzio; this was just the sort of work that he was used to doing. But it should also be noted that, when it came to preparing copies of that sequence of translated letters, the services of a copyist—not Hobbes himself—were used. It should also be borne in mind, finally, that there is absolutely no sign, in the manuscript translation of the *Altera secretissima instructio*, of any correction or intervention by another hand.

The attribution of this translation to Hobbes can also be strengthened by some stylistic considerations, arising from a comparison between this text and the two other major specimens of prose from this period in Hobbes's life: his translations of Micanzio's letters and Thucydides. Of course, since all three items are translations, the comparison does not take place on a level playing field: each text bears the impress of the style of the original, especially where syntactical and structural matters are concerned. (Indeed, out of all three cases, the translation of the *Altera secretissima instructio* is the one most strongly influenced by the style of the original—an almost parodically Tacitean style, which contrives to be antithetical, sententious, and constantly, grimly compressed.) Nevertheless, some common features, particularly at the lexical and semantic level, may be noticed. Some of the more distinctive vocabulary of this text can be found in the Micanzio and Thucydides translations: for example, 'appeacher', 'crimination', 'donative', and 'prank' (with the meaning 'evil deed').[12] Translating Thucydides, Hobbes almost always

12 In this and the following notes, references to the manuscript will be given by section number, and the other two texts will be referred to as 'Micanzio' and 'Thucydides'. Appeacher: section 9; Thucydides, pp. 70 ('appeachment'), 383, marginal note ('appeach'). Crimination: section 9; Thucydides, sig. a4r, pp. 16, 39, 42 ('criminations'). Donative:

uses 'league' and 'confederates' rather than 'alliance' and 'allies'; the same pattern of usage appears here.[13] Also common to this text and the Thucydides translation are the use of 'hardly' to mean 'with difficulty'; the use of 'rifle' as the verb of choice for pillaging or sacking a city; the use of 'obnoxious' (meaning 'liable' or 'subject'); and the use of 'go through' (meaning 'go forth', 'proceed').[14] In the English of this period, there were many phrases using the word 'little' and meaning 'gradually' or 'bit by bit': 'little by little', 'by little and by little', 'by little and little', 'little and little', 'little by little', 'by a little', 'by little'. This manuscript uses 'by little and little', and that is also the form used in the translations of both Micanzio and Thucydides.[15] Another case of variant forms concerns the naming of mountains, where 'Mount X', 'the Mount of X', 'the Mountain of X', and 'the Mountain X' were all possible. This manuscript has 'ye Mountayne Voige' (actually translating a plural, 'Vogesi montes'); that is also the form used in the great majority of cases in the Thucydides translation, which gives, for example, 'the Mountaine *Laurius*', 'the Mountaine *Rhodope*', 'the Mountaine *Scomius*', and 'the Mountaine *Lycaeum*'.[16]

Some slightly distinctive constructions are also common to both texts. This manuscript has 'his loue to one man hindred him of mony', where the verb 'to hinder' takes an indirect object with 'of', with the meaning, 'prevented him from getting money'.[17] The Thucydides translation, similarly, has 'hindered of their liberty'.[18] Again, this manuscript has the phrase 'yor mind . . . imagined kingdomes to it selfe', apparently with the meaning, 'imagined kingdoms being possessed by itself', or 'imagined

section 23; Micanzio, pp. 186, 238, 285 ('donatives'), 256 ('donative'). Prank: section 9 ('prankes'); Thucydides, p. 534 ('some vnlawfull pranke').

[13] In the manuscript the distribution is as follows: 'league' and 'leaguers': seven times; 'confederate': three times; 'allies': once. The Micanzio translation also uses 'league' and 'confederate' (and 'confederacion') almost exclusively.

[14] Hardly: section 16; Micanzio, p. 256; Thucydides, p. 233. Rifle: section 2 ('riflinge'); Thucydides, pp. 4, 97, 285, 491 ('rifled'). Obnoxious: sections 11, 22; Thucydides, pp. 2, 22, 105 (this was the normal meaning of 'obnoxious'; the point is that Hobbes tended to use it in preference to 'liable', 'subject', or 'prone'). Go through: section 18; Thucydides, p. 278.

[15] By little and little: section 19; Micanzio, pp. 206, 233; Thucydides, pp. 229, 273; *OED* 'little', B7.

[16] 'ye Mountayne Voige': section 18; Thucydides, pp. 111, 137, 138, 299.

[17] Section 5.

[18] Thucydides, p. 260: 'lest they should be hindered of their liberty by your example'. Cf. also Micanzio, p. 196 (on the celebration of a coronation): 'the crowne was brought thither in very bad weather wch hindred the vallyes of shott & other tokens of joy'.

itself acquiring kingdoms'.[19] The Thucydides translation has 'imagined to themselues the principality', which uses the same construction.[20] This manuscript has 'the Gallies went out, to the guard of ye Euxine sea', where 'to the guard of' (translating 'ad . . . custodiam') means 'for the guarding of', 'in order to guard'.[21] The Thucydides translation has the following: 'But the *Syracusians* and their Confederates, being out already with the same number of Gallies, they had before disposed part of them to the guard of the open passage'.[22] Also common to the two texts is a peculiar type of fault, arising from a rather erratic use of pronouns which either point to a non-existent noun or have a different person or number from what the sense seems to require. In this manuscript we have the awkward sentence 'The confidence of good fortune when it is gentlest is content with floutinge such as aduise them to moderation, but moued crusheth him that aduiseth'—where 'them' lacks any proper reference, appearing to stand for a general or impersonal object.[23] In the Thucydides translation we find the following: 'And a Citie when it reuolteth, supposeth it selfe to be better furnished, either of themselues, or by their Confederates, then it is'.[24] (In this case 'themselues' and 'their' should clearly be 'itself' and 'its'; but both cases seem to show the same tendency to gravitate towards plural pronouns in cases where there is either an impersonal reference, or no definite reference at all.)[25]

There is one other small but very striking feature of this translation that does seem distinctively Hobbesian. Where the Latin refers to the Ottoman government as 'porta', the usual English translation would have been (in the seventeenth century, as now) 'the Porte'; but this translation uses 'the Gate' instead, even though the translator is clearly

---

[19] Section 2.
[20] Thucydides, p. 314: 'hauing . . . imagined to themselues the principality of all *Peloponnesus*'.
[21] Section 14.   [22] Thucydides, p. 454.   [23] Section 2.
[24] Thucydides, p. 168.
[25] A similar phenomenon occurs quite often in the manuscript of *Leviathan* (BL, MS Egerton 1910): e.g. fo. 27v, 'for let a man (as most men do,) rate themselues at the highest Value they can' (with 'a man' corrected by Hobbes in the MS to 'men', but not corrected in the 1651 edition, p. 42); fo. 38v: 'a vain conceipt of ones owne wisdome, which allmost euery man thinkes he hath in a greater degree, than the Vulgar; that is, than all men but themselues' (corrected in the 1651 edition, p. 61); fo. 64v, 'every man hauing equall right to submit himself to such as they thinke best able to protect them; or if they can, protect themselues by their owne swords' (corrected in the 1651 edition, p. 100). As these examples show, some, but not all, of these errors were picked up in the printing-house. Another instance that went unnoticed is on p. 110 of the 1651 edition: 'every Common-wealth, (not every man) has an absolute Libertie, to doe what it shall judge . . . most conducing to their benefit'.

aware that this is not a term to be understood literally.[26] Thus 'si venerit Hispanus ille, &. . . portam salutârit' is translated as 'if that spaniard come and salute yᵉ Gate', and 'Mehemetus Bassa. . . petit à porta. . . ut cum Gabore agatur de auxilijs' as 'Mahomet Bassa. . . desires at the Gate. . . that Gabor may be dealt withall for ayde'.[27] It is surely significant that, throughout his translations of Micanzio's letters (which make frequent reference to events in Constantinople), Hobbes consistently uses 'the Gate' and not 'the Porte': 'They hope by the Polander and by money att yᵉ gate to have the Transylvanian taken of'; 'The Polackes have spent much at the gate in guiftes and in money'; 'Gabor hath great Intelligence att yᵉ Gate'; and so on.[28]

Finally, one other detail should also be mentioned: at one point in the Thucydides translation, where Hobbes observes that some material is missing, he marks this by putting a row of asterisks in the text and placing the missing material (or, at least, a conjectural restitution thereof) in the margin—exactly the same method as that used for the untranslated sentence in the manuscript here.[29] Of course this method, like many of the other details of usage mentioned above, might also have been adopted by many other writers. The point of mentioning all these details is not to suggest that any one of them—not even, perhaps, the use of 'the Gate'—constitutes conclusive evidence of Hobbes's authorship; rather, it is to show that there is a pattern of internal evidence that tends to confirm, or at the very least is entirely compatible with, all the other evidence indicating that Hobbes was responsible for the translation of the *Altera secretissima instructio*.

The quality of that translation is generally good; it conveys the meaning fluently but economically, with very little embroidery or amplification. The language is for the most part clear and vigorous, with occasional touches of a more colloquial vocabulary ('slubbers', 'lyes pat'), and the overall effect is that of a lively English text. (However, Hobbes has left one element untranslated: the Latin tags, which in the

---

[26] The *OED* records only two examples of 'the gate' being used in this sense, from 1585 and 1599 ('gate', n., 3c). In the first, the term is used as part of an explanation ('the court of the great Lord (which they call the gate)'); in the second, it is itself explained ('The gate of the great Turke, is as much to say, as Constantinople'). In ordinary—unexplained, or non-explanatory—usage, 'Porte' or 'Port' was the standard term in the seventeenth century; so one would expect it to have been used quite automatically by someone translating the Latin word 'porta' in this context.

[27] Section 14.

[28] See Micanzio, *Lettere*, pp. 98, 107, 165; cf. also pp. 109, 161, 173, 182, 231, 239, 253, 276, 286, 314.

[29] Thucydides, p. 480; cf. section 5.

original are set off on the page and printed in italics. These, with one tiny exception, are left in Latin, and presented in larger script for emphasis.[30] Perhaps he felt that he could in this way pay an implicit compliment to Mansfield's linguistic abilities without omitting anything essential from the translation.) In his translation Hobbes sticks quite closely to the Latin syntax: this sometimes produces verbless sentences, or strings of clauses which can be terminated almost indifferently by commas, semicolons, or full points. (That a full point is sometimes followed by a clause not beginning with a capital letter is not an error; this was normal practice in English handwriting in this period, indicating a pause less complete than that between one sentence and another.) In just a few places Hobbes's closeness to the Latin makes him guilty of awkward constructions and/or inadequate translations: 'The confidence of good fortune when it is gentlest is content with floutinge such as aduise them to moderation' would be an example of the former even without its problematic 'them', and 'But for ye Turkes ayd, if Ferenzius get it not wth bribes, the English and Venetian Amb:^rs doubt it much' exemplifies the latter.[31] Very occasionally, his version fails to capture the sense (for instance, giving 'swift' for 'fugacem', which should have been translated as 'apt to flee' or 'timid'), or translates perversely (for example, giving 'That a Prince of Antient power shold not be put downe' for 'Non privandum avitis opibus Principem', which should have been translated as 'That a prince should not be deprived of his ancestral possessions').[32] These rare errors are all the more surprising because Hobbes has elsewhere coped with challenging constructions and some fairly recondite vocabulary. He has also been faced with some quite demanding proper names: his difficulties with finding the modern geopolitical meaning of 'Allobrox' have already been noted, and it may be doubted whether the identity of the rivers 'Visurgis & Albis' (which he correctly translated as 'Weesell, and Elue', i.e. the Weser and the Elbe) would have been apparent to him, without at least some time spent consulting geographical works.[33] (This may add weight to the

---

[30] The exception is in section 26, where '*interluit amnis*' is translated within the text as 'The riuer runs betweene their Prouinces'.

[31] Section 2; section 14 (where the meaning of the Latin is 'However, the British and Venetian Ambassadors doubt whether there will be any Turkish assistance, unless Ferenc obtains it by gifts').

[32] Sections 11, 19.

[33] On 'Allobrox' see above, n. 10. Such homework was not as thorough as it should have been, though: Hobbes apparently thought that 'Wolfenbutelius' was a personal

suggestion, made above, that he had had time to study the text and prepare for his translation before he began writing out the manuscript which we now have.) A few emendations have been made where the Latin was defective: 'deperasset' has been identified as an error for 'desperasset' and 'lacerae' as an error for 'lacernae', and at one point a much less obvious error has been corrected by taking a phrase which is presented in italics in the original as if it were part of a quotation, de-italicizing it, and treating it as part of the commentary instead.[34] The most puzzling feature of this translation is its omission of many minor phrases or sentences. In just one case we can see Hobbes making an omission deliberately, where he has translated the phrase and then deleted it (apparently because, not understanding what it referred to, he thought it did not make sense).[35] In most of the other cases the material omitted is hardly substantive, merely amplifying what has gone before. As has been noted already, it is conceivable that Hobbes was working from a manuscript copy of the Latin text from which, for some reason, all these phrases and sentences were omitted; but there is no independent evidence to support this, and the surviving copies produced by scribes in England do contain all of the missing material.[36] So it seems reasonable to assume that many (possibly all) of these omissions were made by Hobbes—some, perhaps, deliberately, but some unintentionally as his eye passed from the text to his translation and back again.

name (see section 17, at n. 211). He also seems to have thought that 'Caimecamus' (the Ottoman title 'kaimakam') was a personal name (see section 14, at n. 164). Although the earliest version of this title cited from an English text in the *OED* is from 1645, an explanation of it was available in a text which may have been contained in the Hardwick library, though Hobbes would have had to search hard to find this particular passage: 'When the Visier is sent abroad, he makes choice of one of the Bassaes to be his Lieutenant, and to execute his authoritie, and hee is called Chimacham' (R. Knolles, *The Generall Historie of the Turkes*, 3rd edn. (London, 1621), p. 1391: this is from the new material added to this edition by Edward Grimeston). The Hardwick catalogue written by Hobbes in 1627 or 1628 (Chatsworth, MS Hobbes E. 1. A.) has an entry 'Turkish History. Eng. fol.', which presumably refers to Knolles's book; but the edition is not specified.

[34] See section 14 (at n. 174); section 19 (at n. 224); section 10 (at n. 118); the last correction here may already have been made by a copyist.
[35] See section 7 (at n. 71).   [36] See below, Ch. 4 n. 34.

3

The 'Secretissima instructio' Texts

WHAT sort of text, then, was the *Altera secretissima instructio*, and why was it thought so worthy of attention? It was in fact the third in a sequence of pamphlets (though its title, *Altera* . . ., correctly translated by Hobbes as 'A second . . .', suggests that its author was unaware of the second in the sequence); the first, entitled *Secretissima instructio*, had achieved considerable notoriety, becoming one of Europe's most widely read works of political propaganda after its first publication in 1620.

Since the outbreak of the Thirty Years' War in 1618, a flood of pamphlets, newsletters, and broadsheets, both informative and polemical, had poured from the presses. While it might be an exaggeration to speak of a Europe-wide public opinion, it is clear that there were publics in all of the relevant European states whose opinions were thought to matter: considerable efforts were made by rulers and political leaders both to control the flow of such publications and to insert into it works supportive of their own policies. A whole gamut of publications was thus produced, ranging from crude satirical broadsheets to official declarations and Latin treatises by scholars.[1] Readers of all kinds wanted

[1] No Europe-wide overview of this material is available, nor would one be easy to form. The best general account of the writing and circulation of such propaganda is P. Schmidt, *Spanische Universalmonarchie oder 'teutsche Libertet': das spanische Imperium in der Propaganda des Dreissigjährigen Krieges* (Stuttgart, 2001), pp. 51–94. Specific studies include R. Koser, *Die Kanzleienstreit: ein Beitrag zur Quellenkunde der Geschichte des dreissigjährigen Krieges* (Halle, 1874); M. Grünbaum, *Über die Publicistik des dreissigjährigen Krieges von 1626–1629* (Halle, 1880); G. Gebauer, *Die Publicistik über den böhmischen Aufstand von 1618* (Halle, 1892); F. Dahl, 'Gustav II Adolf i samtida engelska ettbladstryck', *Nordisk tidskrift för bok- och biblioteksväsen*, 25 (1938), pp. 173–89; E. A. Beller, *Propaganda in Germany during the Thirty Years' War* (Princeton, 1940); D. Böttcher, 'Propaganda und öffentliche Meinung im protestantischen Deutschland, 1628–1636', *Archiv für Reformationsgeschichte*, 44 (1953), pp. 181–203, and 45 (1954), pp. 83–99; G. Rystad, *Kriegsnachrichten und Propaganda während des dreissigjährigen Krieges: die Schlacht bei Nördlingen in den gleichzeitigen, gedruckten Kriegsberichten* (Lund, 1960); A. E. C. Simoni, 'Poems, Pictures and the Press: Observations on some Abraham Verhoeven Newsletters (1620–1621)', in F. de Nave, ed., *Liber amicorum Leon Voet*

news, of course; most may have enjoyed the entertainment provided by popular satire; and an elite of readers may have wanted to master the official justifications on both sides (concerning the rights to the Bohemian crown, the legal powers of Electors and of the Holy Roman Emperor, and so on).[2] But for a large part of the educated reading public, the pamphlet literature satisfied an interest of a different kind. For more than a generation, educated people had studied the works of writers in the so-called 'reason of state' ('ragion di stato') tradition, and had thought about the unscrupulous methods of political action which those writers both criticized and, to a certain extent, endorsed.[3] As the Thirty Years' War progressed, much of Europe became, as it were, a huge public laboratory in which the theories of reason of state—where high politics, diplomacy, and the use of armed force were concerned—could be tested and demonstrated; and this, for readers who had hitherto studied the practice of reason of state mostly in the works of historians, must have been a fascinating, even an exhilarating, experience.

On several occasions the 'arcana' of international politics were quite dramatically unveiled. During the summer of 1620, a set of compromising letters from the Habsburg side was published, probably by Ludwig Camerarius, a scholar and statesman in the service of the Elector Palatine. In November 1620, in the chaos following the battle of the White Mountain outside Prague, an important collection of Palatine documents (including much confidential correspondence) fell into the hands of the Habsburgs: this was the so-called 'chancery' of the Elector Palatine's chief adviser, Christian of Anhalt-Bernburg. The Habsburgs published a large selection of the most incriminating items in 1621, first in several German editions and then, for Europe-wide consumption, in Latin translation: the main aim of this publication (known as the

---

(Antwerp, 1985), pp. 353–73; T. Cogswell, 'The Politics of Propaganda: Charles I and the People in the 1620s', *Journal of British Studies*, 29 (1990), pp. 187–215; T. K. Rabb, 'English Readers and the Revolt in Bohemia, 1619–1622', in M. Aberbach, ed., *Aharon M. K. Rabinowicz Jubilee Volume* (Jerusalem, 1996), pp. 152–75; P. Arblaster, 'Current-affairs Publishing in the Habsburg Netherlands, 1620–1660, in Comparative European Perspective', Oxford University D.Phil. thesis (1999); J. Miller, *Falcký mýtus: Fridrich V. a obraz české války v raně stuartovské Anglii* (Prague, 2003). I have not seen W. Schumacher, 'Vox Populi: The Thirty Years' War in English Pamphlets and Newspapers', Princeton University PhD thesis (1975).

[2] See the comments on the importance of justificatory pamphlets (on both sides) in the early period of the war in V.-L. Tapié, *La Politique étrangère et le début de la guerre de trente ans (1616–1621)* (Paris, 1934), pp. 410–16.

[3] See below, Ch. 6.

Cancellaria anhaltina) was to scandalize European opinion by revealing the Elector Palatine's attempts to encourage an Ottoman invasion of Habsburg territory. It was not long before the Palatine side had its revenge: a set of letters from the Emperor Ferdinand was captured in late 1621, and published (as the *Cancellaria hispanica*) in the following year. These letters revealed, among other things, that the Emperor had already promised to transfer the Palatine Electorate to Maximilian of Bavaria—something he had kept secret from his ally, the King of Spain. After the surrender of Heidelberg in 1622 more documents from the Palatine side were printed; and further embarrassment was caused when several of Ludwig Camerarius's letters, containing criticisms of key allies, were seized and published in 1627.[4] Never before had the interested public been able to eavesdrop to such an extent on the most confidential counsels and negotiations of their rulers.

It was those rulers themselves who had authorized the release of these documents; they believed that such revelations could do much damage to their opponents, and they were not mistaken. Equally, therefore, they took great care to engage the most able of the intellectuals in their service to edit these works, write authoritative responses to the other side's revelations, and go onto the offensive with their own propaganda pamphlets. Maximilian of Bavaria was particularly active in this field, employing not only his chief counsellor Wilhelm Jocher but also two leading Jesuits, Jakob Keller and Adam Contzen. In 1624–5, for example, Contzen produced for him two (anonymous) pamphlets sharply criticizing Richelieu's foreign policy, *Mysteria politica* and *Admonitio ad Ludovicem XIII regem*; Richelieu had both condemned by the Sorbonne and publicly burnt, and was soon organizing counter-pamphlets of his own.[5] Of course the production of such propaganda was not confined to officially sponsored authors; some writers were

    [4] On these publications see F. Krüner, *Johann von Rusdorf, kurpfälzischer Gesandter und Staatsmann während des dreissigjährigen Krieges* (Halle, 1876), pp. 97–8; Koser, *Die Kanzleienstreit*; F. H. Schubert, *Ludwig Camerarius, 1573–1651: eine Biographie* (Munich, 1955), pp. 117–40; D. Albrecht, *Die auswärtige Politik Maximilians von Bayern, 1618–1635* (Göttingen, 1962), pp. 72–3.
    [5] Schubert, *Ludwig Camerarius*, pp. 138–9; Albrecht, *Die auswärtige Politik*, pp. 155–6; R. Bireley, *The Jesuits and the Thirty Years War: Kings, Courts, and Confessors* (Cambridge, 2003), pp. 69–71. W. F. Church also discusses this episode (*Richelieu and Reason of State* (Princeton, 1972) pp. 121–6), but is unaware of Contzen's authorship. On Keller and Contzen see also R. Krebs, *Die politische Publizistik der Jesuiten und ihrer Gegner in den letzten Jahrzehnten vor Ausbruch des dreissigjährigen Krieges* (Halle, 1890), pp. 183–4, 219–20.

entirely independent, such as the prolific English Puritan Thomas Scott, whose pamphlets, mostly printed in Holland, harshly criticized the foreign policy of James I and Charles I.[6] And some, while not directly employed by any of the powers involved, may have enjoyed semi-official encouragement or assistance. An example is furnished by the case of Giovanni Francesco Biondi, a Dalmatian-Italian Protestant and former diplomatic agent of the Duke of Savoy, who, living as a private citizen in London, told the Palatine ambassador there in late 1626 that he was writing a reply to an Italian anti-Palatine pamphlet; the ambassador promptly wrote to Ludwig Camerarius, asking for his own annotations on the pamphlet and saying how important it was that they should supply Biondi with 'true and solid information'.[7]

Not all the information in these propaganda pamphlets was either solid or true. Some fictions circulated that may have been concocted deliberately to deceive their readers, such as the forged letter from Christian IV of Denmark, criticizing Buckingham, which was taken to be genuine by Buckingham's parliamentary opponents in 1626.[8] But in many cases the pamphlets were more or less transparent fictions, meant to be realistic but probably not intended to deceive. Thomas Scott's most famous production, *Vox populi: Or, News from Spayne* (1620) purported to present the minutes of a meeting of Gondomar (on his return to Spain) with the Spanish Council of State, setting out their agreed policy—both Machiavellian and utterly fanatical—towards England; Scott was presumably surprised to discover that this work was taken by many readers as 'a genuine piece of reportage'.[9] Contzen's anti-French

---

[6] On Scott see S. L. Adams, 'The Protestant Cause: Religious Alliance with the West European Calvinist Communities as a Political Issue in England, 1585–1630', Oxford University D.Phil. thesis (1973), appendix 3 (pp. 448–62), 'The Career of Thomas Scott and Bohemian Propaganda'; P. G. Lake, 'Constitutional Consensus and Puritan Opposition in the 1620s: Thomas Scott and the Spanish Match', *Historical Journal*, 25 (1982), pp. 805–25; S. Kelsey, 'Thomas Scott', *Oxford Dictionary of National Biography* (www.oxforddnb.com).

[7] [L. C. Mieg, ed.,] *Monumenta pietatis & literaria virorum in re publica & literaria illustrium selecta*, 2 vols. (Frankfurt am Main, 1701), ii, p. 391, Rusdorf to Camerarius, 10 December 1626 ('opus est, ut ei suggeramus veras & solidas informationes'). Biondi's pamphlet, if it was ever published, has not been identified; it is not mentioned in the most detailed modern study of Biondi's life and works (V. Kostić, *Kulturne veze izmedju Jugoslovenskih zemalja i Engleske do 1700. godine* (Belgrade, 1972), pp. 52–115).

[8] Adams, 'The Protestant Cause', p. 392. A copy of this letter is PRO, SP 75/7/64: 'S^r. I am crediblie informed that there is a Sub^t in yor Kdome that rules it more then yor selfe, Let him bee remoued, or Ile remoue my Forces, disband them, purchase a Peace wth the Enemy, Neither expect any future helpe from you, nor lend you any. Farewell.'

[9] Kelsey, 'Thomas Scott'.

pamphlet *Mysteria politica, hoc est, epistolae arcanae virorum illustrium sibi mutuò confidentium, lectu & consideratione dignae* (1624) took the form of a series of fictitious letters between statesmen, diplomatic agents, and theologians in Constantinople, Venice, The Hague, Paris, and Turin, all commenting quite realistically on the Palatine issue and French foreign policy. A genre of critical current-affairs commentary had thus developed which hovered somewhere between the publications of genuine documents on the one hand, and, on the other, the fanciful (and, in this period, novel and entrancing) political fictions of Boccalini's *Ragguagli di Parnasso*, with their shrewdly argued discussions between kings, philosophers, and other famous figures of both the present and the past.[10]

This, broadly speaking, is the genre to which the three *Secretissima instructio* pamphlets belonged. It was a genre that permitted some blurring of the borders between fact and fiction, between genuine analysis and satirical exaggeration. And, as was the case with Scott's *Vox populi*, any text which purported to present secret advice was, by its nature, less subject to simple tests of plausibility: the sort of advice that can be given only in secret is bound to differ from what can normally be uttered and avowed. (The story of one text that was highly influential during this period illustrates that principle: the anonymous *Monita secreta*, first published in 1614 and frequently reprinted thereafter, which purported to give the secret instructions issued by the Jesuit order to its members on how to gain political influence and wealth. Despite some rather obviously satirical elements, such as its special concentration on the cultivation of rich widows, this text was widely taken to be genuine.)[11] Most readers, it seems, did understand that the *Secretissima instructio* pamphlets were pro-Habsburg propaganda, and thus not authentic pieces of advice to the Elector Palatine. But in order to work their satirical effect, these texts needed readers who could at least imagine that the Machiavellian suggestions they put forward were

[10] On the popularity and influence of Boccalini see H. Hendrix, *Traiano Boccalini fra erudizione e polemica: ricerche sulla fortuna e bibliografia critica* (Florence, 1995). Scott himself produced a version of Boccalini's *Pietra del paragone*, entitled *Newes from Pernassus: The Politicall Touchstone, taken from Mount Pernassus* (n.p., 1622).

[11] On the history of this text see J. E. Franco and C. Vogel, *Monita secreta: instruções secretas dos Jesuítas: história de um manual conspiracionista* (Lisbon, 2002). One reprinting of it, as an appendix to a work by Caspar Scioppius, gave it the title 'instructio secretissima', perhaps under the influence of the *Secretissima instructio* pamphlets: *Anatomia Societatis Jesu, seu probatio spiritus jesuitarum. Item arcana imperii jesuitici, cum instructione secretissima pro superioribus ejusdem & deliciarum jesuiticarum specimina* (n.p., 1633) (see Franco and Vogel, *Monita secreta*, p. 27 n.).

the sort of thing that might be discussed in the most secret deliberations of princes and their counsellors.

The first *Secretissima instructio* pamphlet was published in at least ten editions, all but one of them at undisclosed places, in 1620. In nine of these the title is *Secretissima instructio gallo-britanno-batava Friderico V. comiti Palatino electori data, ex gallico conversa, ac bono publico in lucem evulgata*; one edition, however, gives Frederick's title as '*Friderico I. electo regi Bohemiae et comiti Palatino electori*'.[12] Since the work purported to be a piece of sympathetic advice written by the Elector Palatine's tutor and confidant, it seems likely that the version using the royal title was the original printing, and that the others were produced by publishers in pro-Imperial territories who baulked at appearing, even fictitiously, to acknowledge his claim to the throne. The general pattern of this first *Secretissima instructio* pamphlet, which was taken as a model by the other two, was as follows. First it surveyed the weaknesses of the Elector Palatine's position, and the problems he faced, concentrating especially on the unreliability of his allies (each of whom had his own 'reason of state' to consider); then it put forward positive recommendations about the best way to proceed. Thus the first part included (in the words of an early, anonymous English translation) the following observations: 'The *Bohemians* are in noe sort yor frindes . . . now they show a more manifest signe of their hatred against yo^u, when they put vpon yo^u such Condicions of governinge, as moderat lords would scarce impose vpon their slaves'; '*Gabor* of *Transilvania* is noe frinde of yo^{rs}, but out of his hatred and feare of the *Emperour*, hath entred into league wth yo^u'; 'Much lesse can yo^u esteeme the *Turke* yor faithfull freinde'.[13] The second part was introduced with the comment: 'Hitherto yo^u haue made yor selfe stronge, by two meanes, wise connterfeitinge [*sic*] and dissemblinge: and speedie execution. The former is now lost and gone: therefore yo^u must rest vpon the latter.' Nevertheless, further deceptions and dissimulations were also recommended. On the Lutheran inhabitants of Bohemia it advised that 'yo^u may deferre the suppression

---

[12] See the listing in W. E. J. Weber, ed., *Secretissima instructio; Allergeheimste Instruction; Friderico V. comiti Palatino electo regi Bohemiae, data; an Friederichen, Pfaltzgrafen, erwehlten König in Böhmen* (Augsburg, 2002), pp. 123–4, and n. 35 below. I do not know on what grounds Jaroslav Miller describes the work as published in Hamburg (*Falcký mýtus*, p. 194). Here and elsewhere I use the term 'editions' in a loose sense; in strict terms, some of these may have been new issues rather than new editions.

[13] BL, MS Sloane 3938, fos. 4v–5r, 7r, 7v; for the original Latin see Weber, ed., *Secretissima instructio*, pp. 44–6, 52, 54.

of the *Lutherans*, whom afterwards when yor affaires are firmely setled, yo^u may easily and comodiously extirpe'; the general advice about Frederick's Bohemian subjects was that 'Yo^u shall bringe them into yor subiection by dissemblinge, by advauncinge some, by removinge others . . . Let *Tiberius* be yor schoole-master in this point, who vsed to bestow extraordinary favo^{rs} on those that he ment to overthrowe.' More dissimulation was called for in Frederick's diplomacy: 'Aboue all thinges beware that yor league wth the *Turke* be not discovered.' And, in conclusion: 'Finally in a kingdome where yo^u haue nothinge but force, yo^u must exercise force but mixt wth cunnyng and fraude, till yo^u haue gott the possession of all.'[14] Commenting on this text in 1624, the prominent jurist and political writer Christoph Besold concluded—with good reason—that 'its purpose seems to have been to make the Bohemian Estates regard the rule of their new king as something hateful and suspect.'[15]

The author of the *Secretissima instructio* has never been identified with certainty. Some modern German library catalogues attribute it to 'Walther von Plessen'; if this is an error for Volrad von Plessen, Frederick's Chancellor and senior adviser on foreign affairs, it suggests that at least some readers have been taken in by the fiction. One copy of one of the early German translations bears the annotation 'Ludovici Camerarij Frid. Reg. Bohem. Consi.', which probably testifies to a similar misunderstanding.[16] Otherwise the only identification with a specific individual is the one made recently by Wolfgang Weber, who attributes the work to Paul Welser, a member of the famous family of merchants and intellectuals in Augsburg. The prime piece of evidence for this attribution is a copy of the *Secretissima instructio* in the Herzog-August Bibliothek, Wolfenbüttel, bearing the early annotation 'auctor Paul Welser Senator Augustae'; further support for this identification is drawn from the fact that one of the 1620 Latin editions and several of the early editions of the German translations of this work (also published in 1620) bear the imprint of Sara Mang, an Augsburg publisher who

[14] BL, MS Sloane 3938, fos. 16r, 21r, 21v–22r, 25v, 26r; for the original Latin see Weber, ed., *Secretissima instructio*, pp. 84, 100, 102–4, 118.

[15] C. Besold, 'Discursus politici IV de arcanis rerumpublicarum' III.1, in his *Spicilegia politico-juridica* (Strasbourg, 1624), p. 259: 'Scopus . . . illius scripti fuisse videtur, ut Ordinibus Bohemicis, odiosum & suspectum redderetur Imperium novi sui Regis'. This discussion comes in a section warning against the use of 'Consilia Machiavellistica' (p. 257).

[16] Cornell University Library, pressmark Rare Books D251.T44v.4, no. 27. (Alternatively, this might be a record of ownership.)

had previously produced one of Welser's own translations, and also from the fact that Paul Welser's brother Marcus had occasionally acted as a political adviser to Maximilian of Bavaria.[17] Weber has made a good case, but not a conclusive one. It might be thought significant that the annotated copy in Wolfenbüttel is of the edition which gave Frederick his royal title (tentatively identified above as the first edition); if the annotation was made immediately on receipt of it, this might represent fresh inside knowledge rather than stale rumour. However, the date at which the annotation identifying Welser was made is simply not known. Nor has that edition been identified as a Sara Mang production; indeed, the fact that all her known editions used the non-royal title might suggest that she was one of the re-printers of the work, not the original printer.[18] In 1620 Paul Welser was in prison, for debt, having been incarcerated in 1615; this could mean that he had both the leisure to write such a work and the incentive to curry favour with Maximilian, but it could also mean that he was not well placed to gather all the latest information on international affairs. Nor does the connection with Maximilian seem strong: in 1620 Marcus Welser had been dead for six years, and his activities as an 'adviser' to the Bavarian ruler had in any case been very slight.[19] The heavy concentration in the *Secretissima instructio* on the internal affairs of Bohemia suggests that its author had some experience of, and a particular interest in, that country—which does not fit the known facts of Paul Welser's biography. And the inclusion in this pamphlet of two letters from the Transylvanian ruler Gábor Bethlen to his Turkish allies (which historians have taken to be genuine) might suggest that it was produced by someone more closely connected with the diplomatic and intelligence services of the Imperial court.[20] Possibly the author,

[17] See W. E. J. Weber, 'Ein Bankrotteur berät den Winterkönig. Paul Welser (1555–1620) und die Secretissima Instructio Gallo-Britanno-Batava Frederico I. Electo regi Bohemiae data (1620)', in M. Häberlein and J. Burkhardt, eds., *Die Welser: neue Forschungen zur Geschichte und Kultur des oberdeutschen Handelshauses* (Berlin, 2002), pp. 618–32, and Weber, ed., *Secretissima instructio*, pp. 7–22. On Sara Mang see J. Benzing, *Die Buchdrucker des 16. und 17. Jahrhunderts im deutschen Sprachgebiet*, 2nd edn. (Wiesbaden, 1982), p. 21.

[18] The only Latin edition to bear her imprint was certainly a later reprint: see below, at n. 35.

[19] See B. Roeck, 'Geschichte, Finsternis und Unkultur: zu Leben und Werk des Marcus Welser', *Archiv für Kulturgeschichte*, 72 (1990), pp. 115–52; here p. 127 n.

[20] For the letters see Weber, ed., *Secretissima instructio*, pp. 62–8, 70–4. They are accepted as genuine in G. Pray, *Gabrielis Bethlenii principatus Transsilvaniae coaevis documentis illustratus*, ed. J. F. Miller, 2 vols. (Pest, 1816), i, pp. 27–30, 74–7;

like Biondi, had received some semi-official assistance—again, a rather unlikely scenario for a man in prison.

The *Secretissima instructio* was written before the final months of 1620—certainly before the battle of the White Mountain in November, of which it shows no knowledge, and necessarily, if Weber is correct, before the death of Paul Welser in late October.[21] An early commentator, the author of the *Mercure françois*, connected it with the meeting of representatives of the Union and the League at Ulm which led to the signing of the Treaty of Ulm on 3 July 1620: 'At gatherings such as the one at Ulm some text is always circulated. Thus the Imperials, not oblivious of this practice, circulated this free discourse or most secret instruction on the state of affairs in Germany, Bohemia, and Hungary, addressed to the Elector Palatine.'[22] One modern historian, Victor-Lucien Tapié, has described the *Secretissima instructio* as 'a pamphlet which circulated very widely at the beginning of 1620', but without presenting his evidence for this dating.[23] Whatever its precise date of publication, its success must have been rapid, as before the end of the year it had appeared not only in the nine further editions already mentioned but also in two translations in German (in a total of nine editions) and one in Dutch.[24] In 1621 a partial French translation

---

S. Katona, *Historia critica regum Hungariae stirpis austriacae*, 42 vols. (Pest, 1779–1817), xxix ('tomulus x'), pp. 634–7 (first letter); S. Szilágyi, *Bethlen Gábor fejedelem kiadatlan politikai levelei* (Budapest, 1879), pp. 149, 468–70 (where the second letter is printed, in Hungarian translation, from a manuscript in the National Museum, Budapest). The first letter is taken as genuine by one of the leading modern authorities on Bethlen, Lászlo Nágy: see his *Bethlen Gábor a független Magyarországért* (Budapest, 1969), p. 102.

[21] Weber, ed., *Secretissima instructio*, p. 22.

[22] *Le Mercure françois*, 6, for 1620 (published in 1621), p. 157: 'Or en telles Assemblies comme celle d'Vlme on faict semer tousiours quelque discours. Aussi les Imperiaux n'oublians pas cette coustume, firent courir ce Libre discours, ou Instruction tres-secrette, sur estat des affaires d'Allemagne, Boheme & Hongrie, addressé à l'Eslecteur Palatin.'

[23] Tapié, *La Politique étrangère*, p. 451 n.: 'Un pamphlet très répandu au début de 1620'.

[24] See the listing in Weber, ed., *Secretissima instructio*, pp. 124–6. One of the German translations was also reprinted in M. C. Lundorp ['Londorpius'], *Der römischen keyserlichen und königlichen Mayestät . . . acta publica*, 2 vols. (Frankfurt am Main, 1627–30), i, pp. 1541–50. The Dutch translation was *Verre-kijcker. Ofte, secrete franschengelsch-hollandtsche instructie ghegheven aen Fredericus de vyfde Paltz-grave aen den Rhijn, ende keurvorst* (n.p., 1620); this is not mentioned by Weber, but is listed in W. P. C. Knuttel, *Catalogus van de pamfletten-verzameling berustende in de Koninklijke Bibliotheek*, 9 vols. (The Hague, 1889–1920), i, part 1, p. 579, no. 3037, where the printer is tentatively identified as Abraham Verhoeven in Antwerp. Some copies of this translation (including BL pressmark T. 2250 (29)) contain an item not present in the original

appeared, consisting of the first nineteen sections (the first part of the text, containing the analysis rather than the policy recommendations). This was published in two different editions: in the volume of the *Mercure françois* covering the year 1620, and in a pamphlet which also contained a strongly anti-Palatine text by the elderly German military commander Hermann Conrad von Friedenberg.[25] And, in addition to these translations, the Latin text of the *Secretissima instructio* would also be reprinted in 1621, 1626, and 1627. These were not the only languages in which the text was read. As we have seen, an English translation survives in manuscript; this may have circulated in scribal copies. There was also an Italian translation, which is preserved in a manuscript in Venice.[26] Possibly this translation was made for the benefit of some of the members of the Venetian government at the end of 1620 or the beginning of 1621, when the adverse comments about Venice in the *Secretissima instructio* became a

Latin, a letter from the Sultan to Gábor Bethlen (pp. 35–6: 'Copie van de toesegginghe des Turcksche Keysers, ghedaen aen Bethlen Gabor'). This was presumably fictitious; it is not the same as the letter from the Sultan published at Bratislava in 1620 (*Dess Türkischen Kaysers Hülff dem Fürsten inn Sieben-bürgen Bethlehem Gabor ... versprochen*), which may be genuine. One of the Latin printings of 1620 was also identified by Knuttel as a Verhoeven production: *Catalogus*, p. 579, no. 3036; this corresponds to no. 7 in Weber's listing.

[25] *Le Mercure françois*, 6, for 1620 (published in 1621), pp. 157–74; *Deux discours tres-beaux et fort remarquables. Le premier: Sur les causes des mouuemens de l'Europe, seruant d'aduis aux roys & princes, pour la conseruation de leurs estats, composé par le baron de Fridembourg, & par le comte de Furstenberg en son ambassade presenté au Roy de France. Le deuxiesme: Secrete instruction au Conte Palatin sur l'estat & affaires de l'Allemagne, Boheme & Hongrie* (Paris, 1621), pp. 20–31. Although the *Secretissima instructio* claimed to have been translated from the French, it is clear that this French version was a translation from the Latin. The text by von Friedenberg was also printed in the *Mercure françois*, 6, for 1619 (published in 1621), pp. 342–70, and was issued as a separate pamphlet in three editions in 1620 and one in 1621. In two of these pamphlet editions it was described as having been sent to the Elector Palatine (*Exhortation aux roys et princes sur le subject des guerres de ce temps ... envoyée au prince palatin* (Paris: Joseph Bouillerot, 1620); *Exhortation aux roys et princes sur le subject des guerres de ce temps ... envoyée au comte palatin par le comte de Fridembourg* (Paris: Abraeh. Saugrain, 1620)); but the *Mercure françois* stated that it had been brought to Paris by the Imperial Ambassador, Count von Fürstenberg, and presented to Louis XIII (p. 341). The edition containing both von Friedenberg's work and the French version of the *Secretissima instructio* has led some modern writers to suppose that von Friedenberg was the author of the latter (see P. Sarpi, *Opere*, ed. G. and L. Cozzi (Milan, 1969), p. 1171 n.). But the style and mental outlooks of the two texts are very different: von Friedenberg's pamphlet is a simplistic and rather blustering piece of work, blaming all the ills of Europe on anti-monarchical sentiment.

[26] Museo Correr, Venice, MS 1093: 'Secretissima Instruzione data a Federico quinto conte palatino elettore'.

matter of political concern to them. In January 1621 they asked their chief publicist, Paolo Sarpi, to draft a reply. What they received from him, however, was not a counterblast to the *Secretissima instructio* but a lengthy essay on how best to respond to hostile propaganda—an essay which, coming as it does from one of the shrewdest controversialists of the age, is of unusual interest where the study of early modern polemical practices is concerned.[27] Sarpi began by affirming that the text was indeed pernicious. It was designed to create 'a tyrant so perfidious, past centuries have never seen the like; it speaks bitingly and injuriously of various princes and peoples, and does not omit the most serene Republic [of Venice], which it discusses in its section 15, where, in very brief and pregnant words, it censures both the past and the present government, and predicts ill success in the future.'[28] It would be a simple matter, he observed, to write a justification of Venice's past and present policies; but this would mean adopting a purely defensive position, and in literary affairs, just as in military ones, to be solely on the defensive is always to be at a disadvantage. He also pointed out that no government is without some imperfections: if a hostile critic points to some of them, it is foolish to seek to hide them, and any attempt to excuse them may seem like an admission that the critic was right. Furthermore, there are some things done by governments 'which, although they are good, perfect, necessary, and praised by the wise, nevertheless look bad when viewed from outside'.[29] The things criticized in the *Secretissima instructio* (Sarpi was evidently thinking above all of Venice's willingness to enter an alliance with a Calvinist, Bethlen, and thus indirectly with

---

[27] Sarpi, *Opere*, pp. 1170–80: 'Del confutar scritture malediche, 29 genaro 1620 [*sc.* 1621]'. This text is discussed in P. Guaragnella, *Gli occhi della mente: stili nel Seicento italiano* (Bari, 1997), pp. 55–122 *passim*, and di Vivo, 'Paolo Sarpi and the Uses of Information', pp. 43–4.

[28] Ibid., p. 1174: 'un tiranno tanto perfido, che li passati secoli non hanno avuto un tale; morde et offende diversi prencipi e popoli, e non tralascia la Serenissima Republica, della quale parla nel cap decimoquinto, dove in brevissime e pregnantissime parole censura tutto il governo passato e presente insieme, augurando cattivo successo all'avvenire'. The argument of section 15 was that Venice, a sham monarchy controlled by an aristocracy, was fundamentally hostile to princely rulers; that it was untrustworthy, always in conflict with its neighbours; and that its policy of allying with Gábor Bethlen (who ruled Transylvania as a vassal of the Turks) against the Habsburgs would lead to Turkish control over Austria, which would prove fatal to Venice's own interests, given that Venice's sycophantic attitude towards the Turks was merely an expression of its own weakness.

[29] Ibid., p. 1173: 'che se ben buone, perfette e necessarie e da savi lodate, hanno però cattiva l'apparenza esteriore'.

the Ottomans, against the Catholic Habsburgs) were in this category: it would be rash to deny them, but pointless to try to defend them, as the general public would not understand the high political reasons that made such things necessary and good. A better approach would be to reveal to the public the malignity of Venice's accusers and their patrons. In the long term, Venice would benefit more from well-written historical works which vindicated Venetian policy—but these were best written by outsiders, not by Venetians. And in the short term it might be necessary to counter enemy propaganda in either of two ways: publishing narrative accounts of recent events which set Venetian policy in an advantageous light, and issuing 'manifestos' or justificatory statements which gave the legal grounds for Venice's actions. However, Sarpi concluded that, while such responses might be necessary in order to counter hostile propaganda, the ideal scenario was one in which the populace did not read about or discuss such matters of state at all.[30]

No response to the *Secretissima instructio*, therefore, was published by the Venetian authorities. But the first printed criticism of the *Secretissima instructio* had already appeared: an anonymous pamphlet entitled *Machiavellizatio qua unitorum animos iesuaster quidam dissociare nititur*, which was published before the end of 1620.[31] In subsequent polemics it emerged that the author of this work was the Calvinist minister Péter Alvinczi, who was based in the town of Košice (Kassa, Kaschau; in modern Slovakia), then under Gábor Bethlen's rule. Alvinczi's pamphlet was concerned mostly with defending Bethlen's actions (and, to a lesser extent, with attacking the Jesuits); he was in fact one of Gábor Bethlen's closest advisers, so his statement that the *Secretissima instructio*'s two letters from Bethlen to the Turks were forgeries should perhaps be given some weight.[32] At the start of his pamphlet Alvinczi described the *Secretissima instructio* as a German production issued under a false Viennese imprint, and reported the rumour that its author had been commissioned or assisted by Péter Pázmány, who was the Catholic Archbishop of Esztergom and the moving spirit of the Hungarian Counter-Reformation:

---

[30] Ibid., pp. 1176–80.
[31] There were two editions: the first (n.p., 1620) was probably printed in Košice; the second had a fictitious imprint ('Saragossa', 1621): see A. Apponyi, *Hungarica: Ungarn betreffende im Auslande gedruckte Bücher und Flugschriften*, 2nd edn., 4 vols. (Munich, 1925–8), ii, pp. 61–2, no. 785.
[32] *Machiavellizatio qua unitorum animos iesuaster quidam dissociare nititur* (n.p., 1620), fo. 4v; cf. above, n. 20.

'they say, my lord Archbishop, that this masked and helmed emissary fights under your protection'.[33] A reply to Alvinczi's work was promptly written by Tamás Balásfi, a Hungarian Catholic cleric (Bishop-elect of Bosnia) who was close to Péter Pázmány; this was printed by Sara Mang in Augsburg, also in 1620.[34] During that year Sara Mang reprinted an earlier pamphlet on Hungarian affairs, attacking Bethlen and defending Pázmány, written by Péter Pázmány himself; although this pamphlet made no allusion to either the *Machiavellizatio* or the *Secretissima instructio*, it was also issued by Mang in a combined printing with the text of the *Secretissima instructio* itself.[35] In 1620 she printed a German translation of the Emperor's edict against Gábor Bethlen, and in 1621 she published another incriminating letter from Bethlen, this time to one of the leaders of the Tatars.[36] These details may perhaps strengthen

---

[33] *Machiavellizatio*, fo. 1v: 'tuo mi d[omi]ne Archiepiscope sub Clupeo ajunt, hunc larvatum ac galeatum militare Emissarium'. Since none of the editions recorded by Weber has a Viennese imprint, the one seen by Alvinczi must have been yet another printing.

[34] T. Balásfi, *Castigatio libelli calvinistici, cui titulus est: Machiavellizatio, quem calvinista quidem praedicans, responsi nomine ad Secretissimam instructionem . . . vulgavit* (Augsburg, 1620). Alvinczi quickly penned a reply, which was published under his own name: *Resultatio plagarum castigatoris autorem Machiavellizationis reverberata in Thomam Balasfi* (Košice, 1620): see G. Borsa et al., *Régi Magyarországi nyomtatványok* (Budapest, 1971–), ii, p. 297, no. 1208. Balásfi responded with *Repetitio castigationis, et destructio destructionum, Petri P. Alvinci, calvinistae cassoviensis praedicantis* (Vienna, 1620): see K. Szábo and Á. Hellebrant, *Régi magyar könyvtár*, 3 vols. (Budapest, 1879–98), iii, part 1, pp. 379–80, no. 1281.

[35] *Falsae originis motuum hungaricorum, succincta refutatio* (Augsburg, 1620); *Falsae originis motuum hungaricorum, succincta refutatio, cui accessit Secretissima instructio gallo-britanno-batava, Friderico V. comiti Palatino Electori data, ex gallico conversa* (Augsburg, 1620). Both these editions were by Mang; however, Apponyi also reports another edition of the second, combined, work with no place of publication (*Hungarica*, ii, p. 59, no. 777; also listed in Č. Zíbrt, *Bibliografie české historie*, 5 vols. (Prague, 1900–12), iv, p. 353, no. 5881). Sara Mang also published a German translation of *Falsae originis*, entitled *Vngerischer Rebellions Brunn* (Augsburg, 1620). *Falsae originis* was first published in Bratislava in 1619, in response to Alvinczi's pamphlet *Querela Hungariae* (n.p. [Košice], 1619). On the involvement of Pázmány and Balásfi in these polemics see V. Frankl, *Pázmány Péter és kora*, 3 vols. (Pest, 1868–72), i, pp. 512–20, and J. Heltai, *Alvinczi Péter és a heidelbergi peregrinusok* (Budapest, 1994), pp. 129–54. Heltai emphasizes Alvinczi's own Palatine connections: he had studied in Heidelberg in 1600–1 (p. 99).

[36] [Ferdinand II,] *Der Röm. Kay. . . . Edictal Cassation der widerrechtlichen . . . Wahl Gabrieln Betlen im Königreich Hungern* (Augsburg, 1620) (see Zíbrt, *Bibliografie*, iv, p. 388, no. 6385); [G. Bethlen,] *Copia eines Schreibens, so Bethlen Gabor den ersten Aprilis Anno 1621. ausz Tirnaw, an einen Fürsten der Tartarn . . . abgehn lassen . . . allen gutherzigen teutscher Nation zu Nachrichtung, und Erinnerung, was hinder desz Bethlen Gabor calvinischen Geist stecke* (Augsburg, 1621) (see Szábo and Hellebrant, *Régi magyar könyvtár*, iii, part 1, pp. 389–90, no. 1317).

the suspicion (shared, evidently, by Péter Alvinczi) that the *Secretissima instructio* came out of a milieu with a special interest in Hungarian and Bohemian affairs and a special animus against Bethlen, which does not obviously fit the attribution to Paul Welser. The publications just mentioned are sufficient evidence to show that Sara Mang was used as a conduit for propaganda publications by Péter Pázmány and some of his friends and supporters; the fact that she had previously printed something by Welser (a translation of Trigault's history of the Jesuit mission in China) may be coincidental. Perhaps the best hypothesis about the *Secretissima instructio*, therefore, is the one formed by those modern Hungarian bibliographers who have studied this issue, namely, that 'this "most secret instruction" probably originated from the circle of Péter Pázmány'.[37]

In 1621 another printed response to the *Secretissima instructio* appeared, a pamphlet (of only 12 pages) entitled *Elenchus libelli famosi, qui inscribitur: Secretissima instructio gallo-britanno-batava, Friderico V. comiti Palatino electori data*. The anonymous author of this work had no surer information about the origins or authorship of the *Secretissima instructio*, merely guessing that it was 'a chicken hatched from an egg laid by one of Loyola's crows', and producing a list of correspondences (some of them rough, at best) between the Machiavellian methods recommended in it—equivocation, dissimulation, regicide, and so on—and the teachings of various well-known Jesuit authors.[38] But this publication, which seems to have enjoyed quite a wide circulation, does at least testify to the continuing notoriety of the *Secretissima instructio*.

So too does the appearance in 1622 of a second *Secretissima instructio* text, which was published (at unspecified places) in at least three

---

[37] Borsa et al., *Régi Magyarországi nyomtatványok*, ii, p. 296: 'Ez a "legtitkosabb utasítás" valószínűleg Pázmány Péter környezetében fogant.' (Note that this hypothesis does not require the assumption that the first printing of the *Secretissima instructio* was by Sara Mang; possibly it was first printed elsewhere, and then passed to Mang by Pázmány or his agents.) Also possibly significant is the fact that the historic collection of the Széchényi Library in Budapest contains no fewer than three copies (in three separate editions, all 1620) of the *Secretissima instructio*: see I. Hubay, *Magyar és magyar vonatkozású röplapok, ujságlapok, röpiratok az Országos Széchényi Könyvtárban, 1480–1718* (Budapest, 1948), pp. 110–11, nos. 523–5. There is also a manuscript copy of the *Secretissima instructio* in the Knihovna Národního Muzea, Prague (MS I C 1, tom. XIV, fos. 611r–633r; I am very grateful to Dr Marta Vaculínová for confirming this).

[38] *Elenchus libelli famosi* [. . .] (n.p., 1621), pp. 3 ('Ex Loyolitici corui ouo pullum hunc'), 4–6. There is also a copy of this work in the Széchény Library: Hubay, *Magyar röplapok*, p. 114, no. 541.

editions during that year.[39] This work followed the established pattern, beginning with a lengthy analysis of the hopelessness of the Elector Palatine's position (a case that could be made even more convincingly, after the defeat at the White Mountain and the loss of most of the Palatinate), and then offering the following cynically ill-founded advice: admit your guilt and declare your submission to the Emperor; work secretly to acquire influence over him; work also on Saxony; dismiss advisers such as Camerarius (but maintain secret contacts with them); convert to Lutheranism; use this to win Saxony for yourself; and finally stir up a religious war, which will enable you to regain Bohemia with the help of the princes of Lower Saxony and the Hanseatic cities.[40] This second *Secretissima instructio* seems to have enjoyed much less popular success than the first, being less revelatory and less shocking in character. If the identification of Welser as the author of the first text is correct, then he was obviously not responsible for the second, which was written after his death. But if Welser did not write the first, then the possibility that both were by the same author must remain open: although the second text says very little about Gábor Bethlen and the Turks, it is stylistically very similar to the first.[41] The only modern historian to have studied all three texts concluded tentatively that they were all by one author, but offered little support for this claim.[42]

It is at least unlikely that the third *Secretissima instructio* pamphlet was written by the author of the second. As has already been noted, the title *Altera secretissima instructio* would surely not have been used by someone who had already produced (or, for that matter, heard of) the second text in this series; either *Tertia secretissima instructio* or *Pars tertia secretissimae instructionis* would have been chosen instead. The third text appeared in two editions in 1626, of which one was entitled *Altera secretissima instructio* and the other *Tertia secretissima instructio*; it can be assumed that the former appeared first, and that the latter was a reprinting

---

[39] Weber lists two (*Secretissima instructio*, p. 127), entitled *Secretissima instructio . . . pars secunda* and *Pars secunda secretissimae instructionis*; a third, entitled *Secretissimae instructionis . . . pars secunda* (n.p., 1622), is in the Staatliche Bibliothek, Ansbach (pressmark 127).

[40] *Pars secunda secretissimae instructionis* (n.p., 1622), sigs. A2v–B1r (analysis), B3v–C2v (advice).

[41] Bethlen and/or the Turks are mentioned briefly: ibid., sigs. B3r, B4r, C2r.

[42] H. Becker, *Die Secretissima Instructio Gallo-britanno-batava, ein Beitrag zur Kritik der Flugschriften des dreissigjährigen Krieges* (Göttingen, 1874). Becker has little to say about the origins of the second text, noting only that it was written before the dismissal of Ernst von Mansfeld in July 1622 (p. 30).

of it by somebody else who was aware of the second text.[43] Indeed, 1626 also saw a reprinting of the first and second texts, the former simply as *Secretissima instructio* and the latter under the title *Secunda secretissima instructio*. In the following year, the first text was reprinted twice under its original title and once as *Prima secretissima instructio*; and the third text was also reprinted (but under its *Altera . . .* title).[44] It thus seems that the third text, a much more talented performance than the second, had created a new wave of interest in this mini-genre of 'most secret instructions', which printers and booksellers had not been slow to exploit.

This third text—which, in accordance with the title page translated by Hobbes, will be referred to here as the *Altera secretissima instructio*—differed in several ways from its predecessors. Its Latin was much more concentratedly Tacitean, constantly striving for effect, and it was more frequently larded with fragmentary quotations from Latin poetry (or pseudo-quotations: some were adaptations, imitations, or sheer inventions); these features indicate an author with more serious literary interests or pretensions.[45] Unlike the other two texts, which declared that they were translated from French, this one described itself (no doubt equally spuriously) as a translation from Dutch; it also had the (fictitious) imprint 'Hagae Comitis, Permissu Senatus' ('The Hague, by permission of the Senate'). These last details might suggest that it was produced in the Spanish Netherlands, where fictitious Dutch imprints were often used for polemical purposes; but a simpler explanation would be that they reflect merely the fact that The Hague was Frederick's place of exile.[46] The only contemporary comment on the

---

[43] This assumption about the order of the two rests not only on the wording of the titles, but also on the character of the printing. The *Tertia . . .* edition (which matches the *Altera . . .* edition line-by-line) is an inferior, hasty production, with poorer typography and paper (and with one gathering, sig. C, produced by a printer different from that of sigs. A, B, and D); it also has several misprints not present in the *Altera . . .* edition.

[44] Weber, ed., *Secretissima instructio*, pp. 127–8 (omitting, however, the 1627 *Altera secretissima instructio*: there is a copy of this in the Staatsbibliothek, Berlin, pressmark 4" Flugschr. 1620/39A).

[45] Comparing the three texts, Hermann Becker noted that in the third 'the presentation is more detailed, and the satire more sharp-edged' (*Die Secretissima Instructio*, p. 36: 'die Darstellung detaillirter, die Satire schneidiger'), but otherwise concluded that 'the language and the method of presentation are also unmistakably the same in all three pamphlets' (p. 41: 'Auch ist die Sprache und Art der Darstellung in allen drei Libellen unverkennbar dieselbe')—a judgement with which it is impossible to agree.

[46] One modern scholar has specified Brussels as the place of publication of the *Secunda secretissima instructio* (1626) and the *Tertia secretissima instructio* (dated by him '1627'),

origins of the *Altera secretissima instructio* comes in a pamphlet by one of Richelieu's propagandists, Mathieu de Morgues, who, stung by its criticisms of France, included it in a list of sixteen recent anti-French 'libelles'. 'It is certain', he wrote, 'that all these pamphlets have been printed in Germany, namely, some at Augsburg and some at Ingolstadt; we can tell this from the paper, the print, and the fact that they have been sold at the Frankfurt fairs by printers from those two towns'.[47] De Morgues also asserted that all of the pamphlets had been written by three people: a 'denatured' Frenchman, an Italian living in Flanders, and 'a Bavarian German'; however, since he confidently identified the Italian as the author of the *Mysteria politica* (which was in fact by the German Jesuit Adam Contzen), the sources of his information must be regarded as suspect.[48]

Internal evidence suggests that the *Altera secretissima instructio* was completed in early August 1626: it refers to the battle of Kalenberg (29 July) but not to the strategically important defeat of the pro-Palatine forces at Lutter-am-Barenberg (27 August), and its author was evidently unaware of the marriage of Gaston d'Orléans (6 August).[49] Until the battle of Lutter-am-Barenberg, the Elector Palatine's prospects were

but without giving reasons for this identification: Cogswell, 'The Politics of Propaganda', p. 191 n.

[47] [M. de Morgues,] *Advis d'un theologien sans passion: sur plusieurs libelles imprimez depuis peu en Allemagne* (n.p. [Paris], 1626), pp. 11–12: 'il est certain que tous ces Libelles ont esté imprimez en Allemaigne, asçauoir vne partie à Augsbourg, & l'autre à Ingolstad: ce qui est recogneu par le papier, par le caractere, par la vente qui en a esté faitte par les Imprimeurs de ces deux Villes aux Foires de Francfort'. De Morgues gave the title only as '*Instructio Gallobritannobataua*', which might refer to any of the three texts; but the pamphlets he attacked were from the period 1624–6, and the author of the *Mercure françois* specified the third text when reproducing de Morgues's comments (*Le Mercure françois*, 12, for 1626 (published in 1627), p. 501). That the *Altera secretissima instructio* was regarded in France as offensively anti-French is suggested by the early annotation on the title page of one exemplum in the Bibliothèque Nationale (pressmark 4-LB36–2425): 'Meschant & pernicieux Liure'.

[48] [De Morgues,], *Advis d'un theologien*, p. 13 ('desnaturé'; 'vn Allemand Bauarois'). He did not say which of these three was responsible, in his opinion, for the [*Altera*] *secretissima instructio*. The Italian he had in mind was presumably the Italian Jesuit Ofondi, who had close contacts with the Imperial generals Tilly and Wallenstein: see Sir Thomas Roe, *The Negotiations of Sir Thomas Roe, in his Embassy to the Ottoman Porte, from the year 1621 to 1628 inclusive* (London, 1740), p. 776, and N. Slangen, *Geschichte Christian des Vierten Königs in Dännemark*, ed. J. H. Schlegel, 2 vols. (Copenhagen, 1757–71), ii, p. 346.

[49] See section 11 (n. 136); section 8 (n. 86). (The marriage of Gaston was effected without prior publicity, and took place in Nantes, which means that news of it would have taken a day or two longer to reach other countries than if it had happened in Paris.) Other evidence, confirming this dating, is presented below.

increasingly uncertain, but not altogether bleak. In December 1625 his most important allies, England, Denmark, and the United Provinces, had made a formal agreement (the so-called Hague Alliance) to work together for the Elector's restitution. This was a positive achievement, though the alliance was not as broad as its promoters had hoped: Sweden's participation was stymied by the death of her envoy on the way to The Hague, and Brandenburg, France, and Venice had decided not to become actively involved. In the early months of 1626 the Elector's prospects seemed to be improving; he accepted an offer by the Margrave of Baden-Durlach to raise an army of 10,000, and received promises from Gábor Bethlen of a new campaign, with Ottoman support, against the Habsburgs' eastern and south-eastern territories. Yet within a few months the situation had deteriorated badly: the Hague Alliance was already showing the strains caused by its members' diverging foreign policy interests; the money pledged by England to Denmark was not paid; Baden-Durlach's plans (which depended on obtaining funding from England, France, or elsewhere) came to nothing; Bethlen's promises were proving exaggerated; and in April the Elector's chief military commander, Ernst von Mansfeld (now in Danish service), was heavily defeated at the battle of Dessau Bridge and had to retreat with the remnants of his army to Silesia.[50]

The writer of the *Altera secretissima instructio* treated the Elector's chances of military success as negligible, and concentrated on the geopolitical situation, mercilessly analysing the internal strains of the Hague Alliance and explaining why other key powers—France, Venice, and the Ottomans—were unlikely to come to the Elector's assistance. In the second part of his text he offered a variety of suggestions, some more implausible than others. First he proposed that Frederick should submit to the Emperor and accept the condition (which had been seriously canvassed by some parties) that his son should be brought up at the Habsburg or Bavarian court as a Catholic—in the hope that Frederick might thereby be allowed to retain at least a remnant of his former territories. Then he suggested trying to gain political power in Holland. Then, in a particularly bold piece of devilment, he recommended that Frederick overthrow Charles I and seize control over England:

[50] See G. Parker, ed., *The Thirty Years' War*, 2nd edn. (London, 1997), pp. 69–70; B. C. Pursell, *The Winter King: Frederick V of the Palatinate and the Coming of the Thirty Years' War* (Aldershot, 2003), pp. 235–41. For the text of the Hague treaty see J. Dumont, *Corps universel diplomatique du droit des gens*, 8 vols. (Amsterdam, 1726–31), v(2), pp. 482–5.

the Puritans would support him, the nobles could be won over by a promise of 'booty', and the whole kingdom was in any case disaffected with Charles because of his loyalty to the hated Buckingham. Other suggestions (in the final sections of the text, missing from Hobbes's translation) included establishing a power-base in a Danish or Swedish port and using it to make naval attacks on Habsburg territories in Europe and the Indies; better still, making such a base in La Rochelle, forming links with the English Puritans from there and planning a landing in Scotland or Ireland; and cultivating the Swiss (who, however, were venal and unreliable). It also warned against fleeing to Constantinople, on the grounds that a free man who becomes the dependant of a tyrant seldom emerges with his freedom intact, and against taking refuge in Sweden, because of the poor climate, internal conflicts, and Polish wars. 'So any helps you get from the Swedish King will be slight, and useless.'[51] The shrewdness of the author's analysis of Frederick's situation in the first part of the work was thus counterposed with a bewildering mixture of partly plausible advice (concerning the Swiss), cunning misdirection (the dismissal of Gustavus Adolphus), and colossal mischief-making (the proposal to foment rebellion in England).[52]

This was a propaganda text of unusual sophistication and complex-ity—indeed, one of the most cleverly designed of any in this period. It managed to address, simultaneously, various different target audiences in a variety of different ways. Its main purpose, self-evidently, was to de-moralize the Elector Palatine and those who supported his cause; this was to be achieved not only by emphasizing the strength of the anti-Palatine alliance (the hardened veterans in its armies, the wealth supporting its campaigns, the fact that it had further resources on which it could yet draw, the growing number of powers that were inclined to assist it, and the increasingly close cooperation between Vienna and Madrid), but also, most importantly, by highlighting the fissiparous nature of the Elector Palatine's own support, and demonstrating all the ways in which his allies' particular interests would lead them sooner or later to abandon or oppose his cause. But, just as it aimed to make the Elector distrust his allies, so also it strove to make them distrustful of him, by suggesting that it was in his interests—once he had understood them correctly,

---

[51] Section 34: 'A Sueco igitur parva auxilia, eaque inutilia.'

[52] The advice against falling into the clutches of the Sultan is harder to categorize. The warning of a loss of freedom of action seems well-founded; but, on the other hand, the prospect of the Ottomans coordinating a European campaign with the other anti-Habsburg powers was one of the things most feared by Imperial strategists.

through the clarifying lens of the pamphlet's analysis—to oppose them or even seek their overthrow. So when it advised the Elector to create 'discord' in the Catholic alliance and argued that such psychological warfare could achieve, without cost, more than entire armies in the field, it was revealing, in a moment of unusual transparency, the very principles on which its own strategy as propaganda was based:

We must try our utmost to use deception to alienate some of them; if you remove a few stones from the arch, the whole vault falls to pieces. Quite often, when we have been defeated, we have renewed the war, at great expense and with greater risk; but it is possible to bring about discord among our enemies with no outlay at all.[53]

Supporters of the Palatine cause, however, were not the only intended readers of this work. On some points, the author seems to have had in mind some of the policy-makers on the anti-Palatine side. For example, he recommended to the Elector that he accept the proposal to have his sons brought up as Catholics, on the grounds that they could use this tactic deceptively to regain some element of power: 'It will be easie to deceaue them, if you deliuer your children to be brought up by ye Spaniard the Emp^r or Bauiere. Religion will get their fauo^r, and some of yor sonnes may haue benefices, and Bishoprickes. This is no small encrease of power.'[54] At the time of writing of the pamphlet, this proposal was being revived by Spanish diplomacy; the author's purpose here seems to have been to warn the anti-Palatine allies against such a plan, on the grounds that the Elector and his sons simply could not be trusted.[55] More generally, when he discussed the strategy Frederick should adopt if he chose to beg for clemency, the author's main aim seems to have been to warn the major Catholic powers against accepting such a move—and, indeed, warn them against those complaisant political leaders on their own side who might invoke a range of rather predictable arguments in its support: 'you know the Crocodiles teares; you shall by those frends wch through hope and your promises you haue yet left you, recouer Caesars fauor. They speake gently of you euery where. And That no peace w^thout restitution. That mercy becomes Catholiques; That a Prince of Antient power shold not be put downe.

---

[53] See section 31; and cf. section 19: 'The mayne thinge is where force succeedes not to ouerthrow their councell.'

[54] See section 21.

[55] This objection was also made by Bavaria, in response to the Spanish proposal, in September 1626: see section 21 (n. 241).

That Dauid spared Sawl. That warre was chargeable.'[56] Again, when the author recommended to the Elector that he stir up the Swiss to attack Imperial territory, this may have been partly intended as a warning to the anti-Palatine powers that they should take more trouble to ensure Swiss neutrality. And, at the same time, the author's comments about Switzerland show that he had some third-party audiences in mind: in this case, he was also trying to persuade the inhabitants of the Catholic cantons that some of their own political leaders had been acting dishonestly when they had declared their cantons' support for an anti-Habsburg policy over the Valtelline.[57]

The *Altera secretissima instructio* was aimed not only at audiences of different political affiliations, but also at readers of varying levels of political sophistication and knowledge. At the lowest level, there may possibly have been some members of the general public who took the text at face value and thought it a scandalous revelation of the Elector Palatine's secret counsels. (As the case of Thomas Scott's pamphlet shows, it would be rash to discount this kind of naivety altogether.) Most general readers, however, might be expected to understand the tongue-in-cheek nature of the work—especially since the nature of the Latin in which it was written would have required a readership with a fairly high level of education. Given that the work was published (presumably) in Imperial or at least pro-Imperial territory, many of those general readers would have been Catholics predisposed to distrust the Palatine side; so even if they understood that the second part of the pamphlet was not a genuine specimen of 'most secret' advice from one of the Elector's counsellors, they may still have felt that it captured something of the unscrupulous and reckless nature of Palatine policy. But—more importantly, perhaps—the author may also have hoped to create a similar impression in the minds of ordinary readers on the other side of the divide. Such readers (in Protestant Germany, the Netherlands, England, and elsewhere), while understanding full well that the text was a cynical piece of pro-Habsburg propaganda, may nevertheless have been subtly influenced by it. Even if the second part of the pamphlet was evidently rather different in character from the first, and was not to be read as a piece of *bona fide* advice, nevertheless the grim accuracy of the first part must have guaranteed that the second could not be discounted as sheer satire. The skill and authority with which the first part of the pamphlet accomplished its task may have inclined them

---

[56] See section 19.   [57] See section 32.

to accept the premise that all political decision-making has to rest on such calculations of interest; they may also have been persuaded by the pamphlet's analysis that the Elector's position was desperate; and they may therefore have been drawn, if only subliminally, to the conclusion that a political leader in such a desperate position might well be impelled to take the most desperate measures.

Whatever the precise impact on the reader of the unstable mix of suggestions in the second part of the text, the effect of the whole work must have depended to a large degree on the sense of authority conveyed by the mass of detailed political information in the first part. Winston Churchill's famous dictum that truth, in wartime, must be attended by a bodyguard of lies needs to be reversed here: this type of propaganda works by surrounding the central lies with a bodyguard of truths. And the quality of those truths—details of political and military events in many parts of Europe—was, in this text, impressively high; some readers, indeed, may have valued the pamphlet simply as a repository of high-level political information. As the modern historian quickly discovers on attempting to supply explanatory annotations to this text, some of the details are extremely recondite, and have been lost to sight by all but the most specialist studies of the period: manoeuvrings in the internal politics of Switzerland, for example, or military preparations in Constantinople, or the secret diplomacy of Gábor Bethlen, or the treatment given by Louis XIII to the envoys of the Landgrave of Hessen-Kassel. One must wonder, indeed, how many readers across Europe would have recognized that a passing mention of 'Amrinus' was a reference to Walter Am Rhyn, a local dignitary of the canton of Lucerne, or that a comment on the burning of 'Praecopium' referred to the (alleged) destruction by Polish troops of the Crimean town of Perekop.[58] Possibly the fact that readers would not have understood all the allusions was also part of the intended effect: in addition to strengthening the general impression that this text was well-grounded and authoritative, such details may have been meant to intimidate political leaders and their advisers on the Palatine side, by making them feel that their opponents' intelligence-gathering was far superior to their own. That the anonymous author was himself involved in the world of intelligence was suggested, subliminally, by various comments in the text. After describing the sinister attitude of the King of Denmark, for example, the author added: 'So much by night-discourse, and free cups,

[58] See sections 32, 34.

wee learned'; commenting on the treacherous intentions of the King of France, he declared: 'Its knowne from o[r] most inward frends, that are of the K[s] Counsayle'; and, discussing French and Venetian machinations in Switzerland, he drew attention to what he said was a secret nocturnal meeting—the sort of thing that might be reported by a surveillance operation—between envoys of those two countries and the Pope, and darkly insisted: 'These things should be investigated.'[59] One detail, about the nature of the complaints made to Charles I by the King of Denmark's special envoy, may possibly have derived from intercepts of that envoy's dispatches.[60] And at several points the author also included comments designed to show that he knew what confidential advice was being given to the Elector Palatine by his own senior counsellors, Camerarius and von Plessen: this, surely, was designed to induce the despairing thought that all their most secret counsels had somehow been penetrated by enemy intelligence.[61] Here, with the Elector himself and his inner circle, we reach the apex of the pyramid of potential readers.

That the author did have access to the sort of intelligence supplied by diplomatic sources and/or secret services is clear: there are some details in this text that could not have been assembled by even the most tireless reader of newsletters and corantos in the public domain. Some kind of officially sanctioned assistance, if not official employment, must have been involved. But from which government? In theory it might be possible to decide on the basis of the nature of the arguments deployed in the text whether the author was writing at the behest of the authorities in Vienna, Munich, Brussels, or Madrid; in practice this seems an impossibly difficult task. The pamphlet's almost certainly false claim that the King of Spain had, when approached for help by rebellious French Huguenots, reported them to the King of France might make one think that the author had a pro-Spanish bias (deriving perhaps from employment in Brussels); but on the other hand the Spanish plan to have the Elector's children brought up as Catholics is discredited in the text, in a way that was in line with Bavarian policy, and probably with Imperial policy too.[62] The geographical spread of the text's subject

---

[59] See sections 8, 11, 33.   [60] See section 5 (n. 50).

[61] See section 20 (n. 235); section 28 (n. 269); section 31 (n. 279); and section 34 (n. 301).

[62] There seems to have been a continuing debate on this question in Vienna. In early 1627 the Emperor's confessor, Wilhelm Lamormaini, drew up a position paper for forthcoming secret negotiations with the Elector Palatine, in which he insisted on the conversion of Frederick or his son as a condition of any restitution of territory; but when

matter may make Madrid a less likely place of composition; but origins in Brussels, Munich, or Vienna would seem to fit the text's geographical coverage more or less equally well. However, although it is known that Maximilian of Bavaria was an assiduous commissioner of high-quality propaganda pamphlets, there is one consideration that weighs against him here: his own diplomatic network was much less extensive than that of the Habsburg powers. Of the three Habsburg power-centres (Vienna, Brussels, Madrid), Brussels had only a slight independent role as a diplomatic centre (sending and receiving some foreign envoys, and having in some ways its own intelligence-gathering agenda), otherwise acting as a sub-section of the Spanish monarchy.[63] Spain had, Europe-wide, a more extensive and more active diplomatic and intelligence network than the Holy Roman Empire; but in Vienna at this time there was such close cooperation with Spain that the Spanish Ambassador, Ossona, was regularly invited to take part in policy discussions in the Emperor's *Geheimer Rat* or Privy Council, and monthly digests of international intelligence were provided to the *Geheimer Rat* by the Spaniards.[64]

Fortunately there is one type of information in the *Altera secretissima instructio* so specialized that its origins can be traced with some confidence: the political and military news from Constantinople. Unlike news from, say, London or Paris, much of which might have been derived from unofficial sources of various kinds, this information is highly likely to have come from diplomatic sources. Spain had no diplomatic representative at the Ottoman capital, but the Empire had a permanent Ambassador (or 'Resident') there; and from the surviving dispatches of that Ambassador—Sebastian Lustrier von Liebenstein, who served there from 1624 to 1629—it becomes clear that his reports provided

instructions were issued to the Imperial negotiators in June 1627, no such condition was included. (See F. von Hurter, *Geschichte Kaiser Ferdinands II und seiner Eltern*, 11 vols. (Schaffhausen, 1850–67), ix, pp. 534–5; R. Bireley, *Religion and Politics in the Age of the Counterreformation: Emperor Ferdinand II, William Lamormaini, S.J., and the Formation of Imperial Policy* (Chapel Hill, NC, 1981), p. 50.)

[63] See T. Osborne, ' "Chimeres, Monopoles and Stratagems": French Exiles in the Spanish Netherlands during the Thirty Years' War', *Seventeenth Century*, 15 (2000), pp. 149–74, esp. pp. 151–4. The Spanish Netherlands was an important centre of intelligence-gathering; the spymaster there served both Brussels and Madrid (with their sometimes differing agendas), but was ultimately answerable to the latter (see M. A. Echevarria Bacigalupe, *La diplomacia secreta en Flandres, 1598–1643* (Vizcaya, 1984), esp. pp. 168–86).

[64] See I. Hiller, *Palatin Nikolaus Esterházy: die ungarische Rolle in der Habsburgerdiplomatie, 1625 bis 1645* (Vienna, 1992), pp. 27–8.

all the detailed information about Ottoman affairs presented in this pamphlet.[65] Thus, for example, the statement that 'They leaped for ioy lately when a rumo^r was spred by a spahee, that Babylon was taken, but that little vse of a false ioy, was recompensed afterward wth an vniuersall sorrow' was based on Lustrier's reports of 30 April and 17 May 1626, which described how a spahi had been brought to the Divan (imperial council) with the news that the siege of Baghdad had been successfully concluded, and related that that news had later turned out to be false.[66] The claim that Mehmed Diak Pasha (the governor of Silistria) was so fearful of revenge attacks by Poland that he wanted the Ottoman government to seek military assistance from Gábor Bethlen ('Mahomet Bassa is afrayd of ye Polackes and desires at the Gate, by Caim-Cam and others, that Gabor may be dealt withall for ayde') was derived from Lustrier's report of 17 May.[67] That report also contained the news that on 9 May the Ottoman government had pledged 400,000 thalers to Hafiz Ahmed Pasha, the commander at the siege of Baghdad, but that he would make no significant move until the autumn because of the excessive summer heat; the pamphlet duly stated that 'Isaffis [sc. Haffis] Mahomet Bassa hath receaued a greate somme of mony. 400^m crownes. on the 9th of may, for the Turkes employments, but by reason of ye heates, he will deferre the warre till Autumne.'[68] Lustrier's next dispatch, dated 25 May and with a postscript section dated 28 May, gave news of the arrival in Constantinople of Bethlen's special envoy Ferenc Bornemisza, whose mission was also discussed in the pamphlet.[69] On 30 May Lustrier reported that the ambassadors of the anti-Imperial powers were alarmed by the news that a Spanish envoy was making

[65] On Lustrier, who went to Constantinople in 1623 and took up ambassadorial duties in 1624, see B. Spuler, 'Die europäische Diplomatie in Konstantinopel bis zum Frieden von Belgrad (1739)', *Jahrbücher für Kultur und Geschichte der Slaven*, 11 (1935), pp. 53–169, 171–222, 313–66; here pp. 332–3. The only Spanish diplomat in Constantinople in this period was a secret envoy who stayed there for a short time in 1625 (p. 365).

[66] Haus-, Hof- und Staatsarchiv, Vienna [hereafter: HHSA], Türkei I, no. 110, liasse January–June 1626, fos. 76–81 (fo. 79r: 'Im 26 dises ist ein Spahi von Babilonia dem Caimecam in offenen diuan fürkhommen, mit Zeitung ab selbiger Vestung erobert'), 89–93.

[67] Ibid., fo. 89v: 'desswegen dann besorgter diack bassa allhie ausgeholten, ds [*sic*] auf allen nothfall der Gabor ime assistiern solle'.

[68] Ibid, fo. 90r: 'den 9. dises 400^m Taller dem Haffis Mehmet Bassa Serdar hilffeniss zugeordnet worden, Vnd demnach beÿ gar Zu grosser hüz in selbigem Landt, disen Sommer nichts sonderliches Zuverrichten wahere Aussgang nechst khommenden herbst oder winter zu erwarten'.

[69] Ibid., fos. 94–7, 110–12.

his way from the Adriatic coast to Constantinople, and that they were offering bribes to the Kaimakam Pasha to get his mission impeded or stopped; but in a postscript to this report, dated 1 June, he explained that 'the arrival of the above-mentioned Hidalgo' was now in doubt because he had suffered a serious fall from his horse and had been forced to return to Ragusa.[70] The *Altera secretissima instructio* not only reported the alarm of the other ambassadors and the misfortune of the fall ('And if that spanish gentleman fallinge from his horse, had not bene forced to goe backe, they had by this time despayred'), but actually used Lustrier's term 'Hidalgo' ('Hispanus ille Hidalgo', translated by Hobbes as 'that spanish gentleman')—even though 'hidalgo' is, of course, not a Latin word.

Two small details provide an even more striking proof that the relevant section of the *Altera secretissima instructio* was derived from these diplomatic reports. Lustrier's dispatches were sent mostly in cipher, with only some innocuous passages or phrases written out *en clair*. As soon as they arrived in Vienna, they were given to a clerk or official who deciphered them and wrote out a fair version of the deciphered text; in most cases both the original message and the deciphered version have been preserved. In the report of 17 May discussing the sending of new funds to Hafiz Ahmed Pasha for the siege of Baghdad (quoted above), the name is given as 'Haffis' in the ciphered original, and the same spelling is used in the deciphered version; but the decipherer's handwriting at that point produces an odd-looking capital 'H', where the left-hand vertical looks just like a capital 'J' with a cross-bar, and the right-hand vertical is a simple line leaning over to the right and strongly resembling a long 's'.[71] This, surely, is the explanation of the *Altera secretissima instructio*'s 'Isaffis': the author must have seen the deciphered version (or, at least, an uncomprehending transcript of it), in which the name appears to be 'Jsaffis'. Another garbling of a name in the pamphlet can also be explained by reference to the decipherer's work. According to the *Altera secretissima instructio*, 'The .3rd. of May the Gallies went out, to the guard of yᵉ Euxine sea, Peghier Bassa is to follow wth yᵉ Army': Hobbes's 'Peghier' here renders 'Pegierius' in the Latin text. This is in fact a garbled version of the name which is spelt

70 HHSA, Türkei I, no. 110, liasse January–June 1626, fos. 113–15, 120–2 (fo. 121v: 'ankhunfft oberermeltes Hidalgo'; fo. 123r: 'durch Vnglückh mit einem Pferde gefallen, vnnd also khranckher vom fall widerumb nach Ragusa zuruck').

71 Ibid., fos. 89r (original), 90r (deciphered version). Lustrier's cipher can be found in HHSA, Türkei I, no. 110, liasse January–June 1625, fo. 107r.

'Recep' in modern Turkish; the 'c' in that spelling represents a sound like the 'j' in English 'jam', and Lustrier's reports normally spelled the name 'Regiep', on Italian phonetic principles.[72] In the relevant section of Lustrier's dispatch of 17 May we find, in the deciphered version, that the name has been falsely given as 'pegier'.[73] In the original cipher, however, the name appears as 'pegiep'; the decipherer has mistaken the final letter because the cipher-symbol used here for 'p' looks very similar to one of the symbols for 'r'.[74] One of the two errors in 'pegier' is thus explained; the other must presumably derive from a mistake by the cipher clerk in Constantinople who, whether through inattention or because the capital 'R' in 'Reciep' looked like a capital 'P', used one of the symbols for 'p' to represent it. But the fact that this doubly erroneous version of the name recurs in the pamphlet constitutes solid proof that the decipherer's transcription was used as a source by the pamphlet's author.

These diplomatic reports from Constantinople also provide some further evidence for the dating of the pamphlet's composition, since in some cases the clerk in Vienna has marked the date on which the report was received there. Of the dispatches just mentioned, the one of 17 May was received on 10 July, and the one of 30 May (with a postscript of 1 June) was received on 12 July. However, the next report to arrive in Vienna was that of 15 June, which was received on 14 August; and it is clear that the contents of this report were unknown to the author of the pamphlet.[75] This confirms that the pamphlet was written in the second half of July and/or the first half of August. The evidence of the diplomatic reports also confirms that the author was acting with official permission and approval: he had been given access to the sort of material that was normally seen only by state officials—indeed, material so sensitive that it had originally been written in cipher. (That he was

---

[72] HHSA, Türkei I, no. 110, liasse January–June 1626, fo. 78r ('Regiep'); Moravský Zemský Archiv, Brno [hereafter: MZA], Collalto archive (G 169), I-1774 (Lustrier letters to Ramboldo Collalto), fo. 31r ('Regiep Bassa'); and cf. n. 75 below.

[73] HHSA, Türkei I, no. 110, liasse January–June 1626, fo. 90r: 'Den 3 dises sindt wider die Cosaggen Zu bewahrung des schwarzen Mehrs Canalen [25] Galleren aussgefahren, wehlsche weillens beÿ 700 sein sollen, der pegier Bassa alss General mit der überigen Armada in wenig tagen nachuolgen wirdet.' (I add the number 25, which appears in the original but was omitted by the decipherer.)

[74] Ibid., fo. 89v: 'der pegiep bassa'.

[75] Ibid., fos. 129–33: this report stated that Recep Pasha had now proceeded with 40 galleys to join the rest of the force in the Black Sea (fo: 131r: 'Questa matina e partito al [*sic*] Regiep Bassa con .40. Galere al mar negro per unirsi colle .20. gia uscite prima')—something expected in the future by the author of the pamphlet.

not himself an official who dealt regularly with this material is, however, suggested by the errors mentioned above: had he been a long-term reader of the dispatches from Constantinople, he would surely have recognized the name 'Haffis' and corrected the erroneous 'pegier'.) Presumably the author had been given access to a whole range of diplomatic and intelligence reports, probably including significant amounts of material supplied by the Spaniards.[76]

This evidence thus strongly suggests a Viennese origin for this text. Of course, other possibilities should also be considered. It might be thought that, given the close relations in these matters between Vienna and the Spanish Habsburgs, the author of the pamphlet was not someone working under Imperial supervision in Vienna, but rather someone in an equivalent position in Brussels, who happened to benefit from full transcripts of the Imperial dispatches from Constantinople. However, we know that the standard practice in Vienna was that when information derived from these dispatches was circulated (to members of the Imperial Council, for example), only a short digest, prepared by one of the *Hofdolmetscher* (court interpreters of oriental languages), was used.[77] It thus seems very unlikely that entire transcripts would have been sent to Brussels; but it is clear, both from the amount of detail presented in the *Altera secretissima instructio* and from its closeness to the original wording of the reports, that the author of the pamphlet had seen the full texts. (It should also be borne in mind that anyone who was regularly employed to write out digests or copies of these materials would have recognized the name 'Haffis', which occurs quite often in the reports from Constantinople, and would probably have corrected 'pegier' too.) The question of timing is also a relevant consideration: the post could take at least two weeks from Vienna to Brussels, which means that a copy of these reports would probably not have reached the latter city before the end of July; yet a writer in Brussels would have had to have finished work on the text and sent it off to be printed before the news of Gaston d'Orléans's marriage (in Nantes, on 6 August) reached that city, and this leaves only a very narrow window of time for his

---

[76] I have not found this type of Spanish material for the relevant months preceding the writing of the pamphlet; but an idea of the likely range is provided by items among the papers of Ramboldo Collalto (the president of the *Hofkriegsrat* in Vienna) for 1624–5, which include copies of letters and reports by Spanish diplomats and officials in Brussels, London, Paris, and Milan, as well as a letter from the Infanta to Ossona (MZA, Collalto archive (G 169), I-1882, fos. 9–12, 15, 29, 41–2, 47–8, 50).

[77] Hiller, *Palatin Nikolaus Esterházy*, p. 73.

work. A writer in the Spanish Netherlands might also be expected to have made good use of the intelligence reports which came to Brussels from that government's agents in England; but the main topic dealt with in those reports during June and July 1626 was the English attempt to assemble a large fleet for anti-Spanish operations—something hardly touched on in the text of the pamphlet.[78]

Overall, therefore, it seems most likely that the *Altera secretissima instructio* was written in Vienna. It was probably worked on intensively during the second half of July, and may perhaps have been completed in the first few days of August.[79] Its author was someone—possibly a secretary, counsellor, or protégé of one of the members of the Imperial Council—who had been given special access to the wealth of up-to-date geopolitical information contained in the official papers of the Imperial government.[80] In modern terminology, he had a high level of security clearance. And this must also make it seem likely that his finished text was, before it went to be printed, scrutinized and given official approval. Under its cloak of anonymity, and for all its idiosyncratic style, this was thus a piece of officially sanctioned propaganda emanating from the very heart of the Imperial government.

The fact that this was such a well-informed and cleverly written piece of work must, at first sight, make it seem surprising that it

---

[78] HHSA, Belgien, PC 63, fos. 28–32, 33–8, 52–3, 54–62 (reports by an unnamed English agent, 23 June–14 July).

[79] The pamphlet's airily dismissive attitude towards Ernst von Mansfeld contrasts with the fact that in the first week of August there was real alarm in Vienna about the news that he had passed successfully through Silesia and seemed about to join forces with Gábor Bethlen (MZA, Collalto archive (G 169), I-1765, fo. 34r: Gerard Questenberg to Collalto, from Vienna, 4 August 1626). The latest datable event referred to in the pamphlet, as noted above, is the battle of Kalenberg of 29 July. Some of the items of news from England, such as the agreement of the London Aldermen to advance £20,000 to the King (on 29 June/9 July: see section 6 (n. 55)) and the retrenchment of the royal household (reported by a London news-writer on 7 [/17] July: see section 6 (n. 62)) may also have reached Vienna only a short time before the completion of the pamphlet.

[80] The only writer previously to have offered an opinion on the author of this text was Hermann Becker, who proposed that it was written—as the *Elenchus* had said about the first *Secretissima instructio* pamphlet—by a Jesuit. This cannot be excluded, even though on one point the author seems to have gone against the views of the most important Jesuit in Vienna, the Emperor's confessor (see above, n. 62); a member of the Imperial Privy Council might well have had a Jesuit as an adviser or confessor, and the level of classical education displayed by the author is consistent with Jesuit training. But the reason given by Becker was merely that the text was 'full of truly Jesuitical trickery' ('voll echt jesuitischer Kniffe': *Die Secretissima Instructio*, p. 41); this probably tells us more about Becker, a Protestant German intellectual in the period of the *Kulturkampf*, than it does about the author of the pamphlet.

did not provoke a storm of answers and refutations. But that fact may itself supply the explanation. The quality of the intelligence marshalled here was too high to be matched by anyone—even with a similar kind of official backing—on the opposing side; against such a formidable bodyguard of truths (and near-truths) no equivalent force could be mustered. The work thus remained unrefuted.

The only printed response to it was something very different from a refutation: a pamphlet entitled *Ad aphorismos tres priores Alterae secretissimae instructionis gallo-britanno-batavae Friderico V datae commentarius*, by a pseudonymous author, 'Philotimus Musaeus', published in Cologne in 1626 (and reprinted or re-issued three times in the following two years).[81] This 43-page work was, as its title indicated, a learned 'commentary' on the first three sections of the text: it went through them almost line-by-line, occasionally adding further illustrations from recent European history, but mostly adducing relevant quotations from classical authors (Xenophon, Livy, Cicero, Seneca, Tacitus, Sallust, Polybius, and so on). Many of these quotations were, as the writer admitted, drawn from Lipsius; indeed, his acknowledged aim was to follow Lipsius's example, and his text managed to combine the two basic methods—of commentary and commonplace-book—on which Lipsius's best-known works had proceeded.[82] Only in his final pages did he offer the Elector Palatine some advice of his own: if he could deceive the Elector of Saxony and invade his territory, that would help his cause, but the most important thing was that he should seek reconciliation with the Emperor and the Emperor's allies.[83] That this curious text was a pro-Imperial production was clear from the outset: it bore a triple dedication, to Tilly (the general of the Catholic League) and to two senior officials of Maximilian of Bavaria, and most (perhaps all) of its editions were

---

[81] The first edition, entitled *Ad aphorismos tres . . .*, was published in Cologne, without the name of a printer; there is an exemplum in the Universitätsbibliothek, Leipzig. The second, entitled *Philotimi Musaei ad aphorismos tres . . .* (Cologne, 1627), bore the imprint 'Aput [*sic*] Johannem Kinckium'; I cite this edition, from the exemplum in the Staatsbibliothek, Berlin (pressmark 4" Flugschr. 1627/17). The third, bearing the same title as the second (but with the misprint '*Insructionis*'), was issued in 1628 with the imprint 'Hagae Comitis' and with no printer's name; there is an exemplum in the Niedersächsische Landesbibliothek, Hanover. The fourth, also bearing the same title and also from 1628, bore the imprint 'Poloniae' and 'Rinoklus' (presumably misprints for, or humorous distortions of, 'Coloniae' and 'Kinckius'); there is an exemplum in the Herzog-August Bibliothek, Wolfenbüttel.

[82] *Philotimi Musaei ad aphorismos tres priores Alterae secretissimae instructionis* (Cologne, 1627), sigs. (†)3v, (*)1r.

[83] Ibid., pp. 42–3.

produced by Johann Kinckius, the main printer of Jesuit works in Cologne.[84] (The ornament on the title page of the 1627 edition was, for good measure, an Austrian double-headed eagle; this ornament appears also on the 1627 reprintings of both the *Secretissima instructio* and the *Altera secretissima instructio*, which were probably produced by Kinckius to accompany this text.)[85] But it is hard to tell whether 'Philotimus Musaeus' had any connection with, or knowledge of, the author of the *Altera secretissima instructio*, whose work he appeared to take entirely at face value, praising the Elector Palatine's loyal adviser for his wise counsel. Was this a case of an earnest *ingénu* failing to get the joke, or was it an attempt—albeit a peculiarly ponderous one—to twist the blade a little further? The latter seems more probable; but that the former cannot be entirely ruled out testifies, perhaps, to some of the uncertainties that must still surround the reception of the *Altera secretissima instructio*.

---

[84] On Kinckius see Benzing, *Die Buchdrucker*, p. 251.

[85] However, while the 1627 *Ad aphorismos tres* bears the imprint 'Aput Johannem Kinckium', the 1627 reprints of the other two texts supply no such details of the printer; the reprint of the *Secretissima instructio* has the imprint 'Hagae Comitis', while that of the *Altera secretissima instructio* has no place of publication. That these items were sold together is suggested by the presence of all three in a volume of pamphlets owned by John Cosin: Durham University Library, pressmark Cosin L.4.23/2–3.

4

The Distribution of the *Altera secretissima instructio* in England

IF little is known about the transmission and reception of the *Altera secretissima instructio* in England, the contents of the text itself help to explain why that is so: here was a pamphlet which, albeit with quasi-satirical intent, openly advocated sedition against the King. No English bookseller could have advertised such a work, and few could have contemplated reprinting it on English soil.[1] Even without its treasonable passages, however, this would still have been a 'hot' work for any bookseller to handle. Since the outbreak of the Thirty Years' War, a series of royal proclamations had been issued, in an attempt to suppress unwelcome commentary on the 'arcana' of foreign policy. The 'Proclamation against Excess of Lavish and Licentious Speech in Matters of State' of December 1620, drafted by Bacon, had commanded James's subjects 'to take heede, how they intermeddle by Penne, or Speech, with causes of state, and secrets of Empire, either at home, or abroad', requiring them to inform the authorities within 24 hours of hearing any such discourse. In September 1623 the 'Proclamation against the Disorderly Printing, Uttering, and Dispersing of Bookes, Pamphlets, &c.' (aimed mainly at publications, such as those of Scott, against the Spanish Match), complained bitterly of 'Printing in the parts beyond the Sea'; and in August 1624 the 'Proclamation against Seditious, Popish, and Puritanicall Bookes and Pamphlets' decreed that any book or pamphlet about 'Religion, Church governement, or State', whether printed in England or imported, must henceforth be licensed

---

[1] Under a statute of 23 Elizabeth, the publication or distribution of any book 'to the encoraging stirring or moving of any Insurreccon or Rebellion' was a felony punishable by mutilation and hanging: see S. A. Baron, 'The Guises of Dissemination in Early Seventeenth-Century England: News in Manuscript and Print', in B. Dooley and S. A. Baron, eds., *The Politics of Information in Early Modern Europe* (London, 2001), pp. 41–56, here p. 46.

by the Archbishops of Canterbury and York, the Bishop of London, or the Vice-Chancellors of Oxford and Cambridge.[2] A government official acted as a regular licenser of newsbooks and political texts in the period 1621–4, and in February 1627 it was announced that there would be an official licenser (under the Secretary of State) of corantos, which 'often times raise disadvantageous and scandalous reports upon the proceedings and successes of his Ma^s frends and Allies'.[3] That these measures were, at least to begin with, quite vigorously enforced is suggested by a passage in a letter from one of the news-gathering correspondents of the Cambridge don Joseph Mead: writing just a month after the 1623 proclamation, he reported that 'The two *Mercurius Gallo-Belgicus* were called in before I could get them. It is said they contained foul and untrue matter concerning our sovereign's speech to the lords about his purpose in sending of the prince into Spain, as also of his approving of the Romish religion.'[4]

At the same time, however, the forbidding of such scandalous works turned them into even more desirable commodities. Small quantities of the printed text of the *Altera secretissima instructio* were brought into the country: as we shall see, early reports indicate that at least two copies were sold in London, and that the printed version could command a colossal price. Seven exempla are held by libraries in the United Kingdom today (though one of these, from Lord Acton's collection, is likely to have been bought from a continental book-dealer in the nineteenth century).[5] It

---

[2] J. F. Larkin and P. L. Hughes, eds., *Stuart Royal Proclamations*, 2 vols. (Oxford, 1973–83), i, pp. 495–6, 583–5, 599–600. Sheila Lambert has down-played the significance of these measures ('Coranto Printing in England: The First Newsbooks', *Journal of Newspaper and Periodical History*, 8 (1992), pp. 1–33, esp. pp. 7–8); but, as Cyndia Clegg has shown, they did form part of a larger policy aimed at limiting public comment on foreign policy and matters of state (*Press Censorship in Jacobean England* (Cambridge, 2001), pp. 177–85).

[3] Clegg, *Press Censorship*, pp. 181–2 (Francis Cottington, who licensed 93 publications in that period); BL, MS Add. 72439, fo. 1r (Edward Conway to the Stationers' Company, 25 February [/7 March] 1626/7; the licenser was Conway's secretary Georg Rudolf Weckherlin—on whom see below, n. 26).

[4] [T. Birch, ed.,] *The Court and Times of James the First* [revd. by R. F. Williams], 2 vols. (London, 1848), ii, p. 421 (anonymous correspondent [Dr Meddus?] to Mead, London, 24 October 1623).

[5] The database www.copac.ac.uk, which records the holdings of 24 academic libraries plus the BL, the National Library of Wales, and the National Library of Scotland (hereafter: NLS), lists exempla of *Altera secretissima instructio* in the BL, Manchester University Library, and the NLS, and of *Tertia secretissima instructio* in the BL and the NLS. The Acton exemplum, not recorded on copac, is in the Cambridge University Library (pressmark Acton d. 34. 596 (31)). The Durham exemplum of the 1627 edition

is even possible that some copies were brought in unwittingly: Mathieu de Morgues, commenting on the distribution of such pamphlets in France, claimed that French booksellers returning from the Frankfurt fairs were surprised to discover copies of the pamphlets surreptitiously inserted into the books they had bought.[6] The original publishers may have used such methods if they were paid by their political masters to do so, but the frequent reprintings of these pamphlets suggest that the profit motive also came to play an important part. The evidence from England indicates that profits were made here too, but that the people best placed to make them were the specialists in the manuscript circulation of news and commentary on current affairs.

As several modern studies have shown, such manuscript transmission played a major role in the political culture of seventeenth-century England.[7] At the heart of this phenomenon were the professional newsletter-writers, whose products, sent to individual subscribers throughout the country, presented information drawn from many sources—oral, manuscript, and printed. As prolific copyists (and/or employers of copyists), the newsletter-writers also produced so-called 'separates', copies of documents or short tracts of current interest such as parliamentary speeches, political discourses, and satires.[8] This could be a lucrative business: while the standard separates of parliamentary reports sold for between 6*d*. and 2*s*. in 1628, the newsletter-writer John Pory offered one of his clients in 1631 a variety of foreign 'discourses' (a 'character' of

---

(see above, Ch. 3 n. 85) is not separately recorded on copac, as it has been treated in the Durham University Library catalogue as part of the 1627 *Secretissima instructio*. Present-day library holdings are, however, a poor guide to the distribution of seventeenth-century ephemeral publications.

[6] [De Morgues,] *Advis d'un theologien*, p. 15. The other method of distribution described by de Morgues involved a network of agents in France who first contributed information to the pamphlet-writers, and then organized the underground circulation of their works; that some underground distribution took place seems likely, but there is more than a touch of paranoia in de Morgues's account.

[7] See especially F. J. Levy, 'How Information Spread among the Gentry, 1550–1640', *Journal of British Studies*, 21 (1982), no. 2, pp. 11–34; R. Cust, 'News and Politics in Early Seventeenth-Century England', *Past and Present*, 112 (1986), pp. 60–90; H. Love, *Scribal Publication in Seventeenth-Century England* (Oxford, 1993), pp. 9–22, 73–89, 191–217; I. Atherton, 'The Itch Grown a Disease: Manuscript Transmission of News in the Seventeenth Century', in J. Raymond, ed., *News, Newspapers, and Society in Early Modern Britain* (London, 1999), pp. 39–65; Baron, 'The Guises of Dissemination'.

[8] Separates are discussed by all the writers listed in n. 7; see also the detailed account in W. Notestein and F. H. Relf, eds., *Commons Debates for 1629* (Minneapolis, 1921), pp. xx–xli, and D. Zaret, *Origins of Democratic Culture: Printing, Petitions, and the Public Sphere in Early-Modern England* (Princeton, 2000), pp. 126–32.

Richelieu, a protest by the princes of the Holy Roman Empire, and so on) at 10*s*. each.[9] Since the newsletter-writers were well connected with printers and booksellers and made it their business to know the latest news and scandals, they were often able to circulate pamphlets or other such materials that could not be licensed (or, indeed, had already been banned); these, naturally, were the most profitable of all. The printers and booksellers were also quite capable of generating such manuscript copies on their own account. As one anonymous informant wrote to the Secretary of State in the early 1620s: 'there bee dyuers stationers soe soone as they heare of anie such bookes, as haue noe publicke authoritie, they indevo[r] vpon whatsoever condicion to gett them in theire hands, and hyres some younge Fellowes, to transcrybe them, & sells them to suche Nuefangle persons, as will not spare anie charges for acqueiringe such trashe.'[10] And, given the high prices charged for such desirable 'trashe', it is understandable that one such professionally produced copy might then breed other, non-professional copies, made by borrowers, or by owners for their friends.

The first report of the existence of the *Altera secretissima instructio* in England comes in a letter dated 2 [/12] February 1627 from one of Joseph Mead's London correspondents (possibly his friend and fellow cleric Dr James Meddus, a man whose hunger for news was almost as voracious as Mead's):

It is much talked of a pamphlet come from Frankfort, of four sheets of paper, called *Instructio Secretissima Frederico*, written by some Jesuit, or ill-willer of our state. The scope is to put a jealousy between his majesty and the Queen of Bohemia, as though the king her husband were advising to make some adventure to get footing in this kingdom, and that he hath here a greater faction of puritans and other enemies of the duke ready to assist him; which lewd libel, they say, is shortly to be burnt in public.[11]

---

[9] Cust, 'News and Politics', p. 64; W. S. Powell, *John Pory, 1572–1636: The Life and Letters of a Man of Many Parts* (Chapel Hill, NC, 1977), p. 56. Cf. also the comments on the high prices charged by Ralph Starkey in I. Atherton, *Ambition and Failure in Stuart England: The Career of John, first Viscount Scudamore* (Manchester, 1999), p. 154.

[10] PRO, SP 14/118/102 (fo. 139r). The letter is undated; it is assigned to 1623 in Clegg, *Press Censorship*, p. 186. The writer emphasized the role of economic motives ('This I take to be the cheefe cause of the soe common dispersinge of such bookes, and incouradgment of light braines or sedicious spirits, to studie to such subiects, is the makinge pryvate gaine by them'), and went on to describe the case of a scrivener who had been commissioned by a stationer to make twelve copies of Scott's *Vox populi*.

[11] [T. Birch, ed.,] *The Court and Times of Charles the First* [revd. by R. F. Williams], 2 vols. (London, 1848), i, p. 190. Despite the slight garbling of the title, it is clear that

It is not known whether such a burning, which would surely have stimulated public interest in the work, ever took place. But interest was clearly spreading: at almost exactly this time Mead's friend Sir Simonds D'Ewes also learned about the text, and within a few days Mead had seen a copy for himself. On 10 [/20] February Joseph Mead wrote from Cambridge to his regular correspondent in Suffolk, Sir Martin Stuteville, enclosing a letter from D'Ewes, their mutual friend, and referring to it as follows. 'I received on Sunday [*sc.* 4 [/14] February] at night a l[ette]re from Sr Symonds Dewes directed to your selfe & vnseald . . . What the book there mentioned containes you may guesse by my intelligence & if I haue so much time I will exscribe you [>a] parcell that you [>may] know ex vngue leonem: I haue not the book but saw it & exscribed a [*sic*] 2 or 3 passages.' The extracts, which Mead did 'exscribe' and send with his letter, were from sections 23 and 24 of the *Altera secretissima instructio*.[12] The circumstances in which Mead had seen a copy (whether printed or manuscript) are not known, but a letter he sent to Stuteville five months earlier gives an idea of his methods: commenting on the notorious pamphlet by the physician Dr Eglisham which accused the Duke of Buckingham of having poisoned James I, Mead wrote that 'A friend passing lately this way showed me a printed copy of Dr. Egglesheim's, which, cutting in pieces, I distributed to three of my pupils to transcribe, and here I send it you to read and return me again sooner or later, as you please.'[13]

As for D'Ewes, it is not known how he had encountered the *Altera secretissima instructio*, but a detail in his autobiography offers an intriguing possibility. In January 1627 he had visited Cambridgeshire and Suffolk, staying in Sir Martin Stuteville's house on the 24th [/3 February]. He then returned briefly to London, where, on the 30th [/9 February], he 'dined with my deare friend Sr Albertus Joachimi the States Embassadour in Ordinarie to the King of Great Brittaine;

---

this refers to the *Altera secretissima instructio*, which has four sheets (A–D_4) and does encourage Frederick to 'get footing' in England. James Meddus was strongly pro-Palatine, and had corresponded in 1620 with Frederick V's adviser von Plessen in Heidelberg: see J. Kočí, J. Polišenský, and G. Čehová, eds., *Documenta bohemica bellum tricennale illustrantia*, 7 vols. (Prague, 1971–81), ii, pp. 224–5.

[12] BL, MS Harl. 390, fos. 201r (letter), 203 (extracts).

[13] [Birch, ed.,] *Court and Times of Charles*, i, p. 149 (16 [/26] September 1626). On Mead's practices more generally as a circulator of news (and of separates) see D. Randall, 'Joseph Mead, Novellante: News, Sociability, and Credibility in Early Stuart England', *Journal of British Studies*, 45 (2006), pp. 293–312.

wheere wee condoled together the sad condicion of Christendome.'[14] His letter to Stuteville must have been written within the next four days. It thus seems possible that D'Ewes was told about the *Altera secretissima instructio*, or even shown a copy of it, by the Dutch Ambassador (who, like D'Ewes, was strongly sympathetic to the Palatine cause—they had first met at the house of Horace, Lord Vere, the leader of the abortive English military expedition to defend the Palatinate in 1620).[15] Among the many manuscripts from D'Ewes's library now in the Harleian collection there are copies of the *Secretissima instructio* and the *Altera secretissima instructio*.[16] The latter (but not the former) is in the hand of Ralph Starkey, a London merchant and antiquarian who was a prolific producer of separates; D'Ewes would acquire the whole of Starkey's remaining stock of manuscripts and books from his executors in 1628, but there is evidence that he had been using Starkey's services occasionally since at least 1623, so it is quite possible that he bought this copy of the *Altera secretissima instructio* from him in early 1627.[17]

The next dated reference to the circulation of this text is provided by Ralph Starkey himself. In a letter to another of his clients, Sir John Scudamore, sent from London in May 1627, he wrote:

S^r I haue sent yo^u herewth the Catologue of Booke yo^u desired to see, I could not procure it sooner by reason the party feared the tymes, also if as yet yo^u haue not seene Secretissima instructio, it is possible I cane nowe procure it yo^u in writinge, but in print it is not to be had, there is two severall bookes of it, the first is prima parse printed an^o. *1620.* the other is Altera parse printed an^o. *1626.* the latter parte .40^s. cannot buye it in printe lett me vnderstand yor Resolucion for hauinge of them, and that it please yo^u to send by the returne of this Caryere .xxx^s. it shalbe sent yo^u by him wthout faile.[18]

While the wording of the final phrases here is a little ambiguous (was 30*s.* the charge for a manuscript copy of the *Altera secretissima instructio* alone, or for copies of both texts?), this colossal price does indicate

[14] BL, MS Harl. 646, fo. 104v (printed in J. O. Halliwell, ed., *The Autobiography and Correspondence of Sir Simonds d'Ewes, Bart, during the Reigns of James I and Charles I*, 2 vols. (London, 1845), i, pp. 351–2).

[15] BL, MS Harl. 646, fo. 87r (meeting of D'Ewes, Joachimi, and Vere, 2 [/12] March 1626).

[16] BL, MS Harl. 252, fos. 75–98r ('Secretissima Instructio'), 99–110r ('Altera secretissima instructio').

[17] See A. G. Watson, *The Library of Sir Simonds D'Ewes* (London, 1966), pp. 24–5, 238, 322.

[18] PRO, C115/108/8578 (dated only 'May 1627'). Italics are used here for underlinings in the MS.

that demand was high.[19] Also striking is the fact that copies of the *Secretissima instructio* were being touted in tandem with copies of the *Altera secretissima instructio*; this may have been a consequence of the recent reprinting of the earlier text on the Continent, but it is also possible that the revival of this otherwise rather stale production was due to the entrepreneurial spirit of copyists such as Starkey, determined to milk the success of the later publication for all it was worth. D'Ewes, as already mentioned, acquired manuscript copies of both texts; but whether he got them at the same time is not known. Nor is there any evidence by which to date the anonymous English translation of the *Secretissima instructio*, which is itself in the sort of neat, workaday secretary hand that was used by professional copyists.[20]

The fullest record of the circulation of the *Altera secretissima instructio* in England is supplied by a number of items in the papers of Sir John Coke, the principal Secretary of State; most of these are undated, but one is a letter written on 4 [/14] August 1627, and the others are clearly related to it. The primary piece of evidence here is an unfinished scribal copy of the *Altera secretissima instructio*, which gets as far as the beginning of section 17: blank pages follow, sufficient for the rest of the text, so it appears to have been seized when the copyist was half way through his work. An endorsement in Coke's hand records: 'John Balle an Attorney of the Common Law dwelling at Amersam d[elivere]d this booke to be copied out to John Waade of Stoke to bee written out for him. Balle had this copie from one Nathaniel Burt a Bookebinder neare Pauls cheine who lent a copie to him wch hee gott copied out by a scholler, This Balle said to Waade.'[21] The phrasing of this note is a little

---

[19] One piece of evidence suggests that the printed texts were also expensive in Holland: Cosin's copy of the *Secretissima instructio*, the *Altera secretissima instructio*, and the *Ad aphorismos tres* (see above, Ch. 3 n. 85) is annotated with the price (apparently for all three together) '5 Rd', i.e. 5 Rijksdaler (Reichsthaler) (Durham University Library, pressmark Cosin L.4.23/2–3). In 1626–8 this was the equivalent of just over £1 2s. (see J. J. McCusker, *Money and Exchange in Europe and America, 1600–1775: A Handbook* (Chapel Hill, NC, 1978), pp. 44, 52, 63). In this period, a large folio volume might cost less than 10s., and an English country schoolmaster might have an annual salary of £10.

[20] BL, MS Sloane 3938.

[21] BL, MS Add. 69911, fos. 90–4, here fo. 94v. (This is a quire of eight leaves, with the second four blank; the foliation ignores the first three of the blank leaves, and resumes with '94' for the final, endorsed, leaf.) I am very grateful to Dr Peter Beal for drawing my attention to the items in this volume of the Coke papers. 'Amersam' is Amersham, in Buckinghamshire; 'Stoke' is probably Stoke Poges, which lies roughly 8 miles to the south of Amersham. Paul's Chain was a little street running southwards from the south side of St Paul's cathedral in London.

ambiguous ('this booke' presumably refers to the text itself, not to this particular unfinished copy), but the overall sequence of events is clear: Nathaniel 'Burt' lent a copy of the text to Balle, who—like Mead in Cambridge—employed a 'scholler' as a copyist, and the resulting copy was then lent to John Waade, so that he could have another copy made from it.

The person referred to by Waade as 'Nathaniel Burt a Bookebinder' was evidently identified by the authorities as Nathaniel Butter, a well-known Stationer who specialized in corantos and current-affairs pamphlets.[22] On further investigation it was established that, in addition to lending a manuscript copy to Balle, Butter had sold two exempla of the printed text, and had circulated a third. In his letter of 4 [/14] August 1627 to Sir John Coke, Butter tried to justify himself as follows:

> May it please yor. honor, As concerning the question made to mee Nathaniell Butter Stationer, about a booke, Intituled *Secretissima Instructio* &c. I will, god willing, set downe the truth to a sillable. One m^r Nathaniell Hall, a Gentleman belonging to Sir Thomas Fanshawes office, a man well knowne to bee both honest and able to make good vse of the worst bookes, a man studious in Antiquities, that hath contynued the storie of our Contrie, where m^r. Samuell Daniell left, one that, for his private, desireth to store himself with any rare manuscripts, or other, Hee desired mee to gett him a couple of the foresaid bookes, wch. after two monethes, with much enquiry, I did procure him. Hee therevpon gaue mee an vnperfect manuscript of the said Booke, wch. lying in my Shopp, I esteemed but as wast paper. A fellowe that had bene a Customer to my Shopp, seeing, desired to read ouer. I denied him often, and told him it was vnperfectlie written, and that hee could not vnderstand it, and that it was a scandalous railing booke, not fitt for euery man to read; notwithstanding hee sent his letter, and still I denied him, till about three weeke agone hee came himself, and made great protestacons, that hee would but read it ouer, and retorne it mee againe within a weeke, but did not performe his promise &c. For the 3.^{d} printed booke, I seeing of it amongst m^r Wakerlins papers, desired him to lend it mee for Sir Robt. Gouldon for 2. or 3. daies, promising to retorne it back againe. This beeing all the hand or dealing that I haue had with the booke aforesaid.[23]

---

[22] On Butter (d. 1664) see H. R. Plomer, *A Dictionary of the Booksellers and Printers who were at work in England, Scotland and Ireland from 1641 to 1667* (London, 1907), pp. 40–1; J. Raymond, *The Invention of the Newspaper: English Newsbooks, 1641–1649* (Oxford, 1996), pp. 8–9, 12–13, 93–4; J. Raymond, *Pamphlets and Pamphleteering in Early Modern Britain* (Cambridge, 2003), pp. 132–4, 149–50.

[23] BL, MS Add. 64892, fo. 59r. I am very grateful to Prof. Thomas Cogswell for drawing my attention to this document. Although Butter gives the title as '*Secretissima*

The 'fellowe' who came (evidently from outside London) and insisted on borrowing a copy was, presumably, the Buckinghamshire lawyer John Balle. But the details given here of the circulation of printed *exempla* indicate a surprisingly close connection between the world of underground distribution and the personnel of the government and the court. Sir Thomas Fanshawe was a long-term servant of the Crown who had risen to the post of Surveyor-General under Charles I; the fact that his employee Nathaniel Hall bought two copies suggests that one of those highly desirable items may have been given to Sir Thomas.[24] Sir Robert 'Gouldon' was probably Sir Robert Gordon, a Scottish nobleman (uncle and guardian of the thirteenth Earl of Sutherland) who was well favoured at Court.[25] And, most surprising of all, the Mr 'Wakerlin' who allowed Butter to borrow a printed *exemplum* was Georg Rudolf Weckherlin, the very official (working under Coke's colleague Lord Conway) who had been appointed licenser of corantos earlier in 1627.[26] These details suggest that the policing of these matters, far from being a black-and-white affair, might often involve some rather complicated and mutually beneficial interactions between gamekeepers and poachers.

On this occasion, however, Butter's connections in high places earned him no immunity. Probably Sir John Coke recognized that his claim about esteeming as 'wast paper' the manuscript copy he kept in his shop

Instructio', there can be no doubt—in view of the date, and the evident connection with the confiscated manuscript—that the *Altera secretissima instructio* was meant.

[24] On Fanshawe see the entry by S. M. Jack in the *Oxford Dictionary of National Biography* (www.oxforddnb.com). Hall's continuation of Daniel (whose two volumes on medieval English history had reached the end of the reign of Edward III) was not published.

[25] There was no one during this period named Sir Robert Goulden (or Gould, Golding, etc.), but there were two people named Sir Robert Gordon, of whom one (of Lochinvar) may be discounted, since he was away on a naval expedition at this time. The uncle of the thirteenth Earl (and younger brother of the twelfth) was born in 1580 and died in 1656; favoured by both James VI and I and Charles I, he served as Gentleman of the Privy Chamber under both of them, was knighted in 1609, and was created the first Knight Baronet of Nova Scotia in 1625. Although his nephew remained in Scotland, Sir Robert spent most of the period 1624–9 in England, frequently at Court. (See Sir William Fraser, *The Sutherland Book*, 3 vols. (Edinburgh, 1892), i, pp. 192–205; P. Hume Brown, ed., *The Register of the Privy Council of Scotland*, ser. 2, vol. iii, for 1629–30 (Edinburgh, 1901), p. 292; Sir James Balfour Paul, ed., *The Scots Peerage*, 9 vols. (Edinburgh, 1904–14), viii, p. 345.)

[26] See above, n. 3. On Weckherlin see L. W. Forster, *Georg Rudolf Weckherlin: zur Kenntnis seines Lebens in England*, Basler Studien zur deutsche Sprache und Literatur, 2 (Basel, 1944).

was bogus; the retention of such a copy was surely a money-making device, which Butter had very likely made a condition of the sale of the two printed exempla. Given the scandalous nature of the text itself, it is not surprising that Butter's punishment was a period of imprisonment. Two undated petitions by Butter survive, both addressed to Coke, and both written in gaol. In the first of these Butter described himself as 'your pet^r according to your Ho^{rs} commaund hauing remayned a prisoner in ye Gateh[*page torn* ous]e at Westm^r for the space of 16. dayes for selling of two [*page torn* inti]tuled Secretissima instructio'.[27] He continued:

And whereas other compl[ain]ts are obiected against y^r p[etitione]^r for printing & selling bookes without licence wch he cannot denie; But wth all affirmeth that he neuer published any in that kind, but such as both stoode for the hono^r of his Matie, his kindred and allies, the good of this state, & the true religion therein maintayned; excepting only the [>sale of the] said twoe bookes, w^{ch} (if y^r Ho[nou]^r: please) y^r p[etitione]^r will recall, and prayeth that his want of vnderstanding in ye Latin tongue may excuse his error therein, he not knowing wherto ye said booke tended: nor neuer heard to the contrary but that he might safely and lawfully sell the same.[28]

Butter's claim that he had 'neuer heard' that he could not 'safely and lawfully' sell them was disingenuous: he can hardly have been unaware of the proclamations of 1623 and 1624, which were very much aimed at this sort of imported item. His claim of complete ignorance of the contents of the text was also scarcely credible: there was no shortage of people who could give him the gist of a short Latin text if he could not read it himself, and, in any case, the huge price he presumably charged for this pamphlet would have testified to his awareness of its nature. (He himself had described it, in his previous letter to Coke, as 'a scandalous railing booke'.) But one part of his statement was quite correct: he did indeed have a record of printing and selling books 'without licence'. In 1621 he had similarly been obliged to petition Coke's predecessor, Sir George Calvert, when he had been imprisoned for more than a month by the Archbishop of Canterbury for 'the printing of a booke Concernynge the Emperor'.[29] And it was also true that, as the wording of his petition insinuated, Butter—like most of those engaged in this

---

[27] BL, MS Add. 69911, fo. 87r.   [28] Ibid., fo. 87r.

[29] W. W. Greg, *A Companion to Arber* (Oxford, 1967), pp. 209–10. Greg identifies the work as the anonymous pamphlet *A Plain Demonstration of the Unlawful Succession of the Now Emperor Ferdinand the Second, because of the Incestuous Marriage of his Parents* ('The Hague', 1620). He dates the imprisonment to 1622; this is corrected in Clegg, *Press Censorship*, pp. 184, 262–3 (n. 92).

kind of pamphlet-publication and news-circulation in England—had been vigorously promoting the cause of the Elector Palatine (the King's 'kindred') and of 'true religion'.[30]

Butter's second petition noted that he had by now been examined by the Secretary of State in person, and complained that he was 'still (to his great expence, hinderance and greife of mynde) most strictly restrayned'. He insisted that 'whereas yor hono^r may iustly suspect, that yor pet^r hath in his custody; or hath disperst many of the said books; he protesteth . . . that he hath neuer sought after; nor soe much as sawe any of that kynd, more then those wherewith he acquainted yor hono^r.'[31] Whether this claim was as disingenuous as most of his other statements cannot be established; but Coke seems to have thought that it was. It is not known how much longer Butter had to stay in gaol.

How many other copies of the *Altera secretissima instructio* may have circulated in England at this time, it is impossible to tell. In addition to the partial transcription confiscated from John Waade, and the copy by Starkey which was acquired by D'Ewes, there is one other copy (in a bound volume of manuscripts in Cambridge University Library) that appears to have been made by an English scribe during this period; it is accompanied by a copy of the *Secretissima instructio*, in the same scribal hand.[32] (There are also transcripts of both texts in one of the manuscripts from Richard Rawlinson's collection in the Bodleian Library; but the hands in that volume are Italian, and it must be doubted whether those transcripts were in England in the 1620s.)[33] Other copies of the

[30] On the link between the market for corantos and interest in the Palatine cause see M. Frearson, 'The Distribution and Readership of London Corantos in the 1620s', in R. Myers and M. Harris, eds., *Serials and their Readers, 1620–1914* (Winchester, 1993), pp. 1–25, esp. pp. 2–4; and Baron, 'The Guises of Dissemination', p. 44 (noting that Butter displayed the Elector Palatine's coat of arms on the title page of his coranto series).

[31] BL, MS Add. 69911, fo. 89r.

[32] Cambridge University Library, MS Ee. 4. 13, fos. 1–25r (*Secretissima instructio*), 26–46 (*Altera secretissima instructio*). I am very grateful to Dr Peter Beal for drawing my attention to this MS.

[33] Bodl., MS Rawl. D 624, fos. 437–464r, 465–98. Similarly, the British Library has a copy of the *Secretissima instructio* in a volume of papers relating mostly to the Carafa family, written in an Italian hand and bound in a late seventeenth-century Italian binding (MS Add. 8296, fos. 312–23); this was acquired by Lord Guilford in the eighteenth century. That the *Secretissima instructio* sparked some interest in Italy is also suggested by the existence of another MS copy (taken, apparently, from the 1626 reprinting of that work) in the Biblioteca corsiniana (now part of the Biblioteca dell'Academia nazionale dei Lincei, Rome): see L. G. Pélissier, 'Inventaire sommaire de soixante-deux manuscrits de la Bibliothèque Corsini (Rome)', *Centralblatt für Bibliothekswesen*, 8 (1891), pp. 176–202, 297–324, here p. 179, referring to MS 677 (pressmark 35 B 6), fos. 366–85.

Altera secretissima instructio may well lie unnoticed in other manuscript collections in England. Comparison of the three (or rather, two-and-a-half) surviving manuscripts with Hobbes's translation suggests that the copy of the Latin which Hobbes used could have derived from Starkey, or from the original used by Starkey, or from the original used by Waade, but not from the Cambridge copy or its original. Some small pieces of evidence suggest that Hobbes's copy may have corresponded particularly closely to the original used by Waade—so perhaps Hobbes used another copy taken from Nathaniel Butter's manuscript copy.[34]

Whether any copies of Hobbes's translation were circulated and still survive (in complete form, unlike the original) in other archives is not known; searches for them have so far proved unsuccessful. But the chances may be slim. For the person who probably commissioned that translation, Viscount Mansfield, was in later life one of the most outspoken critics of the whole practice of circulating news, both printed and—especially—manuscript. In his advice to Charles II, written in the early 1650s, he observed that printed newspapers, both domestic and foreign, 'Should bee forbid . . . as also such fellowes as Captin Rosingame thatt made *500ˡ* a yeare with writinge newse to severall Persons, this did as much hurte as the other iff nott more, for In a letter hee mighte bee bolder then theye durste bee In Printe these to nott onlye to bee forbiden absolutlye, butt to be punishte Severlye iff theye offende In this kinde.'[35] As early as 1626, writing to the Secretary of State about the difficulties he encountered in raising the 'benevolence' (a form of extra-parliamentary taxation) in Nottinghamshire, he had complained

---

[34] One point of divergence between Hobbes's version and the printed Latin text is the omission of a question mark in section 19 (at n. 228); this is also omitted in the Starkey and Cambridge copies. (The Waade copy ends before this section.) The Cambridge copy omits the word 'Bojum' ('the Bavarian', i.e. 'Bavaria') in section 8 (at n. 81), leaving a gap for it (and thus presumably following a manuscript original in which the word was hard to read); Hobbes correctly translates it as 'Bauiere'. The Cambridge copy also has 'causa Caesarum' instead of 'causa causarum' in section 9. The Waade copy omits the word 'Passompirium' (correctly rendered by Hobbes as 'Bassompier') in section 9 (at n. 103), but does not leave a gap, which suggests a simple *Augensprung*. The Waade copy has two features which correspond to peculiarities of Hobbes's text. In section 6 it mistakenly gives 'Regiae' instead of 'regiè' (at n. 61); 'Regiae' makes no sense here, and Hobbes omits the word altogether. And in section 10 the Waade copy has de-italicized the last phrase of a quotation (at n. 118); Hobbes's translation, similarly, assumes that it is not part of the quotation. It should also be noted that none of these three copies makes the numerous omissions that are found in Hobbes's translation (with the exception of the question mark mentioned above).

[35] S. A. Strong, ed., *A Catalogue of Letters and Other Historical Documents exhibited in the Library at Welbeck* (London, 1903), p. 220.

that the people were 'gouerned by ill presedents [*sc.* precedents] . . . God sende them see clerer & nott to be gouerned by theyr Intelegencer, fame thatt neuer speakes trewth.'[36] If he felt so strongly about the influence of ordinary newsletters, it is not hard to imagine what his feelings would have been about the manuscript circulation of the cynical and possibly treasonable *Altera secretissima instructio.*[37]

[36] PRO, SP 16/33/126 (fo. 180r): Mansfield to Lord Conway, 27 August [/6 September] 1626.

[37] Of course it is conceivable that Hobbes's translation of the *Altera secretissima instructio* was commissioned by Devonshire (whose attitude towards the circulation of news was—to judge by his circulation of the Micanzio letters—quite different), and merely passed on by him to Mansfield. However, it is noteworthy that what Mansfield received was not a copy (as one might expect, had Devonshire been circulating this text) but Hobbes's original manuscript. Once the original had passed to Mansfield, the argument sketched here about the unlikelihood of his using it to generate further copies would still apply.

5

Palatine Politics: Cavendish, Mansfield, and Hobbes

THROUGHOUT the 1620s, English public opinion was constantly concerned, and occasionally obsessed, with the issue of the Palatinate. Anyone with access to printed or written news, or with contacts in Parliament and at Court, would have followed the ups and downs—mostly downs—of the Elector Palatine's fortunes and would have held some opinions about the ineffectual attempts of James I and Charles I to help him. This must be all the more true of Thomas Hobbes, since he was closely attached to a prominent political figure, Lord Cavendish, whose sympathies with the Palatine cause were especially strong. Striking evidence of those sympathies—and, at the same time, of his notoriously heavy debts—is provided by a letter written by Lord Cavendish to the Lords of the Privy Council in November 1620, in response to their letter 'inuiting me to a contrebution for the defence of ye Palatinate':

I hope I haue giuen such testemony y^t yow will not beleeue I haue beene the backwardest in y^t seruice... Notwithstanding if my example were now of vse (as peraduenture not long since it was) your LL:^ps should command all y^t my credit could gather, for that is the substance of my present fortunes... I shall neede no more then to remember vnto your LL.^ps the streightness of my present means: for I can not feare y^t your LL.^ps will doubt of my affection, w:^ch I haue approoued before, both by borrowing mony to contribute my selfe, & by diligent & effectuall labour in the country, for the heightening of the former contribution, for w:^ch I dare appeale to my Lord Embassadour the Baron of Dona.[1]

From this it appears that Lord Cavendish had been particularly active in the fund-raising which had taken place earlier in 1620, when the Palatine Ambassador, Achatius von Dohna, had been allowed to solicit

---

[1] PRO, SP 14/117/75 (fo. 136r), 15 [/25] November 1620; the letter is in Cavendish's own hand.

donations to pay for the small volunteer force of English soldiers that went to defend the Palatinate.

Further evidence of Lord Cavendish's interest in Palatine affairs is provided by the long sequence of letters he received from the Venetian friar Fulgenzio Micanzio (Paolo Sarpi's assistant) between 1615 and 1628—letters which were translated by Hobbes, and of which scribal copies were circulated.[2] Of the 75 surviving letters, 37 contain some discussion or mention of the Elector Palatine and his territories. Micanzio's fierce hostility to the Habsburgs—and to the Papacy and the Jesuit order, and hence, more generally, to the whole process of re-establishing Catholicism in Protestant Central Europe—ensured that he was a strong supporter of the Palatine cause, and a critic of English policy. His criticisms of James I were often diplomatically phrased, wrapped in the polite fiction that the King was pursuing a strategy so far-sighted that ordinary observers could not expect to understand its logic. Sometimes he merely reported the critical comments made by others ('For my part I cannot without Impatience heare of those who attribute it all to Irresolution').[3] But from time to time he could not contain his frustration. Commenting in June 1620 on Vere's expeditionary force (which was raised, officially, by Dohna, not by the King), he wrote that 'It is a thing very admirable, that amongst so many tyes of union, of blood, of Religion, of proffitt, of the Cause yett these few soldiers that are sent over are rather by connivance, than decree.'[4] And two years later, discussing the truce which James had negotiated, he exclaimed: 'this Treaty of suspension of Armes which his Matie of Gr. Br. now holds, if it take effect, is even the hand of heaven to assure to ye Spanyards the subjection of Germany quickly, and the totall ruyne of the party adverse.'[5] As for the Spanish Match, James's devotion to this project reduced Micanzio to such despair that his pretence that he was merely reporting other people's criticism became painfully transparent: 'I have ever bene of opinion that though ye world says, nothing could be done worse for ye ruyne of his State Religion and blood . . . yet that Great King hath had his secret end, whereunto he hath directed all, and that it is not as commonly he is slandered for to keepe himselfe in his pleasures and dissolutenes'.[6]

---

[2] See above, Ch. 1 n. 21.   [3] Micanzio, *Lettere*, p. 109.
[4] Ibid., p. 112. 'Admirable' here means 'to be wondered at'.
[5] Ibid., p. 172.   [6] Ibid., p. 233.

Whether Lord Cavendish openly expressed his agreement with any of these views cannot be known, since none of his letters to Micanzio has survived. Occasionally Micanzio's comments (and the marginal annotations made on them by Cavendish) suggest that Cavendish did attempt to justify, or at least excuse, the policy of his sovereign. Thus in January 1621 Micanzio referred to 'the 3 considerations whereuppon your Lo.^{P} sayes was built the Neutrality in ye matter of Bohemia', observing that these were legalistic arguments that might prevail in a court of law but could not carry much weight 'between Soveraignes where one of them proceeds *de facto* & usurpes uppon others': Lord Cavendish's annotation reads 'Censure of reasons in my letter for the K. neutrality in ye matter of Bohemia'.[7] Later that year Cavendish seems to have offered, if not a defence, then at least a reason for the English policy: Micanzio commented that 'The great want of money wch your Lord.^{P} wisely noteth for the cause of those strange proceedings wch wee see is an argument of another want much greater. The holy scripture attributes it to ye wrath of god'.[8] And in the summer of 1622 Micanzio wrote: 'By your Lordship discourse on the state of affayres and of the Court there I gather a great dexterity you have to Interpret things to ye best . . . wherein yor Lordship does your duty towards those that raigne.'[9] But the key fact is that Cavendish circulated copies of these letters, in which Micanzio's vigorous critique of English policy is constantly in the foreground; this made Cavendish an active propagator of criticisms, even if Micanzio's letters did sometimes include (conveniently) remarks suggesting that, somewhere in the background, Cavendish himself did not share all his views.

One thing at least is clear: over a period of many years, Lord Cavendish paid close attention to the unfolding events in and around the Palatine territories, and to the political debates about these and related foreign policy issues. Some further evidence of this can be found in the catalogue of his library which was drawn up, probably in 1627 or 1628, by Hobbes. This includes 'Gallobelgicus 9 peeces', referring to issues of the *Mercurius gallobelgicus*, a continental news-book which summarized recent political and military events in Europe; 'State-pamphlets. Vox populi etc.', for a group of items which contained Thomas Scott's famous attack on the Spanish Match and other such productions; 'Massacro de' Valtelinesi', an Italian translation of a fiercely anti-Habsburg pamphlet (probably by the Zurich theologian Caspar Waser) about the Valtelline,

---

[7] Micanzio, *Lettere*, pp. 126, 128.   [8] Ibid., p. 146.   [9] Ibid., p. 164.

published in 1621; 'Cancellaria Anhaltina, Hispan. etc.', referring to the collections of incriminating documents published in 1621–2; and something described as 'Controuersiae de Regno Bohemiae', which was perhaps a composite volume containing such items as the Habsburg propaganda pamphlets *Jus haereditarium et legitima successio in regno Bohemiae* (n.p., 1620) and *Informatio fundamentalis super hodierno Bohemiae statu* (Frankfurt, 1620), and responses to them such as the widely read *Bohemiae regnum electivum: That is, A Plaine and True Relation of the Proceedings of the States of Bohemia* (n.p. [London], 1620).[10]

Lord Cavendish was not merely a reader about and an observer of events; he was also an active participant in politics, as a member of the House of Commons in the parliaments of 1610, 1614, 1621, 1624, 1625, and 1626. (In the parliament of 1626 he began as a member of the Commons, but moved to the Lords in early March when he succeeded to the earldom of Devonshire.) In the early 1620s he was a key member of the political grouping led by the Earl of Southampton, which campaigned for an anti-Habsburg foreign policy, and, accordingly, strongly supported the cause of the Elector Palatine.[11] Other members of this grouping in the Commons, such as Sir Edwin Sandys (its most prominent member) and Sir Dudley Digges, made impassioned speeches on this topic in the 1621 parliament: as Sandys put it in his speech of 29 May [/8 June], 'Religion rooted oute in Bohemia, in the Pallatinate, in France rootinge out . . . I had rather speak now then betray my country with silence.'[12] When Lord Cavendish discussed

---

[10] Chatsworth, MS Hobbes E. 1. A. The text on the Valtelline was *Vera narratione del massacro degli evangelici fatto da' papisti e rebelli nella maggior parte della Valtellina, nell'anno 1620*, tr. V. Paravicino (n.p., 1621), a version of C. Waser (attrib.), *Veltlinische Tyranney, das ist: aussführliche . . . Beschreibung dess grausamen . . . Mordts so in dem Landt Veltlin gemeinen dreyen Pündten gehörig, Anno 1620* (n.p., 1621). The anonymous *Jus haereditarium* is attributed in some modern catalogues to Pedro Ximenes; the *Informatio* has been attributed to Augustin Schmid von Schmiedebach (Gebauer, *Die Publicistik*, p. 111); Josef Polišenský has suggested that *Bohemiae regnum electivum* was by Sir Thomas Roe (*Anglie a Bílá Horá* (Prague, 1949), pp. 122–4). None of these items is listed in J. Lacaita, *Catalogue of the Library at Chatsworth*, 4 vols. (London, 1879); but that is also true of other items in MS Hobbes E. 1. A.

[11] On Southampton's 'faction' see R. E. Ruigh, *The Parliament of 1624: Politics and Foreign Policy* (Cambridge, MA, 1971), pp. 124–7; Adams, 'The Protestant Cause', p. 286; T. K. Rabb, *Jacobean Gentleman: Sir Edwin Sandys, 1561–1629* (Princeton, 1998), p. 215.

[12] W. Notestein, F. H. Relf, and H. Simpson, eds., *Commons Debates 1621*, 7 vols. (New Haven, 1935), iii, p. 345; cf. similar speeches by Sandys on 30 April (v, p. 119), and by Digges on 26 November (ii, p. 445; iv, p. 437; v, pp. 210–11). On the importance of

these 1621 debates in a parliamentary speech five years later, he praised the House of Commons for having made 'the bravest protestation that ever parliament made' in support of the Palatinate, and commented bitterly that Sandys and Southampton had been imprisoned 'for their forwardness in the Queen of Bohemia's cause'. (He also remarked that Prince Charles's journey to Madrid in pursuit of the Spanish Match had taken place 'to the amazement of the world and terror of all honest men' — terms which suggest that he had shared all of Micanzio's feelings on that subject.)[13]

Southampton, Sandys, Digges, and Lord Cavendish were all active in the Virginia Company, and thus regarded Habsburg power (above all, the power of Spain) as a commercial threat as well as a religious one; the precise mix of religious identification and economic self-interest here is hard to determine, but it is probably fair to say that they were less motivated by commitment to international Calvinism than was the 'puritan' grouping led by the Earl of Pembroke. Lord Cavendish himself was certainly not puritanical by nature. In one of his essays he ridiculed the '*Hypocrisy*' of those who 'wil subscribe to no word that savours not of the Catechisme, accountinge natural, and good speech, as ethnique and unsanctified', and his own personal life included an early period of sexual promiscuity and a succession of unpaid and well-nigh unpayable debts, brought on by uncontrolled expenditure on entertainment, jewels, plate, and other finery.[14] But he does seem to have been strongly anti-Catholic: in the 1621 parliament he supported a motion designed to smoke out any Catholics who might have infiltrated the Commons, and in the 1624 parliament he was appointed to the conference on recusancy,

the Palatine issue in this parliament see S. Adams, 'Foreign Policy in the Parliaments of 1621 and 1624', in K. Sharpe, ed., *Faction and Parliament: Essays in Early Stuart History* (Oxford, 1978), pp. 139–71; T. Cogswell, 'Phaeton's Chariot: The Parliament-men and the Continental Crisis in 1621', in J. F. Merritt, ed., *The Political World of Thomas Wentworth, Earl of Strafford, 1621–1641* (Cambridge, 1996), pp. 24–46.

[13] W. B. Bidwell and M. Jansson, eds., *Proceedings in Parliament, 1626*, 4 vols. (New Haven, 1991–6), ii, pp. 114–15, 120–1 (24 February 1626). The 'protestation' referred to here was the declaration by the Commons on 4 [/14] June 1621 that if James I's diplomatic efforts failed, they would be 'readye to the uttermost of their powers, bothe with their lyves and fortunes, to assist him' in war (R. Zaller, *The Parliament of 1621: A Study in Constitutional Conflict* (Berkeley, 1971), p. 137).

[14] Chatsworth, Hobbes MS D 3, p. 21 ('Of Affectation'); printed in Wolf, *Die neue Wissenschaft*, p. 145. His promiscuity (before his marriage he was reported to have been sleeping with 'many' of his stepmother's gentlewomen) and his debts are discussed in the History of Parliament Trust's article (see above, Ch. 1 n. 12).

proudly assuring the House that no Catholic held any public office in Derbyshire.[15]

After Southampton's death in November 1624 Lord Cavendish seems to have moved (like several other members of Southampton's group) closer to Pembroke. Political alignments became more complicated in this period, after the humiliating failure of the Spanish Match had turned Buckingham into a bitter opponent of the Spanish Habsburgs; however, Buckingham's policies still seemed ineffectual where aid to the Elector Palatine was concerned, and this was one reason why Pembroke's underlying hostility to Buckingham continued. In February 1626 Cavendish was one of the initiators in the Commons of the attack on Buckingham; soon after Cavendish's translation to the Lords in the following month, one of Buckingham's agents wrote an analysis of Pembroke's caucus in the Commons in which he observed that 'the Lord Candishe whiles he was of that house, was the abettor of all that faction'.[16] There were of course non-ideological factors at work here, reasons of personal interest and personal connection: Cavendish was, for example, closely related to one of Pembroke's chief clients, Sir James Fullerton, and it must also be relevant that his two main rivals for local power in Derbyshire were both under Buckingham's patronage.[17] Nevertheless, the fact remains that Cavendish's political alliances would have brought him into contact with people, such as Pembroke, for whom the fate of the Elector Palatine was a matter of

---

[15] These details are also discussed in the History of Parliament Trust's article (above, Ch. 1 n. 12).

[16] C. Russell, *Parliaments and English Politics, 1621–1629* (Oxford, 1979), p. 280; PRO SP 16/523/77, Sir James Bagg to Buckingham, March 1626. 'Candish' was the seventeenth-century pronunciation of 'Cavendish'.

[17] On Fullerton (who was also mentioned in Bagg's letter (above, n. 16)) see Sir Robert Ayton, *The English and Latin Poems*, ed. C. B. Gullans (Edinburgh, 1963), p. 46 n. (where, however, the relationship is misdescribed: Fullerton was Cavendish's wife's stepfather), and the History of Parliament Trust's unpublished article on him for the 1602–29 section (by V. C. D. Moseley); I am very grateful to the History of Parliament Trust for allowing me to see this article in draft. In June 1628 Fullerton was one of several relatives and friends who agreed to pay off Devonshire's debts in return for land from his estates: the indenture for this agreement (Nottinghamshire Record Office, Nottingham, DD P 114/69) names Hobbes as a witness. Other Pembroke clients with personal links to Cavendish included the MPs Sir Francis Stewart, William Coryton, and Dr Samuel Turner: see V. A. Rowe, 'The Influence of the Earls of Pembroke on Parliamentary Elections, 1625–41', *English Historical Review*, 50 (1935), pp. 242–56; Russell, *Parliaments and English Politics*, p. 289 n. On the local rivalry with Buckingham clients (Sir Francis Leek and Sir John Coke) see Dias, 'Politics and Administration', pp. 303–8.

constant concern; and if being pro-Palatine made one more inclined to be anti-Buckingham, the converse may also have applied. Among the pro-Palatine lobby, certainly, Buckingham was always regarded as a hostile element: the Palatine Ambassador, Rusdorf, believed that Buckingham had engineered his removal in January 1627, and Ludwig Camerarius made comments so critical of Buckingham (in his intercepted letters, published by the Habsburgs later in 1627) that Charles instructed his own diplomats to strike Camerarius off their list of correspondents.[18] Whether Devonshire had personal contacts with Rusdorf (as he had had with his predecessor, Dohna) is not known; but we do know from Micanzio's letters that he became well acquainted with Giovanni Francesco Biondi, Rusdorf's fervently pro-Palatine friend.[19]

Devonshire's cousin, Viscount Mansfield, on the other hand, played an almost invisible role in the parliaments of the 1620s (from which he was sometimes excused attendance, because of his wife's medical problems). Nor is he known ever to have shown any active interest in the Palatine cause—unless one includes under that heading the trouble he took to act as host to the young Elector Palatine, Karl Ludwig, and his brother Rupert (and their uncle, King Charles) in 1636, something more easily explained in terms of his constant desire to secure the King's favour for himself. In stark contrast to his cousin, Mansfield was a protégé of Buckingham: twice, in 1621 and 1626, when he was allowed to absent himself from Parliament, he gave Buckingham his proxy vote.[20] While Devonshire's local rivals were Buckingham clients, Mansfield's local opposition came from opponents of Buckingham, and his local supporters included other beneficiaries of Buckingham's patronage such as the Chaworths and the Cecils of Newark.[21] He was a zealous supporter of the royal prerogative, and in late 1626, when some peers (including Devonshire) were resisting the Forced Loan, Mansfield

[18] See E. W. ['E. G.'] Cuhn, ed., *Mémoires et negociations secretes de Mr. de Rusdorf*, 2 vols. (Leipzig, 1789), i, pp. 804, 807–10 (Rusdorf to Frederick, 18/28 January 1627); [L. Camerarius,] *Ludovici Camerarii I.C. aliorumque epistolae nuper post pugnam maritimam in Suedica naui capta captae a victore polono* (n.p., 1627), p. 5 (where Camerarius commented that Buckingham could not do more for the Spanish cause if he were working for the King of Spain); Roe, *Negotiations*, p. 678 (Conway to Roe, 8 [/18] September 1627).

[19] Micanzio, *Lettere*, pp. 158, 176, 186, 214, 217, 239, 283.

[20] G. Trease, *Portrait of a Cavalier: William Cavendish, First Duke of Newcastle* (London, 1979), p. 49; Russell, *Parliaments and English Politics*, p. 286 n. On the latter occasion, when proxy votes became a contentious issue, Mansfield returned to exercise his vote in person.

[21] Dias, 'Politics and Administration', pp. 310–15.

was energetically collecting it. In one of his reports as Lord-Lieutenant he wrote that he had persuaded the people of Nottinghamshire that the Loan was justified by 'the pressing necessity at this instance for defence of God's true religion and the weale publique'.[22] While the 'defence of God's true religion' would have struck a chord with those who favoured a pro-Palatine foreign policy, there is little evidence that Mansfield felt any great enthusiasm for true religion, in comparison with his zeal for the 'weale publique'.[23] His strongest feeling where religion was concerned was his visceral dislike of Puritanism; he seems to have thought of religion mostly in terms of its value as a guarantor of social and political order, and felt much more comfortable with the Catholic gentry and nobility who supported that order than with the Puritans who threatened to subvert it—or who thought that foreign policy should be dictated from the pulpit. So although Devonshire and Mansfield remained personally on very good terms, it seems fair to say that they represented different political positions or attitudes. On the one side there was an exponent of active, oppositional politics, associated with the grand cause of international Protestantism and the more particular interests of trading and colonizing bodies; on the other side there was a supporter of royal power, a lover of tradition and order, someone unmoved by religious idealism and inclined to view religion in instrumental terms. Anachronistically, one might almost describe the former as proto-Whig and the latter as proto-Tory.

The point of this comparison is not to suggest that Mansfield may have taken an interest in the *Altera secretissima instructio* because he sympathized with the Habsburg side; there is no evidence of any such positive sympathies, and, besides, it was not necessary to approve of the text in order to find it interesting (as the case of Sir Simonds D'Ewes, a passionate pro-Palatine, clearly shows). Nor is it to imply that Mansfield could have taken no interest at all in this text, which must therefore have been translated at the request of his cousin; since Devonshire was a good linguist and was very familiar with Tacitean Latin, it seems unlikely that he would have gone to the trouble of commissioning a translation when he could read it well enough in the original. (A more plausible scenario might be that it was Devonshire who first acquired

---

[22] R. Cust, *The Forced Loan and English Politics, 1626–1628* (Oxford, 1987), p. 119 (and cf. p. 102 n. on Devonshire's resistance).

[23] Cf. the comment on his religious 'indifference' by the Queen's papal agent, cited in Trease, *Portrait of a Cavalier*, p. 65.

the Latin text, and then recommended it to his cousin, who required it
to be translated—but any such explanation is necessarily speculative.)
Rather, it is to suggest that, on the Palatine question and a range of
related issues, Thomas Hobbes must have been exposed to two very
different approaches to politics. Which of those approaches, at that
time, was closest to his own?

Unfortunately, the sort of evidence that would enable one to answer
that question with confidence is lacking. Indeed, up until the writing
of Hobbes's first full-length political treatise, *The Elements of Law*—a
work which strongly endorsed the attitudes of Mansfield (by then the
Earl of Newcastle), who commissioned it—there is very little direct
evidence of Hobbes's views, and the indirect evidence that survives
is in most cases either ambiguous or inconclusive. One intriguing
recent discovery is the fact that Hobbes was involved in the collection
of the Forced Loan in September 1627.[24] But this cannot really be
used as any sort of evidence, direct or indirect, of Hobbes's opinions;
he was merely doing his job as secretary to the Lord-Lieutenant of
Derbyshire—who had himself been, at first, a prominent resister of
the Loan.[25]

In the category of indirect evidence can be counted what little is
known about the political attitudes of the circles in which Hobbes
moved, and the friends he cultivated. Here pride of place must go to
Lord Cavendish and his own circle of actively pro-Palatine friends and
allies, many of whom Hobbes would have encountered, certainly at
the Virginia Company and probably when they met with Cavendish
to discuss their parliamentary business. Another figure who may have
exercised some influence on Hobbes was Francis Bacon—who, although
he was known to Lord Cavendish and admired by him, was far removed
from the sort of oppositional politics practised by Cavendish and
his friends. (Until his fall from power in 1621, Bacon had been
quite closely identified with royal policy; thereafter, in his desperate
attempts to regain favour and income, he attached himself all the
more assiduously to his patron Buckingham—though he did also make
an isolated and apparently unsuccessful approach to Southampton.)[26]

---

[24] J. P. Sommerville, *Thomas Hobbes: Political Ideas in Historical Context* (Basingstoke,
1992), p. 170 n. 15; Skinner, *Reason and Rhetoric*, p. 224.
[25] Devonshire was listed as a resister in November 1626, but gave way by the end of
the year; he had also refused to pay the Privy Seal loan (Cust, *The Forced Loan*, pp. 84–5,
102 n., 106).
[26] Bacon, *Works*, xiv, *passim* (Buckingham); p. 454 (Southampton).

After the failure of the Spanish Match, Bacon lobbied for a much more actively anti-Spanish policy, drafting notes and advice on the military weakness of Spain and the reasons for going to war.[27] In the short treatise which he wrote (and addressed to Prince Charles) in 1624, *Considerations touching a War with Spain*, he listed those reasons as follows: 'The recovery of the Palatinate. A just fear of the subversion of our civil estate. A just fear of the subversion of our Church and religion.'[28] His main emphasis was on the second reason: the Spanish desire for a universal *imperium* was an imminent threat to Britain that must be countered. The third reason was almost a sub-set of the second: Spain planned to subvert, and eventually to extirpate, Protestantism in Britain, so pre-emptive action against Spain was needed now. As for the first reason, Bacon still broadly followed the official line of James I's government, which was that Frederick's actions in Bohemia were unjustified, and that any intervention on his behalf should aim only at the restoration of the Palatinate itself.[29] Bacon was thus far from being a pro-Palatine *ultra*; his endorsement of the Elector's claims was only partial, he showed little interest in the advancement of Protestantism in Central Europe, and he placed his main emphasis on a calculation of Britain's national interest. Nevertheless, he was now on the same side as Lord Cavendish and his friends, arguing that a war against Spain would be both profitable and right.

Against these warmongering tendencies, Mansfield may have exerted some countervailing influence in the circles in which Hobbes moved; but, with one exception, those circles do not seem to have contained many people who shared Mansfield's views. The exception is the poet Ben Jonson, to whom Mansfield was a generous patron. Jonson's own writings from the 1620s show that, where the Palatine issue and the associated ferment of public opinion were concerned, he was firmly of Mansfield's opinion. In his *Masque of Augurs* (1622) he celebrated James I's policy of non-intervention; in *Time Vindicated to Himself and to his Honours* (1623) he suggested that those who felt an urge to fight in foreign wars would do better to go hunting; and in many of his works he satirized the news-mongers and their politically presumptuous customers—those who, as he put it in *Neptune's Triumph for the Return*

---

[27] Among these should surely be counted the text entitled 'A Short View to be taken of Britain and Spain' (ibid., xiv, pp. 22–8), which Spedding incorrectly dated to 1619, even though it clearly refers to the negotiations over the Spanish Match as a thing of the past (p. 27).

[28] Ibid., xiv, p. 470.   [29] Ibid., xiv, pp. 471–4.

of Albion (1624), 'relish nothing but *di stato*'.[30] His own disdain for foreign news was openly declared: 'What is't to me whether the French Designe | Be, or be not, to get the *Val-telline*?' This was an attitude far removed from that of Lord Cavendish, who circulated letters from Micanzio in which the likely fate of the Valtelline was a matter of constant concern (though, intriguingly, a fragment from one of those letters surfaces in Jonson's *Discoveries*, the compilation of prose observations and commonplace-book entries which was published after his death).[31] Alongside Jonson, however, we must also place the other person whom Hobbes asked to check the style of his Thucydides translation in 1628: Sir Robert Ayton. And if Jonson represented the Mansfield point of view, Ayton was definitely on the other side, both personally (he was a relative of Lord Cavendish's wife, and a friend of her stepfather, Sir James Fullerton) and politically. His Latin poem 'De rebus bohemicis', which circulated also in an English translation, was a bitter attack on James's non-interventionist policy, concluding that 'This way perhapps a iust Kinge thow mayest seeme, | But men a cruell ffath[r] will thee deeme'.[32]

Hobbes's milieu thus included people of both persuasions, but with a clear preponderance on one side of the argument. Milieux, however, do not necessarily determine how people think. There is another type of indirect evidence which may tell us a little more about Hobbes's attitude: letters to him, from the contents and tone of which it is possible to make some inferences about how the letter-writers thought he might be thinking. The most important piece of evidence in this category is the letter addressed to Hobbes by his friend Robert Mason in December 1622. Mason was a Fellow of St John's College, Cambridge, and seems to have had an appetite for news almost as avid as that of Joseph Mead at Christ's. He evidently regarded Hobbes as a particularly well-placed source of political information, and his comments on this suggest not

---

[30] Jonson, *Works*, vii, pp. 623–47, esp. pp. 643–7; pp. 649–73, esp. pp. 670–3; pp. 675–700, esp. p. 689; cf. S. Pearl, 'Sounding to Present Occasions: Jonson's Masques of 1620–5', in D. Lindley, ed., *The Court Masque* (Manchester, 1984), pp. 60–77; M. S. Muggli, 'Ben Jonson and the Business of News', *Studies in English Literature*, 32 (1992), pp. 323–40.

[31] Jonson, *Works*, viii, p. 219, 'An Epistle answering to one that asked to be Sealed of the Tribe of Ben', ll. 31–2; p. 592, ll. 938–47; Micanzio, *Lettere*, p. 135, ll. 13–21 (letter of 14 May 1621); cf. A. Shillinglaw, 'New Light on Ben Jonson's *Discoveries*', *Englische Studien*, 71 (1937), pp. 356–9. The passage consists not of foreign news, but of Micanzio's praise of Bacon. Jonson's wording differs from Hobbes's; so it would seem that he was shown the original Italian.

[32] Aubrey, '*Brief Lives*', i, p. 365; Ayton, *English and Latin Poems*, pp. 58, 241. (Ayton knew the Elector Palatine personally, having been on an official mission to him in 1609.)

only that the information might be sensitive, but also that it might be thought conducive to criticism of official policy: 'I pray hereafter be as free with me as you see I am wth you', he wrote, 'for you may with the same security impart your news to me, as, I hope, I haue now writt my mind to you'.[33] A clear sense of such criticism is given by Mason's own comments on the recent military débâcle in the Palatinate, where Sir Horace Vere had been forced to surrender the city of Mannheim and had then been permitted to march with his remaining troops to The Hague: responding to the news contained in Hobbes's last letter to him, Mason wrote that 'I am glad to heare Sr Horace Veere is past danger of intercepting, I hope he hath likewise past ye danger of his Majesties displeasure... It is a hard matter for a man to fight against an Enemy with one hand tied behind him.' The disapproval of James's policy was quite audible here; and Mason continued with some dismissive remarks about one of the primary assumptions of that policy—namely, that the Emperor could be persuaded by diplomacy to give back what he and his allies had taken by force. 'It were to be wisht those men had as much Providence [*sc.* foresight] as Charitie, who think if ye Emp^r were once possest of every part in the Palatinate, his Imperial Majesty would then render the whole... As for promises & oaths and such like engagements, they are now adajes accounted of but as weake obligations betwixt a Catholicke Prince & a Heretick, wch are commonly Spurned aside when they ly in their way either to greatnes or commodity.'[34]

Nowhere in this letter did Mason comment directly on any expression of opinion by Hobbes. He did write, however, that 'I trust we shall neither of us be thought immodestly to abuse the libertie of true & loyall subiects... there are many things, as your letter discreetly intimates, whereof it becomes us to be ignorant'.[35] Perhaps Hobbes had adopted the tactic (which he could have learned from Micanzio's letters) of saying that the King must have deep-laid plans so wise and far-sighted that the ordinary subject could not guess at them; by this means he could either have made a veiled criticism of royal policy, or have distanced himself prudently from Mason's own critical comments. Nevertheless, if we assume—as the tone of this letter encourages us to do—that Mason saw Hobbes as broadly sympathetic to his own views, then we may conclude that, in 1622, Hobbes was thought to belong to the pro-Palatine camp. But Mason was hardly a pro-Palatine extremist; his way of discussing these issues was quite untouched by any sort of religious

---

[33] Hobbes, *Correspondence*, i, p. 3.   [34] Ibid., i, p. 1.   [35] Ibid., i, p. 3.

fervour. Rather, he engaged in a cool and slightly cynical analysis of the political situation, praising the Spanish envoy Gondomar for his skill in manipulating English expectations, and remarking on the fact that 'many good Protestants' were now in favour of the Spanish Match because they supposed (though Mason seems to have reserved his own judgement on this point) that it would lead, through the good offices of the Spanish crown, to the restitution of the Palatinate. Religion thus took second place to power politics. It should not surprise us unduly to learn that, within two and a half years of writing this letter, Mason entered the service of the Duke of Buckingham.[36]

The next such piece of indirect evidence comes from November 1629, when Hobbes had left the service of the Devonshire family and was on the Continent with the young Gervase Clifton. It is a letter from a Mr Aglionby (probably George Aglionby), who was apparently acting—in Hobbes's place—as tutor to the Countess's young children. The letter makes no comment on international affairs; but its remarks about domestic politics, written in a light-hearted and knowing tone that clearly presumes the presence of shared assumptions in the mind of its intended reader, take a very definite stance on the political issues of the day. It is a stance that would have gratified Mansfield (whose patronage Aglionby seems also to have enjoyed) and infuriated the second Earl of Devonshire, had he still been living at this time. In this letter, Aglionby ridiculed those members of the House of Lords who had sided with the Commons—as Devonshire had done—over the Petition of Right in the previous year: 'my L^d of Somerset, as it seemes to me hath ingaged himself in a busines wch nothing concernes him, namely ye Liberty of ye Subject.' The Earl of Essex, a prominent opponent of the Forced Loan, who had long called for a war to restore the Elector Palatine, he described as 'a man of the sword, that is to say one of whom there is no use in peace, but he may like old armour be layd up safe'. And, most cuttingly, he dismissed the parliamentarian and physician Samuel Turner (another political ally, a protégé of the Earl of Pembroke, who appears to have attended Devonshire in his final illness, witnessing a codicil to his will) as 'a certain seditious Physician called Dr. Turner, one who disputes of all rule, but obeyes none; no not so much as the rule of civilitie for good manners'.[37] If Aglionby was right

[36] Hobbes, *Correspondence*, ii, p. 856.

[37] Ibid., i, pp. 7–8. Conrad Russell describes Devonshire as 'one of the strongest supporters' in the Lords of the Petition of Right: *Parliaments and English Politics*, p. 370.

to suppose (as he clearly did) that Hobbes would have found these views congenial, then we can conclude that, by 1629, Hobbes had thoroughly repudiated the position of his late master, and was now very much on Mansfield's side of the political divide.

Such a conclusion confirms the impression given by Hobbes's translation of Thucydides, which had been sent to the press in 1628. In his prefatory essay, 'Of the Life and History of Thucydides', he drew special attention to the ill-effects of demagogic politics in popular assemblies:

For his opinion touching the gouernment of the State, it is manifest that he least of all liked the *Democracy*. And vpon diuers occasions, hee noteth the emulation and contention of the Demagogues, for reputation, and glory of wit; with their crossing of each others counsels to the dammage of the Publique; the inconstancy of Resolutions, caused by the diuersity of ends, and power of Rhetorique in the Orators; and the desperate actions vndertaken vpon the flattering aduice of such as desired to attaine, or to hold what they had attained of authority and sway amongst the common people.[38]

Foremost among those 'desperate actions' in Thucydides's history was, of course, a disastrous military expedition. Any wise politician who had argued against it had, Hobbes noted, merely incurred the displeasure of the common people: 'For their opinion was such of their owne power, and of the facility of atchieuing whatsoeuer action they vndertooke, that such men onely swayed the Assemblies, and were esteemed wise and good Common-wealthsmen, as did put them vpon the most dangerous and desperate enterprizes.'[39] When Hobbes wrote those words, calls for a military expedition to reconquer the Palatinate (and/or destroy Spanish power elsewhere) had been a recurrent feature of English politics for most of the previous decade; it is hard to believe that he had only ancient history in mind. Elsewhere he signalled another point of agreement with Mansfield: in a marginal note to Pericles' Funeral Oration in book 2, he commented sardonically on the Athenian passion for news-mongering and political speculation. 'In Athens no man so poore but was a Statesman . . . All the Athenians spend their time in nothing but hearing and telling of newes. The true Character of politicians without employment.'[40] Disdain for parliamentary politics,

---

For an example of Turner and Lord Cavendish acting as parliamentary allies, see Bidwell and Jansson, *Proceedings in Parliament, 1626*, ii, pp. 129–30.

[38] Thucydides, *Eight Bookes*, sigs. a1v–a2r.   [39] Ibid., sig. a1v.
[40] Ibid., p. 103.

distrust of foreign 'enterprizes', and distaste for the culture of political news: on each of these points, Hobbes was distancing himself from the politics of the man who, until his death in June 1628, had been his employer and friend. The essay on Thucydides may have been written only after Devonshire's death; but the whole enterprise of translating the text must have taken up much of Hobbes's time and energy in the preceding years, and it is hard to believe that, during that period, the admiration Hobbes felt for Thucydides can have radically changed its grounds or its nature. Here is the closest thing we have to direct evidence of Hobbes's own political interests and sympathies during this period; and what it suggests is that, if he had shared his employer's views earlier in the decade, at some time in the mid- to late 1620s he had moved decisively in Mansfield's direction.[41]

The other scraps of evidence that have survived from the years preceding the writing of *The Elements of Law* all tend to confirm this alignment. In his letters from the Continent in the mid-1630s Hobbes displayed a perfunctory, almost contemptuous, attitude towards the most important commodity that such letters were meant to supply — political news. Before travelling, he told his former employer Sir Gervase Clifton that he would send him any news he obtained, but then added: 'not that you care [much *deleted*] for them' — a remark which, if correct, may itself reflect the similarity in views between Clifton and Mansfield.[42] Once in Paris, however, Hobbes apologized to Clifton for the fact that he did not send him many letters, commenting rather casually that

[41] One other piece of evidence can be added here which may possibly tell us something about Hobbes's thinking in 1628. Discussing Hobbes's flight from England in late 1640, Aubrey wrote that 'he told me that bp. Manwaring (of St. David's) preach'd *his doctrine*; for which, among others, he was sent prisoner to the Tower. Then thought Mr. Hobbes, 'tis time now for me to shift for my selfe, and so withdrew into France' (*'Brief Lives'*, i, p. 334). The chronology is badly confused here; it is not clear whether the confusion is Aubrey's or Hobbes's, but Aubrey seems the more likely culprit, as he was only 2 years old at the time of Maynwaring's first confinement. Roger Maynwaring caused a scandal in 1627, and was imprisoned by Parliament in 1628, for preaching sermons asserting the King's right to impose extra-parliamentary taxation (the Forced Loan); he was pardoned by the King, and later appointed Bishop of St David's. As a Laudian bishop he was also arrested in 1642 (hence, perhaps, Aubrey's confusion); but Hobbes's comment clearly refers to the 1628 episode. Of course it is possible that Hobbes formed his own political 'doctrine' long after that date, and merely identified retrospectively with Maynwaring; but it is psychologically more plausible to suppose that the reason why Maynwaring's imprisonment made such a strong impression on Hobbes was that, at that very time, he identified with Maynwaring's views.

[42] Hobbes, *Correspondence*, i, p. 21. On the closeness between Clifton and Mansfield see above, Ch. 1 n. 53.

'you should haue mine often, if I had any curiosity towards newes, or lucke in writing them.'[43] The evidence of his other letters suggests that the lack of curiosity was the main thing. Another clue as to Hobbes's political attitudes comes from a letter he sent from Paris in 1636, in which he expressed a desire to read a recent anti-sabbatarian treatise, but added that he feared 'they will put such Thoughts into the Heads of vulgar People, as will conferre little to their good Life. For, when they see one of the ten Commandments to be *Jus humanum* merely (as it must be, if the Church can alter it) they will hope also, that the other nine may be so too.'[44] Worry about the blindly self-interested nature of the 'vulgar People' is combined here with a feeling that certain truths about theological matters are best kept from them—or, to put it another way, that the theological principles which are taught to them might best be selected on the basis not of their truth, but of their conduciveness to peace and social stability. And this leads in turn to another intriguing piece of evidence about Hobbes from the period before the writing of *The Elements of Law*: the first mention of him in the diary-notebook of Samuel Hartlib. At some time shortly before 9 [/19] March 1639 Hartlib recorded what was evidently the first information he had received about Hobbes: 'A fine political brain. An excellent natural philosopher, who has discovered many things at the same time as Descartes. He cannot allow divine and human matters to be treated together. He requires stronger demonstrations in theological matters; otherwise he will believe nothing. He is very much like Mr St Amand where divinity is concerned.'[45] Of Mr St Amand's theological opinions, unfortunately, almost nothing is known.[46] As for the nature of Hobbes's

---

[43] Ibid., i, p. 26.   [44] Ibid., i, p. 30.

[45] Hartlib, 'Ephemerides', 1639: Sheffield University Library, Hartlib Papers (CD-Rom, 2nd edn.; Ann Arbor, 2002), 30/4/5B: 'Ist ein Wacker Politischer Kopf. Ein treflicher Naturalist welcher viel sachen zugleich mit de Cartes erfunden. Er kan nit leiden das man divina vnd Humana zusammen tractire. Will lauter demonstrationes in Theologicis haben. Sonst will er nichts glauben. Er ist mit dem St. Amand sehr modo divino . . . [*marginal reference:*] Hobs.'

[46] John St Amand (*c.*1593–1664) is mentioned several times in Hartlib's 'Ephemerides'. For what little is known of his life I am indebted to the History of Parliament Trust's unpublished article on him for the 1602–29 section (by P. Watson); I am very grateful to the History of Parliament Trust for allowing me to see this article in draft. (See also Ruigh, *Parliament of 1624*, pp. 144–5.) He was educated at Trinity College, Cambridge (1609–13), and later served as secretary to Lord Keeper Williams, Bishop of Lincoln, who helped to ensure his election to Parliament at a by-election in 1624; he was re-elected in 1625, during which year he was also admitted to Gray's Inn. He accompanied the young Duke of Lennox on his grand tour (of France and Spain)

refusal to 'allow divine and human matters to be treated together', that is best explicated by his later works. Some hints of such an attitude may possibly be found in his translation of Thucydides: for example, his marginal comment on the evasive ambiguity of the pagan oracles, 'whether they were the imposture of the Deuill, or of men, which is the more likely', shows a distinct preference for excluding theological assumptions from the study of ancient history.[47] But evidence of this kind is too slender a foundation on which to build any substantial conclusions. All that can be said is that while it is clear, from 1639 onwards, that Hobbes would not have founded politics on religion, and would certainly not have regarded religion, in itself, as a justification for going to war, there is no evidence to suggest that he would have thought any differently in the 1620s.

The contrast between Devonshire's pro-Palatine politics and the attitude of his cousin, Viscount Mansfield, should not be exaggerated, however. While Devonshire was politically more active than most, there is no reason to think that his views were on the extreme wing of the pro-Palatine movement: for all his hostility to Catholicism in England, it does not appear that he derived his foreign policy from any simplistic notion of a Protestant crusade. His correspondent Fulgenzio Micanzio—a Catholic priest—was probably more motivated by anti-Papal zeal than he was; but, more importantly, what dominated Micanzio's analysis was the assumption that any invocation of religious motives on the Catholic side was merely camouflage for the pursuit of temporal interests. Not religion, therefore, but 'reason of state', was the key to understanding. That Devonshire found this assumption congenial is suggested not only by the fact that he circulated Hobbes's translation of Micanzio's letters, but also by all the evidence—from his library catalogue, and his writings—that shows him to have been steeped in the political culture of early modern Tacitism. If we assume that, by the early 1620s, Hobbes

in 1629–32. Little is known of the rest of his life, save that he had a share in the customs on currant imports (1639–41), and was a Royalist in the Civil War. His will contained strong expressions of religious belief. In the period 1638–43 he corresponded with both Hartlib and the Protestant irenicist John Dury, requesting an account of the latter's 'analytical' method of interpreting Scripture, and sending an extract from Grosseteste on faith, the Incarnation, and biblical exegesis (Hartlib Papers, CD-Rom edition, 2/6/8B (Dury to Hartlib), 6/4/49A (Dury to St Amand), 9/1/83B (Dury to Hartlib), 45/6/14A–19B (St Amand to Dury, with Grosseteste extract), 45/6/1A–12A (St Amand to Hartlib); G. H. Turnbull, *Hartlib, Dury and Comenius: Gleanings from Hartlib's Papers* (London, 1947), pp. 20, 179, 186, 194–5, 202–3, 207, 212, 224, 305).

[47] Thucydides, *Eight Bookes*, p. 65.

too had been influenced by this sort of attitude to politics, it becomes a little easier to see how he might have moved, thereafter, towards the political position expressed in his later writings. But in order to explore this issue it is necessary to consider more generally the nature of 'reason of state' theory in this period—a theory of which the *Altera secretissima instructio* was an extreme, and in some ways parodic, expression.

6

'Reason of State' and Hobbes

THE first book to have 'ragion di stato' (reason of state) in its title, and the most influential of all books on this topic, was published by the ex-Jesuit Giovanni Botero in 1589. In his dedicatory epistle Botero explained that he had made many journeys in recent years, and had visited the courts of several kings and princes.

Among the things that I have observed, I have been greatly astonished to find Reason of State a constant subject of discussion and to hear the opinions of Niccolò Machiavelli and Cornelius Tacitus frequently quoted: the former for his precepts relating to the rule and government of peoples, the latter for his lively description of the arts employed by the Emperor Tiberius in acquiring and retaining the imperial title in Rome . . . I was moved to indignation rather than amazement to find that this barbarous mode of government had won such acceptance that it was brazenly opposed to Divine Law, so that men even spoke of some things being permissible by Reason of State and others by conscience.[1]

In the rest of his book, Botero went on to develop a more carefully modulated view of what reason of state could or should be. But those severe opening remarks testify to some simple and important facts: the term 'ragion di stato' already enjoyed wide currency; it was associated with Machiavellianism and Tacitism; and it was used to account for political actions that were, on the face of it, contrary to 'Divine Law' or morality. There is other evidence, from earlier in the sixteenth century, that the term was in common use; but the great popular vogue for 'ragion

---

[1] G. Botero, *The Reason of State*, tr. P. J. Waley and D. P. Waley (London, 1956), pp. xiii–xiv (G. Botero, *Della ragion di stato*, ed. C. Morandi (Bologna, 1930), pp. 3–4: 'tra l'altre cose da me osservate, mi ha recato somma meraviglia, il sentire tutto il dí mentovare Ragione di Stato, e in cotal materia citare ora Nicolò Machiavelli, ora Cornelio Tacito: quello, perchè dà precetti appartenenti al governo, e al reggimento de' popoli; questo, perchè esprime vivamente l'arti usate da Tiberio Cesare, e per conseguire, e per conservarsi nell'Imperio di Roma . . . Ma quel, che mi moveva non tanto a meraviglia, quanto a sdegno si era il vedere, che così barbara maniera di governo fosse accreditata in modo, che si contraponesse sfacciatamente alla legge di Dio; sino a dire, che alcune cose sono lecite per ragione di Stato, altre per conscienza').

di stato' got under way in the last decade of that century (stimulated, no doubt, by the work of Botero and other writers) and continued until the middle decades of the following one.[2] By 1621 the Venetian writer Lodovico Zuccolo could write that even 'barbers... and other artisans of the humblest sort, in their shops and meeting-places, make comments and queries on reason of state, and pretend that they know which things are done for reason of state and which are not'.[3] Indeed, the fact that the efflorescence of reason of state theory during this period went hand in hand with the growth in public interest in matters of state, especially foreign affairs, is surely not coincidental: here was a way of looking at political events that made them more open to discussion, since it both suggested that they needed to be deciphered and supplied some simple rules for their decipherment.[4]

Anyone who studies the theoretical literature developed by Botero and his successors may become absorbed in the subtleties of their various attempts to produce a more acceptable version of 'ragion di stato'. So it is worth bearing in mind at the outset that they operated against a background of ordinary public debate, in which the concept of reason of state was used in a quite simple way. It can be explained most easily using the distinction which was to be found in most elementary discussions of moral theory: between 'honestum' (that which is virtuous or right) and 'utile' (that which is useful or profitable).[5] When a ruler did something which was not virtuous or right (or not in accordance with his religious duties—for example, forming an alliance with heretics or infidels against his co-religionists), but which was useful or profitable for his state, this was ascribed to 'ragion di stato'. The term was thus

[2] On the earlier evidence see K. C. Schellhase, 'Botero, Reason of State, and Tacitus', in A. E. Baldini, ed., *Botero e la 'ragion di stato': atti del convegno in memoria di Luigi Firpo* (Florence, 1992), pp. 243–58, esp. pp. 246, 248–9.

[3] L. Zuccolo, 'Della ragione di stato', in B. Croce and S. Caramella, eds., *Politici e moralisti del Seicento* (Bari, 1930), pp. 23–41; p. 25: 'i barbieri... e gli altri più vili artifici nelle boteghe e nei ritrovi loro discorrono e questionano della ragione di stato e si dànno a credere di conoscere quali cose si facciano per ragione di stato e quali no'.

[4] See the valuable essay by Marcel Gauchet, 'L'État au miroir de la raison d'État: la France et la chrétienté', in Y. C. Zarka, ed., *Raison et déraison d'état: théoriciens et théories de la raison d'État aux XVIᵉ et XVIIᵉ siècles* (Paris, 1994), pp. 193–244.

[5] This distinction, found in Cicero and Seneca among others, was universally recognized in Renaissance Europe. Jean Bodin recommended that readers of history should, when taking notes, categorize every act or saying as 'honestum', 'turpe' (the opposite of honestum), 'utile', or 'inutile' (the opposite of utile), using formulae such as 'C.T.U.', which stood for 'consilium turpe sed utile' ('a wicked but useful plan'): *Method for the Easy Comprehension of History*, tr. B. Reynolds (New York, 1945), pp. 35–6.

partly a descriptive one (this is how rulers act, this is how politics works); but it also suggested something quasi-normative, a value, a ground for justification—not a moral value, however, but one which operated on a different basis (profit, utility) and became most noticeable precisely when it conflicted with morality.

From the late sixteenth century onwards, this notion of utility or profit was increasingly encapsulated in another term, which would itself long outlast the phrase 'reason of state', becoming an almost indispensable piece of political vocabulary: 'interest'. When the French political analyst René de Lucinge (a friend and admirer of Botero) used the term in his influential treatise of 1588, he had to explain what he meant by it. He noted that all actions of princes were motivated by honour or profit, and that the former was often subordinated to the latter: 'We shall therefore concern ourselves only with profit, which we may call "interest".'[6] Botero then popularized the use of 'interest' as a fundamental principle of political analysis: 'It should be taken for certain,' he wrote in *Della ragion di stato*, 'that in the decisions made by princes interest will always override every other argument; and therefore he who treats with princes should put no trust in friendship, kinship, treaty nor any other tie which has no basis in interest.'[7] Nine years later, Botero would sum up his view with the simple phrase, 'reason of state is little else than reason of interest'; the term was by now well established.[8] By the 1620s, when it was used intensively by Richelieu's publicists, and the 1630s, when the eminent Huguenot Henri, duc de Rohan, made it the basis of his influential treatise *L'Interest des princes* (with its memorable opening phrase, 'Princes rule the people, and interest rules princes'), the analysis of geopolitics was unthinkable without it.[9]

[6] R. de Lucinge, *De la Naissance, durée et chute des estats*, ed. M. J. Heath (Geneva, 1984), III.7, p. 222: 'Nous nous attacherons donc seulement au proffit, que nous pouvons nommer interest'. On de Lucinge's connections with Botero and their mutual influence see A. E. Baldini, 'Botero et Lucinge: les racines de la *Raison d'État*', in Y. C. Zarka, ed., *Raison et déraison d'état: théoriciens et théories de la raison d'État aux XVIᵉ et XVIIᵉ siècles* (Paris, 1994), pp. 67–99.

[7] Botero, *Reason of State*, p. 41 (Botero, *Della ragion di stato*, p. 62: 'Tenga per cosa risoluta che nelle deliberationi de' Prencipi l'interesse è quello che vince ogni partito. E per ciò non deve fidarsi d'amicizia, non di affinità, non di lega, non d'altro vincolo, nel quale, chi tratta con lui, non abbia fondamento d'interesse').

[8] G. Botero, *Aggiunte di Gio. Botero Benese alla sua ragion di stato* (Pavia, 1598), fo. 34v: 'ragion di Stato è poco altro, che ragion d'interesse'. The term 'interest' had also been used by Bodin; a full study of its early development has yet to be made.

[9] See R. von Albertini, *Das politische Denken in Frankreich zur Zeit Richelieus* (Marburg, 1951), esp. pp. 176–8; E. Thuau, *Raison d'État et pensée politique à l'époque de*

Once again, the attraction of this term lay partly in the ambiguous way in which it straddled the descriptive–normative divide: it was possible both to say (as Botero did) that rulers generally act out of interest, and to suggest that 'interest' constituted some kind of justification for acting. Interest—unlike sheer desire—might be studied in the light of objective criteria: a person could, after all, be criticized for an action that did not serve his real interests.[10] The nature of that justification, however, was not obviously (and in many cases obviously not) moral: while 'the common good' was a term that was always liable to serve as a hostage to traditional moral theorists and theologians ('bonum commune'), 'the public interest' or 'interest of state' suggested a different set of concerns and, therefore, a different kind of competence to judge them.

The idea that politics should be understood in terms of the pursuit of interest was supported by more general ideas about human nature and human action, derived from many sources, including the Augustinian theological tradition (with its emphasis on man's fallen nature) and the various currents of thought that can be described as Renaissance natural-ism. What they all had in common was an assumption that human beings would not naturally follow the dictates of conscience or 'right reason', and that they would seek a 'good' conceived more narrowly in terms of benefit or advantage; it followed that their interactions might often be conflictual, and that social or political coexistence must depend on artifice and discipline rather than natural harmony. In the modern polit-ical literature, these ideas were most forcefully expressed by Machiavelli and his followers (and by the historian Guicciardini); the Machiavellian influence on the 'ragion di stato' tradition was fundamental.[11] But late Renaissance humanists, searching for models and authorities in the ancient world, found a near-equivalent to Machiavelli's teachings in the writings of Tacitus; and, insofar as Tacitus' imperial Rome differed from the world of small principalities, independent republics, and politically

---

Richelieu (Paris, 1966), e.g. p. 180; Church, *Richelieu and Reason of State*, pp. 116–18; H. de Rohan, 'L'Interest des princes', in his *Le Parfait Capitaine* (n.p., 1639), pp. 261–364, here p. 269. On Rohan's influence, and on later developments in the use of the term, see J. A. W. Gunn, ' "Interest will not lie": A Seventeenth-Century Political Maxim', *Journal of the History of Ideas*, 29 (1968), pp. 551–64; J. A. W. Gunn, *Politics and the Public Interest in the Seventeenth Century* (London, 1969).

[10] For a classic study, arguing that 'interest' functioned as a half-way house between reason and desire, see A. O. Hirschman, *The Passions and the Interests: Political Arguments for Capitalism before its Triumph* (Princeton, 1977).

[11] See the still valuable work by Friedrich Meinecke, *Die Idee der Staatsräson* (Munich, 1924).

active citizenries described by Machiavelli, it seemed actually closer to the world of sprawling monarchies and febrile court-politics they now inhabited. Tacitus' writings offered a radical alternative both to the Aristotelian textbook tradition and to the pious moralism of Christian advice literature; they made politics seem, instead, like a complex and ruthless game in which all players are self-interested and power is the prize. On this view, the common people, though always eager to advance their own crude interests, are stupid and easily tricked; an ambitious demagogue can deceive them, making them think that they will advance their interests when they will in fact only promote his, and a wise ruler can, and in some ways should, deceive them, both by keeping them in awe of unknown powers, and by giving them those 'simulacra' of liberty which will make them content. Much of the art of ruling thus consists of making deceptions of various kinds: these, the 'arcana imperii', were easily identified with the stratagems of the Machiavellian prince.[12]

Part of the attraction of Tacitist political literature was that it offered the reader a key to unlocking all kinds of mysteries of state (the same attraction, indeed, that was exerted by analyses of 'ragion di stato'): politics thus became decipherable and legible. But opinions differed as to whether the discussion of these arcana was, on the one hand, a way of alerting the people to the tricks of their rulers, or, on the other, a way of teaching rulers how to trick the people more expertly (or at least, a way of explaining to some people that such stratagems were necessary and justified): one classic study has divided the Tacitan authors of this period into 'red' and 'black' Tacitists—that is, republican and monarchical—on those grounds.[13] Nevertheless, the

[12] On this identification see R. de Mattei, *Il problema della 'ragion di stato' nell'età della Controriforma* (Milan, 1979), pp. 46–7; M. Behnen, ' "Arcana—haec sunt ratio status." Ragion di stato und Staatsräson: Probleme und Perspektiven (1589–1651)', *Zeitschrift für historische Forschung*, 14 (1987), pp. 129–95; P. S. Donaldson, *Machiavelli and Mystery of State* (Cambridge, 1988), pp. 110–40. On Tacitism more generally see J. von Stackelberg, *Tacitus in der Romania: Studien zur literarischen Rezeption des Tacitus in Italien und Frankreich* (Tübingen, 1960); E.-L. Etter, *Tacitus in der Geistesgeschichte des 16. und 17. Jahrhunderts* (Basel, 1966); G. Spini, 'The Art of History in the Italian Counter Reformation', in E. Cochrane, ed., *The Late Italian Renaissance* (London, 1970), pp. 91–133 (esp. pp. 114–33); K. C. Schellhase, *Tacitus in Renaissance Political Thought* (Chicago, 1976); the essays by P. Burke, 'Tacitism', in T. A. Dorey, ed., *Tacitus* (London, 1969), pp. 149–71, and 'Tacitism, Scepticism, and Reason of State', in J. H. Burns and M. Goldie, eds., *The Cambridge History of Political Thought, 1450–1700* (Cambridge, 1991), pp. 479–98; and R. Tuck, *Philosophy and Government, 1572–1651* (Cambridge, 1993), pp. 31–136.
[13] G. Toffanin, *Machiavelli e il 'tacitismo'* (Padua, 1921).

basic assumptions of these various Tacitist writers about the nature of politics and government did not significantly diverge. Among the most controversial of those was the assumption that religion must be regarded as an instrument of rule. Fear of unknown powers was a very powerful factor in human psychology (here early modern Tacitism went hand in hand with the Epicurean psychology of religion found in Lucretius). It followed that religion should be carefully managed and controlled by the ruler, for more than one reason: because it could shore up his power; because if it lay outside his control, it could be used against him by demagogues and rivals; and because, as Machiavelli had argued, the power of religion over human behaviour was such that a religion of the wrong sort could have a harmful effect on the people, and thus on the strength of the state as a whole.

While the underlying assumptions of the Tacitists about human nature and politics were shared by most writers on 'ragion di stato', this Tacitist (and Machiavellian) instrumentalizing of religion offended many of them deeply. The genre of treatises on reason of state which Botero inaugurated was strongly motivated by a desire to oppose this line of argument; many of the authors of these treatises, indeed, were Jesuits, and if one followed only their self-understanding of what they were doing one would say that they were engaged in a re-Christianizing—or, to be precise, re-Catholicizing—of political theory, fully in the spirit of the Counter-Reformation. (One of their greatest bugbears was the 'politique' tradition of writers such as Bodin, whose experience of the French Wars of Religion had led them to recommend the toleration of religious minorities for the sake of peace; the Jesuit writers saw this as a Machiavellian subjection of religion to the state, and fiercely criticized it.)[14] However, while they thought that they were confronting the Machiavellian-Tacitist doctrine head-on, the fact that they shared so many of its underlying assumptions meant that their whole style of argument tended, in some ways, to run parallel to it, or even to reinforce it. Against the Machiavellian claim that Christianity was enfeebling, and in opposition to any idea that religion should be merely instrumentalized by the state, they wanted to show that Christianity should be the very basis of the state, and that a state so grounded in true religion would

[14] For a valuable study of some of these writers which, however, accepts them rather too easily on their own terms, see R. Bireley, *The Counter-Reformation Prince: Anti-Machiavellianism and Catholic Statecraft in Early Modern Europe* (Chapel Hill, NC, 1990); for a broader perspective, see H. Höpfl, *Jesuit Political Thought: The Society of Jesus and the State, c.1540–1630* (Cambridge, 2004), esp. pp. 84–139.

be more successful and more advantageous.[15] Thus the Spanish Jesuit Pedro de Ribadeneyra insisted that the most secure state was a state based on true religion, and penned an entire chapter demonstrating that Christianity produced successful military commanders.[16] And when Botero introduced the subject of religion into his political treatise, he began with a statement that was fully in line with the Machiavellian tradition,

So great is the power of religion in government that the state can have no secure foundation without it. Hence almost all those who have attempted to found new empires have introduced new faiths or changed the old ones . . .

and then added:

But of all religions none is more favourable to the ruler than the Christian law, according to which not merely the bodies and possessions but even the souls and consciences of his people are subject to him: their affections and thoughts are bound, as well as their hands.[17]

Here, from someone deeply opposed to the instrumentalizing of religion, was a recommendation of Christianity precisely on the grounds that it instrumentally benefited the ruler.

In order to emphasize the difference (as they saw it) between them and their opponents, some of these Counter-Reformation theorists argued that there were two types of reason of state: the acceptable, Christian kind and the unacceptable, Machiavellian variety. As Pedro de Ribadeneyra put it, 'this reason of state is not a single thing, but two: one false and apparent, the other solid and genuine; one deceptive and diabolical, the other certain and divine.'[18] The Sienese theologian and pro-Papal

---

[15] See H. Lutz, *Ragione di stato und christliche Staatsethik im 16. Jahrhundert* (Münster, 1961), pp. 41–2.

[16] P. de Ribadeneyra, *Tratado de la religion y virtudes que deve tener el Principe Christiano, para governar y conservar sus estados* (Madrid, 1595), pp. 1–258, 494–504.

[17] Botero, *Reason of State*, p. 66, adapted (Botero, *Della ragion di stato*, p. 94: 'È di tanta forza la Religione ne' governi, che senza essa, ogni altro fondamento di Stato vacilla: cosí tutti quelli quasi, che hanno voluto fondare nuovi Imperi, hanno anco introdotto nuove sette, o innovato le vecchie . . . Ma tra tutte le leggi non ve n'è più favorevole a Prencipi, che la Cristiana; perchè questa sottomette loro, non solamente i corpi, e le facoltà de' sudditi, dove conviene, ma gli animi ancora, e le conscienze; e lega non solamente le mani, ma gli affetti ancora'). The use of the term 'legge' here ('law') situates the argument in a Machiavellian (and, ultimately, Averroist or Paduan Aristotelian) tradition.

[18] De Ribadeneyra, *Tratado*, sig. ††7r: 'esta razon de Estado no es vna sola, sino dos: vna falsa y aparente, otra solida y verdadera; vna engañosa y diabolica, otra cierta y diuina'.

(anti-Venetian) writer Ventura Venturi similarly distinguished 'blessed' reason of state from 'accursed' reason of state: the former conformed always to true religion, while the latter contravened divine and natural law.[19] In the abstract, of course, this distinction was easily made; indeed, it could be expressed in the simplest possible terms as a matter of 'utile' (profitable) versus 'honestum' (virtuous). As Botero's friend Frachetta put it:

In governing states, the prince considers either the profitable on its own, or the profitable conjoined to the virtuous. If he considers the profitable alone, and proceeds rationally and wisely, choosing the suitable means with which to bring about that profitable result, he will be called cautious and wise; and the art he uses will be called reason of state, and it could be called false prudence, or the shadow or reflection of prudence. But if the prince considers the profitable conjoined to the virtuous, and proceeds rationally and with good counsel, he will be called truly prudent, and his manner of acting will be called true civil prudence. The former is not united with the moral virtues; the latter is.[20]

But the problem, of course, was that in many cases reality did not conform to this simple scheme: following the path of virtue might be profitable in a general, long-term way, but it was often the case that strict adherence to the moral law was seriously disadvantageous, and it was also frequently found that a long-term strategy of virtue could be enhanced by tactical measures which, in themselves, were not virtuous at all. One of the aims of these Counter-Reformation 'reason of state' theorists was, in fact, to show that various forms of apparent immorality and deception were compatible with their overall moral programme: thus Botero, for example, recommended the use of agents and spies to foment mutual distrust among heretical subjects, and de Ribadeneyra allowed his prince not only to equivocate (as was permitted by some

[19] W. J. Bouwsma, *Venice and the Defense of Republican Liberty: Renaissance Values in the Age of the Counter Reformation* (Berkeley, 1968), pp. 381, 447.

[20] G. Frachetta, *Seminario de' governi di stato et di guerra* (Venice, 1613), discorso 12, p. 79: 'nel gouerno de' Stati, ò il Prencipe riguarda l'vtile solo, ò l'vtile congiunto con l'honesto. se l'vtile solo, procedendo con ragione, & sauiezza, & eleggendo i debiti mezzi per conseguir questo vtile, si dirà accorto, & sauio; & l'Arte si chiamerà Ragione di Stato, & si potrà dir falsa prudenza, ò ombra, ò imagine di prudenza. ma se il Prencipe riguarda l'vtile congiunto con l'honesto, procedendo con ragione, & con buon consiglio, si dirà veramente prudente: & l'habito si appellerà vera prudenza ciuile. l'vna non è vnita con le virtù morali, l'altra sí'. Elsewhere in his writings Frachetta referred to these as false and true reason of state. Frachetta, who took minor orders, served as a secretary or adviser to several cardinals.

Catholic casuists) but also, in small measure, to simulate or lie.[21] But their simple dichotomy between good and bad reason of state, with the former presupposing that advantage would always follow naturally in virtue's train, failed to account for much of the actual working-out of their theories—the attraction of which, to contemporary readers, came largely from the ways in which they incorporated much hard-headed advice about the exercise of political power. Nor were the theoretical difficulties much alleviated by the tendency of many of them (including Botero, Frachetta, and de Ribadeneyra) to portray 'good' reason of state as a general form of civil prudence—a kind of practical judgement which applied, in principle, to all activities of government.[22] That a good ruler needed discretion, judgement, and the sort of skill that came from experience was not in doubt. But in assimilating 'ragion di stato' to some all-encompassing kind of practical knowledge, the theorists merely moved further away from those special and awkward cases for which the term had been invented. The danger—as writers such as the 'red' Tacitist Traiano Boccalini and the distinctly 'black' theorist of the 'coup d'état' Gabriel Naudé complained—was that this tendency led to a version of reason of state so sanitized that it could no longer perform any useful function.[23]

A different approach was taken by a number of writers whose attitude was less exaltedly theological than that of the Counter-Reformation theorists. The key exponent of the alternative approach was the Flemish

[21] Botero, *Della ragion di stato*, V.7, p. 154 (*Reason of State*, p. 108); de Ribadeneyra, *Tratado*, pp. 291–2.

[22] Botero defined reason of state as a general art of rule, and presented 'prudence' as the central component of that art: *Della ragion di stato*, I.1, II.1–10, pp. 9, 53–77 (*Reason of State*, pp. 3, 34–53); Frachetta identified civil prudence with true reason of state (see his *Il prencipe* (Venice, 1599), pp. 13–14); de Ribadeneyra identified prudence as the guide to all virtues, and equated it with 'good' reason of state (see his *Tratado*, pp. 405–6, and Höpfl, *Jesuit Political Thought*, pp. 165–7). Maurizio Viroli misrepresents this line of argument, I believe, when he identifies this 'prudence' with the new, immoralist, reason of state, and contrasts it with the traditional (Aristotelian) idea of politics: *From Politics to Reason of State: The Acquisition and Transformation of the Language of Politics, 1250–1600* (Cambridge, 1992), p. 278.

[23] See de Mattei, *Il problema della 'ragion di stato'*, pp. 67–87; J. Freund, 'La Situation exceptionelle comme justification de la raison d'État chez Gabriel Naudé', in R. Schnur, ed., *Staatsräson: Studien zur Geschichte eines politischen Begriffs* (Berlin, 1975), pp. 141–64. An interesting exception to this tendency was Scipione Ammirato, who, although he broadly shared the Counter-Reformation mentality of the Jesuit theorists, was much more steeped in Tacitism than they; on his theory of reason of state as a higher-order principle that overrules ordinary law, see R. de Mattei, *Il pensiero politico di Scipione Ammirato, con discorsi inediti* (Milan, 1963), esp. pp. 124–9.

humanist (and editor of Tacitus) Justus Lipsius, whose treatise on politics, *Politicorum sive civilis doctrinae libri sex*—a work much admired for the elegant way in which it wove together a tissue of quotations from classical sources—exerted a huge influence.[24] Like the Jesuit writers, Lipsius subscribed to some fundamentally Machiavellian and Tacitist assumptions about the nature of politics; unlike them, he did not believe that it was possible to construct, even in theory, a perfectly virtuous 'reason of state', accepting instead that the art of ruling must make some compromises with vice. In his scheme of politics and government, there were three levels of fraudulent behaviour: 'light' (involving dissimulation, the concealment of intentions), 'medium' (involving the active deception, or corruption by bribery, of enemies), and 'great' (involving such actions as breach of treaty). The first, he wrote, was advisable, the second tolerable, and the third unacceptable. His justification for this position was framed, at first sight, in merely quantitative terms: 'Wine does not cease to be wine if it is lightly diluted with water; nor does prudence cease to be prudence, if you add some little drops of fraud.' But he went on to add, importantly, that the permitted frauds were tolerable only when done for the common good; any deception not aimed at that end was a great sin.[25]

The emphasis on the common good here opened up the possibility that this version of reason of state might even be framed as a more convincingly unified theory than that of the Jesuits—something closer to a traditional scheme of natural law, a hierarchical system in which the application of lower-order values could be altered or superseded by the requirements of higher-order ones. But in practice that path was not taken. The Lipsian version of reason of state theory functioned, rather, as something more modest and more realistic than the high-flown, Counter-Reformation variety. Lipsius's term for reason of state was 'mixed prudence', which he described as a mixture of 'honesta' and 'utilia'.[26] As his English disciple Robert Dallington put it:

All Moralists hold nothing profitable that is not honest. Some Politicks haue inuerted this order, and peruerted the sense, by transposing the tearmes in the

---

[24] On Lipsius and his influence see G. Oestreich, *Neostoicism and the Early Modern State* (Cambridge, 1982), pp. 13–117; A. McCrea, *Constant Minds: Political Virtue and the Lipsian Paradigm in England, 1584–1650* (Toronto, 1997), *passim*.

[25] J. Lipsius, *Politicorum sive civilis doctrinae libri sex* (Leiden, 1589), pp. 204–16 (p. 204: 'Vinum, vinum esse non desinit si aquâ leuiter temperatum: nec Prudentia, Prudentia, si guttulae in eâ fraudis').

[26] Ibid., p. 203: 'vtilia honestis miscere'.

proposition: holding nothing honest that is not profitable. Howsoeuer those former may seeme too streight laced, these surely are too loose. For there is a middle way betweene both which a right Statesman must take.[27]

The 'Moralists' here might have included the Jesuit writers (at least, in some of the summaries of their theories, if not in the practical details), while the 'Politicks' (i.e. politiques) represented a caricature version of the Machiavellian tradition. But in reality Lipsius's approach remained loyal to Machiavelli's own belief that a ruler may be obliged to do bad things for the good of the state.

More broadly, Lipsius represented a tradition of argument, partly stemming from Machiavelli and transmitted through widely read authors such as Girolamo Cardano, which insisted that the wise and virtuous man must learn to adapt his external behaviour to the conditions of stupidity and vice that prevailed in the general population; different levels of wisdom would thus be needed, with the highest human level operating, for the most part, only internally.[28] This attitude was very much in tune with Renaissance neo-Stoicism, of which Lipsius was a leading exponent; it was developed further by another influential writer, Pierre Charron, who combined elements of neo-Stoicism, a Montaignian sense of the disjunction between the private and public realms, and a deep admiration for Lipsius.[29] And another widely read author who displayed a similar pattern of thought (though with a more ambivalent attitude to Stoicism) and an evident debt to Lipsius was Francis Bacon, whose essay 'Of Simulation and Dissimulation' put forward what was very evidently an adaptation of Lipsian 'mixed prudence'.[30]

In theory, there were some large differences between the Counter-Reformation reason of state theorists and the Lipsians. The latter were closer to the outlook of the original 'politiques' in the French Wars of Religion: the tranquillity of a well-governed state was to be judged on public criteria, which mere external conformity might satisfy. The former insisted that externalities would not suffice, and that the people must support the state privately, with their souls (as properly directed by the Church) as well as publicly, with their bodies. (Lipsius

[27] R. Dallington, *Aphorismes Civill and Militarie* (London, 1613), book V, aphorism 19, p. 314.
[28] See G. Procacci, *Studi sulla fortuna del Machiavelli* (Rome, 1965), pp. 77–106.
[29] See ibid., p. 100, and R. Kogel, *Pierre Charron* (Geneva, 1972), pp. 50–77, 127–33.
[30] Bacon, *Essayes*, pp. 20–3; McCrea, *Constant Minds*, pp. 87–96.

did recognize—like Bodin—that religious uniformity strengthened a state, and recommended the extirpation of religious dissenters who challenged the secular power; otherwise his argument defended some form of toleration for the sake of civil peace.)[31]

But once the discussion moved away from matters of church and state, and turned instead to the regular business of secular rule, there was in fact much common ground between these two types of reason of state theory. Both took it for granted that the common people were turbulent, fickle, and short-sighted, and that government must involve the management of them in accordance with a superior wisdom which they themselves could not be expected fully to understand. Both accepted that the ruler could properly engage in dissimulation (the concealment of his real thoughts, feelings, or intentions) towards his own subjects and towards foreign powers; the Counter-Reformation writers were more reluctant in theory to allow simulation (that is, positively pretending to have thoughts, feelings, or intentions that one does not have), though they usually found some room for it in practice.[32]

Hovering at the back of all discussions of these topics, of course, was the notorious eighteenth chapter of *The Prince*, in which Machiavelli discussed the relative worth of being thought to possess certain qualities and actually possessing them—the difference between seeming and being. And although most reason of state theorists insisted, understandably enough, that being (virtuous, pious, brave, etc.) was better in the long run, one of the most striking features of their writings is the huge amount of attention they gave to the theme of seeming. The key term here was 'reputation'. In his treatise on reason of state, Botero declared that 'love and reputation' were 'the two foundations of all rule and government'.[33] His later 'additions' to this work included a lengthy discourse on reputation, in which he developed that argument in a more recognizably Machiavellian way. The ruler's authority depends, he explained, on either love, or fear, or reputation; and reputation itself is a combination of love and fear. Love is best *per se*, but least reliable

---

[31] See Bireley, *Counter-Reformation Prince*, pp. 89–90.

[32] For the theological constraints on the notion of simulation, and the various ways of evading them, see J. P. Sommerville, 'The "New Art of Lying": Equivocation, Mental Reservation, and Casuistry', in E. Leites, ed., *Conscience and Casuistry in Early Modern Europe* (Cambridge, 1988), pp. 159–84; P. Zagorin, *Ways of Lying: Dissimulation, Persecution, and Conformity in Early Modern Europe* (Cambridge, MA, 1990).

[33] Botero, *Reason of State*, V.9, pp. 113–14, adapted (*Della ragion di stato*, p. 162: 'essendo due fondamenti dell'Imperio, e del governo, l'amore, e la riputazione').

in practice, because of man's fickle nature; reputation is better than either love or fear taken separately, since 'what it gains from love is the union of the subjects with their ruler, and what it gains from fear is their subjection'; but, in the composition of reputation, fear has the larger part. In any case, however it is analysed, reputation rests 'in the opinion and belief which the people has about him [*sc.* the ruler]'.[34] Frachetta agreed, devoting a whole chapter of his treatise to 'How important reputation is to a ruler in the government of his state'; the English Jesuit writer Thomas Fitzherbert also stressed the importance of reputation, declaring that 'of al external goods it is the principal, & most pretious'.[35] Lipsius also warmed to this theme: all rule depended, he observed, on the 'consensus' (agreement, consent) of the ruled, and that agreement derived from their 'aestimatio' (high opinion) of the ruler: 'take away this, and you take away the kingdom'.[36] (These comments came in a chapter on 'Contemptus'—which is the attitude subjects will adopt towards their ruler if he has lost his reputation with them.) Many later writers on reason of state also attributed special importance to reputation. The duc de Rohan, for example, emphasized its value in both external and internal affairs (commenting that if a ruler is reputed to have an extensive intelligence network, other rulers will be more wary of entering into conspiracies against him), and concluded that 'It is a thing that seems empty, but produces solid effects'.[37] And Richelieu, in his *Testament politique*, gave as the prime reason for not breaking treaties the fact that such breaches would harm the ruler's reputation: 'he cannot break his word without losing his reputation and thereby losing the greatest strength that sovereigns possess.'[38]

As this example shows, the requirements of 'seeming' could have direct consequences for 'being'. There were other ways, too, in which the cultivation of reputation (and 'love') might have real and practical effects. Several of these writers paid special attention to the ways in

[34] Botero, *Aggiunte*, fos. 42–4 (fo. 42r: 'nell'opinione, e nel concetto, che il popolo ha di lui'; fo. 44r: 'ella prende dell'amore l'vnione de' sudditi col Prencipe, e dal timore la soggettione').

[35] Frachetta, *Il prencipe*, pp. 21–6 (p. 21: 'Quanto importi al Prencipe la Riputatione per il gouerno dello Stato'); T. Fitzherbert, *The First Part of a Treatise concerning Policy, and Religion* (n.p. [Douai], 1615), p. 271.

[36] Lipsius, *Politicorum libri sex*, p. 194.

[37] De Rohan, 'De l'Interest des princes', p. 277 ('C'est vne chose vaine en apparence, mais qui produit de solides effets').

[38] Quoted in von Albertini, *Das politische Denken*, p. 185: 'qu'il ne peut violer [*sc.* sa parole] sans perdre sa réputation et par conséquent la plus grande force des souverains'.

which the ruler could increase not only the strength of his state but also the contentment of his subjects by promoting commerce and industry.[39] Botero wrote, more generally, that 'he who wishes to keep his subjects contented and quiet should procure for them plenty, justice, peace, and a certain virtuous liberty'; as Rodolfo de Mattei has pointed out, it is hard to tell whether Botero viewed such things primarily as instrumental means towards successful rule, or as things to be valued in themselves by a virtuous ruler.[40] A similar ambiguity hovers over the notion of 'consent', which was not only implicit in the general argument about reputation, but was also made explicit by writers such as Lipsius (quoted above), Frachetta (who wrote that 'all rulers need the consent of the people, whether immediate or mediate, express or tacit'), and the Spanish Jesuit Juan de Mariana (whose carefully phrased argument was that 'the Prince should never attempt in the commonwealth what it would not be possible to get the citizens to approve').[41] Was this merely a means towards effective rule, or was the obtaining of such consent in some sense a moral duty? The argument was never pursued by the reason of state authors in ways that might have yielded a definite answer to that question. For, in the end, reason of state theory was not a complete body of political philosophy; it put forward a set of techniques and embodied a set of assumptions, but it did not deal in any direct way with the most basic justificatory principles of government and law. That, perhaps, is one reason why the vogue for it came to an end. Once the techniques had been assimilated, it could have little new to offer; and interest shifted towards those styles of political theorizing which could anchor some of the assumptions in philosophical principles of a more abstract and fundamental kind.

In the light of this brief and necessarily schematic sketch of the 'ragion di stato' tradition, some comments may be added both about the nature of the *Altera secretissima instructio*, and about the possible relation to that tradition of Cavendish and Hobbes. That the *Altera secretissima instructio* stands in a close connection to 'ragion di stato' will

[39] See Bireley, *The Counter-Reformation Prince*, p. 129.

[40] G. Botero, *Relatione della repubblica venetiana* (Venice, 1605), fo. 74r ('chi gli vuole tener contenti, e quieti, deue procurare loro l'abbondanza, la giustizia, la pace, & vna certa honesta libertà'); de Mattei, *Il problema della 'ragion di stato'*, p. 56.

[41] Frachetta, *Seminario*, discorso 6, p. 30: 'hanno bisogno del consentimento del popolo, ò immediato, ò mediato, ò espresso, ò tacito'; J. de Mariana, *The King and the Education of the King*, tr. G. A. Moore (Chevy Chase, MD, 1948) [tr. of *De rege et regis institutione* (Toledo, 1599)], p. 345, cited in J. A. Fernández-Santamaría, *Reason of State and Statecraft in Spanish Political Thought, 1595–1640* (Lanham, MD, 1983), p. 99.

be self-evident even to the most casual reader: the text itself refers to 'the great cause, cause of causes, *Reason of State*'.[42] But, once again, the way in which this work makes use of reason of state theory seems, on closer inspection, rather ambiguous. This is a satirical or parodic work which is in some ways meant to be taken seriously; it is also a 'most secret' instruction which is meant to be read as widely as possible. In its most extreme statement, it offers what sounds like a purely parodic version of reason of state, a worst-case example of the sort of 'bad' or 'false' reason of state denounced by the Counter-Reformation theorists: 'you need to use not only forces and stratagems, but also nothing less than criminal acts and things contrary to divine law. To this advice I give first place—and second, and third, and thousandth.'[43] Yet although the phrasing here is clearly designed to shock and repel, many of the details of the argument would not seem so shocking to anyone familiar with the reason of state tradition. The two sentences just quoted form part of a recommendation that the Elector Palatine should try to stir up distrust and disagreement among his enemies—something not very different from Botero's advice on stirring up dissensions among heretical subjects. Elsewhere the author advises Frederick to suborn the counsellors of his enemies; this was specifically allowed by Lipsius, who placed it in his category of 'medium' fraud.[44] The advice that he change religion might also have been thought to belong in the same Lipsian category, since it was well known that Lipsius himself had changed religion more than once.[45] That such actions were described by the author as 'fraud' was not necessarily damning; the same term had been used by Lipsius both for the one category he disapproved of and for the two he permitted. And, as if to emphasize the point, the author accompanied his recommendation of fraud with a comment which many readers would have recognized as an adaptation of one of the most Machiavellian phrases in Lipsius's *Politicorum libri sex*: 'When ye Lions skin is worne out, put on the Foxes case [*sc.* skin]'.[46]

Was the author engaged in a surreptitious satirizing or discrediting of Lipsian reason of state theory? If so, he was being quite unfair, since he omitted Lipsius's key condition (that any frauds be committed for the public good), treating the matter merely as an issue of Frederick's personal survival and advantage. But there is hardly enough evidence to

---

[42] Section 9.   [43] Section 31.   [44] Section 19.   [45] Section 21.

[46] Section 19 (at n. 224). For the use of another phrase which may have had Lipsian associations, see section 25 (at n. 261).

show that the author had any such clear moral purpose. At one point he did comment disapprovingly on the idea of an alliance with infidels, and warned, in true Counter-Reformation style, that the dictates of religion must ultimately prevail: 'And yet I feare that such vngodly aydes, will proue the ruine of them that seeke them. For though in Politique strategems, Religion be last looked at, yet it seemes there is some kingly power aboue that ratifyes the priuiledges of Magistrates, and is iudge of right and wronge.'[47] Yet that warning is noteworthy precisely because it stands out in the text, being quite untypical of it. The only other reference to God comes in the remark that 'To be obstinate against experience is an iniury to God', which seems to be just a rhetorical way of emphasizing the importance of secular experience.[48] Some religious motivation is, at first, attributed to Louis XIII ('Religion drawes him backe. he holds it a great sinne to warre against his bloud'); but Louis's fear of excommunication is explained purely in terms of its secular effects ('He sayes he will not offend the Pope or Popes frends; he feares excommunication. The effectes of it, ye Rebellion of his Princes he abhorres'). Throughout the text, all human action is judged in terms of self-interest; to the rhetorical question, 'does euery man loue himselfe best?', the answer is never in doubt.[49] In the series of case-studies that makes up the first part of the work, the author shows that each of the Elector's allies, no matter how closely connected by blood or friendship, or how strongly bound by solemn promises, will abandon him as soon as that ruler's own interest diverges from his. One could scarcely ask for a more specific substantiation of Botero's comment that 'in the decisions made by princes interest will always override every other argument; and therefore he who treats with princes should put no trust in friendship, kinship, treaty nor any other tie which has no basis in interest'.[50] Not only does the author show that they will follow their own interest; he also notes that, in doing so, they commit frauds of various kinds. (Louis XIII defrauded his own allies; Christian IV seized Bremen by fraud.)[51] Once again, if the analysis in the first part of the text is seen as compelling (as it is surely intended to be), it becomes difficult to dismiss the kind of advice given in the second part as self-evidently satirical. The author seems to be playing a game with reason of state theory: insofar as it is both credible and potentially disreputable, he simultaneously seeks to build on its credibility and

[47] Section 14.   [48] Section 2.   [49] Section 21.   [50] See above, n. 7.
[51] Sections 8, 11.

exploit its disreputability. Reason of state is stretched here, but not to breaking-point.

One other issue deserves consideration: the extent to which the writing and publication of this text could itself be seen as an application of reason of state. Here too things are not as straightforward as they may at first appear. Secrecy was certainly the basic form of dissimulation recommended and required by writers on 'ragion di stato'; the wise and experienced counsellor was also a stock figure in their treatises, and such a counsellor was expected to keep secret not only the sensitive information he received, but also his own advice to the ruler. So to publish a 'most secret instruction' might seem, at first blush, like a subversion of reason of state—were it not for the obvious fact that in this instance the counsel was itself subversive and quasi-satirical, designed not to fortify but to cow and weaken the counselled. It is nevertheless true that this text did include much genuine political information, of the sort that ordinary readers were eager to obtain. And it is also true that many writers on 'ragion di stato' advised rulers that it was not in their interests to let the common people inspect the 'arcana' of politics (a piece of advice that was to be found, paradoxically, in books about those 'arcana' which were sold to the common people in large quantities). One modern historian has concluded that, in the 'ragion di stato' literature, 'the underlying principle was secrecy, not propaganda', and has singled out Paolo Sarpi—who both engaged in pamphlet warfare, and set out the principles of it in his advice to the Venetian Senate—as a startling exception to the rule.[52]

But this is to take too narrow a view of the requirements of reason of state theory; it is to ignore the wider implications of the doctrine of 'reputation', which positively favoured the practice of political propaganda. As these writers emphasized, reputation was not only important for the internal stability of a state under normal conditions; in Frachetta's words, 'reputation matters to the ruler no less in war than in peace'.[53] In any situation of international conflict, a rise in a ruler's reputation would count as an increase of his strength (as it would help to deter enemies and attract allies); equally, therefore, one

---

[52] De Vivo, 'Paolo Sarpi and the Uses of Information', p. 45. (De Vivo notes, however, that Sarpi's advice to the Senate concluded that it would in principle be better to keep the people ignorant of affairs of state, but that if something damaging had been published, it was necessary to counteract it.)

[53] Frachetta, *Il prencipe*, p. 150: 'Non importa meno la riputatione al Prencipe nella guerra che nella pace.' Cf. the statement in section 17: 'Warre depends on fame'.

effective way of reducing the strength of one's opponents would be to undermine their reputations. Such offensive propaganda actions would not necessarily involve fiction and lies; an unmasking of the other side's dissimulations and simulations might be all the more effective because it told the truth. (The duc de Rohan would recommend, as a basic maxim for the French king, a policy of exposing the misuses of Catholicism by Spain and the Papacy, in order to 'make Catholics understand the poison that is hidden underneath'.)[54] The author of the *Altera secretissima instructio* understood that truth, as well as lies, could have a propaganda effect. And in order to achieve his purpose, he was quite happy to exploit both the popular hunger for 'secret' information, and the pleasure which a public brought up on 'reason of state' discourse naturally derived from seeing the workings of such reason of state laid bare.

Among those readers was Thomas Hobbes, whose familiarity with quite a range of literature on 'ragion di stato' can be assumed. By the time he drew up the catalogue of the library at Hardwick in 1627 or 1628, it contained de Lucinge's *De incrementis* (the Latin translation of his *De la Naissance . . . des estats*); a whole collection of works by Botero, including his *Della ragion di stato, Treatise concerning the . . . Greatnes of Cities, Relationi universali, Principi cristiani,* and *Detti memorabili*; Frachetta's *Il Prencipe*; Lipsius's *Politicorum libri sex*; Mariana's *De rege et regis institutione*; Charron's *De la Sagesse*; Dallington's *Aphorismes*; and both parts of Fitzherbert's *Treatise concerning Policy and Religion.*[55] It also contained Machiavelli's *Discorsi* (in Latin and English translations) and his *Florentine History* (in English); several works by Guicciardini (in Italian and English); Paolo Sarpi's *Historia del Concilio Tridentino* and his history of the controversy over the Venetian Interdict; and the

[54] de Rohan, 'L'Interest des princes', p. 280: 'faire comprendre aux Catholiques le venin caché la dessous').

[55] Chatsworth, MS Hobbes E. 1. A. At some stage an incomplete manuscript copy was also acquired of James Mabbe's translation of a Spanish work in the Counter-Reformation 'ragion di stato' tradition, Juan de Santa María's *Tratado de república y policía cristiana para reyes y príncipes* (Madrid, 1615): Chatsworth, MS Hardwick 49. This scribal manuscript was presumably acquired before the publication of the translation (*Christian Policie: Or, The Christian Common-wealth: Published for the good of Kings, and Princes* (London, 1632)); but the manuscript is not listed in MS Hobbes E. 1. A. (The manuscript is a bound volume, containing enough paper for the complete translation, but only the first few leaves are used, giving the dedicatory epistle and chapters 1–4; perhaps a commission to transcribe the entire text was cancelled when it became known that the translation was about to be—or had already been—printed.) On de Santa María's work see Fernández-Santamaría, *Reason of State and Statecraft*, pp. 101–4.

Ragguagli dal Parnaso and *Pietra del paragone* of Boccalini.[56] While some other modern French writers were represented (such as de La Noue and Bodin), it is striking that Italians formed the main concentration of contemporary authors in a foreign vernacular; this suggests that the stay in Venice in 1614–15 may have been an intellectually formative period for both Hobbes and Cavendish (who seems to have cultivated Italian to a much higher level than any other language). And although there is a smattering of Italian belles-lettres, it is also striking that the Italian authors are best represented in the areas of political history, Tacitism, and reason of state. Hobbes may have been responsible for the purchase of many of these books.[57] But the pattern here also tends to confirm what Hobbes himself wrote about the second Earl of Devonshire: 'For his own studie, it was bestowed, for the most part, in that kind of Learning, which best deserueth the paines and houres of Great Persons, *History*, and *Ciuill knowledge*, and directed not to the Ostentation of his reading, but to the Gouernment of his Life, and the Publike good.'[58]

The sheer concentration of editions of, and commentaries on, Tacitus is another noticeable feature of this collection: here too, history and civil knowledge were combined. Among the books listed we find 'Ammiratus in Tacitum' (Scipione Ammirato, *Dissertationes politicae, sive discursus in C. Tacitum* ('Helenopolis', 1609), the Latin version of his *Discorsi sopra Cornelio Tacito* (Florence, 1594)); 'Lipsij opera' (which included Lipsius's commentary on Tacitus); 'Tacitus English' (*The Annales of Cornelius Tacitus*, tr. R. Greenwey (London, 1598)); 'Ammirato. Discorsi sopra Tacito'; 'Tacito Lat. Italian by Dati. 2. vol.' (*C. Cornelij Taciti opera latina, cum versione italica* (Frankfurt, 1612), which included the translation by G. Dati, first published in Venice in 1563); 'Tacito Ital. by Politi' (*Annali, et istorie, di G. Cornelio Tacito*, tr. A. Politi (Venice, 1615–16)); 'Tacitus wth Aphorismes in Spanish' (*Tacito español, ilustrado con aforismos*, tr. B. Alamos de Barrientos (Madrid, 1614)); and 'Tacitus in french' (*Les Oeuvres de C. Cornelius Tacitus*, tr. C. Fauchet and E. de la Planche (Paris, 1584)).[59]

The 'Discourse upon the Beginning of Tacitus', which may have been written by Cavendish with some assistance from Hobbes and was published with Cavendish's other discourses and essays in 1620, shows not only the fruits of a careful study of the Roman historian, but also some familiarity with the reason of state tradition. Self-interest

56 Chatsworth, MS Hobbes E. 1. A.
58 Thucydides, *Eight Bookes*, sig. A1r.
57 See above, Ch. 1 n. 31.
59 Chatsworth, MS Hobbes E. 1. A.

is taken as fundamental: 'most men measuring others by themselves, are apt to think that all men will . . . in all their actions more respect what conduces to the advancing of their own ends, than of truth, and the good of others.'[60] Human beings are naturally foolish and self-deceiving: 'men have generally this infirmity, that when they would fall into consideration of their hopes; they mistake, and enter into a fruitless discourse of their wishes; such impression do pleasing things make in man's imagination.'[61] Dissimulation is given due prominence: Agrippa's failing was that he lacked the 'ability upon just cause, to contain and dissemble his passions, and purposes; and this was then thought the chief Art of government', whereas Tiberius 'knew best of all men how to dissemble his vices'.[62] And the importance of reputation is also acknowledged, in a passage which begins by nodding in the direction of traditional just war theory but then adds:

But this war against the Germans, was to defend the reputation of the Roman Empire, and was necessary, not for the curiosity alone, and niceness, that great Personages have always had, in point of honor, much more great States, and most of all that of Rome, but also for the real and substantial damage (for some man might account the other but a shadow) that might ensue upon the neglecting of such shadows.[63]

Another justification, even further removed from traditional theory, was also put forward: 'And besides this, Augustus might find commodity in this war, by employing therein the great and active spirits, which else might have made themselves work at home, to the prejudice of his authority'; this too was a point made familiar by writers on 'ragion di stato' such as Botero, who had commended foreign wars as a useful safety-valve through which the energies of potentially troublesome subjects could be vented.[64]

The author of this discourse seems to have sympathized in some ways with Tacitus' nostalgia for Republican Rome. On the one hand he took

[60] Hobbes (attrib.), *Three Discourses*, pp. 40–1.   [61] Ibid., p. 62.

[62] Ibid., pp. 57, 64.

[63] Ibid., p. 59. Cf. the comment made nearly twenty years later by the duc de Rohan: 'It is a thing that seems empty, but produces solid effects' (above, at n. 37).

[64] Ibid., p. 59; Botero, *Della ragion di stato*, III.3, pp. 110–11 (Botero, *Reason of State*, p. 77). The idea can be found in Machiavelli: 'Ambition uses against foreigners that violence which neither the law nor the king allows her to use internally; as a result, internal trouble almost always ceases' (N. Machiavelli, *Opere letterarie*, ed. A. Borlenghi (Naples, 1969), p. 154: l'ambizion contra l'esterna gente | usa il furor ch'usarlo infra se stessa | né la legge né il re gliene consente; | onde il mal proprio quasi sempre cessa').

care to explain that the establishment of a republic (after the expulsion of King Tarquin) 'is by the Author entitled, Liberty, not because bondage is always joined to Monarchy', but only because monarchy had been abused by those who held it.[65] On the other hand, the shift to Triumvirate and Principate was referred to by him, repeatedly, as a loss of 'liberty' by 'the people' or by 'Rome'.[66] Of the consolidation of power by Augustus he wrote: 'This encroaching on the liberty of the State, in former times never wanted opposers; but now the stout Patriots were rooted out.'[67] And, most strikingly, he observed:

For though other virtues, especially deep wisdom, great, and extraordinary valor, be excellent ones under any sort of government, and chiefly in a free State . . . yet in the subject of a Monarch, obedience is the greatest virtue . . . Therefore they now study no more the Art of commanding, which had been heretofore necessary for any Roman Gentleman . . . but apply themselves wholly to the Arts of service, whereof obsequiousness is the chief.[68]

Although there are touches or echoes of Hobbes's prose-style in this Discourse, the overall position taken by its author seems to fit what is known about the political attitudes of Lord Cavendish: here is a Tacitist with some sympathies on the red side of the divide (inclined to think, perhaps, that the duty of a 'stout Patriot' in 1620s England was to resist the sort of 'encroachment' represented by extra-parliamentary taxation), who also has a robust 'reason of state' approach to international affairs. Such a person might well have felt that a foreign war could be justified on grounds—such as the defence of reputation and the need to act pre-emptively against Habsburg encirclement—that were rather different from those put forward by Puritan preachers in their pulpits.

For the period of the 1620s, as we have seen, there is too little evidence to enable us to judge exactly what position Hobbes took on such political issues. But there are at least some signs that his judgements, whatever they were, would have been influenced by Tacitist and 'reason of state' ways of thinking. His proximity to Cavendish, and the evidence of the Hardwick library, have already been mentioned. The strongly Tacitist flavour of the letter to Hobbes from Robert Mason in 1622 (which applies to England a quotation from the first book of Tacitus' *Historia*, and invokes the Tacitean concept of 'arcana imperii') should also be borne in mind.[69] A few further indications can be found in

[65] Hobbes (attrib.), *Three Discourses*, p. 33.   [66] Ibid., pp. 34, 36, 38.
[67] Ibid., p. 46.   [68] Ibid., pp. 60–1.
[69] Hobbes, *Correspondence*, i, pp. 1–4.

the prefatory materials to Hobbes's translation of Thucydides. In his Preface to the Readers he famously characterized Thucydides as 'the most Politique Historiographer that euer writ'; in early modern English the adjective 'politique' or 'politic(k)' implied skill and shrewdness in the contrivance, conduct, or understanding of policy, but the notion of 'policy' often had slightly Machiavellian overtones of expediency and the pursuit of secular advantage as opposed to morality or religion.[70] Expanding on this theme, Hobbes wrote that Thucydides excelled at enabling the reader 'to trace the drifts and counsailes of the Actors to their seate': in other words, he made it possible to cut through the public pretexts and official explanations, identifying the motivations that the actors themselves had usually dissembled.[71] In his essay 'Of the Life and History of Thucydides' he defended (against the criticisms of Dionysius of Halicarnassus) the author's method of 'putting first the Narration of the Publique, and auowed cause of this Warre, and after that the true and inward motiue of the same', and commented: 'for without a pretext, no Warre followes. This pretext is alwayes an iniury receiued, or pretended to be receiued. Whereas the inward motiue to hostility is but coniecturall . . . as enuy to the greatnesse of another State, or feare of a iniury to come.'[72] It was in the spirit of the 'reason of state' literature both to think that pre-emption might be an important reason for going to war, and to suppose that such reasons were sometimes best hidden. More generally, Hobbes commended Thucydides as someone who penetrated the façade of dissimulation: his writings offered 'contemplations of those humane passions, which either dissembled, or not commonly discoursed of, doe yet carry the greatest sway with men, in their publique conuersation'.[73] Yet although Thucydides himself had seen through all pretences, his writings still cleverly respected the 'ragion di stato' principle that the common people should not have easy access to the arcana of state: '*Marcellinus* saith, he was obscure on purpose, that the Common people might not vnderstand him. And not vnlikely; for a wise man should so write (thogh in words vnderstood by all men) that wise men only should be able to commend him. But this obscurity is not to be in the Narrations of things done . . . in all w^ch, *Thucydides*

---

[70] Thucydides, *Eight Bookes*, sig. A3v. *OED* 'politic', adj. 2: 'of persons: apt at pursuing a policy; sagacious, prudent, shrewd; of actions or things: judicious, expedient, skilfully contrived'. For a characteristic example of the use of the term, cf. Ben Jonson's naming of the character 'Sir Politick Would-be' in *Volpone*.

[71] Thucydides, *Eight Bookes*, sig. A3v.   [72] Ibid., sig. a4r–v.

[73] Ibid., sig. a4v.

is most perspicuous'.[74] Hobbes's meaning here is partly explicated by
an earlier comment in the same essay, which makes intriguing use of
the notion of 'secrecy': he describes Thucydides as 'hauing so cleerely
set before mens eyes, the wayes and euents, of good and euill counsels,
that the Narration it selfe doth secretly instruct the Reader, and more
effectually then possibly can be done by Precept'.[75] Here is a form
of 'secret instruction' that passes, like a coded message, from a writer
who has understood true reason of state to those readers who have the
capacity to understand it when the causes and consequences of policies
are properly set out. And the origins of this comment are revealed when,
at the end of his essay on Thucydides, Hobbes invokes 'the most true
and proper commendation of him, from *Iustus Lipsius*', quoting the
eulogy of the Greek historian in the *Politicorum libri sex*: 'sound in his
iudgements; euery where secretly instructing, and directing a mans life
and actions'.[76]

   If we now turn to Hobbes's mature political writings, we can find a
number of themes and lines of argument that seem to echo the teachings
of 'ragion di stato' theory. Of course, beyond a certain level of generality,
the fact that Hobbes's attitude was similar to that of the reason of state
writers need not mean that his thinking was influenced directly by
theirs. That he too regarded human beings as naturally conflictual, and
looked to artifice (backed by force) to create viable political structures,
might indicate merely that he shared with those writers some of the
available range of anti-Aristotelian assumptions. Nevertheless, there is a
pattern of similarity that deserves notice.

   That human beings follow what they believe to be their own interests
is a fundamental principle in Hobbes's theory. 'Every man by nature
seeketh his own benefit, and promotion.'[77] Unfortunately, 'the Passions
of men, are commonly more potent than their Reason.'[78] Only the
proper application of reason can tell people where their true interests lie,
and most people will fail to apply reason because they are pursuing those
short-term or seeming benefits to which their passions propel them; 'as
oft as reason is against a man, so oft will a man be against reason.'[79] The

---

   [74] Thucydides, *Eight Bookes*, sig. a4v.   [75] Ibid., sig. a3r.   [76] Ibid., sig. b1r.
   [77] T. Hobbes, *Leviathan* (London, 1651), p. 97. (Page-numbers of this edition can be
found in most modern editions, including those by J. C. A. Gaskin, C. B. Macpherson,
W. G. Pogson Smith, and R. Tuck.)
   [78] Ibid., p. 96.
   [79] T. Hobbes, *The Elements of Law*, ed. F. Tönnies (London, 1889), Epistle Dedicatory, p. xv.

constant threat to political order comes from the fact that people seek a version of their own 'interest' that has been inadequately conceived by them: as one of the speakers in *Behemoth* puts it, 'people always have been, and always will be, ignorant of their duty to the public, as never meditating anything but their particular interest'.[80] What they lack, then, is a proper understanding of what Hobbes calls 'the common interest' or 'the publique interest'; that is what his theory aims to supply. And in so doing, he also aims to persuade them that monarchy is the best form of government, because in it 'the private interest [*sc.* of the monarch] is the same with the publique'.[81]

Another general point of similarity between Hobbes's theory and that of the 'ragion di stato' tradition is the importance both attributed to opinion. As we have seen, for the reason of state theorists, political rule rested on reputation, which was a matter of the opinions held about the ruler by the ruled. This approach involved what might be called a radical psychologizing of political theory: the foundations of rule were to be located not in natural harmony, nor in armies, fortresses, or treasuries, but inside the skulls of the people. Hobbes's views were congruent with this: 'the power of the mighty', explained one of the speakers in *Behemoth*, 'hath no foundation but in the opinion and belief of the people'.[82] In all his political treatises he emphasized the role of false opinion and false doctrine in bringing about the destruction of legitimate rule.[83] It followed that the sovereign power must take an interest in such matters of doctrine and opinion, promoting true and beneficial doctrines and curbing others: 'For the Actions of men proceed from their Opinions; and in the wel governing of Opinions, consisteth the well governing of mens Actions, in order to their Peace, and Concord.'[84]

[80] T. Hobbes, *Behemoth: Or, The Long Parliament*, ed. F. Tönnies (London, 1889), p. 39.

[81] Hobbes, *Leviathan*, p. 96. In his first political treatise, *Elements of Law*, Hobbes did not use the term 'interest' (perhaps because of his awareness of the ways in which its use might conceal the difference between real and ill-conceived interest), preferring terms such as 'benefit' and 'profit' instead; but the argument was essentially the same (e.g. II. V. 1, p. 138: 'the profit of the sovereign and subject goeth always together'). (References to *Elements of Law* include part-, chapter-, and section-numbers, as well as the page-numbers in Tönnies's edition.)

[82] Hobbes, *Behemoth*, p. 16.

[83] Hobbes, *Elements of Law* II. VIII. 4–10, pp. 170–5; *De cive: The Latin Version*, ed. H. Warrender (Oxford, 1983), XII.1–8 (*On the Citizen*, ed. and tr. R. Tuck and M. Silverthorne (Cambridge, 1998), pp. 131–7); *Leviathan*, pp. 168–72.

[84] Hobbes, *Leviathan*, p. 91.

Where specific recommendations about the 'well governing of mens Actions' were concerned, Hobbes's writings were much less detailed than those of the reason of state theorists. As he put it in *The Elements of Law*, he wrote 'Not purposing to enter into the particulars of the art of government, but to sum up the general heads, wherein such art is to be employed'.[85] Nevertheless, some suggestions about 'the art of government' do appear in his works, and several of them agree with those of the 'ragion di stato' writers. In *De cive*, for example, he emphasized the importance of spies or intelligence agents ('exploratores'), who could supply the state with information about 'the plans and movements of all those who have the capacity to do it harm'.[86] Similarly, he explained in *Leviathan* that 'to be able to give Counsell to a Common-wealth, in a businesse that hath reference to another Common-wealth, *It is necessary to be acquainted with the Intelligences, and Letters* that come from thence'.[87] Indeed, when discussing the role of state counsellors (to which he gave special attention), he wrote that they must have a deep knowledge 'of the Strength, Commodities, Places, both of their own Country, and their Neighbours; as also of the inclinations, and designes of all Nations that may any way annoy them'—very much the sort of information that works such as Botero's *Relationi universali* were meant to supply.[88] In *The Elements of Law* he commended 'the aristocracy of Venice' for its wise decision to 'commit the handling of state affairs to a few'; expanding this point in *Leviathan*, he wrote that 'in Deliberations that ought to be kept secret, (whereof there be many occasions in Publique Businesse,) the Counsells of many, and especially in Assemblies, are dangerous'.[89]

Where the ruler's day-to-day government of his own subjects was concerned, Hobbes paid much more attention in *Leviathan* to the promulgation of laws and the instilling of correct doctrines than he did to such matters as the promotion of commerce; but he did make some suggestions about taxation, public welfare, and the role of organizations 'for the well ordering of forraigne Traffique'.[90] In his earlier works he had attempted a more systematic listing of the forms of 'temporal good' which it was the sovereign's duty to promote. Thus in *The Elements of Law* he declared that 'the temporal good of people . . . consisteth in

---

[85] Hobbes, *Elements of Law* II. IX. 1, p. 179.   [86] Hobbes, *De cive* XIII.7, p. 145.
[87] Hobbes, *Leviathan*, p. 135.   [88] Ibid., p. 134.
[89] Hobbes, *Elements of Law* II. V. 8, p. 143; *Leviathan*, p. 136.
[90] Hobbes, *Leviathan*, pp. 119, 181.

four points: 1. Multitude. 2. Commodity of living. 3. Peace amongst ourselves. 4. Defence against foreign power.'[91] In *De cive* the list was slightly different: 'Regarding this life only, the good things citizens may enjoy can be put into four categories: 1) defence from external enemies; 2) preservation of internal peace; 3) acquisition of wealth, so far as this is consistent with public security; 4) full enjoyment of innocent liberty.'[92] This last formulation is quite similar to Botero's statement (quoted above) that 'he who wishes to keep his subjects contented and quiet should procure for them plenty, justice, peace, and a certain virtuous liberty' (where 'virtuous' translates 'honesta').[93] For Hobbes, all these temporal goods could be summarized in the phrase 'salus populi', 'the safety of the people'; 'salus' here had as its most important component the preservation of the people by the maintenance of peace, but also included other forms of well-being. 'The Office of the Soveraign . . . consisteth in . . . the procuration of *the safety of the people* . . . But by Safety here, is not meant a bare Preservation, but also all other Contentments of life, which every man by lawfull Industry, without danger, or hurt to the Common-wealth, shall acquire to himselfe.'[94]

The Latin phrase was derived from the precept 'salus populi suprema lex esto', 'let the safety of the people be the supreme law'. This was a tag often cited by writers in the 'ragion di stato' tradition, as it seemed to express the principle (formulated most clearly by Scipione Ammirato) that reason of state was a higher norm that could supervene on ordinary laws or policies and overrule them. And the idea that the safety and well-being of the people (as assessed and defended by their sovereign) must trump the ordinary norms of behaviour, both legal and moral, was propounded quite emphatically by Hobbes. In his discussion of 'the defence of the people' in *De cive* he argued that sovereign rulers 'may also do anything that seems likely to subvert, by force or by craft, the power of foreigners whom they fear'; this fully encompassed Lipsius's

[91] Hobbes, *Elements of Law* II. IX. 3, p. 179.

[92] Hobbes, *On the Citizen*, p. 144 (*De cive* XIII.6, p. 197: 'Commoda ciuium quae hanc tantùm vitam spectant in quatuor genera distribui possunt. 1. vt ab hostibus externis defendantur. 2. vt pax interna conseruetur. 3. vt quantum cum securitate publica consistere potest, locupletentur. 4. vt libertate innoxiâ perfruantur'). In the translation, 'innocent' should be taken in its literal sense of 'harmless'.

[93] See above, n. 40. Botero's 'peace' referred primarily to not being at war with other states, and 'justice' to one of the essential conditions of internal peace.

[94] *Leviathan*, p. 175; cf. *Elements of Law* II. IX. 1, p. 179: '*Salus populi suprema lex*; by which must be understood, not the mere preservation of their lives, but generally their benefit and good'.

category of 'medium' frauds, and, in its use of the term 'anything', may have gone quite a long way beyond it.[95] Occasionally, indeed, Hobbes's willingness to sanction extreme breaches of moral norms far exceeded anything in the reason of state tradition (with the possible exception of Naudé's admiring account of 'coups d'état'). In *Behemoth* the principal speaker first explains that the Civil War was caused by 'the incitement of Presbyterian ministers' and then estimates that 'near 100,000 persons' died as a result. He suggests: 'Had it not been much better that those seditious ministers, which were not perhaps 1000, had been all killed before they had preached? It had been (I confess) a great massacre; but the killing of 100,000 is a greater.'[96]

In various ways, then, it seems reasonable to align Hobbes's political theory with that of 'ragion di stato': there are general congruities, specific points of agreement, and some elements of a reason of state mentality taken *à l'outrance*. And yet the overall flavour of his work is very different. Just as his writing lacks detailed instructions on 'the art of government', so too it virtually ignores all the case histories of political and military actions and policies, from ancient Greece and Rome and contemporary Europe, which filled so many of the pages of the 'ragion di stato' authors. This is not just a matter of stylistic preference; it reflects Hobbes's most basic assumptions about the nature of political theory. For the study of case histories will yield only the sort of 'prudence' that is derived from 'experience'. Hobbes admits that 'by how much one man has more experience of things past, than another, by so much also he is more Prudent, and his expectations the seldomer faile him.'[97] He allows that a high degree of such prudence is important in a counsellor, and grants that it is necessary in order to govern a kingdom well.[98] But, in the end, prudence offers only a form of conjecture, in which extrapolations are made from past chains of events to future ones; 'such conjecture, through the difficulty of observing all the circumstances', is 'very fallacious'.[99] And in any body of doctrine or belief where certainty is lacking, people are much more likely to twist the doctrines to suit their

---

[95] Hobbes, *On the Citizen*, p. 146 (*De cive* XIII.8, p. 198: 'Quibus etiam addi potest quicquid ad potentiam externorum à quibus metuunt, vel arte vel vi minuendam conducere videbitur').

[96] Hobbes, *Behemoth*, p. 95. Richard Tuck has portrayed *Behemoth* as a very Tacitist work, particularly where its account of Cromwell is concerned ('Hobbes and Tacitus'); for a more qualified judgement see N. Malcolm, '*Behemoth Latinus*: Adam Ebert, Tacitism, and Hobbes', *Filozofski vestnik*, 24 (2003), pp. 85–120.

[97] Hobbes, *Leviathan*, p. 10.   [98] Ibid., pp. 34, 134.   [99] Ibid., p. 10.

particular passions and interests: hence Hobbes's declared disapproval of those 'pretenders to Politicall Prudence' (who may perhaps have included amateur reason of state theorists of the sort satirized by Ben Jonson), whom he compared to little worms nibbling at the bowels of the commonwealth.[100]

What Hobbes aimed to supply was not prudence but science—a system of certain knowledge. This was intended to be not a science of the art of government, but rather, a science that would demonstrate the necessity of government and the need for any government to have certain essential features. Hobbes allowed that the day-to-day management of affairs required prudential and practical skills, and compared those skills to those of a good player at tennis.[101] But, he observed, 'the skill of making, and maintaining Common-wealths, consisteth in certain Rules, as doth Arithmetique and Geometry; not (as in Tennis-play) on Practise onely'.[102] Hobbes's 'scientific' political theory was, at least in part, a science based on definitions and their entailments: an action could be identified with certainty as unjust, for example, if and only if it was in breach of covenant, since justice was defined as action in accordance with covenants made. At the same time, these seemingly analytic jural categories (involving rights and the transfers of rights) were grounded in a descriptive account of human behaviour and the consequences of actions; what exactly the overall nature of this Hobbesian 'science' was, and the extent to which its essential components (a science of 'names' and a science of 'causes') diverged, are questions that have long bedevilled modern commentary on Hobbes. But it is at least clear that he was attempting something that went significantly beyond the sort of theorizing performed by the reason of state writers. This is also shown by the fact that the key categories of his political philosophy were jural ones, such as rights, covenants, and authority—terms little used in the reason of state literature, where the vocabulary was almost entirely descriptive.

To say that Hobbes was going beyond the mental world of the 'ragion di stato' writers does not mean that he was simply dismissing its concerns as irrelevant. In some ways, his political theory can be seen as solving problems which the reason of state literature had raised. The concept of 'interest', for example, had always occupied

---

[100] Ibid., p. 174.   [101] Ibid., p. 136.

[102] Ibid., p. 107. 'Maintaining' here referred not to ordinary government business, but to maintaining the state as a state—for example, not giving away any of the essential powers of the sovereign, as someone ignorant of the true political science might do.

a rather uncertain, intermediate position between the subjective and the objective. Hobbes set out a system of value-terms in which the subjective (and therefore conflicting) use of simple terms such as 'good' and 'bad' was acknowledged, but from which there emerged a higher-level set of values (those relating to the attainment of the one good, self-preservation, on which all subjective evaluators must agree). Those higher values were the ones embodied in the Laws of Nature, the principles of morality, which were objective; the Laws of Nature would never change, though they might in any given set of circumstances be overridden by the immediate requirement of self-preservation. A person's 'interest' would thus have a primary and objective component (whatever increased that person's chances of self-preservation was in his or her true interest), and a secondary, subjective one (relating to the attaining of subjective goods).

Hobbes used the vocabulary of 'utile' and 'turpe' as subjective value-terms, and explained that traditional moral vocabulary expressed the dictates of the Laws of Nature, which set out the optimum rules for the attainment of one's objective interest.[103] But at the same time his argument explained how breaches of the Laws of Nature—immoral acts—might be justified: in any set of circumstances where self-preservation was endangered, an action that would secure it would be not only permitted but required, no matter how contrary it might be to the normal rules of morality. The application of this argument to the case of a sovereign state and its external relations was not straightforward, as Hobbes did not simply transfer the notion of 'self-preservation' to the level of the state itself; a more complex pattern of argument was deployed, involving the natural-law duties of the sovereign.[104] But a similar outcome was achieved: a system of values which could itself explain why its normally applicable values must sometimes be contravened. Unlike the 'ragion di stato' theorists, Hobbes did not have to juggle with two opposing value-scales that proceeded on fundamentally different bases; rather, he showed how they were necessarily related within a single overall system.

Similarly, Hobbes's account of the essential role of consent resolved the ambiguities of the reason of state writers. Consent, for Hobbes, was not merely a psychological prop which it was in the sovereign's interests to strengthen; rather, it was what constituted the very authority

---

[103] Hobbes, *Leviathan*, pp. 24–5 (where Hobbes uses 'pulchrum'/'turpe' for the apparent good/bad, and 'utile'/'inutile' for the means towards it); pp. 79–80.

[104] See Malcolm, *Aspects of Hobbes*, pp. 432–56.

of the sovereign.[105] Hobbes agreed that 'opinion' was thus of essential importance; and what mattered was not just the opinions the subjects held about particular actions or policies adopted by the ruler (the basis of his 'reputation' at any given time), but rather their opinions about the nature of his authority as such. In this way, Hobbes's attention to the topic of 'opinion' was deeper than that of the reason of state writers; and it was also wider, insofar as he had to consider all the other forms of opinion (including, but not confined to, religious beliefs) that might affect people's beliefs about the nature of the sovereign's authority. The control or management of people's beliefs thus became even more important for Hobbes than it was for any of the reason of state writers. And since, as he explained, belief was not subject to the will, and could therefore not be commanded or forced, the only long-term way of ensuring that the right sort of belief was held by the people was to engage in teaching and persuasion.

Could that teaching and persuasion include the inculcating of beliefs which, while politically convenient, were known (by the inculcating ruler) to be false? Hobbes certainly allowed that such a process had taken place in some cases, and that it had conferred some advantage at the time. He noted that 'the first Founders, and Legislators of Commonwealths amongst the Gentiles' had done this, not only with regard to religious practices ('So *Numa Pompilius* pretended to receive the Ceremonies he instituted among the Romans, from the Nymph *Egeria*') but also more generally, when they took care 'to make it believed, that the same things were displeasing to the Gods, which were forbidden by the Lawes'.[106] But there is plenty of evidence elsewhere in Hobbes's writings, in his extended discussions of superstition, priestcraft, and the 'kingdom of darkness', that he regarded such a method as far from optimal: people whose heads were filled with absurdities and false beliefs were much more open to manipulation by interested parties, who could use those beliefs to turn them against their sovereign. The optimal

[105] Hobbes, *Leviathan*, p. 250: 'the authority of all . . . Princes, must be grounded on the Consent of the People'. For an exploration of some aspects of this difference between the reason of state theorists and Hobbes, contrasting the former's techniques for the conservation of power by the ruler with the latter's 'two-way exchange' between authority and obedience, see G. Borelli, *Ragion di stato e Leviatano: conservazione e scambio alle origini della modernità politica* (Bologna, 1993).
[106] Hobbes, *Leviathan*, p. 57. This theme (and the citing of Numa Pompilius as a prime example of it) was a commonplace of the Machiavellian tradition. For a similar attitude to the role of religious beliefs cf. also Hobbes's comments in 1636, cited above, Ch. 5, at n. 44.

strategy involved inculcating true beliefs about the necessity and nature of political rule—the truths which Hobbes's 'science' established. Thus at the outset of his discussion of the duties of the sovereign, Hobbes wrote that 'it is against his Duty, to let the people be ignorant, or mis-informed of the grounds, and reasons of those his essentiall Rights . . . the grounds of these Rights, have the . . . need to be diligently, and truly taught'.[107] Some element of noble lie or pious fraud might have served a purpose at the original foundation of a state, when unruly men had to be quickly brought to order, but it was in the long-term interests of peace and stability that the people should be led towards a true understanding of the nature and justification of authority. Hobbes thus subscribed to a version of the 'principle of publicity' (the principle that the public should have true knowledge about the nature of the state and the rationale of its exercise of power); and his long-term programme for mankind can reasonably be characterized as a project of enlightenment.[108]

This does not mean, of course, that Hobbes elevated truth-telling into an absolute moral requirement. His own political theory, with its strong version of the private/public distinction and its insistence that the externalities, including speech and writing, were all subject to the command of the sovereign, clearly envisaged situations in which simulation or dissimulation might be required; and even a truth-telling philosopher, when it came to such delicate matters as discussion of the publicly authorized religion, might well find himself in such a situation.[109] More generally, Hobbes had a subtle sense of the ways in which ordinary human life requires a kind of theatrical self-presentation, both simulative and dissimulative: once again, there was a gap between the private and the public, and not all the thoughts that ranged freely in a person's mind could be freely expressed to other persons.[110] Moreover, while truth-telling about the necessity and nature of the state was, in

[107] Hobbes, *Leviathan*, p. 175.

[108] See D. Johnston, *The Rhetoric of Leviathan: Thomas Hobbes and the Politics of Cultural Transformation* (Princeton, 1986); R. P. Kraynak, *History and Modernity in the Thought of Thomas Hobbes* (Ithaca, NY, 1990); J. Waldron, 'Hobbes and the Principle of Publicity', *Pacific Philosophical Quarterly*, 82 (2001), pp. 447–74; Malcolm, *Aspects of Hobbes*, pp. 537–45.

[109] For a valuable discussion of this issue, making some connections with writers in the reason of state tradition (but possibly overstating the case where Hobbes's basic concept of philosophy is concerned) see K. Hoekstra, 'The End of Philosophy (The Case of Hobbes)', *Proceedings of the Aristotelian Society*, 106 (2006), pp. 23–60.

[110] For an original investigation of this theme, see M. Brito Vieira, 'Elements of Representation in Hobbes: Aesthetics, Theatre, Law, and Theology in the Construction of Hobbes's Theory of the State', Cambridge University PhD thesis (2005).

his view, important for maintaining the state's authority, it was not the only way, nor, perhaps, the most effective way for at least some elements of the common people: in addition to threats of punishments (which required subjects rational enough to make simple calculations about the costs and benefits of their actions), a certain theatricality of power might also be needed—as expressed in the image of a 'leviathan' that would keep proud people in 'awe'. As for the use of secrecy, dissimulation, and simulation in the actual conduct of government business, Hobbes had no difficulty, as we have seen, in accepting their value in particular circumstances. Nevertheless, his 'principle of publicity' implied that, as a population became more enlightened and therefore more able to accept the true reasons for government policies, the degree of concealment and misdirection should gradually decline: if the people understood that, for example, a pre-emptive war was justified by true political principles, they would not need to have that war presented to them under a simulated pretext. The world of the *Altera secretissima instructio*, in which the most important political truths were always 'most secret' because they could not be publicly avowed, was a world Thomas Hobbes knew well enough. But his aim was to replace it with a better one.

Hobbes's Translation of *Altera secretissima instructio*

BL, MS Add. 70499, fos. 73–83

A second most secret instruction Gallo-britanno-batauian, giuen to Fredericke the V. Translated out of Low Dutch into Latine, and diuulged for the most publique good. At Haghe, by permission of yᵉ Senate. <u>1626</u>

APHORISME .1.

When you began, I helped you, when you grew I applauded, when you reigned, I instructed you. In Banishmʳ. I follow you, I stand faythfull, to yoʳ ruines. *Stant pectore in isto fortunâ titubante fides.*¹ Most are fled. they followed not you, but yoʳ fortune. I am Achates, Thinke me *Theseus* or *Pylades*;² I will be both to you. When you committe to yᵉ sea yoʳ Ship, I will tye my boate to yᵉ sterne, that it may eyther rest in yᵉ same port, or be whirled about wᵗʰ the same tempest. *Nulla meis sine te quaeretur gloria rebus.*³ I may prosper amisse wᵗʰ you, but neuer well without you.

---

¹ The Latin original has 'stat', not 'stant': 'when fortune vacillates, loyalty stays firm in this breast' (adapted from Silius Italicus, *Punica*, XI, ll. 3–4: 'stat nulla diu mortalibus usquam, | fortuna titubante, fides').

Altera secretissima instructio

BL, pressmark 1197.e.35(2)

Altera secretissima instructio gallo-britanno-batava Friderico
V. data. Ex belgica in
latinam linguam versa, et optimo publico evulgata
Hagae Comitis, permissu Senatus, MDCXXVI

APHORISMUS I.

Iuvi prensantem, plausi crescenti, instruxi regnantem, sequor exulem, ruinis tuis fidus adsisto.

> ————*stat pectore in isto*
> *Fortunâ titubante fides.*

Fugêre plerique; Felicitatas illi tuae comites, non tui fuerunt: Achates ego sum, Thesea me, aut Pyladem aestima, utrunque praestabo. Navim tuam ubi fluctibus commiseris, cymbam meam adligabo, ut eodem in portu conquiescat, aut turbine rotetur.

> *Nulla meis, sine te, quaeretur gloria rebus.*

Malè mihi tecum esse potest, bene sine te, esse non potest.

---

² Three figures proverbial for their loyal friendship: Achates, friend of Aeneas; Theseus, friend of Pirithous; Pylades, friend of Orestes.
³ 'I shall not seek any glory in my affairs without you' (Vergil, *Aeneid*, I, l. 278).

2.

This is the sixt time I call vpon you,[4] nor is it yet too late—*Facilis iactura est temporis acti, si lux damna sequens pensauerit*[5]—your hopes haue fayled you these six yeres, and made you to keepe yor instructer of. They were higher then my voyce could reach to, and strong^r then to be altered by the losse and slawghter of yor frends. Great shaddowes of names made you dreame wakinge, and yor mind in a loued error imagined kingdomes to it selfe. Thus reckoneth his interest after he is Bankerupt—*sollicitis Alphius articulis.*[6]—and vaynely pleaseth himselfe wth fancies. Britanny a father in law and Brother in law, France enclininge, Sweden promisinge, Denmarke abettinge, The [Grison *deleted* > Sauoyard] instigatinge.[7] Venice rich, Gabor a frend, the Turke your Patron, Brunswickes,[8] Durlaches,[9] and Mansfelts[10] armies, the strength of the Saxons, and Juitlanders,[11] the relieuinge of *Breda*,[12] the riflinge of Genoa,[13] the rendringe of ye Valteline,[14] the deceauinge of the Swisses,[15] the winninge of Cales,[16] the auersion of ye Indian

---

[4] This statement is puzzling, as there were only two previous *Secretissima instructio* texts and the author was apparently aware of only one of them. The Latin here, 'sexto', means 'six times'; 'for the sixth time' would have been, more correctly, 'sextum'. Possibly the word 'anno' has gone missing ('in the sixth year').

[5] 'It is easy to jettison the past, if the good prospects that follow the loss will compensate for it.' The first phrase seems to contain a reminiscence of Vergil, *Aeneid*, II, l. 646: 'facilis iactura sepulchri'.

[6] 'Alphius [the moneylender] counting on his fingers.' Horace, *Epode* II is a satire on the self-deceiving moneylender Alfius; 'sollicitis articulis' is a phrase from Ovid, *Ex Ponto*, II.3, l. 18. The Latin here also incorporates an allusion to Horace, *Saturae*, II.3, ll. 18–19, 'Postquam omnis res mea Ianum | ad medium fracta est', 'after all my business collapsed at the central arcade of Janus [a place where moneylenders had their stalls in the Roman Forum]'.

[7] 'Sauoyard' is the correct translation (of 'Allobrox'). Carlo Emanuele I, Duke of Savoy, had been an active supporter of the Palatine cause, paying for Mansfeld's troops in 1619 and lobbying other powers (especially Venice and France) for an anti-Habsburg alliance on many occasions in the period 1618–26 (see R. Quazza, 'La politica di Carlo Emanuele I durante la guerra dei trent'anni', in *Carlo Emanuele I: miscellanea*, 2 vols. (Turin, 1930) (= Biblioteca della Società Storica Subalpina, vols. cxx, cxxi), pp. 1–45, esp. pp. 6–29).

[8] Christian of Braunschweig-Wolfenbüttel (1599–1626) was the brother of the Duke of Braunschweig-Wolfenbüttel. A fervent supporter of the Palatine cause (and chivalric admirer of the Winter Queen), he had raised his own forces and fought for the Elector Palatine since 1621. (See H. Wertheim, *Der tolle Halberstädter: Herzog Christian von Braunschweig im pfälzischen Kriege, 1621–1622*, 2 vols. (Berlin, 1929).)

II.

Sexto te demum appello, nec serò tamen:

———*Facilis iactura est temporis acti,*
Si lux damna sequens pensaverit.

Te spes tua, sex annos fefellit, Instructorem arcuit. Altior illa fuit, quàm ut voce mea attingi posset; fortior, quàm ut tuorum cladibus mortibúsque flecti. Magnae nominum umbrae vigilanti insomnia objecêre. amabili errore animus sibi regna finxit. Sic re ad medium Ianum fractâ fenus computat.

sollicitis Alphius articulis.

rerúmque inanis imagine gaudet. Socer Britannus, Affinísque: inclinatus Francus, promissor Suecus, assultor Danus, incentor Allobrox, dites Venetiae, Gabor amicus, Turca Patronus, Brunosviceni, Durlaceni, Mansfeldiani Exercitus, Saxonum vires, Cymbrorúmque. Bredae liberatio, Genuae expilatio, Volterinorum deditio, Helvetiorum deceptio, Gadium occupatio, opum Indianarum auersio, ita mentem tuam

---

⁹ Margrave Georg Friedrich of Baden-Durlach (1573–1638) raised an army of 11,000 men to fight for the Elector Palatine in 1621; this army was defeated in 1622, but Baden-Durlach continued to be an active supporter thereafter.

¹⁰ Count Ernst von Mansfeld (1580–1626), who reconstituted the Elector Palatine's army after the battle of the White Mountain, was the chief military commander on the pro-Palatine side between 1621 and 1626.

¹¹ Christian IV of Denmark (whose kingdom included Jutland) was military leader of the Lower Saxon Circle. 'Juitlanders' here translates, very accurately, 'Cymbrorum': the Cymbri or Cimbri were described by classical geographers as inhabiting a peninsula on the north coast of Germany.

¹² Breda was besieged by the Army of Flanders in the summer of 1624; all attempts to relieve it failed, and it fell on 4 June 1625.

¹³ Genoa, an ally of Spain and a vital communication link for the Habsburgs, was invaded by the Duke of Savoy (with some French support) in March 1625.

¹⁴ The Valtelline formed a strategically important corridor between Austria and Spanish territory in northern Italy. In 1620, after the Catholic inhabitants revolted against their Protestant rulers (the Grisons or Graubünden), Spanish forces occupied it; after pressure from France, Spain handed it over to Papal forces in 1623; in late 1624 French, Swiss, and Grisons troops expelled the Papal soldiers and occupied the territory.

¹⁵ This probably refers to the (successful) attempt by France in late 1625 and early 1626 to persuade the thirteen Swiss cantons to support France's anti-Habsburg policy over the Valtelline (see below, section 32).

¹⁶ 'Cales' was an English name for Cadiz; on the raid on Cadiz, see below, n. 17.

treasure,[17] so ran in yor minde full of hope and empty of matter, and so stopped yor eares, that instruction could haue no accesse. Truth though very stronge cannot go through Shields and Corslets.[18] The confidence

of good fortune when it is gentlest is content with floutinge such as aduise them[19] to moderation, but moued crusheth him that aduiseth. [Instructions *altered to* Instruction] did exasperate you, but by this time the frame of yor vayne Conceipts is fallen asunder, and yor wakinge dreames vanished. yor mind drunke with hope and distorted wth flattery must needes wth so many losses, become sober againe, and rectifyed. To be obstinate against experience is an iniury to God. If wounded you continue kickinge against ye Pricke, with yor safety you will loose also pitty, the comfort of those that perish. Therefore heare ye truth,[20] begin againe wth new aduise.

3

That you will beleeue me I deserue, not aske. you owe it me. When all others spent themselues in Flattery, I onely told you, the danger. Of all yor court, I onely told you the truth. But that which was pleasinge preuayled against that wch was true. The best fortune hath this worst quality to be in it selfe vncertayne, and make a man negligent of ye future. Now the vayne imaginations are vanished, and haue giuen place to the true. The euent hath answered my words to a haire— *Vicitque oracula clades.*[21] Therefore beleeue me also hereafter. From me you shall haue stout, from others pleasinge counsayle. I come a counsello^r to you, not a fidler. I said you were to weake for the Austriackes,[22] *Cuncta tibi aduerso ceciderunt praelia marte.*[23] I prophecyed to you, that seekinge after that which was anothers, you would loose your owne. you haue not now of yor owne to set your foote on. Besides that with so many defeates, you haue worne out yor subiects, and vndone ye Princes that were yor frends. I denyed that ye Bohemians would be faithfull.[24] Their affections, wealth, and gratulations, they haue transferred to y^e

---

[17] In the autumn of 1625 an Anglo-Dutch fleet was formed, for anti-Spanish operations, including the seizure of the treasure fleet from the Americas; but it achieved only an entirely abortive raid on Cadiz in November.

[18] Hobbes (or his manuscript copy) omits two words: 'adamantina texta', through the 'steely fabric' of shields and corslets.

[19] 'Floutinge' means 'mocking', 'scoffing at'; 'them' here has no warrant in the Latin.

spei nimiam, rei vacuam obsederant, aures obturârant, ut omnem instructioni aditum intercluserint. Per scutorum thoracúmque adamantina texta Veritas, quanquam fortissima, penetrare non potuit. Fiducia felicitatis ubi mitissima est, moderata suadentes irridere contenta est, si incitata est monentem obterit: Instructiones te exasperârunt. At nunc soluta est compago futilium, dispulsa vigilantis insomnia. Animum spe ebrium, assentationibus detorsum, reddere sobrium rectúmque debuêre clades. Contra experimenta contumacem esse, Numinis est iniuria. Si contra stimulum ultra saucius calcitrare pergas, cum salute perdes & miserationem, solamen pereuntium. Audi ergo Veritatem, nimis temeritatem luisti. Consilio novo rem auspicare.

III.

Fidem mihi ut habeas, haut rogo, merui: eam tu mihi debes. Omnibus in adulationem effusis, de periculis monui solus, solus in Aula tua verum dixi. sed potentiora veris erant dulcia. Hoc pessimum habet optima Fortuna, ut simul & incerta sui sit; & secura futuri. Nunc vana evanuere, veris dedere locum. Dictis meis ad unguem respondit eventus,

vicítque oracula clades.

Crede igitur & dicturo. Ex me fortia, ex alijs jucunda; Consultor tibi, non Tibicen advenio. Austriacis imparem te dixi.

Cuncta tibi adverso ceciderunt proelia Marte.

Aliena sectantem proprijs excussum iri vaticinatus sum: Pedem ubi in tuo ponas, non habes. Insuper & subditos tot cladibus attrivisti, & amicos Principes evertisti. Bohemos tibi fidos fore negavi, Animos, opes, plausum ad victorem transtulere. Caput deprecationis fuit, à Te tuísque se deceptos. Turcae fidere te vetui: Auxilia pernegauit, pacem

---

[20] Hobbes (or his manuscript copy) omits a phrase: 'nimis temeritatem luisti', 'you have paid the price of your excessive rashness'.

[21] 'And the disaster surpassed what had been predicted.'

[22] See Weber, ed., *Secretissima instructio*, p. 40.

[23] 'In a war that went against you, they killed all your soldiers.'

[24] See Weber, ed., *Secretissima instructio*, pp. 44–6.

victor. It was the beginninge of their Petition for mercy, that they were abused by you and yours.[25] I wished you not to trust to ye Turke.[26] He hath denyed you ayd, and made Peace. An euident miracle in ye Bassaes,[27] not to be drawne into ye warre [>with] mony.[28] I shewed you that Gabo^r would deceaue you.[29] *Medio in discrimine fessum. Destituit fugiens, et sibi consulit.*[30] I would not haue had you trust to the Vnion.[31]

[74r] It hastened your ruine, it heaped it on, and set it goinge. you know your owne and your frends wordes. I warned you of the vncerteny of [>y^e] Princes aydes. They haue eaten vp the Palatinate. They gaue Spinola the best place of ye land to winter in.[32] Conditioninge frendship for themselues,[33] they followed fortune, and some of them warred for ye spaniard. Indeed, all men haue fortune in hono^r,[34] and are afrayde to helpe one that is fallinge, but one fallen they will neuer take vp. I affirmed that succours from Venice would come but leasurely.[35] Their Amb:^r a hundred times entreated, would afford none.[36] To giue you much, he said, would be a burthen to them, and to giue a little would do you no good, and be no hono^r for their Republique. The Grisons complayned that they were ensnared by your fraud.[37] Of France[38] and others, they were Oracles that I told you, and are all come to passe. And this was in ye first Instruction.

4.

I haue made way for credit. Now like a good Tiresias I adde my aduise,[39] and shew you to yor selfe. I will first tell you what you cannot do. Next,

---

[25] No such claim was made in the declaration of submission (the 'Iuramentum') issued by the Estates of Bohemia on 13 November 1620 (Lundorp, *Acta publica*, i (1627), p. 854). But this comment may refer to the public declaration of 21 November 1620, made by those members of the Estates who remained in Prague and addressed to those members who had fled: it accused the Elector Palatine and his general of fleeing in order to 'pursue their own particular private interests', in breach of their oath (ibid., p. 855: 'ihre Particular Priuatsachen durchtreiben'). This, however, is not quite the same claim as the one made in the Latin text here, where 'deceptos' (translated by Hobbes as 'abused') means 'deceived' or 'tricked'.

[26] See Weber, ed., *Secretissima instructio*, pp. 54–6.   [27] Pashas.

[28] Hobbes (or his manuscript copy) omits a phrase: 'oleum & operam Venetus perdidit', 'The Venetian lost his time and trouble' (referring, presumably, to bribes and diplomatic efforts expended by the Venetian bailo in Constantinople).

[29] See Weber, ed., *Secretissima instructio*, pp. 52, 56.

[30] 'Wearied, at precisely the critical moment. He abandoned you as he fled, and consulted his own interest.'

[31] The Evangelical Union (of Protestant princes in Germany), which had been formed in 1606, formally dissolved itself in May 1621.

composuit, miraculum in Bassis evidens, ne auro quidem in bellum trahi potuerunt, oleum & operam Venetus perdidit. Gaborem fallacem ostendi.

——*medio in discrimine fessum*
Destituit fugiens & sibi consulit.

Unioni te credere nolui: Ruinam illa tuam properauit, cumulauit, impulit, nosti tua tuorúmque verba. Incerta esse Principum auxilia monui. Palatinatum illi depasti sunt, Spinolae in optimo terrae loco hyberna dederunt, pacti amicitiam sibi, fortunae obsecundârunt: nonnulli etiam Ibero militârunt. Nimirum omnes Fortunam reverenter habent, casuro assistere formidant, lapso nolunt. Ex Venetis lentum fore auxilium pronunciavi. Legatus centies obtestatus ne exiguum quidem tulit, multa tibi dare, sibi grave: pauca; tibi inutìle esse dictitabant, Reipublicae indecorum. Allobrox insuper dolis se tuis irretitum questus est. De Franco, aliísque, oracula fuêre. Evenere. Atque haec in prima instructione.

IV.

Fidem praestruxi, nunc bonus Tiresias consilium addo, & te tibi aperio. Dicam primò quid non possis. Secundò quid possis: Tu elige quid velis.

[32] Ambrogio Spinola, commander of the Army of Flanders, occupied most of the Lower Palatinate in 1620–1. Despite the use of the word 'winter' here, this seems to refer to the Mainz Accord of April 1621, in which members of the Evangelical Union (see above, n. 31) agreed to a ceasefire with Spinola, which helped him to entrench his control over the areas he had occupied.

[33] Meaning, 'Having stipulated friendship towards them'.

[34] Meaning, 'all men honour fortune'.

[35] See Weber, *Secretissima instructio*, pp. 76–8.   [36] Cf. below, n. 188.

[37] 'Allobrox' here should have been translated as 'Savoy', not 'The Grisons' (see above, Ch. 2 n. 10). The reference may be to the agreement made between Frederick and Carlo Emanuele I of Savoy in May 1619, under which the latter pledged to give the former his active support in return for being promoted as the anti-Habsburg candidate for either King of Bohemia or Holy Roman Empire; three months later, Frederick became King of Bohemia and Ferdinand became Holy Roman Emperor (Quazza, 'La politica', pp. 11–12).

[38] The first *Secretissima instructio* text had in fact said very little about France, offering only the brief warning that the French King might be persuaded to enter the conflict on the Catholic side (Weber, ed., *Secretissima instructio*, p. 96).

[39] The Theban prophet Teiresias was regarded as an infallible oracle. This may allude to Homer, *Odyssey*, XI, ll. 90–138, where Odysseus visits Teiresias in the land of the dead and is given advice about his return journey to Ithaca.

what you can. Choose what you please. The first deliberation is the more laborious, for many thinges you cannot do, wch you thinke [youc *altered to* you] can. The other will be shorter, for you cannot do much. A wise mans care is to consider first, *Quid possint humeri quid ferre recusant.*[40] Fooles by endeauoringe vayne workes, wast the strength they should employ on that wch might do them good. This I would haue you to auoyd. Absteyne from vnprofitable paynes, that you may hold out in profitable. But lets come into ye path.

5.

you cannot be restored by your Brother in Law.[41] For yor owne sake he will not. He hates you out of emulation, he hates you out of iealousie. Neyther are the causes nor the effects of this hatred, secret. He keepes in minde the words of you and yo^rs, and your rough letters to his Father,

[74v] full of contumely towards him.[42] yor Father in Law kept you out of his kingdome, and when he dyed charged his sonne not to admitte you.[43] And he admitted not his sister to come [to *altered to* so] much as to his weddinge [though *deleted* >and *deleted*] wth out other condition then to be present at ye Triumphall feast.

****

[*marginal note against asterisks:* Consules vocari consuerunt inuitauit; ne scilicet venires][44] He remembers that ye nobility denyed to him, the contribution wch in his fathers time they gaue vnto you.[45] Besides, he accuseth you, and affirmes that yor misery hath proceeded from yor owne obstinacy. He made it lately capitall, to disclose the troubles of ye kingdome to forrayners.[46] fearinge least you should know the exulcerated mindes of the nobility, and haue your nayles in ye scabbe.

---

[40] 'What the shoulders can carry, and what they are unable to carry' (adapted from Horace, *Ars poetica*, XI, ll. 39–40: 'quid ferre recusent, | quid valeant humeri').

[41] Charles I. Hobbes (or his manuscript copy) omits the word 'Bello': 'You cannot be restored by war by your brother-in-law'.

[42] Following this sentence, the Latin has a sentence omitted by Hobbes (or by his manuscript copy): 'Ira tua improvida, dictis odia aspera movit', 'Your improvident anger provoked fierce hatreds by what it said.'

[43] Whether James I gave any such instruction to his son is not known; but in October 1623, when Frederick and Elizabeth wanted to go to England to attend the formal reception of Charles after his return from Spain, James did refuse permission (see Pursell, *Winter King*, p. 206).

Prima operosior est consultatio, multa non potes, quae posse tibi videris. Altera strictior. Pauca enim potes. Prima sapientis cura est despicere

Quid possint humeri, quid ferre recusent.

stulti inrita conati, vires, quas in profutura verti oportuit, in ventos effundunt. Hoc cavere te velim. Abstine inutili labore, ut profecturo sufficias. Sed ad orbitam.

V.

Bello per affinem restitui non potes. Non vult tui causâ. Invisus es aemulo, exosus formidanti: odiorum nec causae, nec effecta in occulto, verba tua & tuorum, literasque in Patrem asperas, in se contumeliosas, altâ mente reposuit. Ira tua improvida, dictis odia aspera movit. Regno te Socer arcuit, & moriens filium ne admitteret, obtestatus est. Ille ne ad nuptialia quidem sacra sororem admisit, nec aliâ conditione, quàm ad triumphale epulum.

Consules vocari consuêrunt, invitavit; ne scilicet venires. Meminit nuper sibi à Proceribus negatam tibi decretam vivo Patre pecuniam, Puritanorum in te amorem suspectat. Ultrò te accusat, tuâ te pertinaciâ miserum esse pronunciat. Poenâ capitis nuper sanxit, ne regni turbae foras efferrentur, timet, ne exulceratos Procerum animos cognoscas, & illo sis unguis in ulcere. Incautè tu Buchingami secreta Gallis credidisti. Carolus etiam album pulverem de tua pyxide metuit. Procerum animi discordes, Puritani te opum Ecclesiasticarum pactione Regem

---

[44] The meaning of this sentence would appear to be 'It has been the custom to invite the consuls, and he invited them, no doubt to stop you from coming'. Hobbes's uncertainty presumably arose over the term 'consules' (literally, 'consuls'); he was probably not aware that in Germany and the Netherlands 'consul' was used to refer to a member of a town council (see A. Blaise, *Lexicon latinitatis medii aevi* (Turnhout, 1975), p. 242; J. F. Niedermeyer, *Mediae latinitatis lexicon minus* (Leiden, 1984), p. 261). The claim made here was thus that Charles had invited municipal officials to the wedding feast because he knew that the Elector Palatine would think it beneath his dignity to socialize with them.

[45] Hobbes (or his manuscript copy) omits the phrase 'Puritanorum in te amorem suspectat', 'he is suspicious of the Puritans' love for you'.

[46] This probably refers to Charles's proclamation of 16 [/26] June 1626, 'prohibiting the publishing, dispersing and reading of a Declaration or Remonstrance, drawn by some Committees of the Commons-house': see Larkin and Hughes, eds., *Stuart Royal Proclamations*, ii, pp. 93–5. In this proclamation the King said nothing about capital punishment, but declared that all copies of the remonstrance must be burnt 'upon paine of His indignation and high Displeasure' (p. 94).

you vnaduisedly discouered the secrets of Buckingham to ye French. Charles is afrayd also of y^e *White powder* out of yor Box.[47] The Lords agree not. The Puritanes ayme at you for their Kinge, wth condition to haue the Churches goods. They say the issue royall, the daughter and Nephewes of Kinge James ought to be brought into the kingdome, and Charles to be kept in order by the presence of so many heyres.[48] But now most of them haue altered their mindes and are offended wth you, because they thinke you frend to Buckingham.[49] They suspect that by a royall match for his daughter, he aspires to [a *deleted*] heigth, and would proue an implacable reuenger. Therefore you haue a wolfe by ye eares. If you ioyne with Buckingham, you offend the nobility, who will deny to giue you subsidyes, and w^thout [their *deleted* > the] strength of them ye kinge is weake. If you put Buckingam of, you exasperate the kinge, in whose hands it is to be reuenged not onely wth ease, but also wth profit, by giuinge you nothinge. The Danish Amb.^r shewed vnto ye kinge of Brittany the minde of ye Confederates. That [one mans *deleted* > his] loue to one man hindred him of mony.[50] you know ye instruction. Certaynely he would not haue you flourish least you should inveagle his nobility. He remembers that your sonne about six yeres since at Prague

[75r]　tooke vpon him the Diademe in sport,[51] as in expectation of his death, and that you loue nothinge in him so much as sicknesse, nor hope for any thinge more then his death.

6

He cannot restore you though he would.[52] He is weary of warre. his Kingdome is exhausted, his treasury empty, sauinge towards Norway, that way indeed there is much mony, owinge.[53] The nobility detest warre, cry out for peace, deny and deny againe to giue any mony. The

---

47　See below, n. 252.

48　Hobbes (or his manuscript copy) omits the phrase 'fremunt ista apertiùs, quam ut celari queant', 'they mutter those things so openly that they cannot be hidden'.

49　This is implausible; although Buckingham had become more sympathetic to the Palatine cause after his break with Spain in 1623, the leading proponents of that cause in England were political opponents of Buckingham, and the Elector's agent in London regarded Buckingham as fundamentally hostile (see above, Ch. 5, at n. 18).

50　The Danish Ambassador was Jens Bilde; but this comment probably refers to Johann Zobel, the mayor of Bremen, who was sent by Christian IV as a special envoy to England (arriving at the beginning of June 1626) to demand payment of the moneys that

sibi destinant, stirpem regiam, Iacobi Filiam, & Nepotes in regnum adsciscendos, tot haeredum praesentia Carolum in officio continendum dictitant: fremunt ista apertiùs, quam ut celari queant. At nunc plures eorum mutatis animis tibi sunt infensi, quòd Buchingamo amicum arbitrentur, eum per filiae regias nuptias celsa petere & inexorabilem vindicem fore suspicantur. Lupum itaque auribus tenes. Si Buchingamo jungeris, proceres offendis, qui tibi subsidia negant, sine eorum nervo rex invalidus est. Si Buchingamum abdicas, Regem exasperas, cui in manu est, non modò facilis, sed etiam utilis vindictae modus, si nihil donet. Dani Legatus sociorum mentem Britanno aperuit, Unius amore impediri pecuniam. instructionem nôsti. Certe florere te non vult, ne illicere Proceres valeas: meminit iam ante sex annos filium Pragae ludibrium diadematis suscepisse, expectatione suae mortis, nec esse in se quicquam, quod tu magis ames, quàm invaletudinem, nec quod magis speres, quàm exanimationem.

VI.

Ne potest quidem restituere. Fessus est bello, regnum exhaustum est, aerarium vacuum est, nisi quà Norvvegiam respicit, illâ parte enim aere multo, sed alieno, pressum est. Proceres bellum detestantur, pacem poscunt, aurum abnegant, pernegántque: nobiles negant, Londinenses

were owing. Zobel's reports to Christian placed great emphasis on the problems caused by Buckingham: in his report of 6 [/16] June he said that many patriots hoped Christian would convince Charles that his defence of Buckingham against Parliament was placing both country and Crown in great danger (J. O. Opel, *Der niedersächsisch–dänische Krieg*, 3 vols. (Halle, Magdeburg, 1872–94), ii, p. 512, from a copy of the report in the Royal Archives, Copenhagen). That the author of the *Altera secretissima instructio* knew that this was such a preoccupation of Zobel suggests either that he had well-placed sources of information in London or that some of Zobel's reports were intercepted.

51 In 1620 the Elector Palatine's eldest son, Friedrich Heinrich, was just 6 years old.

52 'Though he would' is Hobbes's addition; a literal translation would be 'Nor, indeed, is he able to restore you'.

53 Norway here stands metonymically for the kingdom of Denmark (of which it was part). Under the Hague accord of 9 December 1625, Charles I was committed to paying the King of Denmark £30,000 per month (E. Weiss, *Die Unterstützung Friedrichs V. von der Pfalz durch Jakob I. und Karl I. von England im Dreissigjährigen Krieg (1618–1632)* (Stuttgart, 1966), p. 89). This was in addition to previous commitments, some still unfulfilled: by May 1626 he owed Christian IV £240,000 (see Pursell, *Winter King*, p. 240).

Lords deny,[54] the Londoners sweare they haue it not, and would be rid of the importunity wth giuinge 20000 pound.[55] At home, there is feare of themselues, disagreement wth ye kinge, and disposinge of Garrisons. Ireland they haue much adoe to keepe wth an army.[56] The Dane calles for Aide, so does the Hollander.[57] Trade fayles. The outpartes of ye kingdome are rifled, ye inpartes pilled. Their ships are intercepted,[58] The Low Contries vnquiet. The Spanish Fleet in readinesse. Auster and Zephirus threaten a storme[59] All their mony is not sufficient, for ye Danish interest,[60] and necessaries of the Kinges house. The Kings household want meate,[61] and are lessened,[62] Nor can ye Kinge compell the Queene to let her Dowry be spent vpon ye Danish warre, vnlesse he meane to go to law wth her.[63] The French are offended;[64] the Confederates[65] alienated. To all this, Ireland is doubtfull,

[54] This emphasis on the nobility and the Lords is puzzling; in the 1626 parliament, resistance to requests for supply came primarily from the Commons.

[55] In June 1626 Charles I demanded a loan of £100,000 from the City of London, on the security of the Crown jewels; the City refused, but after strong pressure from the King the Aldermen agreed (on 29 June [/9 July]) to advance personally the sum of £20,000 (BL, MS Add. 27962D, fos. 207r, 210r; [Birch, ed.,] *Court and Times of Charles I*, i, p. 116; S. R. Gardiner, *History of England from the Accession of James I to the Outbreak of the Civil War*, 10 vols. (London, 1884), vi, p. 124).

[56] Amid fears of a Spanish invasion of Ireland (see below, n. 59), efforts had been made to increase the military forces there, where the small standing army suffered from poor provision, arrears of pay, and low morale. A plan to raise Irish 'trained bands' on the English model was agreed in England in 1625, but abandoned in early 1626 at the request of the Lord Deputy and Council of Ireland, who thought that military formations of Irish Catholics could not be trusted. Soldiers returning from the abortive expedition to Cadiz (see above, n. 17) were diverted to Ireland, but there was no money to pay for them. (See *Calendar of the State Papers relating to Ireland . . . 1625–1632*, ed. R. P. Mahaffy (London, 1900), pp. 77, 110, 130, 142; A. Clarke, 'The Army and Politics in Ireland, 1625–30', *Studia hibernica*, 4 (1964), pp. 28–53, esp. pp. 29–37.)

[57] In addition to the payments to Denmark (see above, n. 53), Charles I was also committed to paying the United Provinces £8,900 per month (for the upkeep of four English regiments there) for the same period.

[58] In April 1626 the entire coaling trade from Newcastle to London was halted after several of the ships had been attacked by pirates from Dunkirk. Shipping in the south-west also suffered heavily from attacks by 'Turks' (pirates from the Barbary states of north Africa) (see *Calendar of State Papers, Domestic . . . 1625–1626*, ed. J. Bruce (London, 1858) [hereafter: *CSPD 1625–6*], pp. 302, 310, 319, 322, 337, 341).

[59] Auster is the south wind, Zephirus the west wind; this refers to the threat of an invasion fleet from the south-west, i.e. from Spain. Following the abortive raid on Cadiz (see above, n. 17), there were strong fears in England of an armada from Spain (and from the Spanish Netherlands: hence the reference to the Low Countries in the previous line). Such fears were well grounded: in the period from November 1625 to February 1626 Philip IV's chief minister, Olivares, was planning both an invasion of Ireland (from Spain) and a raid on England (from the Spanish Netherlands) (H. Lonchay

non habere se pejerant, flagitationem vicenis millibus redimere vellent. Domî sibi metuunt, dissident à Rege, praesidia disponunt. Hyberniam Exercitu vix tuentur, poscit opem Danus, Batavúsque, commercia intercidunt, extima regni spoliantur, intima fraudibus expilantur, naves intercipiuntur, Belgium inquietum est, Hispana classis stat in procinctu, Auster & Zephyrus procellam minantur, aurum in fenus Danicum, & Aulae ministeria non sufficit. Familia regia regiè esurit, minuitur. nec cogere quidem Reginam suam poterit, ut dotem eius in Bellum Danicum insumat, nisi vexari lite Uxoriâ malit. Francus offensus est, socij abalienati; inter haec nutat anceps Hybernia, Scotia contumax, Anglia

and J. Cuvelier, eds., *Correspondance de la cour d'Espagne sur les affaires des Pays-Bas au XVIIe siècle*, 6 vols. (Brussels, 1923–37), ii, pp. 232–3, 241, 250 n.; J. H. Elliott, *The Count-Duke of Olivares: The Statesman in an Age of Decline* (New Haven, 1986), pp. 249–50). Several reports of Spanish preparations reached London in April and May 1626, and on 6 [/16] June the Council discussed a report that 200 ships and 40,000 men were being assembled (*CSPD 1625–6*, pp. 304, 313, 323, 334, 337, 348).

[60] 'Interest' is used here in the financial sense ('fenus').

[61] Hobbes (or his manuscript copy) omits the adverb 'regiè': 'the royal household is royally starving'.

[62] On 16 [/26] June 1626 the King ordered the Lord Keeper to scrutinize excessive costs in the accounts of the Royal Household (*CSPD 1625–6*, p. 360). On 7 [/17] July an anonymous letter-writer in London informed Joseph Mead that 'all the tables at court are to be put down, and the courtiers to be put on board-wages . . . They say likewise that the king meaneth to revoke the greatest part of the pensions'; the same writer later reported that on 10 [/20] July the King 'dissolved all the tables at court save four and his own' ([Birch, ed.,] *Court and Times of Charles I*, i, pp. 125, 129).

[63] Henrietta Maria's dowry, of £240,000, was divided into two equal instalments, the first of which was delivered in 1625 (Russell, *Parliaments and English Politics*, pp. 209, 262; Larkin and Hughes, *Stuart Royal Proclamations*, p. 55 n.). On 14 [/24] April 1626 the Tuscan Resident in London, Amerigo Salvetti, reported that the merchant Philip Burlamachi would soon go to France to collect the second half ('which becomes due in May'), and that 'he will be under instruction to send part of it to Germany, to the King of Denmark and to Mansfeld' (BL, MS Add. 27962D, fo. 162r: 'che matura in Maggio'; 'et havrà ordine di provedere di parte d'essa in Alemagna al Re di Danimarca et al Mansfelt'). The suggestion of litigation here seems very improbable; the marriage treaty did not impose any conditions on how the money must be spent (Dumont, *Corps universel diplomatique*, v(2), pp. 476–7), and, even if it had, there was no court in which such conditions could be enforced. Hobbes has perhaps misunderstood the Latin, where 'nisi vexari lite Uxoriâ malit' could simply mean 'unless he wishes to be vexed by a wifely quarrel' (rather than '. . . wifely lawsuit').

[64] Relations between England and France had deteriorated badly in the winter of 1625–6 over two issues: the treatment of English Catholics, and the treatment of Henrietta Maria. The French Ambassador left in anger in March (see H. Haynes, *Henrietta Maria* (London, 1912), pp. 41–6; Russell, *Parliaments and English Politics*, pp. 263–8).

[65] Denmark and the Netherlands.

Scotland stubborne, England greedy of change, and seeketh occasion of innouatinge. The Kinge runneth into ye displeasure of all, *Defendat vetulum Scoti Iouis vt Ganimedem.*[66] To whom let happen the fate of Seianus,[67] and you will dearely buy his frendship. Notwithstandinge all this, haue you yet a hope, that he will carry a mighty army wth difficult passage and a most difficult warre, into ye Palatinate and there endure a long warre against greater forces then his owne, and ouercome them? or that he can fill the Charybdis[68] of ye Danish auarice? He that feares at home, plays no gambols abroad. When London is on fire; will he carry

[75v] water to Heydlebergh? He is nerest to himselfe, and France by offence giuen is too nere him. And what hope haue wee of victory abroade, when the soldier by imprest[69] and coaction, must be compelled to ye armes he hates? He that fights against his will, will run away of his owne accord.

7

The French kinge will not restore you.[70] He wishes a stoppe to ye power of Spayne, but no encrease to yours. He will walke to his ends another way. He promised wordes and Amb:^rs on yor behalfe but not armes. He hath promised what is yours, to others, if they league wth him. He takes not to heart your misery. He seekes frends for his own Croune, not a crowne for you. He hath also other reasons. He condemned yor actions. Religion drawes him backe. he holds it a great sinne to warre against his bloud, [his sister and his sisters daughter *deleted*].[71] The Grison and Genoa warres[72] he hates, he [wayghes *deleted* > weighes] the hurt it did him, He sought the Peace. He sayes he will not offend the Pope or Popes frends; he feares excommunication. The effectes of it, ye Rebellion of his Princes he abhorres. He neuer thought it reason to

---

[66] 'Even though he defends the Scottish king's favourite [*sc.* Buckingham, favourite of James I] as if he were Jove's Ganymede.' The use of 'vetulus' ('little old man') for 'favourite' here is idiosyncratic.

[67] Sejanus, the scheming favourite of Tiberius, was eventually abandoned by his master, accused before the senate, and summarily executed. Sir John Eliot had caused a scandal when he compared Buckingham to Sejanus in his speech of 10 [/20] May 1626 (J. Forster, *Sir John Eliot: A Biography*, 2 vols. (London, 1864), i, pp. 549–50).

[68] Charybdis, a monster in the Straits of Messina, swallowed the sea three times a day (and spewed it up again).

[69] = impressment (*OED*, 'imprest', n.2).

mutationis avida rerum novandarum quaerit occasionem. Rex omnium offensas incurrit,

> *Defendat vetulum, Scoti Iovis ut Ganymedem.*

Cui Seiani fatum obtingat, amicitiam ejus grauiter lues. Inter ista tu speras fore, ut maximum exercitum difficili aditu, difficillimo bello in Palatinatum ducat & contra majores copias diu bellum trahat, vincátque? aut Danicae avaritiae charybdin impleat? Non lascivit foris, cui metus est domî. An ardente Londino, aquas feret Heydelbergam? Proximus ipse sibi est, & nimiùm vicinus ex offensa Francus. Quae verò nobis spes victoriae foris, cùm miles non nisi pressu & coactu ad exosa arma sit compellendus: at qui pugnat, invitus, spontè fugiet.

VII.

Non reducet bello te Francus. Cursum Hispanae potentiae sisti ille exoptat, non augeri tuam: propositum suum aliâ tentabit viâ. Verba & Legatos pro tua causa, non arma pactus est. Alijs tua pollicitus est, si sibi foederari velint, non est illi cordi miseria tua. Coronae amicos quaerit suae, non tibi Coronam. Habet & alias causas. Nam acta tua damnavit: religione retrahitur. Affinem proritare periculosum ducit, Sorori & Sororis Filiae bellum consanguineum inferre, nefas judicat. Arma Rhetica & Ligustica abominatur. Damna animo pensat, Pacem petijt. Papam & Papae amicos offendere se velle pernegat. Excommunicationem metuit: eius effectus, id est, rebellionem Principum horret. Nunquam unius exulis amicitiam omnium vicinorum paci putavit anteponendam. Habet

---

[70] Hobbes (or his manuscript copy) omits the word 'bello': 'The French king will not restore you by war'.

[71] The Latin has 'Affinem proritare periculosum ducit, Sorori & Sororis Filiae bellum consanguineum inferre, nefas judicat': 'He thinks it dangerous to provoke his brother-in-law, and he holds it a sin to wage consanguineous war against his sister and his sister's daughter'. Philip IV of Spain was Louis XIII's brother-in-law (Louis had married Philip's sister, Anne); Philip had married Louis's sister Elizabeth, and had had three daughters by her by 1626. The most likely explanation of Hobbes's decision to delete the phrase about the sister and her daughter (and to omit the reference to the brother-in-law) is that he assumed that these references were to Charles I and Henrietta Maria; since they had no daughter, and since support for the Elector Palatine would not have involved warring against them, the references would have seemed highly puzzling.

[72] See above, nn. 13, 14.

preferre the frendship of one man and [him *deleted* > him] banished,
before the Peace of all his neighbours. He hath yor enemyes in his
counsell, and in his chamber. The best of ye French Counsailo^{r}s said
playnely, that a monethes warre in Germany did more hurt to France
then three Palatinates were worth. Hence it is, that ye Danish Amb:^{r}
was sent away wth the somme of 50000 frankes[73] rather mocked then
ayded, and beinge angry said in contumely *That the lightnesse* of France
was heauy to Denmarke. Nothinge was giuen to ye Hollanders, but new
conditions put to them, and amendes threatened to be required of them
for betrayinge ye Victory at Rochell.[74] The greatest of his Princes and
his Brother are displeased, some feare discharginge, some his anger, all
fear Richelieu.[75] When there are many frends, and but one enemy, yet
is there no security. But there,[76] there be many enemyes and scarce
one frend.

8.

It is neuer safe to trust to French Papistes. Made they not peace wthout
[76r]   ye knowledge of their allies?[77] yet in that league consisted your safety
and ye growth and glory of all the confederate Kinges. Wee cannot but
remember ye Endeauo^r and labo^r of his Amb:^{r} at ye Hague how he
labo^{r}ed that ye States[78] might not make a Peace wth ye Spaniard. The

[73] In January 1626 Christian IV sent his special envoy Lorenz Wensin first to The
Hague and then to Paris. Richelieu had promised (on 1 January) that France would
give Christian 200,000 livres; but Wensin was given only a promissory note (subject to
further delay) for 150,000 livres. (The Latin text here gives only the figure of 50,000,
not specifying a unit of account; evidently the unit meant here was the écu, which
was equal to three livres.) On his return journey to Christian, Wensin was captured
by agents of the Spanish Netherlands and all his papers were confiscated (Opel, *Der
niedersächsisch–dänische Krieg*, ii, pp. 496, 502–3; Echevarria Bacigalupe, *La diplomacia
secreta*, pp. 56–7). The news that Louis XIII had promised Christian 50,000 écus
for the maintenance of his fleet was in circulation by April 1626 (see B. de Meester,
ed., *Correspondance du nonce Giovanni-Francesco Guidi di Bagno (1621–1627)*, 2 vols.
(Brussels, 1938), ii, p. 736; cf. Roe, *Negotiations*, p. 507).
[74] During the Huguenot rebellion in 1625, when the rebel forces under the duc de
Soubise had achieved naval supremacy on the French Atlantic coast, Richelieu invoked
the Franco-Dutch treaty of 1624 to require the United Provinces to loan ships to France.
A squadron of 20 Dutch vessels under Admiral Haultain van Zoete took part in the
French operation against La Rochelle in September, but in December the States-General

in Consilio & cubiculo hostes tuos, optimus Consiliariorum Gallicorum disertè dixit: Bello Germanico plus damni facturam uno mense Galliam, quàm valeant tres Palatinatus. Hinc Dani Legatus summa 50000. m irrisus magis, quàm adjutus abscessit, & quidem iratus: contumeliosè etiam prolocutus, *Leuitate Gallicâ gravari Daniam.* Batavis nil datum, conditiones novae positae, & jactatae de prodita Rupellana victoria repetundae. Nulla illi causa est tui juvandi, multae deserendi, Principum potentissimi & frater offensus, alij timent exauctorationem, alij offensum, omnes Richelium. Ubi multi amici, unus inimicus, nulla est securitas; at illa in turba multi hostes, vix unus amicus.

VIII.

Nunquam tutum est credere Gallis Papistis. Nonne socijs inscijs pacem fecerunt? Et eo foedere nitebatur tua salus, & sociorum Regum incrementa ac gloria. Non possumus non recordari Legati ejus, Hagae studium & labores, quibus contendebat, ne Status praepotentes pacem cum Ibero inirent: Regis literae omnibus obtrudebantur, etiam

asked for its recall, and the admiral withdrew his force at the beginning of February 1626, a few days before the end of hostilities. Later that month Richelieu addressed a memorandum to Louis XIII, urging him to make much of this 'injure', and to use it to demand further heavy concessions from the Dutch (Richelieu, *Mémoires*, ed. J. Lair et al., 10 vols. (Paris, 1909–31), v, pp. 163–8; [Richelieu,] *Les Papiers de Richelieu: section politique intérieure, correspondance et papiers d'état*, i (1624–1626), ed. P. Grillon (Paris, 1975), pp. 295–7). Hobbes (or his manuscript copy) also omits here the sentence 'Nulla illi causa est tui juvandi, multae deserendi', 'There is no reason why he should help you, and there are many reasons why he should desert you.'

[75] Armand Jean du Plessis, Cardinal Richelieu (1585–1642), chief minister in France since 1624.

[76] Hobbes's 'there' is used for 'illa in turba', 'in that crowd'.

[77] France and Spain made peace, with the Treaty of Monzón, in March 1626. This treaty, which caused huge resentment among the anti-Habsburg powers, was partly disavowed by Richelieu at first, and was not publicly acknowledged until mid-June (see R. Rodenas Vilar, *La política europea de España durante la guerra de treinta años (1624–1630)* (Madrid, 1967), p. 68; A. D. Lublinskaya, *French Absolutism: The Crucial Phase, 1620–1629*, tr. B. Pearce (Cambridge, 1968), pp. 278–81).

[78] Hobbes's 'States' here translates 'Status praepotentes'; 'praepotentes' ('very powerful') is a Latin version of the standard title of the States-General of the United Provinces (see below, n. 114).

kinges letters were thrust vpon euery man, nay mony was brought[79]
[to? *deleted*], but all to that end that the French might haue time to
make their owne Peace, that they might sette their owne affayres in a
safe point, and deriue the extremity of danger vpon the Hollanders, and
boast that ye French were craftier then the craftiest. With ye same fraud
they will deale wth you, suddenly leaue you or ruine you. They now ruine
the Grisons, exhaust the Venetians.[80] First they courted Bauiere, and
endeauo^red to put all into his hands.[81] then you, he fed wth promises,
Now he layes hold on Caesar and Spayne, articlinge yor destruction.
I speake nothinge doubtfull and vncertayne, though [I per? *deleted*] I
tremble to speake it. Its knowne from o^r most inward frends, that are
of the K^s Counsayle,[82] Its knowne both by eye and eare witnesses, I
haue letters in my hand to shew it, That the French Amb:^r not once
or twice, but often and wth much vehemence of speech[83] dealt wth y^e
Count of Oliuares,[84] and wth others for a marriage to be had betweene
ye brother of ye most Christian Kinge[85] and ye daughter of the Emp.^r
and the dowry to be your Prouince and dignity.[86] And that ye Emp.^r
might not stand longe vpon it, this horrible condition was added, that
the French kinge with his whole strength both by sea and land should
ayd ye Emp.^r in the totall pullinge downe of the Palatine. These are the
very wordes. This are they doinge in Spayne. And because they say [yor
deleted] you are at ye lowest already, they are contriuinge to ouerthrow

---

[79]   During the first half of 1625 the French Ambassador at The Hague, Charles Faye
d'Espesses or d'Espeisses (d. 1638), had worked hard to encourage the plan to send
Mansfeld's army to help relieve the siege of Breda; in July he was authorized to promise
that France would pay 500,000 livres in support of Mansfeld's force. In September
Richelieu sent a message to d'Espesses, saying that he should try to stop the Dutch
authorities from making a truce with Spain, and telling him to deliver the 500,000
livres to them. But this message was intercepted and brought to the Infanta in Brussels;
possibly this was the source of the author's information here. (See A. C. Hennequin
de Villermont, *Ernest de Mansfeldt*, 2 vols. (Brussels, 1865–6), ii, pp. 293–4, 310,
317, 321.)

[80]   By signing the Treaty of Monzón (above, n. 77), France settled the issue of
the Valtelline without consulting or even informing its three key allies in the region,
the Grisons (nominal sovereigns over the Valtelline), Venice, and Savoy; all were now
exposed, potentially, to Habsburg retaliation.

[81]   In 1621 France had been keen to support Bavaria as a counterweight to the
Habsburgs, and in 1623 the French Resident in Regensburg had promoted the plan
to transfer the Palatine Electorate to Maximilian of Bavaria; because of this issue,
Maximilian had actively sought a diplomatic *rapprochement* with France during 1623
(see Albrecht, *Die auswärtige Politik*, pp. 87, 93–101). Hobbes's translation omits the
word 'tua': 'illi omnia tradere tua conati', 'endeavoured to put all of your possessions

pecuniae afferebantur; sed omnia eâ mente, ut Francis spacium esset
conficiendae pacis, ut sua ipsi in tuto collocarent, extrema pericu-
lorum in Batavos derivarent: vt jactent versutissimis versutiores esse
Gallos. Eâdem te fraude petunt, inopinatò deserent, aut depriment.
Iam Grisones opprimunt, Venetos exhauriunt. Primò Bojum coluêre,
illi omnia tradere tua conati, deinde te promissis lactarunt; Nunc
Caesarem, Iberúmque prensant, tuum exitium pacti: non dubia aut in-
explorata loquor, quanquam horret animus. Constat ex intimis nostris,
quia regia consilia communicant: constant ex oculatis, auritísque testi-
bus; in manu sunt literarum documenta: Oratorem Francum non semel
iterúmve, sed crebris vicibus magnâ animi orationísque contentione,
apud Comitem Olivarium, aliósque egisse, ut inter Fratrem Regis Chris-
tianissimi, Caesarísque filiam nuptias conciliarent: in dotem cederet tua
dignitas, prouinciâque: Ne verò Caesar cunctaretur, horrenda adiuncta
est conditio: Fore ut Francus summis terrâque maríque viribus, Caesari
auxiliaretur, AD TOTALEM *Palatini* DEPRESSIONEM; haec ipsa verba sunt,
haec in Hispania moliuntur. Quia verò te in ima pressum aiunt, eos qui
sublevare te conantur, Anglum & Danum etiam diruere machinantur,
& tibi superinijcere, ne tantis ruinis erigendis ulla par sit in Europa

into his hands'. But the French policy concerned only the Electorate (i.e. the dignity and
electoral powers within the constitution of the Holy Roman Empire), not the territorial
possessions.

[82] In the Latin this clause is 'quia regia consilia communicant', 'because they are
partakers of the king's counsels [*sc.* deliberations, plans]'; Hobbes (or his manuscript
copy) may have emended 'quia' to 'qui' ('who').

[83] 'Of speech' here abbreviates the phrase 'animi orationísque', 'of mind and of
speech'.

[84] Gaspar de Guzmán y Pimentel, Count of Olivares and Duke of San Lúcar
(1587–1645), chief minister in Spain.

[85] 'Rex christianissimus', 'le roi très-chrétien', was the traditional soubriquet of the
King of France; Louis XIII's brother was Gaston, duc d'Anjou (elevated to the dukedom
of Orléans in August 1626).

[86] The French Ambassador in Spain was Charles d'Angennes, comte du Fargis. There
seems to be no documentary evidence of any such proposals by du Fargis for a marriage,
nor for any such pledge of the Palatinate as a dowry. Richelieu's policy, as set out in his
major memorandum on foreign policy in April 1626, was to restore to German princes
(including the Elector Palatine) the territories they had previously possessed ([Richelieu,]
*Les Papiers de Richelieu: section politique extérieure, correspondance et papiers d'état, Empire
allemand,* i (1616–1629), ed. A. Wild (Paris, 1982), p. 142). And where the marriage
of Gaston was concerned, Richelieu was pressing in the first half of 1626 for a marriage
to Marie de Bourbon, duchesse de Montpensier (which was duly effected on 6 August)
(see G. Dethan, *Gaston d'Orléans: conspirateur et prince charmant* (Paris, 1959), p. 63; A.
Levi, *Cardinal Richelieu and the Making of France* (London, 2000), pp. 96–7, 101).

the English and Dane, that endeauo^r to relieue you, and to tumble
them vpon you, that no power in Europe may be able to rayse againe
so great a ruine. Hence it is that ye Amb:^{rs} of Hessen were deluded,[87]
& Durlach dismissed wth Contumely.[88] Hence it is that that crafty
long-beard said, that also ye French had learned to go a woing for
kingdomes.[89] Count Maurice[90] aduised often, that French ayd was
to be vsed, but theyr fayth not to be trusted to. The Great League
rested vpon the lilies, but they haue pulled away their headles; and
when one hath most neede of them they turne enemyes. Looke what a
horrible sentence is here. Giue me the Palatinate and I will vtterly pull
[76v]   downe the Palatine. Nay whosoeuer stands vp for ye Palatine must be
layd Flatte.

9

But what may be the cause of so great a change? where are his promises?
Neuer aske. the great cause, cause of causes, *Reason of State*. Theres
danger wth you, wealth with the Spaniard. Besides, there are many
particular[91] causes of hatred towards you. He is persuaded that you are
a client of Buckinghams, and a secret enemy of[92] his sister. That you
plotte a diuorce.[93] That you are acquainted with poisoned powders.
That Villers[94] does nothinge without yor priuity. That by yor deuises
the Queene suffers contumely and ye Papists persecution.[95] That you
are the darlinge of ye Hugonots, and priuy to all their secrets. That they
prayse you openly. That if ye kingdome of Britanny fall to you, you

[87]   In early 1626, when Landgrave Moriz of Hessen-Kassel was appealing to Louis XIII
for help (see below, n. 262), the letter he wrote to Louis was taken to Paris by two of his
counsellors. He also had an agent in Paris, Johann Hotomann (C. von Rommel, *Neuere
Geschichte von Hessen*, 3 vols. (Kassel, 1835–9), iii, pp. 621–2). The two counsellors
were kept waiting for an answer for several months; the answer was negative, and they
were sent away in early June with a gift of 4,000 thalers, which barely covered the
expenses of their stay (K. Obser, 'Markgraf Georg Friedrich von Baden-Durlach und
das Projekt einer Diversion am Oberrhein in den Jahren 1623–1627', *Zeitschrift für die
Geschichte des Oberrheins*, NS 5 (1890), pp. 212–42, 320–99; here p. 336).
[88]   In January 1626 Margrave Georg Friedrich of Baden-Durlach (see above, n. 9)
sent his counsellor Tobias von Ponikau to Paris to seek financial and political support
for his plan to raise an army in Switzerland and mount an attack on the territories of
the upper Rhineland, which were garrisoned (rather thinly) by Imperial forces. Although
Richelieu did at one stage seriously consider the use of Baden-Durlach's services (see his
memorandum to Louis XIII of February 1626 in *Papiers de Richelieu*, ed. Grillon, p. 298),

potestas. Hinc illusi Hassorum Legati, hinc cum contumelia dimissus Durlacensis. Hinc callidus ille Barbatus. Didicisse etiam Gallos regna procari. Monuit saepe Mauritius Gallicâ ope utendum, non fidendum fidei. Liga magna super lilia requievit, illa subduxêre caput, & cum maximè egemus eorum operâ, inimica sunt, vide atrociam sententiam. Da mihi Palatinatum, & Palatinum TOTALITER deprimam. Imò quisquis pro Palatino stat, sternendus est.

IX.

Quae causa tantae mutationis? ubi nunc promissa? Ne quaere; causa suprema, causa causarum, RATIO STATUS: Tecum est periculum, cum Hispano opes. Verùm multae sunt odiorum, contra te causae privatim, Buchingami te clientem esse, sororis suae adversarium & insidiatorem persuasus est. Te divortium machinari, pulveres medicatos nôsse. Te inscio nihil ausum Villerium. Tuis artibus Reginae contumelias; Papistis exitium inferri. Te Hugonottis carissimum, cum illis tibi omnium secretorum esse conscientiam. Te ab illis publicè laudari. Tibi si Regnum Britanniae obtingat, Regem etiam Rupellis fore, à nullo sibi maius esse periculum. Dicta, scripta, artes tuae & tuorum ab anno 1619. releguntur,

---

von Ponikau was fobbed off repeatedly, and finally left the French court empty-handed in early June (see Obser, 'Markgraf Georg Friedrich', pp. 332–8).

[89] Hobbes (or his manuscript copy) has emended the Latin here, which in the printed text has a full stop after 'Barbatus' ('long-beard').

[90] The Latin has only 'Mauritius'; 'Count' is Hobbes's addition. The reference is to Maurits, Count of Nassau and Prince of Orange (1567–1625).

[91] 'Particular' here ('privatim') means private or personal.

[92] 'A secret enemy of' here stands for 'adversarium & insidiatorem', 'an enemy of, and plotter against'.

[93] Buckingham's abrasive treatment of Henrietta Maria was notorious, and was a matter of concern to Richelieu (see Richelieu, *Mémoires*, v, pp. 143–4, 148). 'Divorce' here means, presumably, a divorce between her and Charles I—which, since there were as yet no children of the marriage, would have safeguarded the place of the Elector Palatine's children in the succession to the throne.

[94] George Villiers, Duke of Buckingham.

[95] See above, nn. 64, 93. The 'persecution' of Catholics was effected by two royal proclamations, one (at Parliament's request) in August 1625, for 'putting the Lawes against Jesuites and Popish Priests in execution', and the other in January 1626, 'for the better Confining of Popish Recusants' (enforcing a statute of 3 James I, ordering recusants to stay within five miles of their places of abode) (Larkin and Hughes, eds., *Stuart Royal Proclamations*, ii, pp. 52–4, 75–7).

will be Kinge of Rochell too.[96] That no man is more dangerous to him then you. The wordes, writinges, and artes of you and yours, since the yere 1619. are read ouer againe, and all that is odious suggested,[97] and in a manner all is of that nature. Old grudges are not yet forgotten, the actes of Lodowicke, Casimire, and others[98] are repeated.[99] *Funeraque et Lacrymae miserique incendia regni.*[100] and for so many defeates, the Jewells of the Kings house carried in triumph to Heidelbergh.[101] That golden statesman,[102] shewed to ye kinge lately, that his infancy, and beginninge of his reigne was vexed wth ye armes of ye Palatine. and that Bassompier the Scorne of Nations was furnished against him vnderhand at Heidelbergh.[103] That notorious Counsayle was giuen the Hugonots, Bouillon armed, and after his prankes[104] played, defended.[105] And now the attempts of his bretheren also, and the flyinge out of his princes[106] are ascribed to you wth ye English and Sauoyards. And wch is worst of all, they haue now a better fayth in y^e [Spaniards *corrected to* Spaniard] He is a faithfull appeacher[107] of ye traytors, wee their complices. But say he would, how can he? So many mischiefes there are at home. No man of power faithfull to the kinge. towards his brothers emulation or crimination, towards others diffidence. It is the fate of that crowne to

96 'Britanny' here (as elsewhere) means Britain. The fortified city of La Rochelle was the most important power-base of the Huguenots in western France; it had been the centre of rebellions in 1620–2 and 1625–6.

97 'Suggested' here ('suggeruntur') means 'brought to mind'.

98 Armies had been sent from the Palatinate to support Huguenots against the French crown in 1568 (during the reign of the Elector Frederick III), 1576 (during the reign of Ludwig VI), and 1587 (during the regency of John Casimir); the Palatinate had also financed the sending of other troops to the Huguenots in 1569, 1589, and 1591 (see C.-P. Clasen, *The Palatinate in European History, 1555–1618*, 2nd edn. (Oxford, 1966), p. 5).

99 'Are repeated' here ('recensentur') means 'are reviewed'.

100 'Deaths and tears and the burning down of a miserable kingdom.'

101 'Jewells' here translates 'cimelia', which could mean 'treasures' more generally. Henri IV of France had borrowed large sums of money from the rulers of the Palatinate; by 1603 the debt was calculated at 858,404 livres. A repayment of 50,000 livres was made in that year (see L. Anquez, *Henri IV et l'Allemagne d'après les mémoires et la correspondance de Jacques Bongars* (Paris, 1887), pp. 55–6, 58). Possibly this comment refers to some repayment in the form of jewels, plate, or other objects.

102 Meaning, presumably, Richelieu.

103 The meaning here is obscure. Hobbes's translation makes some grammatical sense of the Latin, but he has either emended the punctuation of the printed text (omitting the comma in 'Gentium, contemptum') or worked from a differently punctuated manuscript copy. (I am grateful to Dr J. N. Adams for pointing out that Hobbes's translation also requires a genitive construction with 'contemptum' which is incorrect by the standards of classical Latin.) If, as the printed punctuation suggests, 'adiutum,

quae odiosa sunt suggeruntur, sunt autem penè omnia nigra. Necdum vetera exciderunt; Ludovici, Casimiri, aliorum facta recensentur

Funeráque & Lachrymae, miseríque incendia regni,

& pro tot cladibus Heidelbergam ducta in triumphum Regiae cimelia. Nuper Regi ostendit Polites ille aureus, pueritiam eius & regni primordia Palatinis armis exercita, adiutum, subornatúmque Gentium, contemptum Heidelbergae Passompirium, data consilia Hugonottis atrocia, Bullionium armatum, & post facinora defensum. Nunc verò etiam Fratrum conatus, secessio Principum tibi, Britannis, Allobrogibus imputatur; quod omnibus malis maius est, maior iam fides Hispano; ille proditorum fidus Index habet, nos conscij. Sed fac Velle, quî pote? Tot mala domestica, nemo fidus Regi, qui potens. Fratrum aut aemulatio, aut crimina, aliorum diffidentia. Hoc fatum illius coronae est, agitari, in se collidi, ministros crebrò mutare, rarò meliores substituere, semper esse qui supra, qui contra Regem se efferant.

---

subornatúmque Gentium' was a separate clause, then it looks as if a noun has gone missing from it—perhaps 'motum', 'rebellion'. (The correct translation would then be: 'that the rebellion of the Heathen [*sc.* the Protestants] was aided and equipped; that de Bassompierre was scorned at Heidelberg . . .'.) In his youth François de Bassompierre (1579–1646), military commander and diplomat, briefly visited the Elector Frederick IV at Heidelberg in 1595 (F. de Bassompierre, *Journal de ma vie*, ed. M. J. A. de La Cropte, marquis de Chantérac, 4 vols. (Paris, 1870–7), i, p. 43). Other contacts between him and Heidelberg are not known.

[104] 'Prankes' translates 'facinora' ('crimes'). Cf. *OED*, 'prank', n.2a: 'In early use . . . a deed of wickedness, sometimes rendering Latin *scelus* or *facinus*'.

[105] Henri de la Tour, duc de Bouillon, Prince of Sedan, was a Protestant and an uncle of Frederick V. He had been actively involved, or implicated, in many Huguenot revolts in France, including the major revolt of 1620–2. In the summer of 1622 Frederick had stayed with him in Sedan, and had been joined there by the remnants of Mansfeld's and Braunschweig's armies; Louis XIII then accused Frederick of trying to stir up the Huguenots (see Pursell, *Winter King*, p. 182).

[106] On 6 May 1626 the maréchal d'Ornano, former tutor of Louis XIII's brother Gaston, was arrested on suspicion of plotting against Louis XIII and Richelieu. The Venetian Ambassador reported on 12 May that those suspected of involvement in the conspiracy included Gaston, the prince de Condé, the comte de Soissons, the ducs de Guise and d'Épernon, and the two brothers Vendôme (César, duc de Vendôme, and Alexandre, chevalier de Vendôme, who were illegitimate sons of Henri IV and thus half-brothers of Louis XIII) (N. Barozzi and G. Berchet, eds., *Relazioni degli stati europei lette al Senato dagli ambasciatori veneti nel secolo decimosetto*, ser. 2, vol. ii (Venice, 1859), p. 204). The brothers Vendôme were arrested on 13 June (de Bassompierre, *Journal*, iii, p. 249).

[107] 'Appeacher' means one who informs against a person; this is an accurate translation of 'Index' here.

be turmoyled, and iumbled together. Often to change the ministers of
[77r] state, seldome to put in better. Still to haue some or other to stand
vp¹⁰⁸ aboue or against the kinge. *In tot populis vix vna fides.*¹⁰⁹ Nor is he
a Match for Spayne, and if he were, yet against an equall, the Victory
will be doubtfull. I will not¹¹⁰ grieue you wᵗʰ an vnpleasinge verse but
admonish you. *Bellet et immensâ obluctetur Francus opum vî, Durius
Hispano ferrum est, patientior astus. Flexanimumque aurum,*¹¹¹ so much,
as will serue yᵉ Spaniard to buy as many French men as will suffice
to deliuer the Kingdome into his hands. I thinke there will grow very
great frendship betweene these two Kinges. The K. of Spayne when the
Hugonots sought his ayde, and of their owne accord offered him their
hauens, not onely reiected, but disclosed it.¹¹² And deserues though
our enemy, for refusinge of so profitable a treason, the commendation
of a good Brother in Law. From hence therefore, there is no hope.
Especially when they suspect the originall of yᵉ troubles in his kingdome
disaffection of his Princes, and discord wᵗʰ his Bretheren [>to] proceed
from yᵉ Hollanders, Sauoy, and from you sir. Why shall I trust him
that loues yᵉ Pope? and that hath euery thinge suggested to him by
yᵉ Cardinall?¹¹³ Do you thinke the Cardinall, who by yoʳ destruction,
may get wealth and glory certayne, wᵗʰ the [Spaniard *deleted*] Papists,
had rather take your cause in hand wᵗʰ danger and dishonoʳ? Beleeue
me, all that plot, of yoʳ *totall pullinge* downe, was yᵉ Cardinalles worke,
who seeketh that glory now in your fall, wᶜʰ he could not atteyne in
yoʳ prosperity.

10

The high and mighty states¹¹⁴ of yᵉ Low Contries will not restore you.
the name of an exile lying on their hands is cheape amongst them.
it is a burdensome thinge. And therefore was it also that of late they

---

¹⁰⁸ 'Stand vp' here translates 'se efferant', 'raise themselves up', 'exalt themselves'.

¹⁰⁹ 'In so many nations, scarcely one person is faithful' (Seneca, *Hercules oetaeus*, I, l. 608).

¹¹⁰ Meaning, 'I do not want to'.

¹¹¹ 'Even if France goes to war, and devotes vast resources to its struggle, nevertheless Spain's weapons are stronger, and its cunning is more patient. And gold is what sways people's minds.'

¹¹² It is not known what the source of this claim may have been. Contemporaries thought the opposite: the Venetian Ambassador in France reported in January 1625

In tot populis vix una fides.

Nec par Hispano, & si par esset, dubia tamen esset contra parem victoria. Invidioso carmine te gravare nolo, sed monere.

Bellet & immensa obluctetur Francus opum vî,
Durius Hispano ferrum est, patientior astus.
Flexanimúmque aurum;

quo tot Gallos emere potest Iber, quot regno tradendo sufficiunt. Ego magnam inter illos Reges amicitiam fore auguror. Hispanus Hugonottas auxilia precatos, portus ultro offerentes non reiecit tantùm, sed & indicavit. Magnâ affinitatis bene cultae laude, quamvis hostis noster, merito extollendus, qui proditionem tam fructuosam repudiavit. Hinc igitur spes nulla, praesertim cùm turbati regni, alienatorum Principum, discordia Fratrum ab Hollandis, Sabaudo; téque, ô Domine, originem esse suspicetur. Cur igitur illi fidam, cui Papa non displicet? omnia ingerit Cardinalis? an tu existimas Cardinalem, cui ex tua pernicie opes, gloriáque apud Papistas certa petitur, malle cum dedecore, & periculo, tuam agere causam? crede mihi tota illa machina, de tua TOTALI DEPRESSIONE, opus est Cardinalitium, qui nunc ex tua clade gloriam quaerit, quam ex felicitate habere non potuit.

X.

Non restituent te Potentissimi Status Belgici; vile est apud eos nomen perseverantis exulis; res onerosa. Ideo nuper Lusitanum excusserunt. Fastidiunt pauperem, & in sordibus regiae dignitatis imitamenta

---

that Spain was fomenting Huguenot revolts (Barozzi and Berchet, eds., *Relazioni*, ser. 2, ii, p. 192). During the Huguenots' revolt in early 1625 one of their leaders, the duc de Rohan, asked for Spanish help and was visited by an agent of Olivares: 'Secret negotiations began; a junta of theologians . . . gave its blessing; and although Olivares swore to the papal nuncio in July that Madrid had never given the Huguenots a subsidy, all the indications would seem to point the other way' (Elliott, *The Count-Duke of Olivares*, p. 227; for details of Huguenot–Spanish transactions see *Le Mercure françois*, 12, for 1626 (published in 1627), pp. 195–7; L. Anquez, *Un Nouveau Chapitre de l'histoire politique des réformés de France (1621–1626)* (Paris, 1865), pp. 255–6).

[113] Richelieu.
[114] The Latin is 'Potentissimi Status'; Hobbes's translation uses the standard title given to the States-General of the United Provinces, 'high and mighty' ('hoogmogend').

thrust out ye Portugall.[115] They are squeamish at your pouerty, and laugh in their sleeue at the imitation of dignity royall, in beggary.[116] you know ye sharpe speech of ye secretary,[117] your selfe beinge by. *That you were an hono^r to the Hollanders, for there resided amongst them* [77v] *the greatest Begger of Europe.*[118] Now they begin to hate you to boote. For they thinke they may hate you without cost, but your frendship is chargeable. They beleeue it is for yor sake that ye Emp^r would shut vp the Riuers, and take away yor trafficke;[119] and that they suffer for yor proscription. And that now, he is about to haue them declared enemyes of ye Empire. And that the Emp.^r and Kinge of Spayne were neuer so vnited before,[120] That you the common cause, are he, that make those mighty Princes ioyne. That other kinges and Princes though yor kindred, shake of your company. That a most odious outlaw stickes in their contry, like a thorne in their foote. They had rather you would go into England. They haue also a violent [suspicions *corrected to* suspicion] of the Nassouians and Arminians, as though by naturall ambition you aspired to ye Principality.[121] Besides that, they also haue enough to do to[122] struggle wth their owne losses. Their wonted tribute is decreased,

---

115 In 1597 Emilia, daughter of William I of Orange, had married the exiled Portuguese Don Emanuel (son of Antonio, who had claimed the throne of Portugal in 1580); but the House of Orange had never looked kindly on this connection with a penniless Catholic. In late April 1626 Emanuel moved to the Spanish Netherlands, and Emilia left in early June for Geneva. One Venetian report claimed that they left because of offensive treatment by the States-General ('disgusti ricevuti dagli Stati': P. J. Blok, ed., *Relazioni veneziane: veneziaansche berichten over de Vereenigde Nederlanden van 1600–1795* (The Hague, 1909), p. 213). Other contemporary reports said that they had been tempted by the offer of a pension from the Infanta's court (*Le Mercure françois*, 12, for 1626 (published in 1627), p. 658; de Meester, ed., *Correspondance de Guidi di Bagno*, ii, pp. 738, 755). In fact Emanuel had made a secret deal with the Spanish crown, renouncing his claims to the throne of Portugal in return for a large financial settlement (J. L. J. van de Kamp, *Emanuel van Portugal en Emilia van Nassau* (Assen, 1980), pp. 223–30).

116 There was some truth in these comments. Relations between Frederick and the States-General had been particularly poor in the period 1623–4, but had slightly improved thereafter (see N. Mout, 'Der Winterkönig im Exil: Friedrich V. von der Pfalz und die niederländischen Generalstaaten 1621–1632', *Zeitschrift für historische Forschung*, 15 (1988), pp. 257–72, esp. pp. 264–8).

117 This may refer to Constantijn Huygens (1596–1687), who was secretary to the stadhouder, Frederik Hendrik.

118 In the Latin, 'te praesente' (translated by Hobbes as 'your selfe being by') appears as the final part of this reported remark (given in italics). Either Hobbes (or his manuscript copy) has emended the Latin, de-italicizing this phrase and ignoring the full point after 'nôsti', or the manuscript copy has transposed the phrase.

subsannant. Acre Secretarij dictum nósti. *Honori te Batavis esse, apud eos enim residere grandissimum Europae mendicum, te praesente.* Iam etiam odisse incipiunt; Nam odium tui sine sumptu judicant esse, amicitiam constare impendio. Tuâ causâ credunt, Caesarem velle clausa flumina, sublata commercia, luere se tuam Proscriptionem opinantur; jam etiam illud agi; ut hostes Imperij judicentur. ante nunquam ita Caesarem & Hispanum consensisse, nunc te communem hostem potentium sociare mentem, alios Reges, Principésque etiam cognatos tuam praesentiam excutere; odiosissimum exulem velut spinam suae Patriae infigi; mallent in Britanniam te migrare. Gliscunt etiam Nassoviorum & Arminianorum violentae suspiciones, quasi insolitâ ambitione Principatum tentaveris. Deinde suis ipsi damnis conflictantur; Tributa solita minuuntur, vix tertia pars superest; crescunt impendia; Regum auxilia

---

119 In the summer of 1625 Spanish troops had closed the Rhine and the Ems to all goods destined for the United Provinces (J. Israel, *The Dutch Republic and the Hispanic World, 1606–1661* (Oxford, 1982), p. 217). But the reference here to the Emperor suggests that the author has in mind the discussions between Spanish, Imperial, and Bavarian representatives in Brussels in June and July 1626, during which it was decided to place garrisons on the rivers Elbe and Weser in order to stop all river traffic destined for Holland (de Meester, ed., *Correspondance de Guidi di Bagno*, ii, p. 744; Lonchay and Cuvelier, eds., *Correspondance de la cour d'Espagne*, ii, pp. 271, 275). This decision was communicated to the two commanders in the field, Tilly and Wallenstein, whose joint reply, on 30 July, included a promise to block the rivers (C. M. von Aretin, *Bayerns auswärtige Verhältnisse seit dem Anfange des sechzehnten Jahrhunderts* (Passau, 1839), appendix 2, pp. 232–4). In Hobbes's translation here, the 'yoʳ' in 'yoʳ trafficke' seems unwarranted: the Latin, 'clausa flumina, sublata commercia', just refers to 'rivers closed, commerce taken away'.

120 In May, June, and July 1626 representatives of Spain, the Empire, and the German Catholic princes met in Brussels; the aim was to create a new and more united Catholic League, though this was not in the end achieved (Opel, *Der niedersächsisch–dänische Krieg*, ii, pp. 490–5; Albrecht, *Die auswärtige Politik*, pp. 168–72; Rodenas Vilar, *La politica europea de España*, pp. 78–83). One of the main aims of Spanish policy in these discussions was to persuade the Empire to place the United Provinces under a formal ban; the German Catholic princes refused to support this, as they did not want to commit themselves to war against the Dutch (Lonchay and Cuvelier, eds., *Correspondance de la cour d'Espagne*, ii, pp. 265, 271).

121 'Nassouians' here means supporters of the princely house of Orange-Nassau. After Prince Maurits had died in April 1625 he had been succeeded by his half-brother Frederik Hendrik (1584–1647). Maurits had been strongly anti-Arminian, but Frederik Hendrik was accused of pro-Arminian tendencies, and there had therefore been resistance to the idea of his succeeding Maurits as stadhouder; the charge of pro-Arminianism persisted during 1626 (J. J. Poelhekke, *Frederik Hendrik, prins van Oranje: een biografisch drieluick* (Zutphen, 1978), pp. 188, 194; Israel, *Dutch Republic*, pp. 489–92). That the Elector Palatine aspired to the princedom of Orange was implausible, but the idea had some genealogical basis: his mother, Louise Juliana, was the half-sister of Maurits and Frederik Hendrik. 'Naturall' should perhaps be 'unnatural' ('insolitâ', 'unusual').

122 'Also haue enough to do to' is an expansion of the sense by Hobbes.

that they haue hardly a third part left. Their charge growes. The aydes of kings diminish. yerely pensions, and interest, will shortly be greater then their revenue. Handicrafts beare no price; of all thinges necessary, Wood, brasse, Iron, Cloth, Linnen and ye rest, extreame scarsity.[123] to their domesticke euills, wee may adde their losses by warre, their fleetes taken, sunke, trade by reason of ye danger kept low. Lost within these two yeres, aboue 600 pieces of great Ordinance. No concord amongst the great men nor citties. Frisland demands immunity from tribute, hopeinge for ayd from a child of two monethes old, whom, knowinge the emulation that is betweene kinsmen, they oppose to their hated & expulsed gouerno^r.[124] By this meanes are they also subiect to factions. These men would not I trust, nor will you if you be wise, and obserue them. If Denmarke go on but slowly, or miscarry, they will appease the spaniard with yor head. They haue the example of Carthage and Antyochus kinge of Syria.[125] They storme that the French haue [78r] deceaued, and preuented them.[126] Holland alone, payes yerely 280.^{m} pounds interest.[127] They can make no banke[128] against this. This winde eates vp their bowels; O horrible and pestilent wind.[129] The company of [Am? *deleted*] Roterdam owes .2. millions.[130] Others are quite sunke.

---

[123] The United Provinces was damaged by the Spanish blockade, which caused a severe disruption of business in the eastern provinces and a shortage of imported materials such as salt, lime, iron, and coal (Israel, *Dutch Republic*, pp. 214, 217–20); but the account given here of 'extreame scarsity' is exaggerated. Between February 1624 and August 1626 the price of most commodities in Amsterdam went up by between 5 and 20 per cent: see H. W. Aeckerle, 'Amsterdamer Börsenpreislisten, 1624–1626', *Economisch-historisch jaarboek*, 13 (1927), pp. 86–209, esp. pp. 103–6, 192–6.

[124] A tax revolt against the stadhouder of Friesland, Ernst Casimir of Nassau-Diez, began in Leeuwarden in mid-May 1626 and spread to other towns and villages in Friesland. On 27 May Ernst Casimir left for The Hague to consult the States-General; it was later reported that he went there 'by permission of the people of Leeuwarden, where he was detained' (*Calendar of State Papers . . . in the Archives . . . of Venice, 1625–1626*, ed. A. B. Hinds (London, 1913) [hereafter: *CSPVen. 1625–6*], p. 444). The revolt ended in June after a number of concessions were granted. (See *Le Mercure françois*, 12, for 1626 (published in 1627), pp. 661–3; L. van Aitzema, *Saken van staet en oorlogh in, ende omtrent de Vereenigde Nederlanden*, 7 vols. (The Hague, 1669–71), i, p. 538; Leeuwarder Geschiedeniscommissie, *Rondom de Oldehove: geschiedenis van Leeuwarden en Friesland* (Leeuwarden, 1938), p. 142. The fullest account is given in H. Spanninga, 'Gulden vrijheid: politiek en staatsvorming in Friesland, 1600–1640' Leeuwarden University PhD thesis (forthcoming); I am very grateful to Mr Spanninga for permission to consult this.) It is not clear what the basis is for the claim (made here and below, at n. 245) that the people of Friesland declared a two-month-old baby stadhouder instead; the report in the *Mercure françois* said only that they wanted to replace Ernst Casimir with one of the noblemen of Friesland (p. 662: 'aliquem ex ipsis Proceribus Frisiae').

decrescunt; Pensiones annuae & fenora, mox reditus superabunt, artium Mechanicarum nulla sunt precia, rerum necessariarum, ut lignorum, aeris, ferri; Lanificij, lini, aliarum, summa inopia.

Accedunt malis domesticis bellicae calamitates, classes captae, depressae, negotiationes ob discrimina suppressae; intra biennium sexcenta & amplius grandia tormenta bellica amissa. Proceres concordes nulli, nullae Urbes, Frisij vectigalium immunitatem petunt, opem à Bimestri sperant infante, quem exoso, pulsóque opponunt rectori: non ignari aemulationum inter agnatos. Hinc sunt & ipsi factionibus opportuni. His ego non fidam, nec tu, si sapis & sentis. Si lentè Danus egerit, aut titubârit, tuo capite Iberum placabunt: Exemplum habent Carthaginis altae, Antiochíque Syri. Fremunt se à Franco inlusos & praeventos. Sola Hollandia cùm vicies octies centenis millibus luctatur in annuum fenus, quod nullo aggere excluditur. Ventus ille viscera depascitur. O ventum horribilem atque pestilentem. Roterodamensis societas aeris

---

125 After the defeat of Carthage in 195 BC, Hannibal took refuge with Antiochus III of Syria; but when Antiochus was defeated in his subsequent war against Rome, the Romans demanded that Hannibal be handed over to them, and Hannibal had to flee once again.

126 See above, nn. 77–9.

127 Military expenditure by the United Provinces had risen sharply after 1621, and the public debt of Holland grew rapidly, with new borrowing averaging 1.8 million guilders from 1621 to 1625 and rising to 5.3 million in 1626 (M. C. 't Hart, *The Making of a Bourgeois State: War, Politics and Finance during the Dutch Revolt* (Manchester, 1993), pp. 60–1, 164). In 1626 there were approximately 11 guilders to £1 (McCusker, *Money and Exchange*, pp. 44, 52). The Latin text here gives the figure of 2,800,000 ('vicies octies centenis millibus') without specifying a currency; Hobbes has evidently assumed the currency to be guilders, and has made a rough conversion at a rate of 10 to £1.

128 Although the context here might appear to suggest 'bank' in the financial sense, its meaning is 'embankment' ('aggere'). The phrase alludes to the construction of dikes in Holland.

129 The Latin here, 'O ventum horribilem atque pestilentem', is a quotation from Catullus, *Carmen XXVI*, l. 5. Catullus' poem involves a play of words on the verb 'opponere', which could mean 'to pledge something as surety for a debt': 'Furi, villula vestra non ad Austri | flatus opposita est . . . verum ad milia quindecim et ducentos. | o ventum horribilem atque pestilentem' ('Furius, your little villa has been exposed not to the gusts of the south wind . . . but rather to 15,200 sesterces. O, what a horrible and pestilential wind!').

130 Here too (cf. above, n. 127) the figure in the original, 20,000,000 ('vicies centena millia') has evidently been assumed to be in guilders, and the translation given in pounds. The word translated by Hobbes as 'company' is 'societas', and it presumably refers to the city of Rotterdam as a corporate body. Although merchants in Rotterdam took part in the major trading companies of the day (the West-Indische Compagnie and the Vereenigde Oostindische Compagnie), there was no special Rotterdam company, and the 'Societeit' of Merchant Adventurers from England was not established there until 1635 (R. Bijlsma, *Rotterdams welvaren, 1550–1650* (The Hague, 1918), pp. 143–9, 168–81).

And other Prouinces, as they owe lesse,[131] so haue they lesse meanes to pay. Sure, the Frisians excuse them [the? *deleted*] selues with a great Goddesse *Impossibility*. The credit of them all, is at ye last cast. No man lendes. Besides this, they are very carefull to keepe from ye English Amb:^r and vs, what they are treatinge with Spayne.[132] If it proue Peace, all our secrets will be layd open to ye Spaniard.

11.

There is yet lesse hope in ye Dane. He auoydes battle, and lookes about how to fly. *Martem habet in linguâ, tremolo stant corde pauores.*[133] Oh, but he aemulates the hono^r of Fabius, and calles it Cunctation, [which *deleted*] with this title he slubbers ouer the cowardise[134] wch Christian speakes manfully against.[135] Lately wth a few soldiers Fustenbergh routed and put to flight a huge number of his horse.[136] That great rabble endured not the first brunt. Mony from his confederates he cannot get, but very little, and late. He expecteth a storme to fall on Denmarke.[137] *Nunc socijs grauis incubat exossatque. Nil hosti nocet impauido.*[138] He drawes out the warre longe, like snoringe. He burdeneth ye Saxons with his standinge Campe, that beinge weakened he may adde them to his owne dominion. And now by fraud he hath seazed ye Castle of Breme.[139] He that is ye stronger, neuer wants pretences. Now like a

---

[131] Hobbes (or his manuscript copy) omits 'in singulis', 'each', 'in each case'.

[132] On 2 [/12] June 1626 the Tuscan Resident in London, Salvetti, reported that the Dutch were believed to be engaged in surreptitious negotiations with Spain for a truce or a peace treaty (BL, MS Add. 27962D, fo. 194r). On 19 [/29] June the Dutch Ambassador in London, Albert Joachimi, assured the Privy Council that the rumour was false, and said it was a piece of deliberate misinformation put about by the Habsburgs (*Acts of the Privy Council of England, June–December 1626*, ed. J. V. Lyle (London, 1938), p. 11). In 1626 the person who was head of the English legation at The Hague (though without the status of ambassador) was Dudley Carleton, a nephew of the famous diplomat of the same name (G. M. Bell, *A Handlist of British Diplomatic Representatives, 1509–1688* (London, 1990), p. 197).

[133] 'He talks of war, but there is terror in his trembling heart.' The first phrase may be an adaptation of the proverbial saying, 'bovem habet in lingua' ('he has an ox on his tongue'), used of someone who has been bribed to keep quiet.

[134] To slubber over = 'to daub over so as to cover or conceal' (*OED*, 'slubber', v., 2c); the Latin has 'praeterit . . . inertiam', 'he passes over [or 'omits to mention'] his idleness'.

[135] Quintus Fabius Maximus (*c*.275–203 BC) became known as 'Cunctator', 'the Delayer', because of the tactic of attrition, rather than confrontation, which he adopted towards the Carthaginian army during the second Punic War. 'Christian' here is the King of Denmark, Christian IV ('the Dane').

[136] On 29 July 1626 Egon, Count of Fürstenberg-Heiligenberg (1588–1635), a military commander under Tilly, routed the Danish force which was besieging the

alieni habet vicies centena millia, aliae verò ad fundum venerunt. Aliarum Provinciarum, ut debita in singulis minora sunt, ita difficilior solutio. Frisij certè potentissimâ se Deâ, IMPOSSIBILITATE excusant. Fides omnium extrema stat tegula. mutuum nemo dat: quin etiam Legatum Britannum studiosè celant, & nos quoque quid cum Ibero tractent. Si pax erit, omnia nostra secreta pandentur Hispano.

XI.

Minor etiam spes in Dano. Pugnam detrectat; fugam circumspectat:

Martem habet in lingua, tremulo stant corde pavores.

At Fabij decus aemulatur CUNCTATIONEM vocat, hoc praeterit nomine inertiam, à Christiano masculè exprobatam. pronuper pauco milite ingentem eius equitatum Furstenbergius fudit fugavit, prima in aciem tanta turba non sustinuit. Aurum à foederatis non impetrat, nisi paucum & serum. Ne procella in Daniam ingruat, haud inscius expectat,

Nunc socijs gravis incubat, exossátque.
Nil hosti nocet impavido.

bellum quasi ronchos trahit, Saxones stativis premit, ut debiles Imperio adijciat suo, iam Bremensium arces dolo intercepit. Causa nunquam deest potentiori. Iam nunc belli sumptus ab obnoxijs potens calculator

---

fortress of Kalenberg. The Danes had 7,000 cavalry, plus three infantry regiments; Fürstenberg had 4,000 foot soldiers, and was joined by another unit of the Imperial army consisting of two cavalry regiments (*c*.3,000 men) and 300 musketeers. There was thus some numerical imbalance, but not as much as is suggested here (see Opel, *Der niedersächsisch–dänische Krieg*, ii, pp. 544–6; Villermont, *Tilly*, pp. 200–1).

137 Hobbes (or his manuscript copy) omits a phrase from this sentence: 'haud inscius', 'not at all unaware'.

138 'Now he presses heavily on his allies, and reduces them to pulp. To his enemy, who is fearless, he causes no harm.'

139 Hobbes's translation, using 'now' and 'Castle' (in the singular) is a little misleading: the original is 'iam Bremensium arces dolo intercepit', 'he has already seized by fraud the strongholds of the people of Bremen'. In the spring of 1625 the Archbishop of Bremen, fearing that his territory would be occupied by Imperial troops, asked Christian IV for help; Christian sent Danish forces, which occupied the whole territory in June (but withdrew from all but the southern part later in the year). The accusation of 'fraud' here is unwarranted: the invitation came from the Archbishop on the advice of the cathedral chapter, and the Archbishop also took part in the meeting of leaders of the Lower Saxon Circle that invited Christian to become their military leader (F. W. Wiedemann, *Geschichte des Herzogthums Bremen*, 2 vols. (Stade, 1864–6), ii, pp. 224–8). But the author may have been influenced by the fact that in 1621 Christian had used bribes and threats to get his son Frederik elected coadjutor of the Bremen archdiocese (P. D. Lockhart, *Denmark in the Thirty Years' War, 1618–1648* (Selinsgrove, PA, 1996), p. 94).

mighty auditor he requires his charges of those that are obnoxious to him.[140] Once he threatened to fight, and bled for it. It is he y^t delayes[141] [thy *deleted*>your] exile. Nor is there any hope, but that if he ouercome, he ouercomes for himselfe. He thinkes of his owne augmentation, not at all of yor restitution, but to make it a pretext. Will you know the truth? The ouerthrowes of Mansfeld, Brunswicke, Hessen, he heard of, himselfe wth inward, his familiars wth outward ioy.[142] So much by night-discourse, and free cups,[143] wee learned. There where Weesell, and Elue, brother Riuers, carry forrayne commodityes, he alone would haue the power.[144] And nowe he vnderhand sollicites Caesars frend vmpire of the peace,[145] so secretly, that most perceaue it. For you, he troubles not himselfe about you. for himselfe he is diligent. Howsoeuer it goes, neyther is he a warrio^r, nor are his Captaynes warrio^rs. And of Halberstat, I had no more hope in him, when he liued, then now that he is dead.[146] He would run rashly on, and fall fearefully of, promise much, then threaten, vrge his Brother and againe repent it, a man of a floatinge brayne, vnlike to him selfe.[147] whose frensy did neuer lesse harme then when it killed him. No man doubted but he would haue betrayed his confederates, and ioyned himselfe to ye Emp.^r148 Fuxius[149] euer complayned that he did harme to ye cause, swift,[150] and vncapable of wisedome, glancinge at Mansfelt wth the same censure.

[78v]

---

[140] 'His charges' here translates 'belli sumptus', 'the costs of the war'; 'obnoxious' translates 'obnoxijs', which could mean those 'dependent' on him or 'subject' to him.

[141] 'Delayes' here translates 'moratur', which in this instance appears to mean 'prolongs'.

[142] Respectively, the defeat of Mansfeld at Dessau Bridge (see above, Ch. 3 n. 50), the death of Christian of Braunschweig-Wolfenbüttel, and the capitulation of Moriz of Hessen-Kassel after the siege of Göttingen (see below, nn. 146, 215). There seems to be no justification for the claim made here about the reaction of Christian IV or his 'familiars'. No such *Schadenfreude* is expressed in Christian's personal correspondence of this period (C. F. Bricka, J. A. Fridericia, and J. Skovgaard, eds., *Kong Christian den Fjerdes egenhandige breve*, 8 vols. (Copenhagen, 1887–1947), ii, pp. 12–32); and the British envoy Sir Robert Anstruther described Christian IV as 'treulie . . . much grieued' at the death of Christian of Braunschweig-Wolfenbüttel (PRO, SP 75/7/150, 15 June 1626).

[143] The court of Christian IV was notorious for its heavy drinking; the King himself 'was regularly drunk for two or three days on end' (Parker, ed., *The Thirty Years' War*, p. 201).

[144] The Weser and the Elbe were the two most important watercourses running from central Germany to the North Sea (and serving, respectively, the trading centres of Bremen and Hamburg).

exposcit. Semel pugnam minatus est, & sanguinem dedit. Exilium tuum moratur ipse: Nec spes est, si vincat, sibi vincet, de suo augmento cogitat, de tua restitutione nihil, nisi praetextum habet. Vin' vera scire? Mansfeldicas, Brunosuicenas, Hassicas clades tacito mentis gaudio sensit, familiares aperto; hoc nocturna colloquia, & libera vina nos docuerunt. Solus ipse potens esse vult, quâ Visurgis & Albis fraterna flumina merces externas vehunt. Iam etiam pacis arbitrum Caesaris amicum subornat, tam occultè, ut plerique nôrint. Pro te non sataget, de se anxius, ut ut agat, nec ipse est bellator, nec Bellatores habet Duces. De Halberstadio etiam cum viveret, non magis quàm de mortuo speravi. Ille temeritate praesilire, metu resilire, polliceri multa, post minari, nunc Fratrem pellere, nunc poenitere; homo fluctuantis cerebri, & impar sibi, in quo nunquam innocentior phrenesis fuit, quàm illa, per quam anima expulsa est. Dubium nulli erat, eum proditis socijs se Caesari iuncturum, Alberti veteris exemplo. Fuxius eum, causae nocere semper questus est, fugacem, sapientiae incapacem, pari censura stringens Mansfeldium.

---

¹⁴⁵ It is not clear who is referred to here—possibly the Lutheran Johann Georg I, Elector of Saxony, who had taken a pro-Imperial position during the Bohemian revolt and had played an ambiguous (but broadly pro-Imperial) role since then. There is little evidence that Christian was seeking peace; but when the Infanta made overtures to him he replied politely (on 15 July), and the Emperor's letter to Wallenstein of 9 July shows that he was under the impression that Christian inclined towards peace (see von Hurter, *Geschichte Kaiser Ferdinands II*, ix, pp. 473–4).

¹⁴⁶ Christian of Braunschweig-Wolfenbüttel (see above, n. 8) was known as Christian of Halberstadt because he was administrator of the diocese of Halberstadt. He died of fever on 26 June 1626.

¹⁴⁷ 'Vnlike to him selfe' here translates 'impar sibi', a phrase (used in Horace, *Saturae*, I, 3, l. 19) meaning 'inconsistent in his behaviour'.

¹⁴⁸ Hobbes (or his manuscript copy) omits the final clause of this sentence, 'Alberti veteris exemplo', 'according to the example of old Albert'. It is not clear who is referred to here. Possibly the author had confused Albert V of Bavaria (r. 1550–79) with his predecessor, William IV (r. 1508–50); it was under William IV that Bavaria switched decisively in 1546 from an anti-Habsburg to a pro-Habsburg position.

¹⁴⁹ Johann Philipp Fuchs von Bimbach, who had served in the Imperial army in 1620 but changed sides in 1622, was an adviser to Christian of Braunschweig-Wolfenbüttel in 1623–4 and was appointed General by Christian IV of Denmark in 1625; he was the latter's senior commander at the battle of Lutter-am-Barenberg on 27 August 1626, where he met his death. (See Opel, *Der niedersächsisch–dänische Krieg*, ii, pp. 176–7; Hennequin de Villermont, *Tilly*, pp. 180, 200, 206–10; Bricka et al., *Kong Christians breve*, i, pp. 444–6.)

¹⁵⁰ 'Swift' here does not capture the sense of 'fugacem', which means 'apt to flee', 'timid'.

12

What do wee promise to our selues from Mansfelt. Whence flyes he not? Carelesse of ye warre, greedy of booty, easier to be gotten in peacefull contryes, then in that of ye enemy. Fitter for nothinge, then of frends to make enemyes, and of enemyes victors. Witnesse Lubecke, Saxony, Brandenburgh.[151] Gabor also before the Emp.^{r} complayned of him, saying *I lament not his defeate, he himselfe cares not for it, beinge a man that sets much by* [*pray* altered to *prey*], *but little by the bloud of his soldiers.* By this meanes ye Saxons now are ill affected to yor cause, hauing felt ye hostility of yor frends, and hopelesse of better successe, are panting for an end of the warre. *Vbique vastitas, fames, et dirae mortis imago.*[152] Nor is Sweden at leasure to repayre yor losses, he hath enemyes nere. Poland is prouoked, and denyes Peace. The ouerthrow at Borussia[153] makes them wary; they are angry, and whet their [angry *altered to* anger *deleted*] valo^r, at ye true whetstone.[154] He hath taken the power from his subiects by a Tiranny, and now vseth all his strength to appease his contry. The [79r] sicke cannot helpe ye sicke. *Fasce suo pressus, alienum tollet?*[155]

13.

It is not in ye Turkes power as it was; wee knocke in vayne at ye inexorable Gate. The Bassaes do scarce remember ye name of Palatine, they will not so much as heare yor moaninge. *Claustra strepunt ferro, mentes adamante rigescunt.*[156] They referre our Petitions to ye Emp^r.[157] And that [bod *deleted*] vast body of a Monarchy is shaken wth mighty tempests.[158] It is layd at [by *deleted* >with] mayne strength, by the

---

[151] In the winter of 1625–6 Mansfeld's army was stationed in northern Germany, where it lived off the land, seizing provisions (and booty) and demanding contributions. It ravaged first the duchy of Lüneburg (part of the Lower Saxon Circle), then the duchy of Saxe-Lauenburg. The authorities at Lübeck rejected Mansfeld's demands for money, and defended the approaches to the city, killing 160 of his soldiers in their sorties (*Le Mercure françois*, 12, for 1626 (published in 1627), p. 118). He then took his army through Mecklenburg towards Brandenburg; at the Elector's insistence he promised not to enter the territory, but then did so (in early March), pillaging several towns. (Hennequin de Villermont, *Ernest de Mansfeldt*, ii, pp. 329–32.) In July, partly as a consequence of this, the Elector of Brandenburg sought an alliance with the Emperor (Kočí et al., *Documenta bohemica*, iv, p. 134).

[152] 'Devastation everywhere, and hunger, and the image of terrible death' (perhaps adapted from Vergil, *Aeneid*, II, ll. 368–9: 'crudelis ubique | luctus, ubique pavor, et plurima mortis imago').

XII.

Quid de Mansfeldico nobis promittimus? Vnde non fugit? Incuriosus militiae, avidus praedae, quae ex pacato, quàm hostico est paratior. Nulli rei magis idoneus, quàm ut ex amicis hostes, ex hostibus victores faciat. Testis Lubeca, Saxo, Brandeburgicus. De illo etiam Gabor questus est Caesari: *Cladem eius non lugeo, ipse eam insuper habet, ut cui praeda sit cara, vilis militum sanguis.* Hinc iam à tua causa alienati Saxones, amicorum hostilitatem experti, Nulla spe meliorum successuum ad belli finem anhelant.

> *Vbique vastitas, fames,*
> *Et dirae mortis imago.*

Nec Sueco vacat tuas sarcire clades, vicinos habet adversarios, Polonia inritata est, pacem negat. Clades Borussiae eam cautam facit, iam fortitudinem ad cotem suam acuit irata. Tyrannide potentiam subditis excussit, pacandae Patriae omnes vires insumit. Aeger aegrum sublevare non poterit.

> *Fasce suo pressus alienum tollet?*

XIII.

Magno Turco non est integrum. Frustra non exorandas fores pulsamus: vix nomen Palatini meminerunt Bassae. Ne voces quidem lamentatrices admittunt.

> *Claustra strepunt ferro, mentes adamante rigescunt.*

Preces nostras Caesari referunt. Vastum illud Monarchiae corpus magnis quatitur malis, solida vi pulsatur à Persa, sauciatur à Tartaris,

---

[153] In a strategic move directed against Poland-Lithuania, King Gustavus Adolphus of Sweden had landed on the coast of Ducal Prussia (East Prussia) at the port of Pillau on 6 July 1626, seizing that town and a succession of other coastal towns in quick succession (N. Ahnlund, 'Gustaf II Adolfs första preussiska fälttåg och den europeiska krisen 1626', *Historisk tidskrift*, 38 (1918), pp. 75–115, here p. 107; M. Roberts, *Gustavus Adolphus: A History of Sweden, 1611–1632*, 2 vols. (London, 1958), ii, pp. 321–4).

[154] This alludes to a proverbial saying, mentioned twice by Cicero (*Tusculanae disputationes*, IV.19, para. 43; *Academica priora*, para. 135), that anger is the whetstone of valour. The Latin here, 'ad cotem suam', means 'at its whetstone'; Hobbes's translation, 'at ye true whetstone', seems to assume familiarity with the proverbial saying.

[155] 'Oppressed by his own burden, will he pick up somebody else's?'

[156] 'The lock clatters with its iron bolt; their minds become as inflexible as steel.'

[157] There seems to be no factual basis for this claim.

[158] 'Tempests' here is Hobbes's expansion; the Latin is 'malis', 'ills'.

Persian.[159] it is wounded by the Tartars and Cosackes,[160] and no lesse a plague is in theyr very bowells, the members of it beinge deuided, and fightinge against each other.[161] On a wounded body a wise man will not put new [armes *altered to* armor]. Therefore Gabor also forsakes vs. He seekes for mony, wch gotten, he shewes his [ayde *deleted*] forces, but bringes them not on. He selles vncertaynties, at a certayne price.[162] He also, persuades you to Peace, and condemnes all our Counsells and discloses them. So he gratifyes Caesar.[163]

14

At Constantinople they plyed it; and there were giuen by the Hollander thirty garments of gold and silke to Caim Cam,[164] that is, to the Turkish Buckingham, and other guiftes by others to persuade to a warre against the Emp.^{r} But he will hardly do it; his aemulato^{r}s watch but a new occasion, to send him goinge. Our younge courtiers not longe since, shewed a great deale of ioy, when they heard by ye English Amb.^{r} that it was agreed on betweene the Amb:^{rs} at Constantinople, that Gabo^r

---

[159] In early 1624 Shah Abbas I of Persia had taken advantage of a Janissary revolt in Baghdad to seize both that city and much of the territory of Iraq. An Ottoman army reconquered Iraq and besieged Baghdad in 1625, but failed to take it; this unsuccessful siege was eventually abandoned in the summer of 1627 (J. von Hammer, *Geschichte des osmanischen Reiches*, 10 vols. (Pest, 1829–35), v, pp. 53–66).

[160] The Crimean Tatars had defeated an Ottoman expedition in the summer of 1624, and had formed an anti-Ottoman alliance with the Zaporozhian Cossacks in December 1624. A Cossack fleet in the Black Sea raided Ottoman territory every year during the period 1622–5, and fought a major battle with the Ottoman navy in the summer of 1625. In early 1626 the Tatars made trouble for the Ottomans by raiding Poland and claiming that they had been ordered to do so by the Sultan (von Hammer, *Geschichte*, v, pp. 50–2, 70–1; V. Catualdi, *Sultan Jahja, dell'imperial casa ottomana* (Trieste, 1889), pp. 133–43; A. A. Novoselskii, *Borba moskovskogo gosudarstva s tatarami v pervoi polovine XVII veka* (Moscow, 1948), pp. 113–15; M. A. Alekberli, *Borba ukrainskogo naroda protiv turetsko–tatarski aggressii vo vtoroi polovine XVI—pervoi polovine XVII vekov* (Saratov, 1961), pp. 162–4; T. Gemil, *Ţările române în contextul politic internaţional, 1621–1672* (Bucharest, 1979), pp. 56–62).

[161] Internal dissensions had led to the deposition of two Sultans, Osman II in 1622 and Mustafa I in 1623; during the early years of the new Sultan, Murad IV, there were several minor revolts, and a major rebellion in eastern Anatolia in 1624.

[162] Hobbes (or his manuscript copy) omits a sentence here: 'Frui mavult partis', 'He prefers to enjoy his gains.'

[163] The claim that Bethlen was urging peace on Frederick V, and betraying him to the Emperor, is highly implausible. The suggestion made here about secret complicity with the Emperor seems in line with the claims made in Imperial propaganda against Bethlen

Cosaccísque, nec minor intra viscera pestis pugnantibus membris, & secessionem facientibus. Lacero corpori nemo prudens nova inducit arma. Itaque & Gabor nos deserit: aurum quaerit, post aurum auxilia venditat, non praesentat; certo precio rem incertam vendit. Frui mavult partis. Pacem etiam tibi suadet: omnia nostra consilia improbat, & malè celat: ita Caesari gratificatur.

XIV.

Actum quidem Bizantij feruidè, & à Batavo Caimecamo hoc est, Turcico Buchingamio, datae sericae aureaeque triginta vestes, ab alijs alia dona, ut bellum suaderet in Caesarem, sed vix efficiet. aemuli illius inde evertendi novam occasionem captant. Magna laetitia gestierunt nuper juniores nostri Aulici, cùm ex Britanno Oratore discerent, Bizantij inter Legatos convenisse, ut Gabori in menses quinquaginta talerorum millia

at Constantinople, as described in a Venetian report of April 1626: 'The Emperor is trying to get Gábor distrusted by the Porte, by having delivered to the Kaimakam and the other Viziers letters, whether true or false, written by him to His Majesty, urging him to unite with him against the Ottomans' (von Hammer, *Geschichte*, v, p. 94 n.: 'L'Imperator va procurando di metter il Gabor in mala fede alla Porta col far capitar nelle mani del Caimacham e degli altri Vesiri lettere o vere o false scritte da lui alla Maesta sua con eccitamenti di unirsi contra li Ottomani').

[164] Hobbes was apparently unaware that 'Caimecamus' was a title, not a personal name. The Kaimakam (from the Arabic for 'standing in the station of') Pasha was the Vizier who deputized for the Grand Vizier when the latter was away on a military campaign. The Kaimakam Pasha referred to here was Gürcü Mehmed Pasha ('Gürcü' means 'Georgian') (*c*.1536–1626), the Second Vizier, who had himself served as Grand Vizier in 1622 (von Hammer, *Geschichte*, v, pp. 54, 66–7; F. Ç. Derin, 'Mehmed paşa: Muhammed paşa, gürcü', *İslâm ansiklopedisi: islâm âlemi tarih, coğrafya, etnografya ve biyografya lugati*, 13 vols. (Istanbul, 1940–86), vii, fasc. 76 (1957), pp. 585–7; Ibrahim Alajbegović Pečevija [Peçevi], *Historija, 1520–1640*, ed. and tr. F. Nametak, 2 vols. (Sarajevo, 2000), ii, pp. 328, 346). On his death in July 1626 Sir Thomas Roe wrote: 'This great minister was 96 yeares old, had bene 45 yeares vizier of the bench [*sc.* member of the Divan, the imperial council]; serued 5 emperours, once great vizier, and thrice chaimacham: the most able, and only wise man in this state' (*Negotiations*, pp. 524–5; other sources give his age as 90). The 'Hollander' (Dutch Ambassador) was Cornelis Haga; in October 1626 he reported to the States-General that he had presented Gürcü Mehmed Pasha with gifts worth 30,000 akçes during that year (A. H. de Groot, *The Ottoman Empire and the Dutch Republic: A History of the Earliest Diplomatic Relations, 1610–1630* (Leiden, 1978), p. 176. The akçe was a silver coin, undergoing rapid debasement in this period. In 1625 £1 was worth roughly 350 akçes: see Ş. Pamuk, *A Monetary History of the Ottoman Empire* (Cambridge, 2000), p. 144; McCusker, *Money and Exchange*, pp. 9, 44, 52).

should haue 50^m dollers a moneth payd him by ye Leaguers,[165] and so wth a great army he should inuade the Prouinces of ye Emp.^{r} Which he hath vndertaken to do by Bornomissa;[166] and indeed he already begins to stirre.[167] But neyther will this do vs much good, but procure vs greater malice, and hatred. Gabor sollicites the Turkes,[168] vncertayne and dangerous ayde. Besides its all built vpon a false ground. For ye English[169] had persuaded the Turkes, that Tilly and Fridland,[170] were vtterly ouerthrowne by the K. of Denmarke. and now they know ye truth, they take it ill to haue beene so abused. And y^e [Turkes *altered to* Turke] dissembles not, that without hauinge Boemia and Morauia giuen him he will neuer ayde vs. And yet they beleeue that they cannot be giuen him without bloud. It is true, ye Amb:^{rs} of ye League do what they can; [that *deleted*] but if that spaniard[171] come and salute ye Gate, for all Caimcam, all those wheeles will goe backward. But for ye Turkes ayd, if Ferenzius[172] get it not wth bribes, the English and Venetian Amb:^{rs} doubt it much.[173] And if that spanish gentleman fallinge from his horse, had not bene forced to goe backe, they had by this time despayred.[174] The greater somme had borne downe the lesse.

[79v]

---

[165] On 28 May 1625 Sir Thomas Roe, the English Ambassador in Constantinople, had reported that Gábor Bethlen was seeking 500,000 crowns per year from the allies (England, Denmark, the United Provinces); on 8 May 1626 he reported that (according to Bethlen's envoy in Constantinople) he was seeking 40,000 thalers per month, and that if Louis XIII made an initial payment of 100,000 thalers he would reduce his total demand from 480,000 per year to 400,000 (*Negotiations*, pp. 403, 510). (The units of account mentioned here were similar but not identical: while the English crown was 5s., in 1626 the Reichsthaler—which is specified in the Latin text here—was worth 4s. 7d.: see McCusker, *Money and Exchange*, pp. 63, 69.) Roe did not report any agreed decision on this 'between the Ambassadors' there; however, it is significant that on 1 July 1626 the French Ambassador in Vienna reported that he had news (from Venice) that Bethlen had made just such an agreement with the four ambassadors (*Les Papiers de Richelieu*, ed. Wild, i, p. 183: his report specified 40,000 écus per month, but 'écus' here should evidently have been thalers, since the écu was worth 13s. 7d. (McCusker, *Money and Exchange*, p. 88)).

[166] Ferenc Bornemisza, from Cluj (Kolozsvár), served Gábor Bethlen as an envoy to Constantinople in 1626, arriving there in early May (Roe, *Negotiations*, pp. 510, 516; D. Angyal, 'Erdély politikai érintkezése Angliával', *Századok: a Magyar Történelmi Társulat közlönye*, 34 (1900), pp. 309–25, 388–420, here p. 412). Ludovic Demény and Paul Cernovodeanu write that Bornemisza had also brought a letter to Roe in 1625 (*Relaţiile politice ale Angliei cu Moldova, Ţara Românească şi Transilvania în secolele XVI–XVII* (Bucharest, 1974), p. 84). Vencel Biró describes his mission in 1626 as a secret mission to the French Ambassador (*Erdély követei a Portán* (Cluj, 1921), p. 121), but the evidence from Roe suggests that his purpose was to get the financial support of France, England, the United Provinces, and Venice, promising speedy military action if it were forthcoming. See also above, Ch. 3 n. 69.

[167] 'Begins to stirre' here translates 'movet lacertos', 'moves his forces' (literally, 'moves his arms'; but 'lacertus' was used figuratively for military forces).

à Ligistis solverentur, atque ita ille cum grandi Exercitu provincias Caesaris invaderet, quod ille per Bornomissam facturum recepit, & sanè jam movet lacertos. Verùm nec magnopere nobis hoc proderit, sed odium invidiáque major orietur. Turcas Gabor sollicitat, incertum & periculosum auxilium. Deinde falso omnia nituntur, persuasum erat ab Anglo Turcis, Tillium, Fridlandiúmque à Dano internecione deletum: re intellectâ ludibrio se haberi indignati sunt. Quin Turcae non dissimulant, non alio pacto se auxiliaturos, nisi datâ Bohemiâ & Moraviâ. Nec credunt tamen posse dari sine sanguine; Legati quidem Legistici omnia moliuntur, sed si venerit Hispanus ille, & invito Caimecamo portam salutârit, ne ille machinae retro vertentur. De subsidio tamen Turcico ni Ferenzius donis rem pervicerit, dubitat Britannus & Venetus Orator, & nisi Hispanus ille Hidalgo lapsus equo retrocedere coactus esset, jam deperasset; major pecunia vinceret minorem, ipse Caimecamus

---

168 Bethlen wanted to persuade the Sultan to order the pasha of Buda to attack Habsburg territory, in coordination with Bethlen's own prospective campaign in Silesia (Roe, *Negotiations*, p. 522; M. Depner, *Das Fürstenthum Siebenbürgen im Kampf gegen Habsburg: Untersuchungen über die Politik Siebenbürgens während des Dreissigjährigen Krieges* (Stuttgart, 1938), p. 114). In early July he informed Christian IV that he was certain that the pasha was already preparing an army of 60,000 troops (V. Fraknói, 'Bethlen Gábor és IV. Keresztély Dán Király (1625–1628)', *Történelmi tár* (1881), pp. 98–113, here p. 105). A smaller force, under that pasha's successor, did attack Habsburg territory later in the year.

169 'English' here translates 'Anglo', 'the Englishman', meaning the English Ambassador, Roe.

170 Jean 't Serclaes, comte de Tilly (1559–1632), commander of the army of the Catholic League, conducted a successful campaign in western Germany in the spring and summer of 1626 (see below, n. 215). Albrecht von Wallenstein (1583–1634), Imperial general, had been created Duke of Friedland. He had defeated Mansfeld at the battle of Dessau Bridge in April 1626.

171 See below, n. 174.   172 Ferenc Bornemisza: see above, n. 166.

173 The Venetian Ambassador was Giorgio Giustinian. Hobbes's translation here is awkward: the Latin is 'De subsidio tamen Turcico ni Ferenzius donis rem pervicerit, dubitat Britannus & Venetus Orator' ('However, the British and Venetian Ambassadors doubt whether there will be any Turkish assistance, unless Ferenc obtains it by gifts').

174 A Spanish envoy arrived in Ragusa (Dubrovnik), from Naples, in mid-April 1626 and proceeded overland towards Constantinople; his mission was to conclude a new truce between Spain and the Porte. But after nine days' travel he had a serious fall from his horse, breaking three bones, and was forced to return to Ragusa. Fearing that he would renew his journey, the ambassadors of Venice, England, France, and the United Provinces gave the Kaimakam Pasha a present worth 1,400 thalers to have him stopped; a firman (imperial decree) was then issued, banning the Spaniard from Ottoman territory. (See Roe, *Negotiations*, pp. 508–9, 514; *CSPVen. 1625–6*, pp. 419, 434, 470–1; G. Hering, *Ökumenisches Patriarchat und europäische Politik, 1620–1638* (Wiesbaden, 1968), p. 104 n.; and above, Ch. 3 n. 70.) The Latin here has 'deperasset', evidently a misprint for 'desperasset' (correctly translated as 'had . . . despayred').

Caimcam himselfe would, not vnwillingly, haue giuen way to Gold that goes through in euery place more violently then lightninge. But Gabor to, is mutable, and neuer without pretences to deceaue. The estate of Turky is not such, as to seeke out new warres. They leaped for ioy lately when a rumo[r] was spred by a spahee,[175] that Babylon was taken, but that little vse of a false ioy, was recompensed afterward wth an vniuersall sorrow.[176] The English Amb:[r] there, writes, that all his[177] battayles, and expeditions miscarry, and supplyes are hastened, as in extreamest danger. Isaffis Mahomet Bassa[178] hath receaued [*2 letters deleted*] a greate somme of mony .400[m] crownes.[179] on the 9th of may, for the Turkes employments, but by reason of y[e] heates, he will deferre the warre till Autumne. The .3rd. of May the Gallies went out, to the guard of y[e] Euxine sea,[180] Peghier Bassa[181] is to follow wth y[e] Army.[182] The ouerthrow of the Tartars is now certayne.[183] Mahomet Bassa is afrayd of y[e] [Cosackes *deleted*] Polackes[184] and desires at the Gate, by Caim-Cam and others, that Gabor may be dealt withall for ayde. What can they do in other mens busines that want the helpe of others in their owne? If the Polackes helpe y[e] Cosackes, [*and altered to* or *deleted* >or][185] inuade the Turkes, they will be mightily deiected. and euen now, the more they dissemble their feare, the more it appeares. But Caimcam deales wth the French Amb[r], that there may be a treaty of Peace,[186] from hence therefore the hope is always vncertayne, but mischiefe certayne. And

[80r]

---

175 Spahi, sipahi: cavalryman.

176 'Babylon' here is Baghdad; on this false report see above, Ch. 3 n. 66.

177 *sc.* the Sultan's.

178 This refers to Hafiz Ahmed Pasha, who was in command of the siege of Baghdad; 'Isaffis' (as printed in the Latin original) resulted from a misreading of 'Haffis' (see above, Ch. 3, at n. 71). Hafiz Ahmed Pasha (*c.*1564–1632) was of Bulgarian origin; he married a daughter of Ahmed I, and served as Grand Vizier from February 1625 to December 1626 (and in 1631–2) (O. F. Köprülü, 'Hâfiz Ahmed paşa', *İslam ansiklopedisi: islâm âlemi tarih, coğrafya, etnografya ve biyografya lugati*, 13 vols. (Istanbul, 1940–86), v(1), fasc. 39 (1948), pp. 71–7; İ. H. Danişmend, *Osmanlı devlet erkânı* (Istanbul, 1971), pp. 33–4; Pečevija, *Historija*, ii, p. 342 n.).

179 The unit of currency is not specified in the original; the diplomatic report from which this information was derived specified thalers (see above, Ch. 3 n. 78).

180 The Black Sea, where the Ottomans had been attacked by Cossack naval forces (see above, n. 160).

181 This name ('Pegierius') derived from 'pegier', a distorted version of 'Recep' (see above, Ch. 3 n. 74). Recep Pasha (d. 1632) was a Bosnian who had been appointed Vizier and Kapudan Pasha (commander of the Ottoman navy) in 1623; he succeeded Gürcü Mehmed Pasha as Kaimakam Pasha in 1626 (S. Bašagić, *Znameniti hrvati, bošnjaci i hercegovci u turskoj carevini* (Zagreb, 1931), p. 63; Danişmend, *Osmanlı*

auro, quod fulmine violentiùs perrumpit, non inlubenter cederet. Sed & Gabor mutabilis semper speciosas habet causas fallendi. Non est ille Turcarum status ut nova bella quaerant. Gestiente nuper laetitiâ ferebantur, didito per Spachium quendam, de capta Babylonia, rumore. Sed falsa gaudij usura luctu cuncta complevit. Scribit Britanni Regis Orator, omnia proelia, omnes expeditiones infeliciter cecidisse: supplementa properantur ut in summo periculo. Isaffis Mehemetus Bassa magnam pecuniam quadringentorum millium accepit nono Maij, in rem Turcicam; sed ob calores aestatis in autumnum bellu[m] differet. Tertio die Maij triremes ad Ponti Euxini custodiam egressae sunt, cum Exercitu sequetur Bassa Pegierius. De clade Tartarorum iam constat, Tiaccus Mehemetus Bassa sibi metuit à Polonis, petit à porta per Caimecamum aliósque, ut cum Gabore agatur de auxilijs. Quid illi praestare in aliena causa poterunt, qui in sua alienis auxilijs indigent! Si Cosaccis Polonì succurrant, aut regnum invadant, magna erit consternatio, nunc metus Turcorum quò magis dissimulatur, eò magis sese prodit. Caimecamus tamen cum Legato Franco agit, ut de pace tractetur. Itaque hinc incerta

---

devlet erkâm, p. 188; Z. Danişmen, ed., *Naîmâ târihi*, 6 vols. (Istanbul, 1967–9), ii, pp. 917, 956).

[182] 'Army' here correctly translates 'Exercitu'; but the author of the text had misunderstood the diplomatic report from which he derived his information, where the word used was 'Armada', meaning a naval force (see above, Ch. 3 n. 73).

[183] See below, n. 305.

[184] Hobbes (or his manuscript copy) has curtailed the name of this pasha: in the original it is 'Tiaccus Mehemetus Bassa'. Mehmed Diak Pasha was appointed beylerbeyi (chief governor) of the province of Silistria in 1625; his province, which ran northwards up the Black Sea coast, was contiguous at its northern end with the western tip of the Khanate of the Crimean Tatars, and thus also close to Polish territory. He was known to be hostile to Poland (see B. Baranowski, *Polska a Tatarszczyzna w latach 1624–1629* (Lodz, 1948), p. 40). When the Tatars raided Polish territory in early 1626 the Poles mustered some forces to drive them out; the Tatars left of their own accord, but the Poles told Mehmed that they blamed the Turks for ordering the raid (ibid., p. 51), and he probably feared Polish retaliation. (Cf. above, Ch. 3 n. 67.)

[185] Hobbes first wrote 'and', then altered it to 'or', then deleted it and added 'or' as an interlineation. The Latin has 'aut'.

[186] The French Ambassador was Philippe de Harlay, comte de Cézy (1582–1652). It is not clear with whom this peace was to be concluded—not the Poles, as the Ottoman Empire was already at peace with Poland, having signed a formal agreement in 1623 (V. Ciobanu, *Politică şi diplomaţie în Ţările Române în raporturile polono-otomano-habsburgice (1601–1634)* (Bucharest, 1994), pp. 212–13). The most likely candidate is the Empire; in 1627 the Venetian Ambassador complained that de Cézy had previously advised the Kaimakam Pasha to pursue a peace treaty with the Empire (M. P. Pedani-Fabris, ed., *Relazioni di ambasciatori veneti al senato: Constantinopoli, relazioni inedite (1512–1789)* (Padua, 1996), p. 616).

yet I feare that such vngodly aydes, will proue the ruine of them that
seeke them. For though in Politique strategems, Religion be last looked
at, yet it seemes there is some kingly power aboue that ratifyes the
priuiledges of Magistrates, and [he *deleted*] is iudge of right and wronge.
The English Amb:ʳ professes that helpe is to be sought for in any land
Acheronta mouenda.[187] But what if Cerberus be angry to.

15

The state of Venice is in worse case now, then when it denyed you
both much and little [aydes *altered to* ayde].[188] The Complayntes
of their subiects and citties groninge vnder yᵉ burthen grow euery
day greater, and greater. Verona sayes, and other cittyes say, that
since the time of their foundation, they were neuer so grieuously
oppressed as now. [In *deleted*>Amidst] these complayntes the fierce
soldier lyes vpon them, and commands their griefe to keepe silence.[189]
Contarini[190] himselfe despayres, Tornio[191] despayres, the [Generall
deleted>Duke] himselfe[192] foretelles [*2 letters deleted*] calamityes. Their
affayres miscarryinge, the Reformed can do lesse in the Colledge then
before.[193] They haue lately spoken much against the French, and will
neuer league wᵗʰ them any more, The halfe of them [>not] long
since perswaded to peace and frendship[194] with the Pope and Popish

---

[187] 'One must rouse the underworld' (adapted from Vergil, *Aeneid*, VII, l. 312:
'flectere si nequeo superos, Acheronta movebo', meaning 'if I cannot persuade the upper
Gods to change their minds, I shall rouse the underworld').
[188] This probably refers to 1620, when Venice declined both a request for 8,000
troops (in June) and a request for 100,000 ducats (in August and October) (see H. von
Zwiedineck-Südenhorst, *Die Politik der Republik Venedig während der dreissigjährigen
Krieges*, 2 vols. (Stuttgart, 1882–5), i, pp. 104–5).
[189] In this sentence the Latin first describes the soldier as 'violentus' ('boisterous',
'violent'), then adds the adjective 'ferox' ('haughty', 'fierce'). Hobbes translates the first
adjective as 'fierce', and ignores the second. Conditions were bad in Verona in the 1620s,
not only because of large increases in taxation (the tax burden had risen from 47,000
ducats in 1590 to 174,000 in 1625) but also because of excesses committed by soldiers
billeted on the population (see V. Cavallari et al., *Verona e il suo territorio*, 7 vols. (Verona,
1950–2003), v(1), pp. 394–5). The tax burden rose further in March 1626 when the
Senate decided to extend the 'extraordinary tithe' from the city of Venice to the entire
Terrafirma (Girolamo Priuli, 'Cronache', for 1626: Österreichische Nationalbibliothek,
Vienna, MS 6230, fo. 226). It may be significant that in 1626 Ferdinand II contemplated
a plan to occupy the territory of Verona (Cavallari et al., *Verona*, v(1), p. 33); possibly the
reports which formed the basis of the author's comments here also lay behind that plan.

semper spes, certa pernicies. Quanquam vereor, ne tam impia auxilia petentibus exitiosa sint. Quamvis enim in politico stratagemate pietas extrema sit, videtur tamen esse aliquod numen regium, quod Magistratus jura sanciat: cui sit aequi & iniqui judicium. Profitetur Legatus Angliae in omni terra quaerenda auxilia, Acheronta movenda; quid si tamen & Cerberus sit iratus?

XV.

Venetorum res deteriore loco est, quàm illâ tempestate cum magna pariter, modicáque negarent auxilia. Urbium, subditorúmque querelae sub onere gementium, in dies crescunt; negat Verona, negant aliae Urbes à conditu suo, unquam se tam acerbâ vexatione oppressas. Querimonijs tantis violentus miles incubat, & doloris silentium ferox imperat. Desperat ipse Contarenus; desperat Turnius, Dux ipse clades praedicit, rebus malè cedentibus, Reformati minus possunt in Collegio. Nuper multa in Francum dicta, nunquam ejus foedera suscipient. Nuper dimidía pars pacem, amicitiam, foedus cum Pontefice, & papistico foedere

---

190 The various branches of the Contarini family supplied many officers of state during this period; in 1626 these included Ambassadors to the Netherlands, England, the Papacy, and France. But this reference appears to be to someone resident in Venice: most probably Nicolò Contarini (1553–1631), author of the *Historie venetiane*, who became Doge in 1630. He had been notably hawkish in his attitude towards the Habsburgs earlier in the 1620s (G. Cozzi, *Il doge Nicolò Contarini: ricerche sul patriziato veneziano agli inizi del seicento* (Venice, 1958), esp. pp. 169–95).

191 The Latin here is 'Turnius'; Hobbes, apparently not understanding the reference, has italianized it. Count Heinrich Matthias von Thurn (1567–1640) was one of the original leaders of the Bohemian revolt in 1618, and continued to support the causes of Frederick V and Gábor Bethlen thereafter. In January 1625 Venice appointed him commander of its land forces, hoping to benefit from his expertise while preparing against a possible Habsburg invasion; he remained in Venice, in this capacity, until April 1627 (H. von Zwiedineck-Südenhorst, 'Graf Heinrich Matthias Thurn in Diensten der Republik Venedig: eine Studie nach venetianischen Acten', *Archiv für österreichische Geschichte*, 66 (1885), pp. 257–76, esp. pp. 265–70).

192 The Doge ('Duke') of Venice was Giovanni Corner or Cornaro (d. 1629).

193 The 'Colledge' (Collegio) was the chief governing body in Venice, composed of the Doge and his advisers, the chief justices, and the 'Savii' (a group of senior statesmen elected by the Senate). 'Reformed' here ('Reformati' in the original) refers presumably to those elements, such as Fulgenzio Micanzio and Domenico Molino, who favoured a pro-Calvinist or generally pro-Protestant foreign policy (E. O. G. Haitsma Mulier, *The Myth of Venice and Dutch Republican Thought in the Seventeenth Century* (Assen, 1980), pp. 10, 89–92).

194 The Latin has 'pacem, amicitiam, foedus', 'peace, friendship, and an alliance'.

League.[195] And though they be iealous of and hate yᵉ Austrian Power, yet they had rather Caesar were mighty then they perish. It is incredible what the states Ambʳ[196] writeth of the contentions in yᵉ Colledge, *Nec*

[80v] *tantos Austro ciet adria fluctus nec coro superum mare*[197]

16

you see what you cannot do, and by whom you cannot; nor are there any others by whom you canne. your hope depends on other mens ayde, in which there be two thinges doubtfull,[198] their *Will* and their *Power*.[199] and the same will hardly[200] continue when you haue them. In the beginning of your fall you fownd that most were *Vnwillinge*, now you finde them *Vnable*[201] to. *Miserum est alieno incumbere fulcro*.[202] for our fall is then at yᵉ discretion of others. But Caesar though he [be troubled *deleted*] receaue hurt, yet hath he large and fertile Provinces, and vnited wealth, Thence comes strength and soldiers. His Imperiall command helpes him to, for they giue, that wish *vt nec bene vertat*.[203] His army is formidable to our men. The Spanish wealth and power, *Finitimis* [*inuidiessa* corrected to *invidiossa* [sic]] *locis*,[204] may yet last. That enuy gets you confederates not frends. If some other passion preuayle aboue their enuy and emulation, as it begins to do,[205] you shall be quite forsaken. He is not a warrior of one yere, nor a giuer of one ducat;[206] There come in yerely to that kinge from the [*2 letters deleted*] rootes of the mountaynes Ingots of molten gold, *Ditiaq*[*ue*] *argenti deducunt aequora lamnas*.[207] He wearyes all men with warre, and if he be a good

---

[195] In the first three months of 1626 a pro-Papal element in the Venetian Senate had called for reconciliation with the Papacy over the Valtelline. The majority had rejected this idea after hearing a speech to the Senate on 28 March by the French Ambassador, who promised resolute French military action; but the pro-Papal element gained strength soon afterwards when the Ambassador's credit was destroyed by news of the Franco-Spanish peace treaty of Monzón (see L. von Pastor, *Geschichte der Päpste seit dem Ausgang des Mittelalters*, 16 vols. (Freiburg im Breisgau, 1901–33), xiii(1), pp. 295–7).

[196] Johan Berck (1565–1627) served as Ambassador of the United Provinces in Venice from 1622 to 1627 (O. Schutte, *Repertorium der nederlandse vertegenwoordigers, residerende in het buitenland, 1584–1810* (The Hague, 1976), pp. 87–9).

[197] 'The Adriatic does not whip up so many waves in the south wind, nor does it do so in the wind from the north-west.'

[198] The Latin has 'incertissimae', 'extremely doubtful'.

[199] The word 'Power' has been altered from normal script to large script.

suasit. Et quamvis Austriacam potentiam exosam & suspectam habeant, malunt tamen Caesarem esse potentem, quàm se perire. Incredibilia sunt, quae Legatus Statuum de concertationibus Collegij scribit.

— Nec tantos Austro ciet Adria fluctus.
Nec Coro superum mare.

XVI.

Vides quid non possis, & per quos non possis; nec alij sunt per quos possis. Spes tua alieno nititur auxilio; in quo duae sunt res incertissimae. VOLUNTAS & POTENTIA. Earundem rerum difficillima est perseverantia. Sensisti initio ruinae tuae plerisque deesse VOLUNTATEM, nunc etiam POTENTIAM;

Miserum est alieno incumbere fulcro:

nam lapsus est in alieno arbitrio. At Caesar licet afflictus, vastas tamen habet, & fertilitate nativa dites Provincias, opésque junctas: Inde miles & nervus; Imperio etiam sublevatur; dant enim illi qui optant

Vt nec bene vertat.

Exercitus eius nostris est formidabilis. Hispanae opes & potentia

— Finitimis invidiosa locis.

durare potest. Invidia illa tibi socios, non amicos conciliavit; si Livorem & aemulationem alius vicerit affectus, uti jam fieri coeptum, deserêre. Non est bellator unius anni, nec donator unius aurei. Illi Regi de montium radicibus in annos singulos ramenta metalli fluentis,

Ditiáque argenti deducunt aequora Lamnas.

---

[200] 'Hardly' here is used in its sense (now obsolete) of 'with difficulty' (see *OED*, 'hardly', 6–7). The Latin has 'difficillima est perseverantia', meaning that they will continue only 'with extreme difficulty'.

[201] The word 'Vnable' has been altered from normal script to large script.

[202] 'It is miserable to lie on someone else's couch' (adapted from Juvenal, *Saturae*, VIII, l. 76: 'miserum est aliorum incumbere famae').

[203] 'That it may not turn out well' (adapted from Vergil, *Eclogae*, IX, l. 6: 'quod nec bene vertat').

[204] 'Envied by neighbouring territories' (Ovid, *Heroides*, VII, l. 120).

[205] See above, n. 120.   [206] 'Ducat' here translates 'aurei', 'gold coin'.

[207] 'The rich sheets of silver are turned into coins.'

husband[208] may weary them out. [Hee *altered to* He] is able therefore to vngergo [*sic*] a very long warre. He hath euery yere some new degree of Power, new Prouinces, new veynes of Gold and siluer.

17

His Confederates are not weake. The Pope is come to him,[209] and more are comminge, perhaps the Venetian to. And though they feele ye smart of the warres, yet they hate a trecherous Peace, and such as aymes at occasion of Mischiefe. They haue an [har? *deleted*] army hardened wth vse, whose sight our men endure not[.][210] your selfe lately read letters from Wolfenbutelius,[211] pitifull ones, and full of despayre. Namely that for many and most weighty causes, the Dane was vnable to relieue the Citties by Tilly besieged, An[d][212] consequently wth no lesse dammage of the army, then Infamie, y[^{ose}][213] garrisons were murthred in ye sight of an Idle kinge and fearfu[ll][214] Campe.[215] Warre depends on fame, and that they haue cast away, when they not onely not excuse so great a couardise, but flatly deny that they are able to relieue them for ye future. What then doth he so nere the wretches? That they may perish with a witnesse?

[81r]

18

The warre therefore is on all hands difficult. If you hasten fight, you fight against valiant and old soldiers, and victorious, wch is neuer without danger, seldome wth out a defeate. If you prolonge the warre, the enemy can longest hold out, both [*2 letters deleted*] with his owne wealth and ours. For both the Palatinates, are husbanded to their vse, and the seate

---

[208] 'Husband' here translates 'oeconomus', 'manager of a household'.

[209] Pope Urban VIII had been notably less enthusiastic than his predecessor, Gregory XV, in his support for the Imperial cause (Bireley, *Jesuits and the Thirty Years War*, pp. 64–5, 84). In 1625 Urban did urge the German bishops, and the King of Spain, to give money to Bavaria and the Emperor; but he excused himself from making large contributions, as he had to pay for raising a Papal force to drive the French out of the Valtelline. However, after the Franco-Spanish treaty of Monzón (which made such a force unnecessary) he became more active in support of the Catholic forces in Germany, sending encouraging letters to the Emperor, the Duke of Bavaria, and the Archbishop of Mainz in early June 1626 (von Pastor, *Geschichte der Päpste*, xii(1), pp. 299–300).

omnes bello fatigat, & si oeconomus esse velit, evincet, longissimo itaque bello par est. In annos singulos novus illi potentiae gradus additur; novae Provinciae, novae metallorum venae.

XVII.

Ne foederatis quidem invalidae vires, Accessit illis & Papa, jungentur alij, forsan & Veneti. Et licet belli damna sentiant; insidiosam tamen pacem, & nocendi occasionibus intentam oderunt. Firmatum usu exercitum habent; aspectum eius ferre nostri non possunt, legisti ipse nuper literas Wolffenbütelio scriptas, sanè miserabiles, & desperatione plenas; Nimirum ob plurimas gravissimásque causas, non posse Danum, Urbibus à Tillio obsessis occurrere. Itaque non minore damno exercitus, quàm infamiae flagitio, praesidia nostra in conspectu ociosi Regis, & castrorum paventium contrucidantur. At bella constant famâ; famam autem prodegerunt, qui non modò tantam inertiam non excusant, sed etiam in posterum negant auxiliari se posse. Quid ergò miseris assident? an ne sine teste pereant.

XVIII.

Difficile igitur est undiquaque bellum. Si acceleras, contra validos, & veteranos exercitus, contra victores victo pugnandum est: quod nunquam periculo, rarissimè clade caret. Si bellum trahis; hostis diutiùs durabit, opibus & suis & nostris. Nam Palatinatus uterque eorum bono

---

210 This punctuation mark is lacking; but some mark seems to be required by the sense.

211 The city of Wolfenbüttel; Hobbes gives the impression that he thinks this is a personal name.

212 The 'd' is obscured by the binding.

213 This reading is uncertain; the contraction is something more extensive than 'yᵉ', but the last part of it is obscured by the binding. The Latin has 'praesidia nostra', 'our garrisons'.

214 The 'll' is obscured by the binding.

215 In 1626 Tilly (see above, n. 170) besieged the small fortress-town of Münden (near Kassel) from 5 to 9 June, and the city of Göttingen from 17 June to 9 August. The garrison of the former was massacred; that of the latter was permitted to leave on 11 August. Neither place was literally 'in the sight' of King Christian or his army (based in Wolfenbüttel), but they were within a few days' march.

of ye warre is in our ground. They are at great charges, but yet they
go through,[216] and encrease their forces. nor haue they yet cast forth
the holy Anchor,[217] nor set on foot the Crusado, nor yet armed the
Clergie. And all this they would do, if we should put them to their
vtmost. They take heart at our threatninges. Wee threatned lately a
warre from Denmarke, England, Sweden, but the greatest storme by the
way of Lorrayne and ye Mountayne Voige.[218] presently[219] they oppose
their forces. Deuxponts, and [*Saru? deleted*] Sara,[220] too nere your *heu
quondam*[221] subiects dearly buy that threatninge. This is an argument,
they meane not [*2 letters deleted*] to shrinke. Euery thinge is in that
estate, and so shut vp, that wth out a most long warre, and a most difficult
iourney, the Palatinate can neuer be recouered. No hope therefore from
ye armes of yor frends. *Sola potest victo pax reddita ferre salutem.*[222]

19

By force, the way is barred. This way you can do nothinge. in vayne are
yor treasures spent, yor contry wasted, and bloud spilt. Giue ouer. you
can do nothinge in spight of successe.[223] Goe not ye bloudy way. There
rest onely two pathes to be trodden, Prayers, and Fraud. The prayers
of kinges are powerfull, of banisht men, pitifull. For Fraud theres place
[81v]   euery where, euen against the fraudulent. When ye Lions skin is worne
out, put on the [*Foxs C? deleted*] Foxes case.[224] If by entreaty you can

---

216   'Go through' here translates 'evadunt', which has the general sense of 'go forth',
'proceed', 'carry on'.

217   The Latin here has 'Necdum sacram anchoram levarunt', 'they have not yet raised
the holy anchor'. Traditionally, a ship would have one extra-large anchor, known as the
'sacra ancora', that was used only in emergencies; to cast the 'holy anchor' was thus a
proverbial phrase for an action of the last resort. Hobbes's use of 'cast forth' to translate
'levarunt' (the opposite procedure, in fact) suggests that he was familiar with the proverb.
Following this clause, the Latin has another clause which Hobbes has not translated:
'necdum Ecclesias oppignorârunt [a misprint for 'oppignerârunt']', 'they have not yet
mortgaged the churches'.

218   Richelieu's advice to Louis XIII in February 1626 (see above, n. 88) proposed two
campaigns against Germany, one from the north (organized primarily by Denmark) and
one from the west (organized by France, England, and the United Provinces). In that
same month it was reported in the Spanish Netherlands that Louis XIII was planning an
attack on the Lower Palatinate through the Duchy of Zweibrücken (Deux-Ponts) (see de
Meester, ed., *Correspondance de Guidi di Bagno*, ii, p. 713). On 3 March Maximilian of
Bavaria wrote to warn Archduke Leopold that French forces were gathering for an attack
on Zweibrücken or upper Alsace; alarmed, Leopold wrote to the Infanta in Brussels on
30 March, asking for reinforcements (Obser, 'Markgraf Georg Friedrich', p. 340). That

colitur, & sedem belli in nostro collocat. Magno sumptu gravantur, sed evadunt tamen, & novo semper accessu vires adaugent. Necdum sacram anchoram levarunt, necdum Ecclesias oppignorârunt, necdum crucem praedicârunt bellicam, nec dum clerum armârunt: & illâ tamen facturi sunt, si extrema tentemus. A minis nostris animis recipiunt, bellum è Dania, Britannia, Suecia nuper minabamur, praecipuam verò per Mediomatrices, aut Vogesi montes tempestatem, at illi mox copias opponunt; minas luit Bipontinus, & Sara nimiùm vicinus tuis, heu quondam Civibus. Indicium hoc est cedere nolentium. Omnia verò ita constituta atque obsepta sunt, ut nonnisi diutissimo bello, difficillimo itinere recuperari Palatinatus possit. Nulla itaque spes in armis amicorum.

Sola potest victo, pax reddita ferre salutem.

XIX.

Praeclusa est, quae sit vi via, Hâc nihil potes. incassum tot opes effusae, Provinciae vastatae, fusus sanguis. Absiste, nihil ages invito successu. Vias cruentas ambulare noli; supersunt tibi semitae duae, mutuo nexu concordes, precum & fraudum. Regum preces sunt validae, Exulum miserabiles. Dolis ubique locus est, etiam contra dolosos. Leoninae lacerae vulpina succedanea esto. Precibus si partem à Caesare impetrabis,

France had entertained such plans was confirmed by the documents seized from Wensin (von Aretin, *Bayerns auswärtige Verhältnisse*, appendix 2, p. 192; cf. above, n. 73). If it had aimed at the Lower Palatinate, the French army would thus have passed through Lorraine, the Saar, and the Vosges mountains ('Vogesi montes' here).

219 'Presently' here has the sense of 'soon' or 'immediately' ('mox').

220 See above, n. 218; these two territories were now garrisoned by Imperial forces.

221 'Alas, former!'   222 'Only the return of peace can bring safety to the defeated.'

223 'In spight of successe' here translates 'invito successu' (literally, 'when success is unwilling'; meaning 'when success [*sc.* the outcome] goes against you').

224 'Case' here means 'the skin or hide of an animal' (*OED*, 'case', n., 2 (4.a)); the Latin has 'lacerae', which Hobbes or his manuscript copy has evidently (and sensibly) emended to 'lacernae' (from 'lacerna', a cloak). This may be an echo of Lipsius, *Politicorum libri sex*, IV.13, p. 205: 'Et ex Spartani regis monito: . . . Vbi Leonina pellis non pertingit, oportet Vulpinam assuëre' ('And, as the king of Sparta advised, "where the lion's skin does not reach, it must be patched up with the fox's" '). Lipsius took this quotation from Plutarch's *Life of Lysander* (VII, 4); but behind all discussions of the lion-fox theme by political writers of this period there lay one of the most famous passages in Machiavelli, *The Prince*, ch. 18, where it is said that the prince must have the qualities of both the lion and the fox.

get of ye Emp.^{r} but part of your contry, that part may draw the whole. Archimedes vsed to say that if he had another world to stand in, he could by his art, moue this world out of his place. If you can get part of yor Contry to stand in, you will gather wealth by little and little, and getting an army together secretly, oppresse your neighbours before they heare of it. The reason and way of this, the deputies of Holland haue lately taught.[225] And surely the Husbandmen could do this at Anassus,[226] and cannot Fredericke? be not ashamed of entreatinge, Turnus entreated Aeneas, *Victos non dedecent vittaeque et verba precantum.*[227] Not you but yor fortune begges. Its she that will blush to haue had so much power ouer you,[228] and she also, when she shall be stronger will kill the Emp.^{r} you know the Crocodiles teares; you shall by those frends wch through hope and your promises you haue yet left you, recouer Caesars fauor. They speake gently of you euery where. [>And] That no peace wthout restitution.[229] That mercy becomes Catholiques; That a Prince of Antient power shold not be put downe.[230] That Dauid spared Sawl. That warre was chargeable.[231] Loade these men wth [hopes *deleted*] promises, fill them wth hopes. you know euery where, who is in fauo^r and wherein he can preuayle. The mayne thinge is where force succeedes not to ouerthrow their councell. Feare nothinge. No Prince is without his Achitophell, that can both giue euil Counsayle, and so cloake it that it may passe for good.[232] Of other Princes Counsailors, all haue that opinion. Princes thinke so of any princes counsayle; but of their owne none, or but one or two.[233]

---

[225] This probably refers to Dutch encroachment on the neighbouring territory of East Friesland. Mansfeld had stationed his army there in 1623, occupying Emden and establishing other fortified positions close to the Dutch border; when he left, in 1624, the Dutch in turn occupied some of these positions.

[226] 'Anassus' is the river Enns, in Austria; this comment refers to the Peasants' War in Upper Austria in 1626. The area had been placed under Bavarian administration in 1620, and the Bavarians had begun the forcible conversion of the (mostly Lutheran) population to Catholicism. After most of the leaders of a protest delegation were executed, a large peasant revolt took place in the spring and early summer of 1626, during which the rebels seized several towns near Linz (including Steyr and Enns, both on the river Enns). The revolt was finally crushed in November 1626. (See G. Heilingsetzer, *Der oberösterreichische Bauernkrieg 1626* (Vienna, 1976).)

pars illa totum trahet. Archimedes movere mundum arte se posse dictitabat; si alium mundum in quo pedem poneret, haberet. Tibi si pars Provinciae detur, in qua pedem ponas, opes sensim colliges, & clàm exercitum, quo famam praeveniens vicinos opprimas; Rationem modúmque nuper deputati Batavi docuerunt. Et sanè potuerunt hoc rusticani ad Anassum, non posset Fredericus? Nec dedignare preces, etiam rogavit Turnus Aeneam.

> *Victos non dedecent*
> *Vittaeque & verba precantum.*

Non tu, sed fortuna tua precabitur, erubescet illa in te tantum sibi licuisse? illa eadem cùm fortior erit, Caesarem occidet. Nôsti Lacrymas Crocodili. Caesaris gratiam per amicos tuos parabis, quos spe & promissis adhuc tenes. De te illi, ubique mollia loquuntur; Nullam nisi te restituto fore pacem. Catholicos Clementiam decere. Non privandum avitis opibus Principem. Davidem pepercisse Sauli: nimis bellum esse sumptuosum. Hos promissis onera; spe impleto. Scis quo quisque loco sit gratiosus, ubi polleat. Caput rei est, cùm vis, non succedit, consilia destruere. Pone metum, nulli Principum suus deest Achitophel, qui & mala consilia det, & ita palliet, ut bona videantur, de alijs Principibus omnes & singuli, de singulis Principibus Principes id credunt, de suis nemo, vel duo, vel nemo.

---

[227] '[Proffering] sacrificial head-bands and the words of supplicants is no disgrace for those who have been defeated' (adapted from Vergil, *Aeneid*, VII, l. 237: 'Praeferimus manibus vittas ac verba precantum'). Turnus, king of the Rutili, made war against Aeneas and was defeated by him.

[228] In the Latin this phrase is a question: 'erubescet illa in te tantum sibi licuisse?' ('will she blush at having taken such a liberty in your case?'); possibly the manuscript copy used by Hobbes omitted the question mark. (See above, Ch. 4 n. 34.)

[229] The Latin has 'nisi te restituto' ('without your restitution').

[230] The Latin has 'Non privandum avitis opibus Principem' ('That a prince should not be deprived of his ancestral possessions').

[231] 'Chargeable' here translates 'nimis . . . sumptuosum' ('extremely expensive', or 'excessively expensive').

[232] See 2 Samuel, chs. 15–17.

[233] The Latin here ('nemo, vel duo, vel nemo') is taken from Persius, *Saturae*, I, ll. 2–3, 'nemo? | vel duo, vel nemo' (usually translated as 'Nobody? One or two, or nobody').

20

[82r] But in what order will you proceed? Will you do it before the Dyet?²³⁴ your owne aduiser, would haue you do it wᵗʰ teares and lamentation in the Dyet it selfe.²³⁵ And to this aduise he giues the garland; I thinke it nothinge worth. For though your Calamity, may moue to pitty such as you haue done no harme to, yet will it not appease the offended. Euery man feeles his owne losse. They all lay the fault vpon you. Euery mans owne payne pinches him. Whilest he is yet in choller, he will exclude pitty. They will all reckon their dammages, and require amends. Ten [plo? *deleted*] Palatinates will not serue to stop up so many mouthes. And though there be specially two that hold your Prouinces, the Spaniard and Bauiere,²³⁶ yet others haue pretty skirtes of it, so that yoʳ patrimony is amongst a dozen of them, and those great ones, of wᶜʰ not one will render.²³⁷ *Boius propositi est tenax Iberque parto cedere nescius.*²³⁸ And there is no lesse an impediment on our partes.²³⁹ For they cannot deale with you publiquely, without acknowledginge your fault and crying mercy,²⁴⁰ wᵗʰ [prop . . . ? *altered to* promise] to obey hereafter, and security for satisfaction. Caesar will not dissemble his great losses, he will exact amends. If you vndergo this you [stey? *deleted*] stayne your dignity, and oblige your [*word altered to* selfe] to all. For what can he complayne of, that confesseth himselfe guilty of so many crimes? They will not perdon all iniuries. They obiect to yoʳ longe stubbornesse, and yᵉ seekinge of the ruine of the Empire by the Turkes and Tartars. The prayers of yᵉ French will be but cold, as one that had rather please yᵉ Papistes. The prayers of yᵉ English will be contemned as one of no power. And yᵉ prayers of yᵉ Dane will be reiected wᵗʰ hatred, as of an enemy.

21

If there be no place for entreaty, there remayneth fraud. It will be easie to deceaue them, if you deliuer your children [to the Spaniard *deleted*]

²³⁴ The Imperial Diet (Reichstag) had not met since 1613. A meeting planned for 1624 had not taken place; a Diet of Deputies (Deputationstag), called for August 1625 in Ulm, had been twice delayed and in the end did not take place either. But the reference here is apparently to an Imperial Diet, at which princes of the Empire appeared in person; no such diet was held until 1640.

²³⁵ This probably refers to Frederick's senior adviser and Chancellor, Volrad von Plessen, who recommended that Frederick make a formal submission and promise of

XX.

Verùm quo perges ordine? An Comitia antevertes? in ipso te Conventu lachrymis & querelis agere consultor tuus jubet, & isti consilio palmam tribuit; ego ne algam quidem. Etsi enim calamitas tua movere posset inlaesos, non tamen placabit infensos. Sua quisque detrimenta sentit; causam in te conferunt omnes, suus quemque dolor urit; ille miserationem tui excludit, dum adhuc fervet, omnes damna computabunt, res repetent, tot votis ne deni quidem Palatinatus sufficient. Et quamvis à duobus praecipuè tuae Provinciae teneantur, Ibero, & Boio, Lacinias tamen sat magnas alij quoque tenent; ita ut inter duodecim sit ditio tua, & quidem potentes, divisa, quorum nemo sponte reddet.

> *Boius propositi est tenax*
> *Ibérque parto cedere nescius.*

Nec minus à nobis impedimentum objicitur: publicè tecum agi nihil potest, nisi agnitâ culpâ veniam poscas, pariturum pollicearis, satis dandi cautionem praestes. Caesar gravia damna non dissimulabit; compensationem exiget. Ista si subibis dignitatem minues, & cunctis te obligabis. Quid enim queri potest, tot criminum se reum professus? Iniurias non omnes condonabunt, contumaciam longam objectant, & ex Tartaris Turcísque quaesitam Imperij ruinam. Franci preces erunt frigidae, vt qui placere Papistis malit, Britanni contemnentur, ut impotentis, Dani vt inimici cum odio reiicientur.

XXI.

Si precibus locus non erit, superest dolus. Fallere autem promptum erit, si Hispano, Caesaríve, aut Boio liberi tradantur educandi, religio favorem

---

satisfaction to the Emperor (in return for full restitution of the Palatinates) in February 1626, and again in November (see A. Gindely, *Friedrich V von der Pfalz, der ehemalige Winterkönig von Böhmen seit dem Regensburger Deputationstag vom Jahre 1622 bis zu seinem Tode* (Prague, 1885), p. 22).

[236] The Upper Palatinate was occupied by Bavaria; the Lower Palatinate was occupied primarily by forces from the Spanish Netherlands.

[237] Hobbes (or his manuscript copy) omits 'sponte' ('of his own accord').

[238] 'The Bavarian is firm of purpose; the Spaniard does not know how to withdraw from what he has acquired.' (The phrases 'tenax propositi' and 'cedere nescius' are both taken from Horace: *Odes* III.3, l. 1, and I.6, l. 6.)

[239] 'An impediment on our partes' here means 'an objection raised on our side' ('à nobis impedimentum objicitur').

[240] Meaning, 'without your acknowledging your fault and begging for mercy'.

[82v] to be brought up by ye Spaniard the Emp^r or Bauiere.²⁴¹ Religion will get their fauo^r, and some of yor sonnes may haue benefices, and Bishoprickes. This is no small encrease of power. To some of them some portion of yor territory may be restored. The English will neuer be offended with the so easie sellinge of Religion. nor will it be a dishono^r to you to [returne *altered to* turne], you but returne to your ancestors, who were Papists. Onely Frederique ye 3^d and your Father were of ye Reformed Religion; few Lutherans.²⁴² I wonder that they Contemne you and yours so much, not onely in England but in Germany, that they bee not called to some Protestant Cathedrall Churches; for that lyes pat for men banished. Is it contempt? or want of loue? or does euery man loue himselfe best?²⁴³

22.

But if yor owne resolutions restrayne you, and you will not suffer yor children to be taught any other Religion, wee must then goe another way to worke. See what you can get in Holland. Ernest of Nassaw is fallen of. it may be Henry²⁴⁴ may be set goinge. Shall a child of .2. monethes old be put, or required to ye Helme of Frisland,²⁴⁵ and stand you still? The Arminians loue Henry, but ye Gomaristes, especially ye Magistrates hate him.²⁴⁶ He is somewhat of a rough nature, obnoxious to accusation.²⁴⁷ you they [that? *deleted*] hate to, but you must labo^r to get ye affections of ye great ones. Lift euery stone,²⁴⁸ theres treasure vnder some. He can loose nothinge by troublinge the water²⁴⁹ that hath nothinge. Aske some [ch? *deleted*] Command for yor selfe or children, occasions may rise of getting vp againe. nothinge misbecomes that carries profit with it.

---

²⁴¹ In 1623 plans had been seriously canvassed (and promoted by James I) for a settlement of the conflict to be accomplished by betrothing Frederick's elder son either to a daughter of the Emperor (with the son to be brought up at the Imperial court, obtaining the Palatine territories and electoral title on coming of age), or to a niece of the Duke of Bavaria; both plans were firmly rejected by Frederick (see Pursell, *Winter King*, pp. 200, 203–5, 208–9). In early August 1626 the idea was revived by the Spanish diplomat Gondomar in Brussels, who proposed a full restitution of the territories and dignities of the Elector Palatine on condition that (*a*) some territory be kept by Bavaria as a surety until all war-reparations were paid, and (*b*) Frederick's children be brought up as Catholics, some at the Imperial court and some in Bavaria (von Aretin, *Bayerns auswärtige Verhältnisse*, appendix 2, p. 204, account of meeting between Gondomar and the Bavarian envoy to Brussels, 10 August 1626; cf. p. 208 for Bavaria's rejection of this idea). Cf. also above, Ch. 3, at nn. 55, 62.

²⁴² As a statement about Electors Palatine this is correct, since John Casimir (another Calvinist) acted only as regent. Frederick III (r. 1559–76) was the first Calvinist Elector

conciliabit, filijs quibusdam Sacerdotia & Episcopatus patebunt. Magnum hîc potentiae incrementum; alijs de Provincia portio reddetur; nec Britanni offendentur, facili religionis nundinatione. Nec dedecori erit illa transitio, majoribus tuis accedes, qui Papistae fuerunt, solus Fridericus tertius & Pater tuus, reformatae religionis fuere, pauci Lutherani. Miror sanè, non modò in Anglia, sed etiam in Germania, ita te tuósque contemni ut ne ad Evangelicas quidem Ecclesias Cathedrales vocentur, cùm id Exulibus commodissimum foret: An ille contemptus est? an alienatio? an sibi quisque bene esse, quàm alijs mavult?

XXII.

Si tamen tua te decreta tenent, nec filios aliâ religione imbui permittis, alia tentanda est via. In Batavia vide, si quid obtinere possis. Ernestus Nassovius excidit, forsan impelli posset Henricus: Puer duorum mensium claro Frisiorum admovetur, aut petitur, tu cessas? Henricum Arminiani amant; Gommaristae, praesertim Magistratus, oderunt. asperioris est ingenij, accusationibus obnoxius, te quoque exosum antè dixi, sed adlaborandum, ut potentium tibi animos concilies. omnem move lapidem, sub aliquo thesaurus erit. Rebus turbatis nihil perdere potest, qui nihil habet. Pete vel tibi vel filijs, quamcunque Praefecturam, occasio erit emergendi, nihil dedecet, quod utile est.

Palatine; his successor, Ludwig VI (r. 1576–83) reintroduced Lutheranism; and Ludwig's younger brother, Frederick IV (Frederick V's father; r. 1592–1610) was a Calvinist, having been brought up under the influence of his uncle John Casimir, who ruled the Palatinate during his minority.

[243] This translates 'an sibi quisque bene esse, quàm alijs mavult?' ('does everyone prefer his own well-being to that of others?').

[244] 'Ernest' was Ernst Casimir, stadhouder of Friesland (see above, n. 124). 'Henry' was Frederik Hendrik, Prince of Orange (see above, n. 121), stadhouder of Holland, Zeeland, Utrecht, Overijssel, and Gelderland.

[245] For the claim that a baby had been declared stadhouder of Friesland, see above, at n. 124.

[246] 'Gomarists' (followers of the theologian Franciscus Gomarus) were strict Calvinists, opponents of the Arminians. In some towns the members of the town councils ('Magistrates' here) were anti-Arminian even though Arminians formed a significant part of the population. In one such case, Utrecht, Frederik Hendrik instructed the council in February 1626 that it could no longer use army troops to quell Arminian meetings (see Israel, *Dutch Republic*, p. 492).

[247] 'Obnoxious' here ('obnoxius' in the original) means 'liable' or 'subject'.

[248] For this proverbial phrase see D. Erasmus, *Adagiorum opus* (Basel, 1533), p. 141, I.4.xxx, 'Omnem mouere lapidem'.

[249] 'Troublinge the water' here translates 'Rebus turbatis' ('by stirring things up').

23.

If it succeed not, or but slowly in Holland, attempt England. in that kingdome all is swolne. you will driue out ye young King[250] at first dash, as one that is hated by the nobility. There will be a iust cause of reuenge, the defendinge of Buckingham that killed your Father in law.[251] You the sonne in law do but [the *deleted*] reuenge the death of your father

[83r] in law which his sonne neglecteth. Nothinge can be more acceptable to ye kingdome, to which nothinge is more odious then Buckingham. To gayne you their affections, none [g *deleted*] could haue better done it, then the kinge, that has alienated them from himselfe. All delayes are hinderances. begin, by yor frends and Complices. They are yet aliue, and flourish that make y^e *White Powder*, and gaue it to Hamilton,[252] and your Father in law. Vndertake the cause, the kingdome will take you into her bosome. Draw away yor Brother in lawes frends, when he is alone, you will get him downe. Shew the Donatiue, the Bishops and Clergies wealth. The Puritans allured with that bayte, will carry you into ye throne vpon their shoulders. The Scotch nobility is dry and couetous, promise them booty. They are displeased with the impuritanity[253] of ye Bishops replanted there by your Father in law,[254] augment their discontents. In England the Noble men, are for ye most part needie, ambitious, prodigall, luxurious, emulators of each other. your Vertue may make vse of these mens vices to yor hono^r:[255] All such are weary of ye present, changeable wth expectation of the future,[256] easie to be won with promises, By these you may subuert Charles, and by yo^{r}selfe these.

24

Nor will ye French in ayd of his sister hinder you. The lilies goe not ouersea. The French ride, not sayle. The Hollanders lately ouer-came

250 At the time of writing of this text, Charles I was 25 years old; 'young' here translates 'adolescentem', which, in classical Latin, could be used of someone under the age of 30 or even 40.

251 The claim that Buckingham had poisoned James I was made by the Scottish physician George Eglisham (see his *Prodromus vindictae in Ducem Buckinghamiae, pro virulenta caede potissimi Magnae Britanniae Regis Iacobi* (Frankfurt am Main, 1626), esp. pp. 43–8), and was widely circulated; Buckingham responded to it in the House of Lords on 15 [/25] May 1626 (S. R. Gardiner, ed., *Notes of the Debates in the House of Lords . . . 1624 and 1626*, Camden Society, NS xxiv (London, 1879), p. 193).

252 James Hamilton, second Marquess of Hamilton (1589–1625), died of a fever at Whitehall on 2 [/12] March 1625, three and a half weeks before the death of James

XXIII.

Si Batavica vel minùs, vel lentè sub manum succedant; Britannias aggredere, omnia in illo regno tument, Regem adolescentem primo impetu propelles, utpote invisum proceribus; justa vindictae causa, defensus Buchingamius, Soceri interfector, Gener necem Soceri, quam filius negligit, ulcisceris. Nihil regno gratius, cui nihil odiosius est Buchingamio. Iungere animos tibi meliùs nemo potuit, quàm Rex, qui eos à se abalienavit: omnis tibi mora obstat, per amicos & conjuratos rem incipe, Vivunt, floréntque albi pulveris architecti, qui Hamiltonio, Soceróque miscuerunt: Causam suscipe, te sinu suo regnum suscipiet, Affini amicos subtrahes, solitarium excuties. Donatiuum ostenta, Praesulum & Cleri opes, Purae religionis sectatores illâ illecebrâ inescati, humeris suis in thronum te extollent. Scotiae nobilitas, arida est, & avida, praedas pollicere. Offensa est impuritate Episcoporum, quos socer reposuit, offensas auge. In Anglia Proceres plerique sunt egentes, ambitiosi, sumptuosi, luxuriosi, aemuli aliorum, alienis vitijs tua virtus ad summum decus consequendum utatur. Omnes tales, praesentium sunt fastidiosi, futurorum expectatione mobiles, regnantibus infidi, pollicentibus faciles. Per eos Carolum, per te illos everte.

XXIV.

Nec Francus obsistet, ut sororio adsistat. Lilia non tranant aequora. Equitat non navigat Francus. Nuper pro illo Batavi vicêre. nec sermones

---

I. George Eglisham (see above, n. 251) had been brought up with Hamilton and had remained under his patronage; in his pamphlet he also claimed that Hamilton had been poisoned by Buckingham (*Prodromus vindictae*, pp. 22–43). Specifically, he wrote that Buckingham had given James I a 'poisonous white powder' (p. 46: 'pulverem album virulentum'), which the king had taken in a glass of wine.

253 This word (translating 'impuritate') appears to be Hobbes's coinage. *OED* has an entry for the noun 'impuritan' ('a hostile term for one not a Puritan or opposed to Puritanism': it gives citations from 1617 and 1627), but none for 'impuritanity'.

254 The moribund Scottish episcopate was resuscitated by James VI and I, who increased the number of bishops and strengthened their powers. Presbyterian opposition to this focused not so much on the qualities or beliefs ('impuritanity') of the bishops themselves as on the various changes in practice that accompanied this development—especially those specified in the Five Articles of Perth (1618), which included kneeling at communion and the celebration of Holy Days (D. G. Mullan, *Episcopacy in Scotland: the History of an Idea, 1560–1638* (Edinburgh, 1986), pp. 95–113, 151–65).

255 'To yor hono^r' here translates 'ad summum decus consequendum' ('to attain the highest honour').

256 Hobbes (or his manuscript copy) omits the phrase 'regnantibus infidi' ('disloyal to their rulers').

for him.²⁵⁷ Feare not what men say. Successe makes any defence iust. He that is Vanquished, is he that is guilty. Victory seekes not Aduocates but breedes them. If the French allowed of yoʳ Bohemian action, he will not condemne this of England, they are [*word altered to* alike] iust [of *deleted* >or] alike vniust. Besides, yoʳ sonne may chance to haue a wife out of yᵉ land of yᵉ lilies. your Brother in law deserues to be put out, because he ayded you slowly. And it is iust that yᵉ British nobility should perish, because they delay the kinge, and had rather Buckingham should dye then you liue. But this you must dissemble. When you haue the power in yoʳ handes, then off wᵗʰ the ouertoppinge Poppies heades.²⁵⁸

[83v]

25

Seeme these thinges hard and dangerous? *Nil sine magno vita labore dedit mortalibus.*²⁵⁹ To attempt great thinges, is an act of your owne. But if you like somewhat else better, that is easie, and wᵗʰout vnquietnesse. Sell yoʳ whole Prouince to yᵉ French or some other mighty Prince together wᵗʰ all yoʳ rights and priuiledges for meate and drinke, and sit still. The buyer will seeke the possession of it with his sword; and you the while may be out of the way of Jupiter and his lightninge. Euery one will consult seriously, and fight lustily for his owne. The People of Rome haue taken [her? *deleted*] armes heretofore for those that put themselues into their protection. Many will come to [by? *deleted*] buy another title, if it be sold cheape. The Saxons sold themselues to yᵉ Dane,²⁶⁰ at first wᵗʰ good conditions, though now they be tyed to hard lawes, and heare this, *Vri. Secari.*²⁶¹ They find the Fencer vexinge them vnder yᵉ name of Patron more heauy then yᵉ enemy, and do therefore begin to looke backe to Caesar.

---

²⁵⁷ On the loan of a Dutch squadron to France in 1625–6, see above, n. 74.

²⁵⁸ The Latin here, 'metes eminentia papaverum', alludes to the story of King Tarquin of Rome, who, when asked what should be done with the leaders of the Gabii, gave no verbal response but struck off the heads of poppies with his stick (Florus, *Epitome*, I.1, 'eminentia forte papaverum capita virgula excutiens'; Frontinus, *Stratagemata*, I.1, 'virga eminentia papaverum capita . . . decussit').

²⁵⁹ 'Life has given nothing to mortals without great labour' (Horace, *Saturae*, I.9, ll. 59–60).

metue. successu omnis defensio justa redditur, qui victus est, nocens habetur. Victoria non quaerit advocatos, sed parit; si Bohemica probavit Francus, non damnabit Britanna. Pari jure pollent, aut pari injuriâ. Quin & filio tuo obtingere possunt nuptiae de terra liliorum. Affinis tuus meruit excidere, quia tardè juvit. Proceres Britanniae perire justum est, quia Regem morantur, & mori malunt Buchingamium, quàm te vivere. Verùm ista dissimulabis: rerum potitus metes eminentia papaverum.

XXV.

Ardua ista videntur & periculosa?

> — —*Nil sine magno*
> *Vita labore dedit mortalibus.*

Factum tuum est magna aggredi. Si aliud placet, quod facile, quietúmque est. Provinciam tuam universam, Franco aut alteri potenti, juráque omnia divende, & pactus alimenta quiesce. Emptor evictionem sibi gladio praestet, Tu sede procul Iove & fulmine. Pro suis quisque rebus consultat seriò, pugnat fortiter. Olim pro deditis Quirites arma sumpsere. Alienam litem si vili veneat, multi ibunt praestinatum. Saxones se Dano vendidere, bonâ initiò conditione. licet nunc duris legibus auctorentur, & illud audiant: *Vri, secari*: Graviorem sentiunt Lanistam, nomine Patroni saevientem, quàm hostem, ideòque Caesarem respectant.

---

²⁶⁰ This probably refers to the decision by the Lower Saxon Circle in April 1625 to appoint Christian IV 'Kreisoberst' (military leader of the Circle).
²⁶¹ 'To be burned; to be cut' This phrase (used in the Latin translation of Aristotle's *Categories*, sect. 4 (2a4), where 'to cut, to burn' are given as examples of acting, and 'to be cut, to be burned' are given as examples of being the subject of another's action) derived from a medical phrase, current in both Greece and Rome. Cicero gave it a political application, saying that in the state, as in the body, we allow a harmful limb 'to be burned and cut' ('uri secarique') so that the rest of the body may be saved (*In M. Antonium*, VIII, para. 15); this remark attracted public controversy when Lipsius paraphrased it and applied it to the extirpation of religious dissent (see Lipsius, *Politicorum libri sex*, IV.3, p. 109; G. Güldner, *Das Toleranz-Problem in den Niederlanden im Ausgang des 16. Jahrhunderts* (Lübeck, 1968), pp. 97, 100–2).

26

Why will you not imitate Hessen, and in a iuster cause? he offred to ye French Kinge his Castles, Citties, subiects, and ye wealth and bloud of himselfe and children,[262] and least it should not seeme in ernest, he gaue vp the Boies that had endured his campe amongst them two yeres together to be sacrificed at vnawares by the veterane legions, that by such a sacrifice he might ratify his french seruitude.[263] Nor ought it to trouble you, that like a base fugitiue he was contemned, and his poore Amb^rs at Paris forced to wayte vpon ye heeles of ye Cardinalls and great men in vayne.[264] The accesse to the Rocke of Rhine is hard and farre of.[265] The riuer runs betweene their Prouinces. Also the Contry is rugged. *Non Bacchi Cererisue ferax, Francica faecundas quaerunt sibi lilia [glebos? altered to glebas].*[266] As for the opinion of the lawiers that may [thinge? *altered to* thinke] it an vnwise part because by offeringe to alienate that wch is holden in fee of the [*word deleted*] Empire, you abdicate yor selfe; and vpon this ground thinke Hessen to be w^thout a master and by escheate, vpon ye flyinge of, of the [*catchword:* vassall][267], *to have fallen vacant and to be in need of being transferred to someone else: that does not harm your case in any way. Your luck is assured; you will give what you do not have, and will receive what you were not hoping for.*

27

Again, does it seem cowardly to give up your right? But you have been thrown out of possession. The thing itself is gone; the legal fiction is worthless.

[262] Landgrave Moriz of Hessen-Kassel had enjoyed close relations with Henri IV, had stayed in France in 1602, and was regarded as particularly pro-French (*Recueil de quelques discours politiques, escrits sur diverses occurrences* (n.p., 1632), pp. 62, 226; Anquez, *Henri IV et l'Allemagne*, p. 58). He wrote to Louis XIII on 20 February 1626 imploring him to give his help and 'protection' (von Rommel, *Neuere Geschichte von Hessen*, iii, p. 621 n.). On 14 April 1626 Maximilian of Bavaria wrote to the Electors of Mainz, Trier, and Cologne, warning that one of Landgrave Moriz's envoys to Paris (see above, n. 87) was offering Louis XIII 'his land, people, goods and possessions, but above all his fortress of Rheinfels on the river Rhine' (von Aretin, *Bayerns auswärtige Verhältnisse*, appendix 2, p. 169: 'seine Landt vnd Leüth, hab vnd guett, vornemblich aber sein vesstes an den Rheinstrom gelegenes Paashauss Rheinfelss'). It is not clear what the grounds for this claim were.

[263] This claim about the 'sacrifice' of troops (where 'amongst them' has no equivalent in the Latin) refers presumably to the massacre of the garrison of Münden (and, allegedly, Göttingen: see above, n. 215); the idea that this was connected with Moriz's diplomacy towards France seems to be baseless.

XXVI.

Cur in justiore causa non imitaberis Hassum: Arces ille, Urbésque & Populos, suum insuper, filiorúmque cum opibus sanguinem Franco obtulit; & ne parum seria videretur addictio, inscios agrestes biennij pene stativa passos, veteranis legionibus obtulit sacrificandos, ut illâ victimâ sanciret Gallicam servitutem. Nec movere te debet, quòd tanquam vilis Transfuga contemptus sit, legatíque eius inglorij Parisijs Cardinalium & Potentium vestigia lambant invito conatu. Nimium arduus est ad Rheni petram accessus, & nimiùm vastus Provincias.

interluit amnis.

aspera etiam regio est.

Non Bacchi Cererísve ferax,
Francica, foecundas quaerunt sibi lilia glebas.

Quòd verò Iurisperiti imprudens factum existimant, quasi feudum Imperij exteris offerendo, ipse se abdicârit, Hassiámque ideo sine domino esse censeant, & transfugio Vasalli caducam alij tradendam, tuae causae nihil officit. Fortuna tua tuta est, dabis quod non habes: recipies quod non sperabas.

XXVII.

Ignavum videtur rursum de tuo jure cedere? At possessione deturbatus es. res abijt, fictio juris inanis est. Verùm aliud animosius propono. Iterum

---

264 See above, n. 87.

265 This refers to Rheinfels ('rock of the Rhine'), a castle on the Rhine which belonged to the Landgrave of Hessen-Kassel, although it was not contiguous with the rest of his territory. Spanish forces had tried to gain control of it in 1624, as it was of strategic importance for the 'Spanish road'; on 9 July 1626 the Landgrave signed a document promising to place it under Imperial 'protection', and it was occupied by Spanish forces (after a month-long siege) on 3 September of that year. (See Dumont, *Corps universel diplomatique*, v(2), pp. 497–8; von Aretin, *Bayerns auswärtige Verhältnisse*, appendix 2, p. 201; J. Kessel, *Spanien und die geistlichen Kurfürsten am Rhein während der Regierungszeit der Infantin Isabella (1621–1633)* (Frankfurt am Main, 1979), pp. 204–6; and cf. above, n. 262.)

266 'It is not productive of grapes or corn; the French lilies require fertile soil.' The first line is a reminiscence of Seneca, *Hercules furens*, l. 697: 'Estne aliqua tellus cereris aut bacchi ferax?'

267 Hobbes's translation (or rather, the surviving part of it) ends here.

However, I have a different and bolder suggestion. Once again, incite rebellion and stir up insurrections, using ministers of religion and crafty politicians. That enterprise turned out badly in Italy, France, and Germany; seditions seldom produce a happy result, and in many cases the harm they cause rebounds on those who started them. But what are you afraid of? Fortune bears down on you; the defeats of your friends render you notorious; it is good to die as the world collapses.[268]

> *You go, still a great man, as an exile from the warring peoples.*
> *And in your departure you take your followers with you.*

It is true that insurrections produce more enemies; but you are regarded as powerful.

28

I do not disapprove of the bold advice you receive, even though it comes from a harbourless pilot.[269] *He recommends that you seek some port from your brother-in-law, or from the Dane, or the Swede, and use it as a base from which to rule the Ocean, acquire riches, harden your sons for warfare, and raid the coasts of Spain, Italy, and the Indies. Nor is it a new thing for a king to become a pirate. Jephthah committed robberies when he had been expelled from his home,*[270] *and nevertheless was made leader of Israel. Your brother-in-law will perhaps refuse, for fear of a conspiracy. The Dane will permit it; but those provinces are rather a long way away from your enemies. I would send you to Africa, were it not for the fact that the inhabitants of Barbary are utterly untrustworthy, and extremely avaricious.*

29

Indeed, the man with the golden gauntlets[271] *urges you to go yourself to the Sultan; he says that you may be granted a place of refuge in the Aegean Sea. He notes that even David was given Ziklag;*[272] *from which it follows that*

---

[268] The Latin here, 'iuvat mundo ruente mori', seems to be adapted from Claudian, *In Rufinum*, II, l. 19: 'everso iuvat mundo mori' ('it is good to die as the world is overturned'), part of a nihilistic speech uttered by the rebellious praetorian prefect Rufinus as he planned to drag the Roman world into war.

[269] The Latin here has 'anormis', apparently a coinage from the Greek adjective ἄνορμος, meaning 'without a harbour', and 'Pilotj', from 'pilotus', a term used in medieval, but not classical, Latin. It is not clear who is referred to here—perhaps Ludwig Camerarius, whose (alleged) suggestion that Frederick move to Sweden is discussed in more detail in section 34, below.

per verbi Ministros, per Catos Politicos seditionem move, tumultus cie, male cessit in Italia, Gallia, Germania illa molitio. Seditionum exitus rarò felix, plerumque in auctores vertitur noxa[.] Sed quid metus? Fortuna te premit, amicorum clades nobilitant, iuvat mundo ruente mori,

> *Vadis adhuc magnus populis pugnantibus exul.*
> *Exitióque trahis comites.*

ex tumultibus quidem crescunt hostes, tu tamen potens haberis.

XXVIII.

Consilium forte, sed anormis Pilotj non improbo. Portum aliquem ab affine, vel Dano, aut Sueco petere suadet, ex illo Oceanum regnare, rem parare, filios ad bella durare, Ibera, Itala, Inda littora incursare. Nec nova res ex Rege pirata. Iephte domo pulsus Latrocinia exercuit, & tamen Ductor Israelis factus est. Affinis fortè negabit conspirationis metu. Danus concedet; sed longiùs absunt ab hostibus illae Provinciae. Ad Afros te mitterem, sed nulla fides Barbaris, summa avaritia.

XXIX.

Hortatur quidem te Manicaureus, vt Ottomanidem ipse adeas, in aegeo mari asylum dari posse. Datam & Davidi Sicelegam. Ex ea posse te

---

[270] See Judges 11: 3.

[271] 'Manicaureus' does not appear in classical Latin; it seems to be a coinage from 'manica' (sleeve, gauntlet) and 'aureus' (golden). The only reference to golden 'manicae' in classical literature is in Silius Italicus, *Punica*, IV, ll. 155–6: 'auro virgatae vestes, manicaeque rigebant | ex auro' ('his clothes were striped with gold, and his gauntlets were stiff with gold'). That passage is a description of Crixus, a vainglorious military commander of the Boii (a Celtic tribe). The Boii were regarded by some writers as the ancestors of the Bohemians (and/or as the ancestors of the Bavarians: cf. above, at n. 238). So it is possible that this is a reference to Frederick's supporter the Bohemian military commander Heinrich Matthias von Thurn (see above, n. 191)—though the method of allusion does seem peculiarly abstruse. This identification might be strengthened by two further points: the fact that von Thurn himself had spent time in Constantinople (as a lobbyist for Gábor Bethlen) after the defeat at the White Mountain, and the reference, immediately following here, to Venice, von Thurn's current place of residence.

[272] 1 Samuel 27: 5–6: 'And David said unto Achish, If I have now found grace in thine eyes, let them give me a place in some town in the country . . . Then Achish gave him Ziklag that day'.

you can emulate an anointed king who was, however, a fugitive. But Venice disapproves of this plan, having considered the protection of its commercial interests. Nor would I want you to become a plaything of the Sublime Porte, or to kiss the purple robes of the pashas. Therefore I pay no heed to the swollen-veined ship-owners of Rotterdam.[273] Anyone who, as a free man, sneaks into the house of a tyrant, abandons his freedom. Nevertheless, it is better to do this than to undertake nothing at all.

30

I urge you, rather, to go to La Rochelle. For the Rochelais themselves wish for it; they think they would do honour to themselves by giving refuge to kings, and they also hope that you would bring some reinforcements with you. Everything there is favourable to you. There is one and the same religion (except for a few details, which are ignored in time of war). There you will have a partnership in the same actions, and by means of that partnership kings can be attacked.[274] There is an opportunity to harm the French King, who abandoned you; and there is an opportunity to strengthen the Calvinists. From this place you will be able to send advice to your friends, the Puritans in Britain, who are the enemies of the King, and you can do so without raising any suspicions; you will receive visits from all of them, under the pretext of negotiating. If you gather forces from there, and go to the coasts of Ireland or Scotland, you cannot fail to succeed; it is better to do that than to mope, open-mouthed, weighed down by a royal title, reading about other people's deeds, and hearing about the defeats and complaints of your allies. But they too are pursuing their own interests. Whoever does the ploughing, sowing, and harrowing for himself, it remains uncertain who will be the reaper. And you, what will you do?

> *Do you not want to undertake the task to win fame for yourself?[275]*
> *Take pity on your sons.[276]*

31

You should stir up quarrels again among your enemies; for this purpose you need to use not only forces and stratagems, but also nothing less than

---

[273] This reference is obscure, though the general sense must be that Dutch merchants hoped that a closer connection between the Elector Palatine and the Ottomans would lead to the latter adopting a more actively anti-Habsburg policy, to the commercial advantage of the United Provinces.

Regem unctum, sed profugum aemulari. Verùm hoc Venetus improbat, mercibus suis cavendum ratus. Nec magnae Portae te ludibrium fieri vellem, Bassarúmque purpuram basiare. Itaque varicosos Roterodamensium Naucleros non audio. Quisquis liber Tyranni domum subintrat, liber esse desinit. praestat tamen hoc agere, quàm nihil moliri.

XXX.

Ego potiùs Rupellam te voco: nam & ipsi Rupellani id cupiunt, honorificum sibi aestimant, asylum dare Regibus, nonnullas vires etiam allaturum sperant. Omnia illic tibi secunda sunt. Religio una, eadémque exceptis paucis, quae inter arma negliguntur. Societas eorundem facinorum, quâ Reges impetuntur. Opportunitas nocendi Gallo, qui te deserit; occasio reformatos roborandi. Hoc loco tuos amicos, Puritanos in Britannia, Regis inimicos instrues, consilia communicabis, sine suspicione, negotiationum praetextu omnes recipies. si illic vires colligas, si Hyberniae, Scotiae littora adeas, non poteris à fortuna destitui, praestat illa agere, quàm regio titulo oneratum in Hiantia desidere, & aliorum acta legere, & sociorum audire clades, & querelas. Et illi tamen res suas agunt; quisquis sibi arat, serit, occat, messor in incerto est. Tu quid agis?

> *Non super ipse tua moliris laude laborem?*
> *Arcanios miserare tuos.*

XXXI.

Concitanda iterum inter hostes discordia, ad hunc finem non modò vires artésque, sed scelera etiam ipsa nefásque adhibenda sunt. Huic

---

[274] The Latin here, 'Societas eorundem facinorum', appears to echo Cicero, *Philippicae*, XXXVII, 17, 36: 'omnium facinorum . . . societas' ('a partnership in all his actions'). 'Facinus' can mean 'crime'; but the Ciceronian phrase is neutral.

[275] Adapted from Vergil, *Aeneid*, IV, l. 273: 'nec super ipse tua moliris laude laborem'.

[276] 'Arcanios' in the Latin is evidently a misprint for 'Ascanios'. The line just adapted from the *Aeneid* (see n. 275) was spoken in reproof to Aeneas, who was dallying with Queen Dido instead of pursuing his Roman destiny; in the same speech Aeneas was also urged to think of the future of his young son, Ascanius.

criminal acts and things contrary to divine law. To this advice I give first place—and second, and third, and thousandth. I admit, indeed, that up until now, everything has been dared, everything has been tried, and yet too little has been accomplished. You must try again: perhaps something will be achieved. The body of your enemies (joined now by the Pope) is too strong and too great. The strong chains in which it binds us cannot be broken or moved by our own strength; but if it drinks up the hidden poison of discord, it will be loosened by paralysis, break up, and collapse in self-destruction. Our own Union dissolved itself in the most self-seeking way;[277] *the great alliance of the kings has now fallen apart;*[278] *but although there is no lack of quarrels among the Papists, their alliance and common strategy remain in being. We must try our utmost to use deception to alienate some of them; if you remove a few stones from the arch, the whole vault falls to pieces. Quite often, when we have been defeated, we have renewed the war, at great expense and with greater risk; but it is possible to bring about discord among our enemies with no outlay at all. Our orator*[279] *suggests that new hopes are to be had from Strasbourg;*[280] *the situation in the Danube region is highly inflamed;*[281] *it astonishes us that Gábor remains at rest and does not seize this ripe opportunity.*[282] *The Bear*[283] *is carried forward by his own impetus; the Cock*[284] *practises frauds, but is revealed by his crowing. Nothing distresses me more, I am torn apart in my mind, I am shattered by pain at the thought that we may lose this opportunity: if those things pass us by fruitlessly, I shall hang myself.*

> *Are neither the French King,*[285] *nor Gábor, nor the Turk and Venice taking up their arms?*[286]
> *Oh, what degenerate times we live in!*[287]

---

[277] See above, n. 31.

[278] This apparently refers to the alliance between Charles I and Christian IV (as cemented in the Hague treaty of December 1625), perhaps with some allusion also to the cooperation of Louis XIII.

[279] 'Fronto' in the Latin: this refers, presumably, to Marcus Cornelius Fronto (AD 90–168), a famous orator. The allusion may be to Frederick's adviser Ludwig Camerarius (see below, n. 301), a humanist scholar who was noted for the elegance of his Latin.

[280] Strasbourg, which had a mainly Lutheran population, had been placed under Imperial control. In 1624 the Council of Strasbourg had entertained a French diplomat, who told them that Louis XIII would help defend their liberties; this meeting attracted the ire of the Emperor. In 1626 the people of Strasbourg may have been angered by

consilio primas, secundas, tertias, millesimas do. Hactenus quidem nihil inausum, nihil intentatum est relictum, parum actum fateor. Iterum tentandum, fortè aliquid agetur. Nimis est robustum, nimis grande corpus hostium, cui jam accessit & Papa. forte vinculum, nostris viribus, nec frangi, nec loco moveri potest, occultum discordiae venenum si combibat, paralysi solvetur, ipsum se dividet, & in se collisum ruet. Nostra se unio cupidissimè dissolvit, jam magna Regum liga dissilijt, at inter Papistas etsi non desint querelae; manet tamen foedus, & communia consilia. Extremâ vi fraudum connitendum est, ut aliquos di vellamus; pauca saxa si fornici subtrahis, tota concameratio concidit. Victi saepius bellum renovavimus, magno sumptu, maiore periculo, discordiam hostium nulla impensa moliri licet. Fronto noster Argentorato novas spes ostentat, ad Istrum res fervet, miramur Gaborem quiescere, & occasionem capillatam non prendere. Vrsinus suo fertur impetu. Alectryon dolos agit, sed cantu prodit. Nulla me res magis angit, discrucior animi, dolore rumpor occasionem nobis perire: illae si transeant irritae, laqueo me induam.

> *Non Gallus, non arma Gabor, non Turcus & Adria?*
> *ô tempora, ô mores!*

the appointment of the Emperor's 13-year-old son as Administrator of the bishopric of Strasbourg; but the precise reasons for the claim made here are not apparent. (See R. Reuss, *L'Alsace au dix-septième siècle*, 2 vols. (Paris, 1897–8), i, pp. 67–8.)

[281] This refers to the revolt in Upper Austria: the river Enns joins the Danube just north of the town of Enns (see above, n. 226).

[282] The Latin here, 'occasionem capillatam' ('hairy opportunity'), alludes to the Renaissance iconography of Occasio, depicted as a female figure with a lock of hair at the front of her head and a bald pate at the back—meaning that she can be seized as she is approaching us, but that we shall grasp nothing if we wait until she has passed (see e.g. C. Ripa, *Iconologia*, ed. P. Buscaroli (Milan, 1992), p. 322).

[283] It is not clear who is referred to here, nor why the adjectival form is used ('ursinus', meaning 'pertaining to a bear', or 'bear-like'). The Orsini family does not supply a suitable candidate in this period. Conceivably there may be an implied play of words in German involving 'Bayern', 'Bayrisch' (Bavaria, Bavarian) and 'Bär' (bear).

[284] The Latin has 'Alectryon', a person who was turned into a cock by Mars; the reference is presumably to Louis XIII, via an implied pun on 'gallus' ('cock').

[285] 'Gallus' in the Latin.

[286] In the Latin, 'arma' is apparently accusative, and a verb (such as 'movent') is implied but not stated. (Cf. the opening sentence of section 32: '. . . rapite arma'.) 'Venice' here translates 'Adria' ('the Adriatic').

[287] The Latin here uses the stock exclamation, 'ô tempora, ô mores', employed several times by Cicero (e.g. *In Catalinam*, I.2.1).

32

You at least, brave men of Switzerland, take up your arms. If you want it, Swabia is yours.[288] *You, allies who share our religion, and you who have subscribed to the new alliance of Uri, Schwyz, and Unterwalden.*[289] *Was it to no purpose that the French and Venetian officials went about their work among the people of Fribourg, Lucerne, and Solothurn?*[290] *They have already boasted that those people were ensnared by the cunning of a few men. But if you do not act quickly, the eagerness of the people of Uri and their allies will grow cool,*[291] *and in the other cities the people on our payroll will be in danger, since they are forcing both the citizens and the senators to join our alliance unwittingly. For even if something else is decided in the council, the people who are present for the purpose of taking the notes and compiling the minutes, the chairman and the secretary, turn everything to our benefit, and change the decisions of the senate to suit their own wishes. All praise to you, Am Rhyn!*[292]

> *The Seine takes precedence over the deep Rhine.*[293]

So if we are forcing the most Papistical people of Switzerland to join our side against their will, and if just a few men are all that is needed to effect that, why do we not try to get all the rest?

33

However, I am fearful of the Venetians and the Swiss. The King of France is becoming Hispanophile again, and it is absolutely certain that he is

[288] Swabia, to the north-east of Switzerland, was a 'Circle' (Kreis) of the Holy Roman Empire, with a mixed Catholic and Protestant population; its most important component was the duchy of Württemberg.

[289] Uri, Schwyz, and Unterwalden formed the original alliance (in the thirteenth century) from which the Swiss Confederation grew. This reference is to the exclusively Catholic 'golden' or 'Borromean' league formed by those cantons and four others (Lucerne, Zug, Fribourg, Solothurn) in 1586.

[290] Between November 1625 and February 1626 de Bassompierre (see above, n. 103) had served as Extraordinary Ambassador in Switzerland, and had worked with the resident French Ambassador, Robert Miron, sieur du Tremblay (1569–1641), to persuade the cantons to support France's anti-Spanish and anti-Papal policy over the Valtelline (see above, n. 14). A special Diet of the cantons was held at Solothurn (13–20 January 1626), at which the French position was upheld. The French diplomats used pressure and bribery to obtain the agreement of the Catholic cantons; Solothurn agreed before 12 January, Lucerne only on the 27th, and Fribourg not until 12 February. Venice's

XXXII.

Vos saltem, ô Helueta pectora, rapite arma. Si vultis; Suevia vestra est. Vos ô Socij fidei nostrae, & vos adscriptitij novae ligae Uranij, Suitzeri, Subsylvani. An frustra in Friburgensibus, Lucernatibus, Soloduranis sategerunt Gallici Venetíque quaestores? Iam paucorum astu illaqueatos iactârunt. Verùm nisi citò rem agitis, fervor Uraniorum & sociorum intepescet, in aliis Urbibus pensionarij nostri erunt in periculo; nam & Cives & Senatores inscios in foedus nostrum cogunt; Etsi enim in consilio aliud decernitur, qui tamen scribundo & relegundo adsunt, Praetor & Archigrammateus, nostris rebus cuncta addicunt, & suo arbitrio Senatus consulta temperant. Macte animi Amrine!

praeit altum Sequana Rhenum

Quod si Helvetios Papistissimos invitos cogimus esse nostros, idque valent pauci, cur non & reliquos tentamus?

XXXIII.

Verùm & Venetos & Helvetios timeo, & Gallus iterum Hispanissat, certo certius nostra consilia tradit Ibero: uti & aliorum, omnibus. Quid

policy was supportive of France, but its diplomacy in Switzerland does not seem to have been closely coordinated with the French efforts (E. Rott, *Histoire de la représentation diplomatique de la France auprès des Cantons Suisses, de leurs alliés et de leurs confédérés*, 10 vols. (Bern, Bumpliz, 1900–23), iii, pp. 945–56).

[291] The Catholic cantons, having ratified the French actions in the Valtelline (see above, n. 290), came under strong pressure from the Pope to withdraw their assent to it; the resident French Ambassador had to work hard to retain their support (Rott, *Histoire de la représentation diplomatique*, iv, pp. 89–97).

[292] Walter Am Rhyn (*c.*1569–1635), a member of a patrician family from Lucerne and an 'avoyer' (senior magistrate) of the canton of Lucerne, was appointed colonel of a Swiss regiment in Louis XIII's service in November 1625. He corresponded with the French diplomats in Switzerland, and exerted a pro-French influence, playing a key role in preventing the Catholic cantons from returning to a pro-Spanish position in February 1626 (see E. Rott, *Inventaire sommaire des documents relatifs à l'histoire de Suisse conservés dans les archives et bibliothèques de Paris*, 5 vols. (Paris, Bern, 1882–94), ii, pp. 58, 74, 76, 84; Rott, *Histoire de la représentation diplomatique*, iii, pp. 913, 959; iv, pp. 96, 101(n.); M. Godet et al., *Dictionnaire historique & biographique de la Suisse*, 8 vols. (Neuchâtel, 1921–34), i, p. 308).

[293] This tag plays on Am Rhyn's name, suggesting that he was more devoted to the interests of France than to those of his own region (though his name was in fact derived not from the river Rhine but from the Rin, a stretch of the river Wyna, in central Switzerland).

betraying our plans to the King of Spain—as he is betraying others' plans to everyone. Why was there a nocturnal meeting at Lucerne between the Venetians, Miron, and the Papal Nuncio?[294] *The Venetians, moreover, were on their way to Basel, then to Holland and England.*[295] *What was the reason for holding it by night, if it were just a matter of protocol? These things should be investigated. French regiments are threatening the Alps, and pretexts for action are being prepared. Moreover, Durlach is already trying to sell his services to the Emperor; I think he is looking for a military command against the peasants,*[296] *having been denied such a post by the Duke of Savoy.*[297] *Indeed he has great hopes from that source, though I fear that the concerns of religious worship*[298] *may thwart his attempts. The Papists find it easy to share their secrets with one another; but the mystery of the new Mass is not to be entrusted lightly to anyone. We can milk the Swiss people only if we trick them. I am speaking of the Papists; Bern is loyal.*[299] *If they choose you to be their leader, accept the task. But know this: the first time fortune goes against them, they will flee,*

Too cunning to bear their share of the yoke.[300]

Painted rays do not shine by night; they reflect light only on a bright day. With these people nothing can be achieved except by bribery; when coins have shed their light, these people reflect the sparkle. But when the money-box is closed,

Sad clouds cover their bovine faces.

---

[294] 'The Venetians' were Marc'Antonio Correr and Angelo Contarini, who were on their way to England as Extraordinary Ambassadors. Miron was the French Ambassador in Switzerland (see above, n. 290). The Papal Nuncio in Switzerland from 1621 to 1628 was Alessandro Scappi (d. 1650), Bishop of Campagna (and later Bishop of Piacenza) (Rott, *Histoire de la représentation diplomatique*, iv, p. 89; p. B. Gams, *Series episcoporum ecclesiae catholicae* (Regensburg, 1873), pp. 747, 865). In a report to the Venetian Senate sent from Basel on 25 May, Correr and Contarini said that when they came to Lucerne they were given a 'banquet' by Miron in his house, and added that 'the Nuncio Scappi only sent to us very late'. They also gave an account of the meeting with Scappi (which was evidently separate from that with Miron), saying that the Nuncio had criticized French policy and that they had defended it. (See *CSPVen. 1625–6*, pp. 423–4.) The suggestion here of a conspiratorial meeting between all three parties was thus either a mistake or, more probably, a piece of mischief-making.

nocturnus Lucernae conventus, Venetorum cum Mironio & Nuncio Papali? at illi ibant Basileam, in Hollandiam, Angliam. Quid opus erat nocte, si Caerimoniae solae agebantur? Haec penetrare oportet; prement Francae legiones Alpes, causae praetexuntur. Quin & Durlachius jam Caesari se venditat, credo Praefecturam bellicam contra agrestes ambit, à Sabaudo negatam. Magna quidem inde spes, sed vereor vt fida silentia conatus premant. Papistae sibi facilè mutuò secreta aperiunt. Novae Missae mysterium non facilè cuiquam committendum. Gens Helveta non nisi decepta à nobis mulgebitur. De Papistis loquor. Berna fida est. Ducem si te legerint rem suscipe. Hoc tamen scito, ad primum fortunae ictum fugituros.

Ferre iugum pariter dolosi

Radij picti nocte non lucent, in sereno tantum relucent, cum his nihil nisi dando peragitur, ubi fulsit nummus renident, si clausa est arca,

Tristia taurinos obvolvunt nubila vultus.

---

[295] Correr and Contarini (see above, n. 294) were in Basel on 25 May, were at The Hague on 15 June, and reached England on 26 June (*CSPVen. 1625–6*, pp. 423, 443, 454).

[296] See above, nn. 226, 281.

[297] The claim that Baden-Durlach (see above, n. 9) was offering his services to the Emperor is entirely false. Throughout the period 1625–6 he lobbied ceaselessly, applying both to Paris and to London, for support for his plan to raise an army to attack the upper Rhineland (see above, n. 88; for his lobbying of Charles I see Rusdorf, *Mémoires*, i, pp. 764–5; ii, pp. 143–4). He did also approach Carlo Emanuele, Duke of Savoy, sending his son Christoph to Turin in April–May 1626 and another representative in June–July. On the latter occasion Carlo Emanuele showed some interest in the idea of recruiting Swiss troops (hoping to use them himself, in place of the French troops that were withdrawing after the Franco-Spanish peace treaty); but nothing definite was agreed (Obser, 'Markgraf Georg Friedrich', pp. 342–50).

[298] The Latin here, 'fida silentia' ('faithful silences'), is a phrase for religious devotions from Vergil, *Aeneid*, III, l. 112.

[299] Bern seems to have been particularly anti-Habsburg: when news of the Franco-Spanish peace treaty reached Switzerland, the canton of Bern issued a special protest against it (M. Stettler, *Annales oder gründtliche Beschreibung der fürnembsten Geschichten unnd Thaten welche sich in gantzer Helvetia . . . verlauffen*, 2 vols. (Bern, 1626–7), ii, p. 571).

[300] From a description of false friends in Horace, *Odes*, I.35, l. 28.

34

I would urge you to travel to Sweden with your Nestor,[301] *but there are many reasons not to do so: the roughness of the climate and of the way of life; the haughty nature of the young King;*[302] *the Polish war;*[303] *the internal seditions, stirred up by great interests;*[304] *the victories of the Poles; the defeats of the Tatars; the burning of Perekop; the pillaging of other towns;*[305] *the fact that the place where the tyrant resides is surrounded by arms.*[306] *So any helps you get from the Swedish King will be slight, and useless.*

A tiny skiff is of no use for the vast ocean.

He who gives small helps to someone who is in need of great ones, ensures that that person lives longer in misery; crumbs thrown to the starving do not help to fill them, but exacerbate their hunger.

35

These things come from someone who is loyal and experienced. Make use of them. War is long, life is short,[307] *the expense is certain, the outcome is doubtful, your enemy is persistent, your allies are inconstant, those hostile to you are unanimous, your confederates are quarrelsome, your exile is at hand, hope is far-off, and no one will lift a weapon for your benefit unless it serves his benefit too. The spirits of your enemies have been raised by success;*

[301] Nestor, one of the Greeks who fought at Troy, was famed for his wisdom and prudence (and great age). This probably refers to Frederick V's old adviser Ludwig Camerarius, who, while stationed in The Hague, had become an adviser to the Swedish Ambassador there in 1623. He visited Sweden in 1622 and 1623, and again in March–April 1626, when he was appointed Swedish Ambassador to the Netherlands (Schubert, *Ludwig Camerarius*, pp. 248, 308–13). He was convinced (correctly) that Swedish intervention could bring about the reversal of Frederick's fortunes.

[302] At the time of writing of this text, Gustavus Adolphus was 31 years old; 'young' here translates 'adolescens' (see above, n. 250).

[303] Gustavus Adolphus had committed large forces to his campaigns against Poland in Lithuania in the periods 1621–3 and 1625–6; contrary to the impression given here, those campaigns had been largely successful.

[304] Sweden was generally peaceful, but there had been some agitation (Catholic plots, and a minor rebellion in the province of Småland) in 1623–4—some of which was probably instigated by Poland (Roberts, *Gustavus Adolphus*, i, pp. 109–11).

XXXIV.

Iter Suecicum cum Nestore tuo suaderem, sed multa obstant. aëris victúsque asperitas, fastus Regis adolescentis, Polonicum bellum, seditiones domesticae, magnis agitatae causis. Polonorum Victoriae, Tartarorum clades, incinerata Praecopia, aliarum spolia Urbium, armis circumdata sedes Tyranni. A Sueco igitur parva auxilia, eáque inutilia.

Non facit ad vastum, parvula cymba mare.

Qui magnis egenti dat parva, vitam illi prorogat ad miseriam, micae esurientibus iniectae sunt irritamenta famis, non adiumenta satietatis.

XXXV.

Haec animo fido consultóque. Tu utere. Bellum longum, aetas breuis, sumptus certus, eventus anceps, hostis pertinax, socij mobiles, inimici unanimes, symmachi discordes, exilium prasens, spes in longinquo, nemo tui commodi causa sine suo commodo sagittam tollet. Hostes

---

[305] These four clauses apparently refer to the retreat of the Tatars from their raid on Poland in early 1626 (see above, n. 160). In fact the Tatars did not undergo any defeat, and neither the town of Perekop (one of their strongholds, in the Crimea) nor any of their other settlements was burnt down or pillaged. But Polish diplomacy spread reports of a major victory over the Tatars (Pope Urban VIII sent King Sigismund a special message of congratulation: Baranowski, *Polska a Tatarszczyzna*, p. 50), and these seem to have been taken up enthusiastically by the author here.

[306] In late July and throughout August 1626, Gustavus Adolphus's headquarters were at Dirschau, on the river Vistula, south of Danzig (Gdansk). He was there with the main body of his army, and was not surrounded by any hostile forces; the Polish army sent to oppose him did not reach the area until September, after this text was written (Roberts, *Gustavus Adolphus*, i, pp. 324, 328–30). So, in the light of the preceding clauses, it seems more likely that this comment refers to the Khan of the Crimean Tatars, Mehmed Giray III—though his position is even more thoroughly misdescribed by it.

[307] Adapted from the proverbial saying, 'ars longa, vita brevis' ('the art is long [to learn], life is short'), which derived from a version of a maxim of Hippocrates cited in Seneca, *De brevitate vitae*, I.1, l. 8.

those of your friends have been worn down by defeat; many of your friends
are still free, but their intentions are doubtful. Out of many evils, choose
one; out of great evils, choose the least. That is my opinion. And I fear the
strange things that may be done by Britain,

> *Such things as would be scorned neither by Capaneus nor by bold Amphiaraus,*
> *Nor by the fierce priestess of Bacchus with the ivy-berries held upside-down.*[308]

THE END.

---

[308] Capaneus went to fight in the Theban war and was struck dead by Jupiter for blasphemy (he appears as a blasphemer in Dante's *Inferno*, XIV, ll. 43–72); Amphiaraus, who also fought at Thebes, ordered his son to kill his (the son's) mother; the priestesses of Bacchus (or Maenads) took part in the dismembering of Pentheus (king of Thebes), which was led by his own mother. Apart from the Theban theme, the connection between these three seems, therefore, to consist of outrageous and unnatural acts (with a suggestion of impending inhumanity by Charles I towards his sister and brother-in-law). The Latin here appears to bear some relation to a passage about Bacchantes in Persius, *Saturae*, I, ll. 99–102, in which the words 'torva', 'Maenas', and 'corymbis' also occur; however, that passage was offered by Persius as a specimen of grossly inflated poetic

successu feroces, amici cladibus fessi, liberi multi, ingenia dubia. Ex multis malis unum; è magnis, minimum elige. Ita censeo. & Britanna ostenta metuo;

> *Qualia non capaneus, non audax amphiaraus;*
> *Sperneret, inverso nec Moenas torva corymbo.*

FINIS.

diction. (It was traditionally, though incorrectly, regarded as a quotation from a poem by the Emperor Nero: see Aules Persius Flaccus, *Satiren*, ed. W. Kissel (Heidelberg, 1990), pp. 241–4.) In Persius' verses the corymbi (clusters of ivy-berries) are used by the Maenas to guide a lynx; the significance of the corymbus being held upside-down here is not immediately apparent, but I am very grateful to Dr Patrick Finglass for the following suggestion. The Maenas in question was Agave, mother of Pentheus, who returned to Thebes with her son's head stuck on her thyrsus. The thyrsus was a rod decorated with an ivy-cluster at one end; normally that end would be uppermost, but in this case the head (stuck on the other end) was lifted aloft and the ivy was, unusually, at the downwards-pointing end.

List of Manuscripts

BAKEWELL, DERBYSHIRE

Chatsworth House

Hardwick 27: 2nd Earl of Devonshire and widow, receipts.
Hardwick 29: 1st Earl of Devonshire, accounts.
Hardwick 49: Mabbe, translation of de Santa María.
Hardwick 51: Bacon, treatises.
Hardwick 64: 2nd Earl of Devonshire, translation of Castiglione.
Hardwick 143/12: Baron Cavendish, promise of gift to son.
Hobbes D 3: 2nd Earl of Devonshire, essays.
Hobbes D 6: 'A Narration of Proceedings'.
Hobbes E. 1. A.: Hardwick library catalogue.
Hobbes, unnumbered: 'Translations of Italian Letters'.
Indenture H/301/16: grant of Cleisby manor, 1639.

BRNO

Moravský Zemský Archiv

Collalto archive (G 169), I-1765: Questenberg, letter to Collalto.
Collalto archive (G 169), I-1774: Lustrier, letter to Collalto.
Collalto archive (G 169), I-1882: Collalto papers.

CAMBRIDGE

Cambridge University Library

Ee. 4. 13: *Secretissima instructio, Altera secretissima instructio.*

LONDON

British Library

Add. 8296: *Secretissima instructio.*
Add. 11309: Micanzio, letters.

Add. 27962D: Salvetti, reports.

Add. 33572: Harrison, letter.

Add. 64892: Butter, letter to Coke.

Add. 64893: Devonshire, Mansfield, et al., letter to Coke.

Add. 69911: Butter, petitions; *Altera secretissima instructio* (incomplete).

Add. 70499: 'A second most secret instruction'; 2nd Earl of Devonshire, letter to Bates; Hobbes, letters to Mansfield.

Add. 72439: Conway, letter to Stationers' Company.

Add. 72441: Trumbull, letter to his son.

Egerton 1910: Hobbes, *Leviathan.*

Harl. 252: *Secretissima instructio; Altera secretissima instructio.*

Harl. 390: Mead, letter to Stuteville.

Harl. 646: D'Ewes, autobiography.

Harl. 3360: Hobbes, optical treatise.

Harl. 4955: Andrews, poems.

Sloane 3938: translation of *Secretissima instructio.*

National Archives (Public Record Office), Kew

C115/108/8578: Starkey, letter to Scudamore.

microfilm Prob. 11/154: 2nd Earl of Devonshire, will.

SP 14/117/75: Cavendish, letter to Lords of Privy Council.

SP 14/118/102: Anonymous letter.

SP 16/33/126: Mansfield, letter to Conway.

SP 16/523/77: Bagg, letter to Buckingham.

SP 75/7/64: 'Christian IV', forged letter.

NOTTINGHAM

Hallward Library, University of Nottingham

Pw 1 54: Christian Cavendish, letter.

Pw 1 59: Christian Cavendish, letter.

Pw 1 60: Christian Cavendish, letter.

Pw 1 61: Christian Cavendish, letter.

Pw 1 63: Christian Cavendish, letter.

Pw 25/19: Mansfield papers.

Pw 25/44: Mansfield papers.

Pw 25/48: Mansfield papers.

Pw 25/49: Mansfield papers.

Pw 25/57: Mansfield papers.

Pw 25/139: Mansfield papers.

Pw 26/196: Mansfield papers.
Pw V 522: Mansfield papers.
Pw V 872: Mansfield papers.
Pw V 944: Mansfield papers.
Pw2 V 213: Mansfield papers.

NOTTINGHAM

Nottinghamshire Record Office
DD P 114/69: Cavendish indenture.

OXFORD

Bodleian Library
Rawl. D 624: *Secretissima instructio; Altera secretissima instructio.*

PRAGUE

Knihovna Národního Muzea
I C 1, tom. XIV: *Secretissima instructio.*

ROME

Biblioteca dell'Academia nazionale dei Lincei
Corsiniana 677: *Secretissima instructio.*

SHEFFIELD

Sheffield University Library
Hartlib Papers (CD-Rom, 2nd edn.; Ann Arbor, Mich., 2002)
2/6/8B: Dury, letter to Hartlib.
6/4/49A: Dury, letter to St Amand.
9/1/83B: Dury, letter to Hartlib.
30/4/5B: Hartlib, 'Ephemerides', 1639.
45/6/14A-19B: St Amand, letter to Dury, with Grosseteste extract.
45/6/1A-12A: St Amand, letter to Hartlib.

STAFFORD

Staffordshire Record Office
D 4038/I/33: 2nd Earl of Devonshire, legal document.

VENICE

Museo Correr
1093: 'Secretissima Instruzione'.

VIENNA

Haus-, Hof- und Staatsarchiv
Belgien, PC 63: English agent, reports.
Türkei I, no. 110: Lustrier cipher; Lustrier dispatches.

Österreichische Nationalbibliothek
6230: Girolamo Priuli, 'Cronache'.

Bibliography

[NOTE: classical texts referred to in the explication of quotations and allusions are not separately listed here; the editions used are those of the Loeb, Teubner, or Oxford Classical Texts series.]

Acts of the Privy Council of England, June–December 1626, ed. J. V. Lyle (London, 1938).

Adams, S. L., 'The Protestant Cause: Religious Alliance with the West European Calvinist Communities as a Political Issue in England, 1585–1630', Oxford University D.Phil. thesis (1973).

——'Foreign Policy in the Parliaments of 1621 and 1624', in K. Sharpe, ed., *Faction and Parliament: Essays in Early Stuart History* (Oxford, 1978), pp. 139–71.

Aeckerle, H. W., 'Amsterdamer Börsenpreislisten, 1624–1626', *Economisch-historisch jaarboek*, 13 (1927), pp. 86–209.

Ahnlund, N., 'Gustaf II Adolfs första preussiska fälttåg och den europeiska krisen 1626', *Historisk tidskrift*, 38 (1918), pp. 75–115.

van Aitzema, L., *Saken van staet en oorlogh in, ende omtrent de Vereenigde Nederlanden*, 7 vols. (The Hague, 1669–71).

von Albertini, R., *Das politische Denken in Frankreich zur Zeit Richelieus* (Marburg, 1951).

Albrecht, D., *Die auswärtige Politik Maximilians von Bayern, 1618–1635* (Göttingen, 1962).

Alekberli, M. A., *Borba ukrainskogo naroda protiv turetsko–tatarski aggressii vo vtoroi polovine XVI—pervoi polovine XVII vekov* (Saratov, 1961).

Altera secretissima instructio Gallo-Britanno-Batava Friderico V data, ex belgica in latinam linguam versa, et optimo publico evulgata ('The Hague', 1626).

[Alvinczi, P.,] *Querela Hungariae* (n.p. [Košice], 1619).

——*Machiavellizatio qua unitorum animos iesuaster quidam dissociare nititur* (n.p. [Košice], 1620).

——*Resultatio plagarum castigatoris autorem Machiavellizationis reverberata in Thomam Balasfia* (Košice, 1620).

Angyal, D., 'Erdély politikai érintkezése Angliával', *Századok: a Magyar Történelmi Társulat közlönye*, 34 (1900), pp. 309–25, 388–420.

Anquez, L., *Un Nouveau Chapitre de l'histoire politique des réformés de France (1621–1626)* (Paris, 1865).

——*Henri IV et l'Allemagne d'après les mémoires et la correspondance de Jacques Bongars* (Paris, 1887).

Apponyi, A., *Hungarica: Ungarn betreffende im Auslande gedruckte Bücher und Flugschriften*, 2nd edn., 4 vols. (Munich, 1925–8).

Arber, E., ed., *A Transcript of the Registers of the Company of Stationers of London, 1554–1640 AD*, 5 vols. (London, 1875–94).

Arblaster, P., 'Current-affairs Publishing in the Habsburg Netherlands, 1620–1660, in Comparative European Perspective', Oxford University D.Phil. thesis (1999).

von Aretin, C. M., *Bayerns auswärtige Verhältnisse seit dem Anfange des sechzehnten Jahrhunderts* (Passau, 1839).

Atherton, I., *Ambition and Failure in Stuart England: The Career of John, first Viscount Scudamore* (Manchester, 1999).

—— 'The Itch Grown a Disease: Manuscript Transmission of News in the Seventeenth Century', in J. Raymond, ed., *News, Newspapers, and Society in Early Modern Britain* (London, 1999), pp. 39–65.

Aubrey, J., *'Brief Lives', chiefly of Contemporaries*, ed. A. Clark, 2 vols. (Oxford, 1898).

Ayton, Sir Robert, *The English and Latin Poems*, ed. C. B. Gullans (Edinburgh, 1963).

Bacon, F., *The Works*, ed. J. Spedding, R. L. Ellis, and D. D. Heath, 14 vols. (London, 1857–74).

—— *Essays and Colours of Good and Evil*, ed. W. Aldis Wright (London, 1875).

—— *The Essayes and Councels, Civill and Morall*, ed. M. Kiernan (Oxford, 1985).

—— *Philosophical Studies, c.1611–c.1619*, The Oxford Francis Bacon, vi, ed. G. Rees (Oxford, 1996).

Balásfi, T., *Castigatio libelli calvinistici, cui titulus est: Machiavellizatio, quem calvinista quidem praedicans, responsi nomine ad Secretissimam instructionem . . . vulgavit* (Augsburg, 1620).

—— *Repetitio castigationis, et destructio destructionum, Petri P. Alvinci, calvinistae cassoviensis praedicantis* (Vienna, 1620).

Baldini, A. E., 'Botero et Lucinge: les racines de la *Raison d'État*', in Y. C. Zarka, ed., *Raison et déraison d'état: théoriciens et théories de la raison d'État aux XVIᵉ et XVIIᵉ siècles* (Paris, 1994), pp. 67–99.

Balfour Paul, Sir James, ed., *The Scots Peerage*, 9 vols. (Edinburgh, 1904–14).

Baranowski, B., *Polska a Tatarszczyzna w latach 1624–1629* (Lodz, 1948).

Baron, S. A., 'The Guises of Dissemination in Early Seventeenth-Century England: News in Manuscript and Print', in B. Dooley and S. A. Baron, eds., *The Politics of Information in Early Modern Europe* (London, 2001), pp. 41–56.

Barozzi, N., and G. Berchet, eds., *Relazioni degli stati europei lette al Senato dagli ambasciatori veneti nel secolo decimosetto*, ser. 2, vol. ii (Venice, 1859).

Bašagić, S., *Znameniti hrvati, bošnjaci i hercegovci u turskoj carevini* (Zagreb, 1931).

de Bassompierre, F., *Journal de ma vie*, ed. M. J. A. de La Cropte, marquis de Chantérac, 4 vols. (Paris, 1870–7).

Becker, H., *Die Secretissima Instructio Gallo-britanno-batava, ein Beitrag zur Kritik der Flugschriften des dreissigjährigen Krieges* (Göttingen, 1874).

Behnen, M., ' "Arcana—haec sunt ratio status." Ragion di stato und Staatsräson: Probleme und Perspektiven (1589–1651)', *Zeitschrift für historische Forschung*, 14 (1987), pp. 129–95.

Bell, G. M., *A Handlist of British Diplomatic Representatives, 1509–1688* (London, 1990).

Beller, E. A., *Propaganda in Germany during the Thirty Years' War* (Princeton, 1940).

Benzing, J., *Die Buchdrucker des 16. und 17. Jahrhunderts im deutschen Sprachgebiet*, 2nd edn. (Wiesbaden, 1982).

Besold, C., *Spicilegia politico-juridica* (Strasbourg, 1624).

[Bethlen, G.,] *Copia eines Schreibens, so Bethlen Gabor den ersten Aprilis Anno 1621. ausz Tirnaw, an einen Fürsten der Tartarn . . . abgehn lassen . . . allen gutherzigen teutscher Nation zu Nachrichtung, und Erinnerung, was hinder desz Bethlen Gabor calvinischen Geist stecke* (Augsburg, 1621).

Bidwell, W. B., and M. Jansson, eds., *Proceedings in Parliament, 1626*, 4 vols. (New Haven, 1991–6).

Bijlsma, R., *Rotterdams welvaren, 1550–1650* (The Hague, 1918).

[Birch, T., ed.,] *The Court and Times of Charles the First* [revd. by R. F. Williams], 2 vols. (London, 1848).

——— *The Court and Times of James the First* [revd. by R. F. Williams], 2 vols. (London, 1848).

Bireley, R., *Religion and Politics in the Age of the Counterreformation: Emperor Ferdinand II, William Lamormaini, S.J., and the Formation of Imperial Policy* (Chapel Hill, NC, 1981).

——— *The Counter-Reformation Prince: Anti-Machiavellianism and Catholic Statecraft in Early Modern Europe* (Chapel Hill, NC, 1990).

——— *The Jesuits and the Thirty Years War: Kings, Courts, and Confessors* (Cambridge, 2003).

Biró, V., *Erdély követei a Portán* (Cluj, 1921).

Blaise, A., *Lexicon latinitatis medii aevi* (Turnhout, 1975).

Blok, P. J., ed., *Relazioni veneziane: veneziaansche berichten over de Vereenigde Nederlanden van 1600–1795* (The Hague, 1909).

Boccalini, T., *Newes from Pernassus: The Politicall Touchstone, taken from Mount Pernassus*, tr. T. Scott (n.p., 1622).

Bodin, J., *Method for the Easy Comprehension of History*, tr. B. Reynolds (New York, 1945).

Borelli, G., *Ragion di stato e Leviatano: conservazione e scambio alle origini della modernità politica* (Bologna, 1993).

Borsa, G., et al., *Régi Magyarországi nyomtatványok* (Budapest, 1971–   ).

Botero, G., *Aggiunte di Gio. Botero Benese alla sua ragion di stato* (Pavia, 1598).

——— *Relatione della repubblica venetiana* (Venice, 1605).

___ *Della ragion di stato*, ed. C. Morandi (Bologna, 1930).

___ *The Reason of State*, tr. P. J. Waley and D. P. Waley (London, 1956).

Böttcher, D., 'Propaganda und öffentliche Meinung im protestantischen Deutschland, 1628–1636', *Archiv für Reformationsgeschichte*, 44 (1953), pp. 181–203, and 45 (1954), pp. 83–99.

Bouwsma, W. J., *Venice and the Defense of Republican Liberty: Renaissance Values in the Age of the Counter Reformation* (Berkeley, 1968).

Bricka, C. F., J. A. Fridericia, and J. Skovgaard, eds., *Kong Christian den Fjerdes egenhandige breve*, 8 vols. (Copenhagen, 1887–1947).

Brito Vieira, M., 'Elements of Representation in Hobbes: Aesthetics, Theatre, Law, and Theology in the Construction of Hobbes's Theory of the State', Cambridge University PhD thesis (2005).

Burke, P., 'Tacitism', in T. A. Dorey, ed., *Tacitus* (London, 1969), pp. 149–71.

___ 'Tacitism, Scepticism, and Reason of State', in J. H. Burns and M. Goldie, eds., *The Cambridge History of Political Thought, 1450–1700* (Cambridge, 1991), pp. 479–98.

Calendar of State Papers, Domestic . . . 1625–1626, ed. J. Bruce (London, 1858).

Calendar of State Papers . . . in the Archives . . . of Venice, 1625–1626, ed. A. B. Hinds (London, 1913).

Calendar of the State Papers relating to Ireland . . . 1625–1632, ed. R. P. Mahaffy (London, 1900).

[Camerarius, L.,] *Ludovici Camerarii I.C. aliorumque epistolae nuper post pugnam maritimam in Suedica naui capta captae a victore polono* (n.p., 1627).

Castiglione, B., *De curiali sive aulico libri quatuor*, tr. B. Clerke (London, 1571).

Catualdi, V., *Sultan Jahja, dell'imperial casa ottomana* (Trieste, 1889).

Cavallari, V., et al., *Verona e il suo territorio*, 7 vols. (Verona, 1950–2003).

Cavendish, M., *The Life of the Thrice Noble, High and Puissant Prince William Cavendishe* (London 1667).

[Cavendish, W.,] *A Discourse against Flatterie* (London, 1611),

___ *Horae subsecivae: Observations and Discourses* (London, 1620).

Church, W. F., *Richelieu and Reason of State* (Princeton, 1972).

Ciobanu, V., *Politică și diplomație în Țările Române în raporturile polono-otomano-habsburgice (1601–1634)* (Bucharest, 1994).

Clarke, A., 'The Army and Politics in Ireland, 1625–30', *Studia hibernica*, 4 (1964), pp. 28–53.

Clasen, C.-P., *The Palatinate in European History, 1555–1618*, 2nd edn. (Oxford, 1966).

Clegg, C., *Press Censorship in Jacobean England* (Cambridge, 2001).

Cogswell, T., 'The Politics of Propaganda: Charles I and the People in the 1620s', *Journal of British Studies*, 29 (1990), pp. 187–215.

___ 'Phaeton's Chariot: The Parliament-men and the Continental Crisis in 1621', in J. F. Merritt, ed., *The Political World of Thomas Wentworth, Earl of Strafford, 1621–1641* (Cambridge, 1996), pp. 24–46.

Cozzi, G., *Il doge Nicolò Contarini: ricerche sul patriziato veneziano agli inizi del seicento* (Venice, 1958).

Cuhn, E. W. ['E. G.'] ed., *Mémoires et negociations secretes de Mr. de Rusdorf,* 2 vols. (Leipzig, 1789).

Cust, R., 'News and Politics in early Seventeenth-Century England', *Past and Present,* 112 (1986), pp. 60–90.

—— *The Forced Loan and English Politics, 1626–1628* (Oxford, 1987).

Dahl, F., 'Gustav II Adolf i samtida engelska ettbladstryck', *Nordisk tidskrift för bok- och biblioteksväsen,* 25 (1938), pp. 173–89.

Dallington, R., *Aphorismes Civill and Militarie* (London, 1613).

Danişmen, Z., ed., *Naîmâ târihi,* 6 vols. (Istanbul, 1967–9).

Danişmend, İ. H., *Osmanlı devlet erkâmı* (Istanbul, 1971).

Demény, L., and P. Cernovodeanu, *Relaţiile politice ale Angliei cu Moldova, Ţara Româneasca şi Transilvania în secolele XVI–XVII* (Bucharest, 1974).

Depner, M., *Das Fürstenthum Siebenbürgen im Kampf gegen Habsburg: Untersuchungen über die Politik Siebenbürgens während des Dreissigjährigen Krieges* (Stuttgart, 1938).

Derin, F. Ç., 'Mehmed paşa: Muhammed paşa, gürcü', *İslam ansiklopedisi: islâm âlemi tarih, coğrafya, etnografya ve biyografya lugati,* 13 vols. (Istanbul, 1940–86), vii, fasc. 76 (1957), pp. 585–7.

Dethan, G., *Gaston d'Orléans: conspirateur et prince charmant* (Paris, 1959).

Dias, J. R., 'Politics and Administration in Nottinghamshire and Derbyshire, 1590–1640', Oxford University D.Phil. thesis (1973).

Donaldson, P. S., *Machiavelli and Mystery of State* (Cambridge, 1988).

Dumont, J., *Corps universel diplomatique du droit des gens,* 8 vols. (Amsterdam, 1726–31).

Echevarria Bacigalupe, M. A., *La diplomacia secreta en Flandres, 1598–1643* (Vizcaya, 1984).

Eglisham, G., *Prodromus vindictae in Ducem Buckinghamiae, pro virulenta caede potissimi Magnae Britanniae Regis Iacobi* (Frankfurt am Main, 1626).

Elenchus libelli famosi, qui inscribitur: Secretissima instructio gallo-britanno-batava, Friderico V. comiti Palatino electori data (n.p., 1621).

Elliott, J. H., *The Count-Duke of Olivares: The Statesman in an Age of Decline* (New Haven, 1986).

Erasmus, D., *Adagiorum opus* (Basel, 1533).

Etter, E.-L., *Tacitus in der Geistesgeschichte des 16. und 17. Jahrhunderts* (Basel, 1966).

Exhortation aux roys et princes sur le subject des guerres de ce temps . . . envoyée au comte palatin par le comte de Fridembourg (Paris, 1620).

Exhortation aux roys et princes sur le subject des guerres de ce temps . . . envoyée au prince palatin (Paris, 1620).

Feingold, M., 'The Humanities', in N. Tyacke, ed., *The History of the University of Oxford,* iv: *Seventeenth-Century Oxford* (Oxford, 1997), pp. 211–357.

[Ferdinand II,] *Der Röm. Kay. . . . Edictal Cassation der widerrechtlichen . . . Wahl Gabrieln Betlen im Königreich Hungern* (Augsburg, 1620).

Fitzherbert, T., *The First Part of a Treatise concerning Policy, and Religion* (n.p. [Douai], 1615).

Forster, J., *Sir John Eliot: A Biography*, 2 vols. (London, 1864).

Forster, L. W., *Georg Rudolf Weckherlin: zur Kenntnis seines Lebens in England*, Basler Studien zur deutsche Sprache und Literatur, 2 (Basel, 1944).

Fowler, A., *The Country House Poem: A Cabinet of Seventeenth-Century Estate Poems and Related Items* (Edinburgh, 1994).

Frachetta, G., *Seminario de' governi di stato et di guerra* (Venice, 1613).

Fraknói, V., 'Bethlen Gábor és IV. Keresztély Dán Király (1625–1628)', *Történelmi tár* (1881), pp. 98–113.

Franco, J. E., and C. Vogel, *Monita secreta: instruções secretas dos Jesuítas: história de um manual conspiracionista* (Lisbon, 2002).

Frankl, V., *Pázmány Péter és kora*, 3 vols. (Pest, 1868–72).

Fraser, Sir William, *The Sutherland Book*, 3 vols. (Edinburgh, 1892).

Frearson, M., 'The Distribution and Readership of London Corantos in the 1620s', in R. Myers and M. Harris, eds., *Serials and their Readers, 1620–1914* (Winchester, 1993), pp. 1–25.

Freund, J., 'La Situation exceptionelle comme justification de la raison d'État chez Gabriel Naudé', in R. Schnur, ed., *Staatsräson: Studien zur Geschichte eines politischen Begriffs* (Berlin, 1975), pp. 141–64.

von Friedenberg, H. C., *Deux discours tres-beaux et fort remarquables. Le premier: Sur les causes des mouuemens de l'Europe, seruant d'aduis aux roys & princes, pour la conseruation de leurs estats, composé par le baron de Fridembourg, & par le comte de Furstenberg en son ambassade presenté au Roy de France. Le deuxiesme: Secrete instruction au Conte Palatin sur l'estat & affaires de l'Allemagne, Boheme & Hongrie* (Paris, 1621).

Gabrieli, V., 'Bacone, la riforma e Roma nella versione Hobbesiana d'un carteggio di Fulgenzio Micanzio', *The English Miscellany*, 8 (1957), pp. 195–250.

Gams, P. B., *Series episcoporum ecclesiae catholicae* (Regensburg, 1873).

Gardiner, S., *The Devotions of the Dying Man* (London, 1627).

Gardiner, S. R., ed., *Notes of the Debates in the House of Lords . . . 1624 and 1626*, Camden Society, NS 24 (London, 1879).

——— *History of England from the Accession of James I to the Outbreak of the Civil War*, 10 vols. (London, 1884).

Gauchet, M., 'L'État au miroir de la raison d'État: la France et la chrétienté', in Y. C. Zarka, ed., *Raison et déraison d'état: théoriciens et théories de la raison d'État aux XVIe et XVIIe siècles* (Paris, 1994), pp. 193–244.

Gebauer, G., *Die Publicistik über den böhmischen Aufstand von 1618* (Halle, 1892).

Gemil, T., *Ţările române în contextul politic internaţional, 1621–1672* (Bucharest, 1979).

Gindely, A., *Friedrich V von der Pfalz, der ehemalige Winterkönig von Böhmen seit dem Regensburger Deputationstag vom Jahre 1622 bis zu seinem Tode* (Prague, 1885).

Godet, M., et al., *Dictionnaire historique & biographique de la Suisse*, 8 vols. (Neuchâtel, 1921–34).

Greg, W. W., *A Companion to Arber* (Oxford, 1967).

de Groot, A. H., *The Ottoman Empire and the Dutch Republic: A History of the Earliest Diplomatic Relations, 1610–1630* (Leiden, 1978).

Grünbaum, M., *Über die Publicistik des dreissigjährigen Krieges von 1626–1629* (Halle, 1880).

Guaragnella, P., *Gli occhi della mente: stili nel Seicento italiano* (Bari, 1997).

Güldner, G., *Das Toleranz-Problem in den Niederlanden im Ausgang des 16. Jahrhunderts* (Lübeck, 1968).

Gunn, J. A. W. ' "Interest will not lie": A Seventeenth-Century Political Maxim', *Journal of the History of Ideas*, 29 (1968).

——— *Politics and the Public Interest in the Seventeenth Century* (London, 1969).

Haitsma Mulier, E. O. G., *The Myth of Venice and Dutch Republican Thought in the Seventeenth Century* (Assen, 1980).

Hakewill, G., *An Apologie of the Power and Providence of God in the Government of the World* (Oxford, 1627).

Halliwell, J. O., ed., *The Autobiography and Correspondence of Sir Simonds d'Ewes, Bart, during the Reigns of James I and Charles I*, 2 vols. (London, 1845).

von Hammer, J., *Geschichte des osmanischen Reiches*, 10 vols. (Pest, 1829–35).

't Hart, M. C., *The Making of a Bourgeois State: War, Politics and Finance during the Dutch Revolt* (Manchester, 1993).

Haynes, H., *Henrietta Maria* (London, 1912).

Heawood, E., *Watermarks Mainly of the 17th and 18th Centuries* (Hilversum, 1950).

Heilingsetzer, G., *Der oberösterreichische Bauernkrieg 1626* (Vienna, 1976).

Heltai, J., *Alvinczi Péter és a heidelbergi peregrinusok* (Budapest, 1994).

Hendrix, H., *Traiano Boccalini fra erudizione e polemica: ricerche sulla fortuna e bibliografia critica* (Florence, 1995).

Hennequin de Villermont, A. C., *Ernest de Mansfeldt*, 2 vols. (Brussels, 1865–6).

Hering, G., *Ökumenisches Patriarchat und europäische Politik, 1620–1638* (Wiesbaden, 1968).

Hiller, I., *Palatin Nikolaus Esterházy: die ungarische Rolle in der Habsburgerdiplomatie, 1625 bis 1645* (Vienna, 1992).

Hirschman, A. O., *The Passions and the Interests: Political Arguments for Capitalism before its Triumph* (Princeton, 1977).

Historical Manuscripts Commission, *Thirteenth Report*, 'MSS of his Grace the Duke of Portland', ii (London, 1893).

History of Parliament Trust, 1602–29 section, draft article on Lord Cavendish (by V. C. D. Moseley).

_____ 1602–29 section, draft article on Sir James Fullerton (by V. C. D. Moseley).

_____ 1602–29 section, draft article on John St Amand (by P. Watson).

Hobbes, T., *Leviathan* (London, 1651).

_____ *Opera philosophica quae latine scripsit omnia*, ed. W. Molesworth, 5 vols. (London, 1839–45).

_____ *Behemoth: Or, The Long Parliament*, ed. F. Tönnies (London, 1889).

_____ *The Elements of Law*, ed. F. Tönnies (London, 1889).

_____ *De cive: The Latin Version*, ed. H. Warrender (Oxford, 1983).

_____ *The Correspondence*, ed. N. Malcolm, 2 vols. (Oxford, 1994).

_____ (attrib.), *Three Discourses*, ed. N. B. Reynolds and A. W. Saxonhouse (Chicago, 1995).

_____ *On the Citizen*, ed. and tr. R. Tuck and M. Silverthorne (Cambridge, 1998).

Hoekstra, K., 'The End of Philosophy (The Case of Hobbes)', *Proceedings of the Aristotelian Society*, 106 (2006), pp. 23–60.

Höpfl, H., *Jesuit Political Thought: The Society of Jesus and the State, c.1540–1630* (Cambridge, 2004).

Hubay, I., *Magyar és magyar vonatkozásu röplapok, ujságlapok, röpiratok az Országos Széchényi Könyvtárban, 1480–1718* (Budapest, 1948).

Hulse, L., 'William Cavendish, first duke of Newcastle upon Tyne', *Oxford Dictionary of National Biography* (www.oxforddnb.com).

Hume Brown, P., ed., *The Register of the Privy Council of Scotland*, ser. 2, vol. iii, for 1629–30 (Edinburgh, 1901).

von Hurter, F., *Geschichte Kaiser Ferdinands II und seiner Eltern*, 11 vols. (Schaffhausen, 1850–67).

Huxley, A., 'The *Aphorismi* and *A Discourse of Laws*: Bacon, Cavendish, and Hobbes, 1615–1620', *Historical Journal*, 47 (2004), pp. 399–412.

Israel, J., *The Dutch Republic and the Hispanic World, 1606–1661* (Oxford, 1982).

Jack, S. M., 'Sir Thomas Fanshawe', *Oxford Dictionary of National Biography* (www.oxforddnb.com).

Johnston, D., *The Rhetoric of Leviathan: Thomas Hobbes and the Politics of Cultural Transformation* (Princeton, 1986).

Jonson, B., *Works*, ed. C. H. Herford, P. Simpson, and E. Simpson, 11 vols. (Oxford, 1925–52).

van de Kamp, J. L. J., *Emanuel van Portugal en Emilia van Nassau* (Assen, 1980).

Katona, S., *Historia critica regum Hungariae stirpis austriacae*, 42 vols. (Pest, 1779–1817).

Kelliher, H., 'Donne, Jonson, Richard Andrews and the Newcastle Manuscript', in P. Beal and J. Griffiths, eds., *English Manuscript Studies, 1100–1700*, iv (1994), pp. 134–73.

Kelsey, S., 'Thomas Scott', *Oxford Dictionary of National Biography* (www.oxforddnb.com).

Kessel, J., *Spanien und die geistlichen Kurfürsten am Rhein während der Regierungszeit der Infantin Isabella (1621–1633)* (Frankfurt am Main, 1979).

Knolles, R., *The Generall Historie of the Turkes*, 3rd edn. revised by E. Grimeston (London, 1621).

Knuttel, W. P. C., *Catalogus van de pamfletten-verzameling berustende in de Koninklijke Bibliotheek*, 9 vols. (The Hague, 1889–1920).

Kočí, J., J. Polišenský, and G. Čehová, eds., *Documenta bohemica bellum tricennale illustrantia*, 7 vols. (Prague, 1971–81).

Kogel, R., *Pierre Charron* (Geneva, 1972).

Köprülü, O. F., 'Hâfiz Ahmed paşa', *İslam ansiklopedisi: islâm âlemi tarih, coğrafya, etnografya ve biyografya lugati*, 13 vols. (Istanbul, 1940–86), v(1), fasc. 39 (1948), pp. 71–7.

Koser, R., *Die Kanzleienstreit: ein Beitrag zur Quellenkunde der Geschichte des dreissigjährigen Krieges* (Halle, 1874).

Kostić, V., *Kulturne veze izmedju Jugoslovenskih zemalja i Engleske do 1700. godine* (Belgrade, 1972).

Kraynak, R. P., *History and Modernity in the Thought of Thomas Hobbes* (Ithaca, NY, 1990).

Krebs, R., *Die politische Publizistik der Jesuiten und ihrer Gegner in den letzten Jahrzehnten vor Ausbruch des dreissigjährigen Krieges* (Halle, 1890).

Krüner, F., *Johann von Rusdorf, kurpfälzischer Gesandter und Staatsmann während des dreissigjährigen Krieges* (Halle, 1876).

Lacaita, J., *Catalogue of the Library at Chatsworth*, 4 vols. (London, 1879).

Lake, P. G., 'Constitutional Consensus and Puritan Opposition in the 1620s: Thomas Scott and the Spanish Match', *Historical Journal*, 25 (1982), pp. 805–25.

Lambert, S., 'Coranto Printing in England: The First Newsbooks', *Journal of Newspaper and Periodical History*, 8 (1992), pp. 1–33.

Larkin, J. F., and P. L. Hughes, eds., *Stuart Royal Proclamations*, 2 vols. (Oxford, 1973–83).

Lee, S., 'William Cavendish, second earl of Devonshire', revised by V. Stater, *Oxford Dictionary of National Biography* (www.oxforddnb.com).

Leeuwarder Geschiedeniscommissie, *Rondom de Oldehove: geschiedenis van Leeuwarden en Friesland* (Leeuwarden, 1938).

Levi, A., *Cardinal Richelieu and the Making of France* (London, 2000).

Levy, F. J., 'How Information Spread among the Gentry, 1550–1640', *Journal of British Studies*, 21/2 (1982), pp. 11–34.

Lipsius, J., *Politicorum sive civilis doctrinae libri sex* (Leiden, 1589).

Lockhart, P. D., *Denmark in the Thirty Years' War, 1618–1648* (Selinsgrove, PA, 1996).

Lonchay, H., and J. Cuvelier, eds., *Correspondance de la cour d'Espagne sur les affaires des Pays-Bas au XVIIe siècle*, 6 vols. (Brussels, 1923–37).

Love, H., *Scribal Publication in Seventeenth-Century England* (Oxford, 1993).

Lublinskaya, A. D., *French Absolutism: The Crucial Phase, 1620–1629*, tr. B. Pearce (Cambridge, 1968).

de Lucinge, R., *De la Naissance, durée et chute des estats*, ed. M. J. Heath (Geneva, 1984).

Lundorp ['Londorpius'], M. C., *Der römischen keyserlichen und königlichen Mayestät . . . acta publica*, 2 vols. (Frankfurt am Main, 1627–30).

Lutz, H., *Ragione di stato und christliche Staatsethik im 16. Jahrhundert* (Münster, 1961).

McCrea, A., *Constant Minds: Political Virtue and the Lipsian Paradigm in England, 1584–1650* (Toronto, 1997).

McCusker, J. J., *Money and Exchange in Europe and America, 1600–1775: A Handbook* (Chapel Hill, NC, 1978).

Machiavelli, N., *Opere letterarie*, ed. A. Borlenghi (Naples, 1969).

Malcolm, N., *De Dominis (1560–1624): Venetian, Anglican, Ecumenist and Relapsed Heretic* (London, 1984).

——*Aspects of Hobbes* (Oxford, 2002).

—— 'Behemoth Latinus: Adam Ebert, Tacitism, and Hobbes', *Filozofski vestnik*, 24 (2003), pp. 85–120.

——and J. A. Stedall, *John Pell (1611–1685) and his Correspondence with Sir Charles Cavendish: The Mental World of an Early Modern Mathematician* (Oxford, 2005).

de Mariana, J., *De rege et regis institutione* (Toledo, 1599).

—— *The King and the Education of the King*, tr. G. A. Moore (Chevy Chase, MD, 1948).

de Mattei, R., *Il pensiero politico di Scipione Ammirato, con discorsi inediti* (Milan, 1963).

——*Il problema della 'ragion di stato' nell'età della Controriforma* (Milan, 1979).

de Meester, B., ed., *Correspondance du nonce Giovanni-Francesco Guidi di Bagno (1621–1627)*, 2 vols. (Brussels, 1938).

Meinecke, F., *Die Idee der Staatsräson* (Munich, 1924).

Le Mercure françois, 6, for 1619 and 1620 (published in 1621).

—— 12, for 1626 (published in 1627).

Micanzio, F., *Lettere a William Cavendish*, ed. R. Ferrini and E. De Mas (Rome, 1987).

[Mieg, L. C., ed.,] *Monumenta pietatis & literaria virorum in re publica & literaria illustrium selecta*, 2 vols. (Frankfurt am Main, 1701).

Miller, J., *Falcký mýtus: Fridrich V. a obraz české války v raně stuartovské Anglii* (Prague, 2003).

[de Morgues, M.,] *Advis d'un theologien sans passion: sur plusieurs libelles imprimez depuis peu en Allemagne* (n.p [Paris], 1626).

Mout, N., 'Der Winterkönig im Exil: Friedrich V. von der Pfalz und die niederländischen Generalstaaten 1621–1632', *Zeitschrift für historische Forschung*, 15 (1988), pp. 257–72.

Muggli, M. S., 'Ben Jonson and the Business of News', *Studies in English Literature*, 32 (1992), pp. 323–40.

Mullan, D. G., *Episcopacy in Scotland: The History of an Idea, 1560–1638* (Edinburgh, 1986).

'Musaeus': *see* 'Philotimus'.

Nágy, L., *Bethlen Gábor a független Magyarországért* (Budapest, 1969).

Niedermeyer, J. F., *Mediae latinitatis lexicon minus* (Leiden, 1984).

Notestein, W., and F. H. Relf, eds., *Commons Debates for 1629* (Minneapolis, 1921).

———— and H. Simpson, eds., *Commons Debates 1621*, 7 vols. (New Haven, 1935).

Novoselskii, A. A., *Borba moskovskogo gosudarstva s tatarami v pervoi polovine XVII veka* (Moscow, 1948).

Obser, K., 'Markgraf Georg Friedrich von Baden-Durlach und das Projekt einer Diversion am Oberrhein in den Jahren 1623–1627', *Zeitschrift für die Geschichte des Oberrheins*, NS 5 (1890), pp. 212–42, 320–99.

Oestreich, G., *Neostoicism and the Early Modern State* (Cambridge, 1982).

Opel, J. O., *Der niedersächsisch–dänische Krieg*, 3 vols. (Halle, Magdeburg, 1872–94).

Osborne, T., '"Chimeres, Monopoles and Stratagems": French Exiles in the Spanish Netherlands during the Thirty Years' War', *Seventeenth Century*, 15 (2000), pp. 149–74.

Pamuk, Ş., *A Monetary History of the Ottoman Empire* (Cambridge, 2000).

Parker, G., ed., *The Thirty Years' War*, 2nd edn. (London, 1997).

Pars secunda secretissimae instructionis (n.p., 1622).

von Pastor, L., *Geschichte der Päpste seit dem Ausgang des Mittelalters*, 16 vols. (Freiburg im Breisgau, 1901–33).

Pázmány, P., *Falsae originis motuum hungaricorum, succincta refutatio* (Bratislava, 1619; 2nd edn. Augsburg, 1620).

———— *Falsae originis motuum hungaricorum, succincta refutatio, cui accessit Secretissima instructio gallo-britanno-batava, Friderico V. comiti Palatino Electori data, ex gallico conversa* (Augsburg, 1620).

———— *Vngerischer Rebellions Brunn* (Augsburg, 1620).

Pearl, S., 'Sounding to Present Occasions: Jonson's Masques of 1620–5', in D. Lindley, ed., *The Court Masque* (Manchester, 1984), pp. 60–77.

Pečevija [Peçevi], Ibrahim Alajbegović, *Historija, 1520–1640*, ed. and tr. F. Nametak, 2 vols. (Sarajevo, 2000).

Pedani-Fabris, M. P., ed., *Relazioni di ambasciatori veneti al senato: Constantinopoli, relazioni inedite (1512–1789)* (Padua, 1996).

Pélissier, L. G., 'Inventaire sommaire de soixante-deux manuscrits de la Bibliothèque Corsini (Rome)', *Centralblatt für Bibliothekswesen*, 8 (1891), pp. 176–202, 297–324.

'Philotimus Musaeus', *Ad aphorismos tres priores Alterae secretissimae instructionis gallo-britanno-batavae Friderico V datae commentarius* (Cologne, 1626; 2nd edn. Cologne, 1627).

A Plain Demonstration of the Unlawful Succession of the Now Emperor Ferdinand the Second, because of the Incestuous Marriage of his Parents ('The Hague', 1620).

Plomer, H. R., *A Dictionary of the Booksellers and Printers who were at work in England, Scotland and Ireland from 1641 to 1667* (London, 1907).

Poelhekke, J. J., *Frederik Hendrik, prins van Oranje: een biografisch drieluick* (Zutphen, 1978).

Polišenský, J., *Anglie a Bílá Horá* (Prague, 1949).

Powell, W. S., *John Pory, 1572–1636: The Life and Letters of a Man of Many Parts* (Chapel Hill, NC, 1977).

Pray, G., *Gabrielis Bethlenii principatus Transsilvaniae coaevis documentis illustratus*, ed. J. F. Miller, 2 vols. (Pest, 1816).

Procacci, G., *Studi sulla fortuna del Machiavelli* (Rome, 1965).

Proctor Williams, W., 'Paper as Evidence: The Utility of the Study of Paper for Seventeenth-Century English Literary Scholarship', in S. Spector, ed., *Essays in Paper Analysis* (Washington, 1987), pp. 191–9.

Pursell, B. C., *The Winter King: Frederick V of the Palatinate and the Coming of the Thirty Years' War* (Aldershot, 2003).

Quazza, R., 'La politica di Carlo Emanuele I durante la guerra dei trent'anni', in *Carlo Emanuele I: miscellanea*, 2 vols. (Turin, 1930) (= Biblioteca della Società Storica Subalpina, vols. cxx, cxxi), pp. 1–45.

Rabb, T. K., 'English Readers and the Revolt in Bohemia, 1619–1622', in M. Aberbach, ed., *Aharon M. K. Rabinowicz Jubilee Volume* (Jerusalem, 1996), pp. 152–75.

———*Jacobean Gentleman: Sir Edwin Sandys, 1561–1629* (Princeton, 1998).

Randall, D., 'Joseph Mead, Novellante: News, Sociability, and Credibility in Early Stuart England', *Journal of British Studies*, 45 (2006), pp. 293–312.

Rawley, W., 'The Life of the Honourable Author', in F. Bacon, *Resuscitatio*, ed. W. Rawley (London, 1657), sigs. b2–c4.

Raymond, J., *The Invention of the Newspaper: English Newsbooks, 1641–1649* (Oxford, 1996).

———*Pamphlets and Pamphleteering in Early Modern Britain* (Cambridge, 2003).

Recueil de quelques discours politiques, escrits sur diverses occurrences (n.p., 1632).

Reuss, R., *L'Alsace au dix-septième siècle*, 2 vols. (Paris, 1897–8).

de Ribadeneyra, P., *Tratado de la religion y virtudes que deve tener el Principe Christiano, para governar y conservar sus estados* (Madrid, 1595).

Richelieu, A. J. du Plessis, Cardinal, *Mémoires*, ed. J. Lair et al., 10 vols. (Paris, 1909–31).

――― *Les Papiers de Richelieu: section politique intérieure, correspondance et papiers d'état*, i (1624–1626), ed. P. Grillon (Paris, 1975).

Richelieu, A. J. du Plessis, Cardinal, *Les Papiers de Richelieu: section politique extérieure, correspondance et papiers d'état, Empire allemand*, i (1616–1629), ed. A. Wild (Paris, 1982).

Ripa, C., *Iconologia*, ed. P. Buscaroli (Milan, 1992).

Roberts, M., *Gustavus Adolphus: A History of Sweden, 1611–1632*, 2 vols. (London, 1958).

Roberts, R. S., 'The London Apothecaries and Medical Practice in Tudor and Stuart England', London University PhD thesis (1964).

Robertson, G. C., *Hobbes* (Edinburgh, 1886).

Rodenas Vilar, R., *La política europea de España durante la guerra de treinta años (1624–1630)* (Madrid, 1967).

Roe, Sir Thomas (attrib.), *Bohemiae regnum electivum: That is, A Plaine and True Relation of the Proceedings of the States of Bohemia* (n.p. [London], 1620).

――― *The Negotiations of Sir Thomas Roe, in his Embassy to the Ottoman Porte, from the year 1621 to 1628 inclusive* (London, 1740).

Roeck, B., 'Geschichte, Finsternis und Unkultur: zu Leben und Werk des Marcus Welser', *Archiv für Kulturgeschichte*, 72 (1990), pp. 115–52.

de Rohan, H., 'L'Interest des princes', in his *Le Parfait Capitaine* (n.p., 1639), pp. 261–364.

von Rommel, C., *Neuere Geschichte von Hessen*, 3 vols. (Kassel, 1835–9).

Rott, E., *Inventaire sommaire des documents relatifs à l'histoire de Suisse conservés dans les archives et bibliothèques de Paris*, 5 vols. (Paris, Bern, 1882–94).

――― *Histoire de la représentation diplomatique de la France auprès des Cantons Suisses, de leurs alliés et de leurs confédérés*, 10 vols. (Bern, Bumpliz, 1900–23).

Rowe, V. A., 'The Influence of the Earls of Pembroke on Parliamentary Elections, 1625–41', *English Historical Review*, 50 (1935), pp. 242–56.

Ruigh, R. E., *The Parliament of 1624: Politics and Foreign Policy* (Cambridge, MA, 1971).

Russell, C., *Parliaments and English Politics, 1621–1629* (Oxford, 1979).

Rystad, G., *Kriegsnachrichten und Propaganda während des dreissigjährigen Krieges: die Schlacht bei Nördlingen in den gleichzeitigen, gedruckten Kriegsberichten* (Lund, 1960).

de Santa María, J., *Tratado de república y policía cristiana para reyes y príncipes* (Madrid, 1615).

――― *Christian Policie: Or, The Christian Common-wealth: Published for the good of Kings, and Princes*, tr. J. Mabbe (London, 1632).

Sarpi, P., *Opere*, ed. G. and L. Cozzi (Milan, 1969).

Schellhase, K. C., *Tacitus in Renaissance Political Thought* (Chicago, 1976).

____ 'Botero, Reason of State, and Tacitus', in A. E. Baldini, ed., *Botero e la 'ragion di stato'*: atti del convegno in memoria di Luigi Firpo (Florence, 1992), pp. 243–58.

Schmid von Schmiedebach, A., *Informatio fundamentalis super hodierno Bohemiae statu* (Frankfurt, 1620).

Schmidt, P., *Spanische Universalmonarchie oder 'teutsche Libertet': das spanische Imperium in der Propaganda des Dreissigjährigen Krieges* (Stuttgart, 2001).

Schubert, F. H., *Ludwig Camerarius, 1573–1651: eine Biographie* (Munich, 1955).

Schumacher, W., 'Vox Populi: The Thirty Years' War in English Pamphlets and Newspapers', Princeton University PhD thesis (1975).

Schutte, O., *Repertorium der nederlandse vertegenwoordigers, residerende in het buitenland, 1584–1810* (The Hague, 1976).

Scioppius, C. [Schoppe, K.], *Anatomia Societatis Jesu, seu probatio spiritus jesuitarum. Item arcana imperii jesuitici, cum instructione secretissima pro superioribus ejusdem & deliciarum jesuiticarum specimina* (n.p., 1633).

Secretissima instructio gallo-britanno-batava Friderico I. electo regi Bohemiae et comiti Palatino electori data, ex gallico conversa, ac bono publico in lucem evulgata (n.p., 1620).

Secretissima instructio gallo-britanno-batava Friderico V. comiti Palatino electori data, ex gallico conversa, ac bono publico in lucem evulgata (n.p., 1620).

Secretissima instructio . . . pars secunda (n.p., 1622).

Secretissimae instructionis . . . pars secunda (n.p., 1622).

Shillinglaw, A., 'New Light on Ben Jonson's *Discoveries*', *Englische Studien*, 71 (1937), pp. 356–9.

Simoni, A. E. C., 'Poems, Pictures and the Press: Observations on some Abraham Verhoeven Newsletters (1620–1621)', in F. de Nave, ed., *Liber amicorum Leon Voet* (Antwerp, 1985), pp. 353–73.

Simpson, P., *Proof-Reading in the Sixteenth, Seventeenth and Eighteenth Centuries* (Oxford, 1935).

Skinner, Q., *Reason and Rhetoric in the Philosophy of Hobbes* (Cambridge, 1997).

Slangen, N., *Geschichte Christian des Vierten Königs in Dännemark*, ed. J. H. Schlegel, 2 vols. (Copenhagen, 1757–71).

Sommerville, J. P., 'The "New Art of Lying": Equivocation, Mental Reservation, and Casuistry', in E. Leites, ed., *Conscience and Casuistry in Early Modern Europe* (Cambridge, 1988), pp. 159–84.

____ *Thomas Hobbes: Political Ideas in Historical Context* (Basingstoke, 1992).

Sorbière, S., *Relation d'un voyage en Angleterre* (Paris, 1664).

Soverus, B., *Curvi ac recti proportio* (Padua, 1630).

Spanninga, H., 'Gulden vrijheid: politiek en staatsvorming in Friesland, 1600–1640', Leeuwarden University PhD thesis (forthcoming).

Spini, G., 'The Art of History in the Italian Counter Reformation', in E. Cochrane, ed., *The Late Italian Renaissance* (London, 1970), pp. 91–133.

Spuler, B., 'Die europäische Diplomatie in Konstantinopel bis zum Frieden von Belgrad (1739)', *Jahrbücher für Kultur und Geschichte der Slaven*, 11 (1935), pp. 53–169, 171–222, 313–66.

von Stackelberg, J., *Tacitus in der Romania: Studien zur literarischen Rezeption des Tacitus in Italien und Frankreich* (Tübingen, 1960).

Stettler, M., *Annales oder gründtliche Beschreibung der fürnembsten Geschichten unnd Thaten welche sich in gantzer Helvetia . . . verlauffen*, 2 vols. (Bern, 1626–7).

Strong, S. A., ed., *A Catalogue of Letters and Other Historical Documents exhibited in the Library at Welbeck* (London, 1903).

Szábo, K., and Á. Hellebrant, *Régi magyar könyvtár*, 3 vols. (Budapest, 1879–98).

Szilágyi, S., *Bethlen Gábor fejedelem kiadatlan politikai levelei* (Budapest, 1879).

Tapié, V.-L., *La Politique étrangère et le début de la guerre de trente ans (1616–1621)* (Paris, 1934).

Tertia secretissima instructio Gallo-Britanno-Batava Friderico V data, ex Belgica in latinam linguam versa, et optimo publico evulgata (n.p., 1626).

Thuau, E., *Raison d'État et pensée politique à l'époque de Richelieu* (Paris, 1966).

Thucydides, *Eight Bookes of the Peloponnesian Warre*, tr. T. Hobbes (London, 1629).

Toffanin, G., *Machiavelli e il 'tacitismo'* (Padua, 1921).

Trease, G., *Portrait of a Cavalier: William Cavendish, First Duke of Newcastle* (London, 1979).

Tuck, R., *Philosophy and Government, 1572–1651* (Cambridge, 1993).

——— 'Hobbes and Tacitus', in G. A. J. Rogers and T. Sorell, eds., *Hobbes and History* (London, 2000), pp. 99–111.

Dess Türkischen Kaysers Hülff dem Fürsten inn Sieben-bürgen Bethlehem Gabor . . . versprochen (Bratislava, 1620).

Turnbull, G. H., *Hartlib, Dury and Comenius: Gleanings from Hartlib's Papers* (London, 1947).

Verre-kijcker. Ofte, secrete fransch-engelsch-hollandtsche instructie ghegheven aen Fredericus de vyfde Paltz-grave aen den Rhijn, ende keurvorst (n.p., 1620).

Vickers, B., *Shakespeare, Co-Author: A Historical Study of Five Collaborative Plays* (Oxford, 2002).

Viroli, M., *From Politics to Reason of State: The Acquisition and Transformation of the Language of Politics, 1250–1600* (Cambridge, 1992).

de Vivo, F., 'Paolo Sarpi and the Uses of Information in Seventeenth-Century Venice', in J. Raymond, ed., *News Networks in Seventeenth-Century Britain and Europe* (London, 2006), pp. 35–49.

Waldron, J., 'Hobbes and the Principle of Publicity', *Pacific Philosophical Quarterly*, 82 (2001), pp. 447–74.

Waser, C. (attrib.), *Veltlinische Tyranney, das ist: ausführliche . . . Beschreibung dess grausamen . . . Mordts so in dem Landt Veltlin gemeinen dreyen Pündten gehörig, Anno 1620* (n.p., 1621).

_____ *Vera narratione del massacro degli evangelici fatto da' papisti e rebelli nella maggior parte della Valtellina, nell'anno 1620*, tr. V. Paravicino (n.p., 1621).

Watson, A. G., *The Library of Sir Simonds D'Ewes* (London, 1966).

Weber, W. E. J., 'Ein Bankrotteur berät den Winterkönig. Paul Welser (1555–1620) und die Secretissima Instructio Gallo-Britanno-Batava Frederico I. Electo regi Bohemiae data (1620)', in M. Häberlein and J. Burkhardt, eds., *Die Welser: neue Forschungen zur Geschichte und Kultur des oberdeutschen Handelshauses* (Berlin, 2002), pp. 618–32.

_____ ed., *Secretissima instructio; Allergeheimste Instruction; Friderico V. comiti Palatino electo regi Bohemiae, data; an Friederichen, Pfaltzgrafen, erwehlten König in Böhmen* (Augsburg, 2002).

Weiss, E., *Die Unterstützung Friedrichs V. von der Pfalz durch Jakob I. und Karl I. von England im Dreissigjährigen Krieg (1618–1632)* (Stuttgart, 1966).

Wertheim, H., *Der tolle Halberstädter: Herzog Christian von Braunschweig im pfälzischen Kriege, 1621–1622*, 2 vols. (Berlin, 1929).

Wiedemann, F. W., *Geschichte des Herzogthums Bremen*, 2 vols. (Stade, 1864–6).

Wolf, F. O., *Die neue Wissenschaft des Thomas Hobbes: zu den Grundlagen der politischen Philosophie der Neuzeit* (Stuttgart, 1969).

Worsley, L., 'The Architectural Patronage of William Cavendish, Duke of Newcastle, 1593–1676', University of Sussex D.Phil. thesis (2001).

Ximenes, P. (attrib.), *Jus haereditarium et legitima successio in regno Bohemiae* (n.p., 1620).

Zagorin, P., *Ways of Lying: Dissimulation, Persecution, and Conformity in Early Modern Europe* (Cambridge, MA, 1990).

Zaller, R., *The Parliament of 1621: A Study in Constitutional Conflict* (Berkeley, 1971).

Zaret, D., *Origins of Democratic Culture: Printing, Petitions, and the Public Sphere in Early-Modern England* (Princeton, 2000).

Zíbrt, Č., *Bibliografie české historie*, 5 vols. (Prague, 1900–12).

Zuccolo, L., 'Della ragione di stato', in B. Croce and S. Caramella, eds., *Politici e moralisti del Seicento* (Bari, 1930), pp. 23–41.

von Zwiedineck-Südenhorst, H., *Die Politik der Republik Venedig während der dreissigjährigen Krieges*, 2 vols. (Stuttgart, 1882–5).

_____ 'Graf Heinrich Matthias Thurn in Diensten der Republik Venedig: eine Studie nach venetianischen Acten', *Archiv für österreichische Geschichte*, 66 (1885), pp. 257–76.

Index